This book, containing a lucid account of Bentham's ontology and epistemology and an assessment of its significance, will be welcomed by both Bentham scholars and historians of philosophy more generally. Not since C.K. Ogden's pioneering work in the 1930s have we seen such a stimulating work on this under-appreciated and yet fascinating and important area of Bentham's thought.

Philip Schofield, University College London, UK

Piero Tarantino's work explores Bentham's fascinating and profoundly original theory on the ontology of normativity. The book provides an illuminating and impressive interpretation of all the pieces Bentham put together to develop a theory of normativity out of a general ontological framework. Everyone with an interest in the deepest questions in the philosophy of normativity will derive much instruction from the book. I highly recommend it.

Peter Stemmer, University of Konstanz, Germany

Philosophy, Obligation and the Law

This book presents a comprehensive investigation of the notion of obligation in Bentham's thought. For Bentham, obligation is a fictitious – namely linguistic – entity, whose import and truth lie in empirical perceptions of pain and pleasure, 'real' entities.

This work explores Bentham's fictionalism, and aims to identify the general features that ethical fictitious entities (including obligation) share with other kinds of fictitious entities. The book is divided into two parts: the first examines the ontological and epistemological foundations of Bentham's distinction between real and fictitious entities; the second part addresses the normative and motivational aspects of moral and legal notions.

This book reveals the centrality of the following issues to Bentham's legal reform: logic, theory of language, physics, metaphysics, metaethics, axiology, moral psychology, the structure of practical reasoning and action with reference to the law.

Dr Piero Tarantino is a researcher at Centre Bentham, Sciences Po Law School, Paris, France.

Routledge Research in Constitutional Law

This series features thought-provoking and original scholarship on constitutional law and theory. Books explore key topics, themes and questions in the field with a particular emphasis on comparative studies. Where relevant, titles will engage with political and social theory, philosophy and history in order to offer a rounded analysis of constitutions and constitutional law.

Series Editor: David Marrani

Available titles in this series include:

Philosophy, Obligation and the Law
Bentham's Ontology of Normativity
Piero Tarantino

The Internet and Constitutional Law
The Protection of Fundamental Rights and Constitutional Adjudication in Europe
Edited by Oreste Pollicino and Graziella Romeo

Engineering Constitutional Change
A Comparative Perspective on Europe, Canada and the USA
Edited by Xenophon Contiades

Colonial and Post-colonial Constitutionalism in the Commonwealth
Peace, Order and Good Government
Hakeem O. Yusuf

The Legal Philosophy and Influence of Jeremy Bentham
Essays on 'Of the Limits of the Penal Branch of Jurisprudence'
Edited by Guillaume Tusseau

Constitutionalism in the Global Realm
A Sociological Approach
Poul F. Kjaer

The Accountability Gap in EU law
Marios Costa

Philosophy, Obligation and the Law

Bentham's Ontology of Normativity

Piero Tarantino

Routledge
Taylor & Francis Group
LONDON AND NEW YORK

First published 2018 by Routledge

2 Park Square, Milton Park, Abingdon, Oxfordshire OX14 4RN
52 Vanderbilt Avenue, New York, NY 10017

Routledge is an imprint of the Taylor & Francis Group, an informa business

First issued in paperback 2020

British Library Cataloguing in Publication Data
A catalogue record for this book is available from the British Library

Library of Congress Cataloging in Publication Data
A catalog record for this book has been requested

ISBN: 978-1-138-49657-6 (hbk)
ISBN: 978-0-367-58934-9 (pbk)

Typeset in Galliard
by Swales & Willis Ltd, Exeter, Devon, UK

To my mother Carmela, my father Giacomo,
and my sister Paola for their unshakable love and
never-ending support

Contents

Foreword

Guillaume Tusseau

PROFESSOR OF PUBLIC LAW

SCIENCES PO LAW SCHOOL, MEMBER OF THE INSTITUT UNIVERSITAIRE DE FRANCE

It truly is a great benthamic *pleasure* to write a foreword to Piero Tarantino's study ambitiously entitled *Philosophy, Obligation and the Law*, and (only apparently) more modestly presented in the subtitle as an exploration of "Bentham's ontology of normativity".

Legal and political theorists have never denied or underrated the originality and importance of Jeremy Bentham's reflections on jurisprudence and legal reform. In recent times, there has been a growing interest in Bentham's thought, especially thanks to the continuous publication of new authoritative editions of his texts, which have made them available to a wider public in a reliable form. The conditions for historical studies – purporting to restate Bentham's actual thought – as well as conceptual studies – focusing on what contribution Bentham's theories could offer to abstract philosophical debates – have flourished from several parts of the world. Different methodological perspectives have been adopted in order to illuminate the manifold and often neglected contributions which Bentham's writings offered and can still offer to the advancement of a variety of fields of human knowledge, not confined only to the area of law and political science.

Piero Tarantino's book is representative of these current debates and this current attitude towards Bentham. By adopting several of the aforementioned perspectives in a very original fashion, and especially by focusing on conceptual problems without neglecting the dimension of intellectual history, it provides a substantial and cutting-edge contribution to the understanding, assessment and discussion of Bentham's philosophy.

With two forthcoming collections on public deontology and on the possibility of codification, Tarantino's research is one of the major achievements of the project *CodeBentham* (ANR-11-IDEX-0005–02), which jointly involved Sciences Po Law School, Paris xiii University, and Paris iii University. The project gathered jurists, philosophers, historians, political scientists, anglicists and economists in order to explore the birth, development, circulation and reception of the idea of codification, which was conceived by Bentham as a social and cultural construction regarding not merely law but, more deeply, any form of guidance of human behaviour.

Tarantino's book investigates Bentham's treatment of the normative component of the practical domains, especially morality and law, and the obligations they entail. In pursuit of these aims, it examines the ontological framework of the physical world – or at least of its representation by human beings – and, then, of the ethical realm. The concept of codification entails a consistent systematization of a body of rules and standards of behaviour with the purpose of designing the infrastructure of society and, thus, regulating and coordinating human conduct. In this sense, codification has a prescriptive character: its objective is not only to design institutions but also to guide and direct people towards specific ends, which are envisaged by the author of the code, namely in Bentham's case: the greatest happiness of the greatest number. Nevertheless, the "guidance claim" a code necessarily expresses is by no means self-evident. It involves many crucial concepts such as normativity, practical reason, motivation, bindingness, obligatoriness, mandatoriness, obedience, compliance, etc. Although most of them are crucial to the understanding of the functioning of normative systems, and especially legal orders, be it from a legal, a moral or a sociological viewpoint, they remain what Gallie illuminatingly called "essentially-contested concepts". One of Tarantino's contributions is precisely to elucidate and discuss Bentham's position – or positions, inconsistencies and hesitations – in this respect. Having had the privilege to discuss it with him, my feeling is that what is at stake is not so much arriving at a definitive picture of what Bentham thought, as following Tarantino's peregrination in Bentham's writings, both published and unpublished. As they are lively presented and analysed here, one cannot help but be somehow fascinated by Bentham's efforts at determining a theoretical position that would allow him, from an operational viewpoint, to imagine the ideal code, able to evolve depending on the requirements of the principle of utility.

As is suggested in Tarantino's book, the normativity of a code presupposes that the world it aims to regulate is somehow "adapted" to such a regulation. This is where the ontological dimension appears. As is made evident, Bentham's practical and concrete reflections about the ends of the law, how behaviour must be guided, what laws should be enacted, how a statute should be drafted and promulgated, etc., cannot be severed from a more fundamental, theoretical and abstract topic: how can the world be made "available" for utilitarian reformism? What intellectual tools can be imagined to offer the appropriate "reading" or "picture" of social reality? From this point of view, Tarantino considers it necessary to connect four sub-questions concerning the ontological, epistemological, normative and motivational facets of an obligation, which remains Bentham's central legal concept to understand the law. These four questions provide him with a guideline for an overall exploration of the concept of normativity in Bentham's philosophy. But the very modal possibility of this normativity presupposes a fictional construction of the world, which leads Bentham to a very specific theory of language. Hence the subtitle: the ontology of normativity, which according to my reading needs to be understood both as (i) the nature of normativity in Bentham's conceptions of law, morality, religion and more generally human intercourse, and (ii) the world that is conceptually or practically needed for this very normativity to be conceivable.

Is the world that is regulated by norms independent from norms, and does it pre-exist norms? On the contrary, do the normative authorities contribute to shape the social world they deal with? Many scholars would, as I personally have, struggle with Bentham's manuscripts in order to decide whether he is closer to realism or to constructivism. For the first time, Tarantino offers a third possibility. By means of the introduction and adoption of a new historiographical category, i.e. "empirical constructivism", he elucidates Bentham's version of fictionalism, which underpins the philosopher's view of the ontological nature of the different fields of knowledge, including physics, mathematics, morality, law and religion. Tarantino shows the conceptual unity of Bentham's theoretical system: it turns out to be the harmonious combination of empirical realism inasmuch as it admits the reality of perceptions at the basis of our representation of the world, and rational constructivism, inasmuch as it acknowledges the power of the mind to create a framework to think of the world and act. This allows Tarantino to guide the reader from Bentham's "ontology of fiction", regarding the linguistic construction of the framework of the world from perceptual grounds, to his "normativity of fiction", specifically concerning the nature of the practical domains. The detailed explanation of Bentham's theory of real and fictitious entities provides the theoretical premises for the clarification of the specific constitution of the ethical subsets.

This is not the place to review all the merits of Tarantino's study, and I am confident that the reader will naturally find his or her own many ways to benefit from it. Let me just point to what struck me when I discovered Tarantino's manuscript: the value of the insightful hypotheses he labels "empirical constructivism", and then develops as "fictionalist" and "internalist". Shouldn't this idea lead us to explore a kind of pragmatist reading of Bentham's philosophy? One needs indeed to remember that William James' lectures on *Pragmatism* were dedicated to John Stuart Mill, who can be portrayed at least partially as Bentham's heir, and presented as "A New Name for Some Old Ways of Thinking". Might not the adoption of a pragmatist lens shed light on Bentham's ontology and epistemology? How could it help to reconsider the question of the fact-value distinction in utilitarian philosophy? How could it contribute to identifying the very specificities of Bentham's conception of jurisprudence, which is not merely censorial or merely expositive? How much could it lead, in the broader context of Dewey's writings, to offer new interpretations of Bentham's theory of democracy and public deliberation? As is evident from these questions, not only does Tarantino offer a brilliant self-contained study of Bentham's philosophy, it also paves the way for new understandings of it.

A last aspect deserves mention. Tarantino's interpretative work largely benefits from very recent editorial work. It is no coincidence that his book indirectly provides the first and, to date, unique commentary of the metaphysical and metaethical sections of Bentham's *Preparatory Principles*, a book that might seem to an inexperienced reader as a morass of annotations without a specific thematic focus. In addition, Tarantino's reconstruction takes advantage of as yet unpublished Bentham manuscripts on logic and grammar, which, along with his writings on ontology and language, are crucial to the treatment of the sources of normativity; unfortunately, these manuscripts are still available only in the imprecise Bowring edition, on which almost all the existing scholarship is based. Thanks to access to these unedited manuscripts, Tarantino gained an accurate knowledge of Bentham's thoughts according to their precise textual formulation and theoretical evolution. This form of intimacy allows Tarantino to cast light on Bentham's intellectual and practical struggles, and how he might himself have realized how much language was the true matter and texture of intellectual and practical achievements.

Tarantino's book entices us to read Bentham's texts and consider his words without historiographical prejudices, but with the genuine curiosity and also the pleasure to discover in them the roots of certain ideas which inspire the present. *Philosophy, Obligation and the Law: Bentham's Ontology of Normativity* offers a thorough interpretation of Bentham's thought, firmly grounded on the critical assessment of his writings. Thanks to that, this book overcomes still persistent tendencies to reductive and oversimplified reconstructions of Bentham's philosophy and has the merit of shedding light, from a new fictionalist perspective, on pivotal concepts such as normativity and practical reason which are at the heart of our moral life and legal practice. Tarantino tracks down the thread that ties Bentham's philosophy to the current reflections on the foundations of practical reality, and clearly shows how Bentham's insightful and underexplored fictionalist approach can help us possibly to handle and settle, but most of all to express, crucial questions of our times.

Acknowledgements

Philosophy, Obligation and the Law: Bentham's Ontology of Normativity is the outcome of a long, often tortuous, but always fruitful intellectual (and also physical) journey which I began at the University of Konstanz in 2008 and ended at the Centre Bentham, Paris in 2017. Two events were crucial in determining the direction of this journey: the meeting with Professor P. Stemmer, who aroused my curiosity on the subject of normativity, and the meeting with Professor G. Tusseau, who led me to the discovery of the richness and fecundity of Jeremy Bentham's thought. This singular convergence between two seemingly separate lines of research, namely the normative question and Bentham studies, is at the origin of this book.

Between 2008 and 2017, I carried out my project in various prestigious universities, where I had the great opportunity to interact with a large number of scholars and researchers. Although I am not able to mention all of them here, I would like to express appreciation to them as they contributed in many ways to the development of my research and influenced to different extents my methodological approach. I wish to thank Professors P. Stemmer (Department of Philosophy, University of Konstanz), G. Kohler and F. Cheneval (Centre for Ethics, University of Zurich), J.-F. Kervégan (*NoSoPhi* Team, Paris 1 Panthéon-Sorbonne University), H. Steinfath (Department of Philosophy, University of Göttingen), and G. Tusseau (Sciences Po Law School – Paris) for supervising my work from time to time and offering me the best conditions for pursuing my research. Taking advantage of their expertise and collaborating with their research groups allowed me to optimize my project on Bentham and normativity and broaden my skill set. My research activities were financed by a series of institutions, which I gratefully acknowledge: the University of Bari, the State Secretariat for Education and Research SER – Swiss Confederation, the Government of the French Republic, the German Academic Exchange Service – DAAD, and Sciences Po – Paris.

My book was mostly written during my fellowship at the Sciences Po Law School and my membership at the Centre Bentham. Here, I found the ideal academic environment, including administrative assistance, to prepare my manuscript for publication. I am indebted to the people working at the Law School, to all members of the Centre Bentham and to the participants in the Project

CodeBentham (involving Sciences Po, Paris iii University and Paris xiii University) for the numerous seminars, meetings and friendly conversations which enabled me to shape and share my scholarship. My deepest gratitude goes to Professor G. Tusseau: without his intelligent guidance, generous support and constant encouragement my longstanding project would hardly have been brought to completion. Furthermore, I owe him the idea of writing a book about the topics I was studying.

A special word of thanks is due to Professor P. Schofield for giving me access and permission to quote his transcription of Bentham's original manuscripts on *Logic* and *Universal Grammar*, which were indispensable for my study. I wish to extend my thanks to Professor E. De Champs for supplying me with her transcription of Bentham's correspondence to D'Alembert (UC 169.052–066).

I would like to thank Professors G. Pellegrino, Schofield, Stemmer and Tusseau, and the anonymous reviewers who read early versions of my manuscript and provided me with detailed commentaries, inspiring criticisms and helpful suggestions. I am also grateful to the participants in the Workshop of the Department of Ethics and Philosophy at the Université Catholique of Lille (29 January 2014), the International Symposium *Peut-on tout codifier? Ambitions et limites d'un paradigme* (20 May 2015, Sciences Po – Paris), and the ISUS Conference 2016 "Utilitarianism and Institutional Design" (6–8 July, Université Catholique of Lille) for their thought-provoking remarks, which helped me work out the direction I wanted to take. Finally, I would like to express my gratitude to the Editor, Professor D. Marrani, and the Editorial Board for taking my book into their series Routledge Research in Constitutional Law.

Abbreviations

Bowring:	*The Works of Jeremy Bentham. Published under the Superintendence of his Executor, John Bowring.*
A Comment on the Commentaries; *A Fragment on Government*:	*A Comment on the Commentaries and A Fragment on Government*, edited by Burns J. and Hart H., London: The Athlone Press, 1977.
Correspondence:	*The Correspondence of Jeremy Bentham*, various volumes in *The Collected Works of Jeremy Bentham* (full references in bibliography).
Deontology; *A Table of the Springs of Action*; *Article on Utilitarianism*:	*Deontology together with A Table of the Springs of Action and Article on Utilitarianism*, edited by Goldworth A., Oxford, UK: Clarendon Press, 1983.
IPML:	*An Introduction to the Principles of Morals and Legislation*, edited by Burns J. and Hart H., London: The Athlone Press, 1970.
UC:	Bentham Manuscripts, University College London Library (UC 101.088: box 101, folio 088).

From the normative question to Bentham

A discourse of 768VO pages has been written on the import of this single term Obligation. I have written page after page myself upon the same subject, which have gone into the fire. So long as we have not as yet acquired a clear conception of our subject, there is no end to what we write.[1]

Jurists in general, have not known what foundation to give to obligation. If you inquire what is its principle, you will find the clouds thicken around you.[2]

The title of this book, *Philosophy, Obligation and the Law: Bentham's Ontology of Normativity*, might appear quite clear at a glance. It suggests that the subject of the book is a reconstruction of Bentham's treatment of the notion of obligation. This idea is also supported by reference to a mysterious *ontology of normativity*, which intuitively seems to be related to the concept of obligation. However, when reflecting carefully on such a title, a reader might be perplexed about the meaning of some words included in it and, in particular, by the notion of normativity to which an ontological character is ascribed. Moreover, it seems puzzling to talk of an ontology of normativity in Bentham's work, as he never used the noun normativity because it was unknown to him.

This title, then, requires a terminological explanation which entails conceptual and historical clarification. The meaning of normativity, the centrality of the notion of obligation involved in it, and its relation with Bentham's philosophy need to be specified. This is the task to which this introduction is devoted. It aims to outline a theoretical path from the contemporary debates on practical normativity to the Benthamite reflection on ethics, with special regard to its constitutive idea of obligation.

Expressions such as *normative principle*, *normative grounds* and *normative reasons* are increasingly recurrent. They are employed in various fields of knowledge, especially with reference to human behaviour, with the purpose of identifying and qualifying their foundations. Despite this large and growing usage, the meaning

1 *Preparatory Principles*, 146.
2 *General View of a Complete Code of Laws*, Bowring iii, 180.

of the technical word *normativity*, along with its cognate *normative*, still remains general and quite opaque;[3] furthermore, attempts to clarify it and its historical developments have often proved controversial.

By and large, normativity concerns the principles, grounds or reasons for something, such as an action, a system of laws, a discipline and so forth.[4] In this sense, we can talk of the normativity of a legal rule punishing an individual who commits a crime, the normativity of a moral standard involving not lying and the normativity of a religious command prohibiting idolatry; normativity in these contexts means the ability of such norms to direct human behaviour. A legal rule, a moral standard and a religious command are, indeed, ought-statements, that is, prescriptions pointing out that something ought to be done or that someone ought to behave in accordance with them.[5]

Likewise, values and virtues, such as goodness, rightness, prudence, probity, beneficence and so forth, are normative since, when they qualify an act, a habit, a disposition and a propensity, they do not merely express a belief about these things, but they recommend their approval and adoption.[6] Values and virtues guide those who acknowledge them: compliance with what is regarded as valuable or virtuous is needed. Holding that something is good or right means that it is worth being adopted or pursued and, then, that it ought to be adopted or pursued. So, an agent who regards an action as right feels bound to perform it.[7]

What do we mean when we say that the elements making up practical reality, such as rules, standards, commands, values and virtues, are *normative*? What does their *normativity* consist in? Practical notions, such as norms and values, entail an obligation, inasmuch as they exercise the prerogative to make a claim on their subjects' conduct in order to influence and direct it. Their normativity consists in this prerogative, namely in this guidance claim, having a binding force. Hence, the notion of obligation is at the heart of the concept of normativity. An investigation into the normativity of practical reality is an investigation into the requirements derived from it.

3 See, for example, Copp 2004, 8; Stemmer 2008, 12.

4 In theoretical sciences also we may acknowledge a form of normativity: saying that a principle is normative means that it is a reason to believe in a certain state of affairs depending on or deriving from it.

5 On the notion of *ought*, see Kelsen 1945, 35–7.

6 About the idea that moral elements are endowed with normativity, see, for example, Copp 2004, 7: "Moral thought and discourse concern how we are to act, what we are to choose, and how we are to live; they involve us in evaluating, prescribing, and recommending. I use the term 'normative' to speak of this phenomenon." In other words, normativity concerns the action-guiding and choice-guiding prerogative of the elements making up the ethical domain.

7 The normativity of practical reality is clearly explained by Korsgaard 1996a, 8–9: "ethical standards are *normative*. They do not merely *describe* a way in which we in fact regulate our conduct. They make *claims* on us; they command, oblige, recommend, or guide. Or at least, when we invoke them, we make claims on one another. When I say that an action is right I am saying that you ought to *do* it; when I say that something is good I am recommending it as worthy of your choice." See also Korsgaard 1996a, 11: "when you think an action is right, you think you ought to do it – and this consideration at least frequently provides you with a motive for doing it."

These requirements should not only compel an agent to do something but also motivate him/her to conform his/her behaviour to them. Normativity proves to be deeply intertwined with motivation. Compliance with practical elements, which constrain the will to do something, is to be obtained through an agent's decision.[8]

Normativity is the constitutive property of practical reality and, as Stemmer (2008, 3) makes clear, this property is intimately related to the concept of obligation, consisting in the fact that people ought to do something.[9] The existence of rules, orders, commands, standards, norms, values and virtues lies in their normativity, i.e. in their binding character. They aim to compel or orient an agent's deliberation when he/she is involved in a reasoning on what to do. Practical reality is, thus, built on the idea of obligation and, by virtue of this, it is different from physical reality.

Such considerations on the ontological structure of the practical domain lead us to a foundational issue, concerning the grounds of the obligation to do something under which an agent is placed when reflecting on that action. What are the sources of the normativity of the practical world, that is, of the claim of practical elements to regulate our behaviour? Answering this question consists in settling the so-called *normative question*, which is framed by Korsgaard as an investigation into "what *justifies* the claims that morality makes on us"; in this sense, it involves the seeking of "a philosophical foundation for morality" that does not merely consist in "an explanation of moral practices."[10] The normative question concerns the foundations of practical reality, namely the grounds or reasons on which the obligations that practical elements impose on us are based. It aims to justify the constraints that practical notions put on our will.

The understanding of the claim that an obligation makes on us to obtain compliance is the objective of the normative question. It requires the enlightenment of the roots of practical disciplines such as morality, law and religion. It is important to clarify why moral, legal and religious values and standards have an action-guiding authority, thereby uncovering what endows them with a normative feature. The ultimate purpose of the normative question, therefore, is to justify the prerogative of morality, law and religion to impose a constraint on the agent's conduct.

The topic of normativity has lately aroused considerable interest in the area of practical philosophy, especially in the field of morality, leading to a major debate and a flurry of literature. From the 1970s onwards, an increasing number of scholarly works dealing with normativity have been written. Today, the normative

8 On the connection between normativity and motivation, and its problematic nature see Korsgaard 1996, 44: "The idea that moral conduct is obligatory, like the idea that moral judgments express internal reasons, is intended to capture both elements of the normativity of morality: both its power to motivate and to bind."

9 More generally, on the ontology of normativity see Stemmer 2008, 1–13.

10 Korsgaard 1996a, 9–10: "When we seek a philosophical foundation for morality we are not looking merely for an explanation of moral practices. We are asking what *justifies* the claims that morality makes on us. This is what I am calling 'the normative question'."

question lies at the core of contemporary philosophical debates and is relevant to the grounds of morality, law and religion. Normativity is acknowledged as the distinctive property of practical reality, inasmuch as practical entities, such as moral values, legal norms and religious orders, provide standards of conduct.

The understanding of normativity in terms of *reasons for action* is common in the current debate. This interpretation was first suggested by Raz, who states that "the normativity of all that is normative consists in the way it is, or provides, or is otherwise related to reasons."[11] By *reason for action* philosophers mean "a consideration that counts in favour of" the performance of an action.[12] The normative character of practical elements, such as social rules, moral considerations, religious beliefs and legal directives, lies in their ability to give rise to reasons that influence and modify people's behaviour, by compelling their practical deliberation and choice. Consistent with this approach, the majority of scholars have focused their attention on normative reasons, investigating their sources, their nature, their authoritative power over an agent's reflection and decision, and their relation to motivation.[13]

As regards the normative question, a new and promising research path, complementary to a purely systematic approach, consists in tracing it back to its historical roots. Leading thinkers, such as Darwall, Korsgaard and Schneewind, agree in identifying the seventeenth- and eighteenth-century British moral tradition as the philosophical context from which the so-called normative question, in the sense of an investigation of the foundations of morality, arises, before finding its mature exposition in Kant's practical thought. As Korsgaard observes:

> Many of the moves in the contemporary debate were anticipated in the debate between the Rationalists and the Sentimentalists of the eighteenth century. At the center of their dispute was the notion of *obligation*, a term they used primarily to refer to the *normativity* of duty. The term "obligation" is a source of confusion, because "an obligation" is sometimes used loosely as synonym for "a duty," a required action. But "obligation" refers not so much to the action as to the *requiredness* of the action, to its normative pull. We say that we *feel* obliged, or are *under* an obligation, to express our sense that the claims of morality are claims *on us*.[14]

In a nutshell, again with Korsgaard's words, we may state that "the moral philosophy of the modern period can be read as a search for the source of normativity."[15] Hence, the examination of the normative question brings us back to its origins,

11 Raz 1999, 67.
12 See, for example, Scanlon 1998, 17; Korsgaard 2008, 207–8.
13 See, for example, Korsgaard 2008, 207–29; Raz 1990, 15–48; Redondo 1999, 13–64; Scanlon 1998, 17–77; Stemmer 2008, 87–134.
14 Korsgaard 1996, 44.
15 Korsgaard 1996a, 18.

to the philosophical context within which this foundational issue takes shape, at least as we know it nowadays.

The current understanding of the notion of normativity has its natural point of departure in modern British moral philosophy, roughly beginning with Hobbes and ending with Bentham. Philosophers of the likes of Locke, Shaftesbury, Hutcheson, Hume and so forth, included in this long period, have been all together identified as *British moralists* by recent historiography.[16] The lively and highly productive context in which these philosophers operated was particularly characterized by a concern with the requirements and demands of morality.

The roots of the contemporary debates on normativity can be found in such a context, distinguished by a crucial turn in conceiving the idea of obligation. Darwall acknowledges "fundamental changes involving the concept of obligation in British ethics of the early modern period, as it developed in the direction of the view that obligatory force is a species of motivational force – an idea that deeply informs present thought."[17] So, a distinctive aspect of practical reality in the modern British tradition appears to be the relation between obligation and motivation, which is now a matter of contention among scholars dealing with normativity.

British moralists aimed to discover the grounds of morality and to justify them. Their reflection developed on two interrelated levels: the former pertained to the clarification of the nature of the obligation implied by morality and the latter to the explanation of the binding feature of morality.[18] Both levels were connected in the general investigation of the sources of the normativity of morality. Questions concerning the foundations of the practical domain and their normative force were at the heart of the interests and debates of British moralists, whose attempts to tackle them produced a variety of theories.

Within such debates, the notion of obligation was put under scrutiny, with the consequence that it was subject to a process of "radical rethinking and revision" of its import.[19] In particular, obligation began to be related to the idea of the autonomy of the moral agent. It was seen as springing from the agent's judgement on what to do and no longer as deriving from an authority external to him/her, such as God or nature, as asserted by natural law theorists. As Schneewind argues, "The moral philosophies of Reid, Bentham, and Kant are the final eighteenth-century efforts to articulate the normative belief about the dignity and worth of the individual that led to conceptions of morality as self-governance."[20] So, as a

16 See Selby-Bigge 1987; Raphael 1969.

17 Darwall 1989, 133. See also Darwall 1995, 2.

18 Darwall (1995, 2) has rightly identified the two interrelated questions at the core of British moralists' thought: "In what might the universal bindingness of morality consist? What makes morality obligating?" and, more fundamentally, "What is for anything to be binding? What is bindingness, obligation, or, as moral philosophers are inclined to say these days, *normativity* itself? In what does an *ought to do* consist?"

19 Cf. Darwall 1989, 135–6: "the whole matter of what exactly moral obligation is (or, perhaps more accurately, what it *could be*) was undergoing radical rethinking and revision in the period following Hobbes. [. . .] With the appearance of Shaftesbury's *Characteristics*, however, we shall see that a radical shift must have been underway."

20 Schneewind 1998, 6.

conclusion of this process of redefinition of obligation, it is the individual that provides himself/herself with duties.

Bentham's philosophy came to maturity in a similarly lively and highly productive period, distinguished by reflection on the foundations of morality. Bentham is certainly one of the prominent figures in the general process of the rethinking of moral entities, including the leading notion of obligation. One of Bentham's major contributions to practical philosophy lies in conceiving of obligation, along with other ethical elements, as a fictitious construction of the human mind, based on sensory experience, and in applying this idea to the legal field. Notwithstanding certain historiographical tendencies to detach Bentham's philosophy from his time, the examination of his thought in the eighteenth-century British moral tradition seems to be fundamental to understanding that the originality of Bentham's proposal derives from the intellectual climate of the time. On the other hand, focusing on Bentham's reflections concerning the foundations and the requirements of morality and law adds to and completes the picture of modern philosophy.

Bentham was deeply influenced by the view of an empirical basis of morality. Yet he reconciled that sensory approach with the idea of the linguistic construction of ethical elements. This new connection between empiricism and constructivism emerges in Bentham's attempt to tackle fundamental issues in morality and law, as well as in physics. Bentham understood the concept of obligation as a fictitious entity created by the human mind in relation to the feelings of pleasure and pain, which are regarded as real entities. The desire to enjoy pleasure and avert pain makes binding the action instrumental in fulfilling that desire. Obligation is thus the result of harmonious cooperation between sensibility and intellectual activity, including particularly the faculties of language and imagination. Such an ontological perspective on ethics, linking desire and duty, might be called *empirical constructivism*, as an alternative to Kant's more famous form of *transcendental constructivism*.[21]

The fictitious notion of obligation has meaning and truth only if it is referred to pleasure and pain: they are the pillars on which the human mind builds the practical domain. The binding and motivating force of an obligation, in which its character consists, springs from pleasure and pain, which are individually perceived. So, the investigation of the nature of an obligation is joined to an investigation of its normative foundations. The ontological and normative – as well as the epistemological and motivational – features of an obligation depend on pleasure and pain. From these empirical roots the mind can create a fictitious ontology endowed with normativity. Ethical elements turn out to be human artefacts, anchored to physical reality: they can make a guidance claim on us by virtue of their constitutive relation with pleasure and pain, which have the form of reward or punishment.

21 On the Kantian form of constructivism, see Rawls 1980, 515–72. For an examination of the normativity of morality and law in Kant's thought, see Kervégan 2010, 89–109; 2015, 63–92.

Nonetheless, Bentham's original contribution to the normative question, that is, to the shaping of the early modern idea of obligation as an internal requirement of a self-governing moral agent's thinking, has largely been overlooked and is sometimes minimized. Distinguished scholars, dealing with the historical sources of normativity, neglect to examine Bentham's treatment of the notion of obligation as the core element of his fictitious ontology of the practical world.

Even though Bentham's reflection is certainly a fundamental step in the "autonomist internalist tradition"[22] of modern British ethics, it is not taken into account by Darwall, who explicitly restricts his analysis to the British moralists' works produced between 1640 and 1740.[23] Korsgaard, on the other hand, draws attention to Mill, who is read as an upholder of "the reflective endorsement method."[24] Only Schneewind explicitly acknowledges Bentham's role in the path to morality as autonomy, but he surprisingly adds that it is unclear how Bentham provided a foundation for this new view of morality.[25]

Many reasons might be advanced to explain why Bentham's contribution has been neglected and consequently underrated. One of these is that his writing style is not as easy and appealing as that of some of the British empiricists such as Hume or Locke. A number of repetitions, ambiguities and inconsistencies make interpreting Bentham's texts somewhat difficult. Bentham was a very prolific writer: he preferred to devote his time to the drafting of his ideas rather than to giving clarity and consistency to his writings. Furthermore, only a small part of what he wrote, especially *An Introduction to the Principles of Morals and Legislation* and *A Fragment on Government*, received the attention of the wider public.[26] Generally speaking, philosophers have failed to recognize the importance of Bentham's theory of real and fictitious entities, and its import in the shaping and settlement of the normative question.

Only in recent times, thanks to the meritorious work of the Bentham Committee, and the scholars and researchers involved in the Bentham Project, have new and revised editions of his texts been available to readers. In this way, the Bowring edition, which for a long time has been and still is the main reference point for Bentham's manuscripts, notwithstanding the serious inaccuracies

22 Darwall 1995, 21. Roughly speaking, internalists maintain that moral considerations, including duties, depend on the agent's states of mind, such as desires, dispositions, needs and interests; they oppose externalists, who challenge such a connection and claim the independence of moral notions from the agent's states of mind.

23 See Darwall 1995, 1–22.

24 Korsgaard 1996a, 78–84.

25 Cf. Schneewind 1998, 423 and also 6 with the related note 4. On p. 423 Schneewind alleges that Bentham, with his greatest happiness principle, was more concerned in "settling disputes and guiding social change," in which "the balance of utilities was obvious," than in the investigation of individual practical reason, based on "the actual balances of pleasure and pain." Bentham "never fully explained [. . .] how individuals were to get from the principle of utility a method for making private decisions." Hence, according to Schneewind, Bentham's foundation of morality as self-governance, entailing "that individual agents be able to reason out for themselves what they ought to do," remains unclear.

26 Cf. Twining 2004, 1–2. See also Elster 2013, 140–1.

resulting from the way they were transcribed, selected and collected, has been partly superseded and is destined to be fully superseded by more precise, accurate and even more attractive editions.

Taking advantage of this impressive editorial work,[27] along with the increasingly sophisticated literature on Bentham's utilitarianism and recent works in the areas of practical philosophy, with particular reference to the topics of normativity and fictionalism, the present book, *Philosophy, Obligation and the Law: Bentham's Ontology of Normativity*, affords a comprehensive investigation of Bentham's treatment concerning the ontological and epistemological foundations of the normative and motivational character distinguishing morality and law; this is an important subject which has hitherto been largely unexplored.

The methodological strategy adopted in this book involves addressing the question of normativity outlined above and teasing out the answers which Bentham's writings can give. Bentham's assessment of the normative claim of morality and law thoroughly depends on his idea of ethics as a fictitious construction. *Philosophy, Obligation and the Law: Bentham's Ontology of Normativity* aims to disclose Bentham's original view of the action-guiding prerogative of morality and law. In pursuit of this general objective, this book is divided into two parts: the first part examines the ontological and epistemological aspects of Bentham's distinction between real and fictitious entities, whose interrelations provide the framework of the ethical realm, as well as the physical world; the second part throws light on both the normative and motivational aspects of Bentham's ethics.

The handling of these issues provided Bentham with the theoretical basis for his project of State reform; in fact, the institutional design, which Bentham worked out, is intimately related to his fictionalist conception of the normativity of the practical world. This is the reason why Bentham's important and innovative achievements in the area of constitutional law cannot be fully understood as long as their philosophical premises are not clarified.

Although fictitious, an obligation purports to direct human behaviour. Bentham's ontological fictionalism has a distinct practical character that needs to be scrutinized in its normative and motivational facets. Bentham's account of ethics is intertwined with his theory of real and fictitious entities; consequently, his ontological and linguistic fictionalism provides the key to interpreting his constructivist view on morality and law.

Moral and legal elements are fictitious entities, that is, experience-based products of the human mind, whose structures and operations have to be identified and analysed in order to uncover the intimate nature of morality and law and their function in regulating human action. It is important to understand Bentham's treatment of fictitious entities and its bearing on his conception of ethics. When

27 As an example, this book, *Philosophy, Obligation and the Law: Bentham's Ontology of Normativity*, greatly benefits from the very recent edition of Bentham's *Preparatory Principles* (2016), which is an irreplaceable source of his philosophical thought.

conceiving of an obligation as a fictitious entity, one needs to explain how it can influence an agent's conduct by obtaining his/her compliance. Dealing with such issues requires first a reconstruction of Bentham's theory of real and fictitious entities and then the examination of its application to the ethical field, in order to clarify and justify the reason-giving ability of morality and law.

Bentham's texts may be a source of inspiration for settling the normative question, because they provide useful insights to its understanding.[28] They invite us to rethink certain central aspects of the contemporary debates on normativity from a new point of view, harmonizing realism and fictionalism, objectivism and subjectivism, sensibility and rationality: in short, empiricism and constructivism. Classical philosophical questions strictly related to the question of normativity, such as the working of practical reason, the causation of action and the freedom of the will, may benefit from such a point of view. Bentham's ideas may help to throw light on the ontological structure of the practical domain and its normative component.

28 Darwall (1995, 20) argues that "a study of the British moralists on obligation might yield significant philosophical benefits, including, perhaps, some clarifications of the issues underlying contemporary debates about internalism." This opinion is certainly valid for Bentham's reflection on obligation.

The ontology of fiction

The theory of real and fictitious entities and its relation with the normative question

Bentham thinks of the notion of obligation as a fictitious entity, underlying the ethical dimension of human life. Understanding, from Bentham's perspective, what an obligation is and how human beings become aware of it brings us to an investigation into the general nature of a fictitious entity, as it is opposed to or contrasted with a real entity. Only by throwing light on the framework of the human representation of the world, basically articulated according to the connection between real and fictitious entities, can the ontological and the epistemological character of the notion of obligation be identified and, consequently, the structure of ethics disclosed. Obligation is, in fact, the constitutive ingredient of practical reality as a whole, characterizing with its normative force each single component. Along with obligation, on which our present focus lies, practical concepts such as virtues, values, standards and norms have a guidance function. They make a normative claim on us, which needs to be explored in the light of the distinction between real and fictitious entities.

The notion of obligation belongs to ethical fictitious entities, which are a subset of fictitious entities. So, the definition of a fictitious entity and the clarification of the way we know it enables us to understand the ontological and epistemological status of ethics and, thus, of its fundamental notion of obligation. My work is committed to exploring Bentham's fictionalism, with the purpose of identifying the general features that ethical fictitious entities, including obligation, share with other kinds of fictitious entities, such as *physical concepts*,[1] and, then, of bringing out the particular aspects which distinguish the ethical domain from other fictitious domains of the world, such as physics. In this way, it is possible to trace, in Bentham's philosophy, a path that guides us from the comprehensive definition of a fictitious entity, with reference to its relation to a real entity, to the characterization of its ethical specifications and, finally, to the grasping of the normative

1 At first glance, the expressions *physical concepts* and, similarly, *physical notions* seem to be ambiguous, since they suggest something that is both real and abstract at the same time. In this case, by *physical concepts* and *physical notions* I mean abstract objects or elements belonging to the field of physics such as motion, relation, force, cause and so on: according to Bentham they are not empirical perceptions but mental constructions. By using the terms *concept* and *notions* and qualifying them as *physical* I aim to emphasize the intellectual character of these particular objects or elements.

function of an obligation, which is the core element in the constitution of the practical sphere.

When dealing with Bentham's theory of real and fictitious entities, we are faced with both a textual or editorial question and an interpretative question. Numerous remarks pertaining to fictitious entities are scattered through Bentham's writings and yet the bulk of his doctrine may be identified in a group of manuscripts concerning ontological, logical, linguistic and grammatical issues. They were composed circa 1813–15 and posthumously gathered by Bowring, who organized and divided them into four compilations entitled *A Fragment on Ontology*, *Essay on Logic*, *Essay on Language* and *Fragments on Universal Grammar*. Around the same period, the pedagogical book *Chrestomathia*, which contains a long and telling excursus about real and fictitious entities (Appendix iv *Nomenclature and Classification*), was written.[2] In all these works the character and the properties of fictitious entities are carefully scrutinized, leaving in the background their disciplinary specifications. Even though these texts were not conceived by Bentham as part of a general project on real and fictitious entities, they provide a major and consistent account of Bentham's fictionalism.

The Bowring edition of the texts dealing with ontology, logic, language and grammar is, however, unsatisfactory, since it is incomplete and presents many inaccuracies in the transcription of the original handwritten manuscripts. An attempt to isolate Bentham's treatment of the distinction between real and fictitious entities was pursued in 1932 by Ogden, who tried, under the label of *theory of fictions*, to give it a sort of unity by putting together a large number of passages from the Bowring edition and introducing them with a detailed commentary. This collection provided the textual reference point for a series of studies of Bentham's fictionalism. However, Ogden just reproduces Bowring and, consequently, all the scholarship is based on inadequate texts.

In addition, the material selected by Ogden, mostly taken from Bentham's writings on ontology, logic, language and grammar, dates back to a later stage of the so-called theory of fictions, which had already taken shape about thirty years before, in the early 1770s, as can be seen from certain remarks in *A Fragment on Government* and especially in his works on mathematics.[3] Despite his lifelong concern with real and fictitious entities, Bentham provides a quite uniform and consistent treatment of them in his writings. Very probably, he matured his view on the distinction between real and fictitious entities, especially with reference to ethical and legal objects, at an early stage in his career, and later developed and enriched it, setting out its ontological foundations and extending its investigation to physics.

A preliminary attempt to overcome such editorial problems has come from Schofield's publication of Bentham's English manuscripts on ontology in the book *De l'Ontologie et autres textes sur les fictions* (1997), with an introduction,

2 For a detailed history of its composition see *Chrestomathia*, xi–xxix and, particularly, xx–xxviii.
3 Cf. Schofield 2006, 8–9.

a commentary and an accompanying French translation by Cléro and Laval. This book, in which the grounds of the theory of real and fictitious entities are laid down, appears to be addressed especially to the French-speaking public and does not fully adhere to the criteria actually pursued in *The Collected Works of Jeremy Bentham*. Consequently, an authoritative edition of Bentham's writings on ontology, logic, language and grammar, to replace the inadequate Bowring edition and serve as new basis for Bentham scholarship, is greatly needed.

The textual examination of Bentham's handwritten manuscripts on ontology, logic, language and grammar is crucial to the reconstruction of his fictionalist view and its influence on ethics. Professor Schofield, who is Director of the Bentham Project at University College London and General Editor of the *Collected Works of Jeremy Bentham*, is planning to produce a new authoritative edition of Bentham's essays on *Logic* and *Universal Grammar*. He gave me access to his preliminary version and thus a part of my reconstruction and interpretation of Bentham's theory of real and fictitious entities is based on this unpublished material, from which the related quotations inserted into my book are selected.[4] Therefore, the textual gap due to the unsatisfactory Bowring edition of Bentham's manuscripts on ontology, logic, language and grammar is destined to be filled with the preparation of a new and authoritative edition of the writings that Bentham devoted to these topics.

Bentham's writing style along with the editorial arrangement of his materials makes the reconstruction of his thought on the ontological, logical, linguistic and grammatical matter more complex. Apart from a few exceptions, such as his first two books *A Fragment on Government* and *An Introduction to the Principles of Morals and Legislation*, published in 1776 and 1789,[5] the structure and organization of Bentham's works are the outcome of an editor's decision rather than the author's choice. Especially in the case of the books dealing with logic, ontology, language and grammar, edited by Bowring, Bentham's writings are closer to a collection, and sometimes to a juxtaposition, of notes than to a revised and finished book, as revealed by the presence of repetitions, discrepancies, controversial points, abrupt interruptions, compositional observations and personal notes. Besides, Bentham also used to write similar texts only making a few changes or adding some new information.

In Bentham's texts it is not rare to find theoretical ambiguities and lexical anomalies, as in the case of the treatment of the notions of *idea*, *substance*, *body* and especially *existence*, which are core concepts of his ontology. They are employed in a way that does not fit completely with their definitions, oscillating between a realist and constructivist perspective. A key to understanding

4 When quoting a passage from Bentham's writings on *Logic* and *Universal Grammar*, transcribed and collected by Schofield, I point out the identification number of the original manuscript, which is reported by Schofield himself, along with, in most cases, the pages of the Bowring edition containing Bowring's often imprecise and incomplete transcription of that passage.

5 An *Introduction to the Principles of Morals and Legislation* was however printed in 1780.

Bentham's thought consists in the acknowledgement of "some persistent tensions in his personality and some ambivalences in some of his central ideas" opposed to "the overall coherence of his work," as argued by Twining: "many of Bentham's ideas invite conflicting interpretations. 'Benthamic ambiguity' is an important thread in reading Bentham."[6]

The theory of real and fictitious entities is a *locus classical* of Bentham's work, from which the particular, ambivalent character of his reflections plainly emerges and openly challenges any interpreter to account for it. A suitable interpretative criterion in reading Bentham's writings should be based on the disclosure, and not on the concealment, of his textual discrepancies by attempting to give an explanation or justification for them. These theoretical ambiguities and lexical anomalies, which often remain puzzling to the reader, do not seem to be merely due to imprecision or inaccuracy, but might also be considered as the traces of the inner tension between realism and constructivism, running throughout Bentham's fictionalism and, thus, throughout his account of the world. The understanding of these two alternatives, i.e. realism and constructivism, would allow us to throw light on Bentham's handling of the normative problem, ascertaining the ontological and epistemological nature of the obligation which constitutes an ethical and a legal system.

Let us take into consideration the interpretative question regarding Bentham's theory of real and fictitious entities. After the studies made by Steintrager (1977, 20–43) and Long (1977, 65–83), mainly focused on the role of fictitious entities in politics and law, a substantial treatment of Bentham's fictionalism by Harrison (1983, 47–105) provided an overall examination of the notion of a fictitious entity, not confined only to the legal area, but including its application to physics. The number of scholarly works on Bentham's theory of real and fictitious entities has increased significantly since the late 1990s, during which time Bentham scholars, especially those working at the Bentham Project in London (Quinn, Rosen, Schofield and Tyler) and the Centre Bentham in Paris (Bozzo-Rey, Cléro, De Champs, Laval and Tusseau), have begun a lively debate on the character of a fictitious entity.[7] They have emphasized the controversial and problematic nature of fictitious entities, which still remains puzzling, as it wavers between existence and non-existence, reality and unreality, or, we might say, empiricism and constructivism.

During this time, it has been ascertained that Bentham's utilitarianism thoroughly depends on his fictionalism. There is now a widespread belief among scholars that the distinction and the connection between real and fictitious entities provide the framework of Bentham's philosophical system, shaping not only his legal theory but all other aspects of his thought, including morality, mathematics,

6 Twining 2004, 7–8.

7 See, for example, Bouveresse 1993, 87–98; Bozzo-Rey 2007, 2008, 2009b; Cléro 1993, 1998, 2007, 2014a; De Champs 1999; Guidi 1987/8, 253–62; Laval 1994; Poggi 2006; Postema 2002a; Quinn 2012; Schofield 2006, 1–27; 2009, 50–3; 2015; Tusseau 2011a; Tyler 2004, 685–703.

physics, and natural sciences. To put it differently, the theory of real and fictitious entities lies at the basis of Bentham's philosophy. Schofield clearly outlines this new interpretative approach in Bentham studies: "It is often assumed that the starting-point for Bentham's thought is the principle of utility. There is, however, a deeper aspect to his thought, on which the principle of utility itself is founded. This is his ontology, and his theory of logic and language which is linked to it."[8] This new and promising line of research into Bentham's philosophy as conceptually grounded on fictionalism seems to be still in its infancy and needs to be explored in all its ontological and epistemological complexity and breadth.

Moreover, the concern about Bentham's fictionalism has also been indirectly boosted by consideration of the contribution it can make to the current controversy surrounding the status of mathematical, physical, moral, legal and religious fictions.[9] Bentham's theory of real and fictitious entities is a milestone in the history of fictionalism, a metaphysical subject currently arousing increasing interest in philosophy of science, ethics and legal thought. In order to examine the nature of mathematical, physical, moral, legal and religious notions, Bentham throws light on their ontological status as fictitious entities. His original fictionalist view, concerning the meaning and truth of conceptual objects, offers inspiring insights to researchers and scholars interested and involved in the controversy over the ontology of the theoretical and the practical domain.

To the best of my knowledge, very few books are exclusively devoted to Bentham's theory of real and fictitious entities, two such being Laval 1994 and Tusseau 2011a, despite the ever increasing number of articles on this topic. There are, however, sections of monographs which deal with the theory of real and fictitious entities as an introduction to certain features of Bentham's thought (for example Schofield 2006, 1–27) or to fictionalism (for example Cléro 2014, 16–21, 49–54).

Notwithstanding the growing interest in it, Bentham's theory of real and fictitious entities is an area of research in which much work remains to be done, as Schofield also recently remarked.[10] Furthermore, this area of research involves an investigation of ethical fictitious entities, encompassing the notion of obligation, the peculiarities of which deserve to be clarified within Bentham's general treatment of fictitious entities. It is not an exaggeration to speak of a form of *ethical fictionalism* in Bentham's thought as a specification of his *fictionalism*.[11] To understand Bentham's answer to the normative question, concerning the action-guiding and binding character of ethics, we need, in the first place, to

8 Schofield 2009, 50.

9 See, for example, Cléro 2000; 2004, 203–31, 436–7, 445–53; 2014, 16–21, 49–54; Quinn 2015; Rosen 2005; Tusseau 2009, 2011.

10 Cf. Schofield 2009, 159.

11 Although in the history of thought forms of moral and legal fictionalism might be tracked down in meta-ethical non-realist and non-cognitivist positions, conceptions of fictionalism with reference to morality and law have explicitly appeared only in recent time. See, for example, Mackie 1977. For a general view, cf. Joyce 2005; also Olson 2011.

elucidate what a fictitious entity is, by attempting to grasp its mysterious and maybe ambiguous nature.

This book, *Philosophy, Obligation and the Law: Bentham's Ontology of Normativity*, seeks to offer a general examination and a critical assessment of Bentham's concepts of real entity and fictitious entity, with a particular focus on their application in the ethical field with reference to the notion of obligation, on which the normative question depends. A clarification of the nature of obligation in Bentham's work runs up against a crucial interpretative difficulty of his theory of real and fictitious entities, consisting in the clarification of the status of fictitious entities and of their relation to real entities. This difficulty concerns the type of existence or reality of fictitious entities, whether it derives from an external physical element or whether it is an internal product of the activity of the human mind.

When reviewing the state of the art regarding Bentham's theory of real and fictitious entities, we have to acknowledge three main crucial gaps: the first is that the origin and sources of Bentham's distinction between real and fictitious entities remain puzzling as they have hitherto never been explored, with a few exceptions;[12] second, notwithstanding the successful efforts to clarify the ontological character of fictitious entities and throw light on their connection with real entities, scholars have neglected to examine the rich and manifold application of Bentham's fictionalist approach to several of the various domains of knowledge, focusing their attention especially and often exclusively on his treatment of politics and law;[13] third, no attempt has ever been made to outline the legacy of Bentham's thought concerning fictitious entities in the shaping of the concept of normativity.

When investigating Bentham's theory of real and fictitious entities, I adopt a threefold strategy: I attempt to trace Bentham's ontological distinction between real and fictitious entities back to its possible historical sources, which at present remain obscure; I focus on Bentham's multidisciplinary approach to fictitious entities, clarifying its application to certain fields of knowledge; and I throw light on the contribution of Bentham's fictionalism to the modern normative question.

As regards the historical reconstruction of Bentham's theory of real and fictitious entities I think that it is possible to identify at least three main sources: the Aristotelian tradition handed down by Sanderson's *Logicae Artis Compendium*, a very popular and largely influential textbook in seventeenth- and eighteenth-century English universities, especially at Oxford and Cambridge, which underpins and informs Bentham's methodological approach; D'Alembert's conception of reality and his definition of *être fictif*, which inspired Bentham's fictionalism; and the nominalist idea of universals as *entia ficta*, namely as figments without correspondence to real objects.

12 See, for example, De Champs 1999, 2015, 45–9; Murphy 2014, 61–7.

13 As an exception, along with the above-mentioned treatment by Harrison (1983, 47–105) of Bentham's physics, we can consider Cléro 2000. This article investigates how the theory of real and fictitious entities can provide the foundations of sciences.

The theoretical structure of Bentham's treatises on ontology, logic, language and grammar was influenced by the Aristotelian tradition. In the preface to *Essay on Logic* Bentham expresses his debt to Aristotle: "In this sense the logic of Aristotle may be said to have formed the basis of this work. In that storehouse of instruction he [the author of *Essay on Logic*, i.e. Bentham himself] found at any rate a considerable number of the tools or instruments which he has had to work with."[14] Bentham probably had no first-hand knowledge of Aristotle's logic; he learned it through the reading and study of Sanderson's *Logicae Artis Compendium*,[15] which is devoted to formal logic and philosophy of language. In particular, Sanderson's textbook summarizes and interprets Aristotle's *Organon*, showing particular interest in the empirical bases of scientific knowledge. Although Bentham distanced himself from the Aristotelian tradition, especially from its underlying realism, his theory of real and fictitious entities took shape in a period highly characterized by reflection on Aristotle's logic, which lies behind that theory and nourishes it.[16]

Bentham explicitly attributes to D'Alembert the merit of inspiring his ontological view based on the distinction between real and fictitious entities:

> *D'Alembert* is the *author in whose works* the notion of this distinction was first observed by me; – *étre fictif* is the expression employed by him for the designation of the sort of object, for the designation of which the appellation *fictitious entity* has ever since been employed.[17]

Again, Bentham makes it clear that "the distinction between names of *real entities* and names of *fictitious entities*" is:

> [a] distinction which, in some of his Encyclopædical remarks, D'Alembert was, it is believed, the first to bring to view, and which will be found to pervade the whole mass of every language upon earth, actual or possible.[18]

Bentham's gratitude to D'Alembert for inspiring him with the idea of fictitious entity is also expressed in his letter addressed to D'Alembert in Spring 1778,

14 *Essay on Logic*, UC 101.088 (Bowring viii, 218).

15 Cf. *Essay on Logic*, UC 101.088 (Bowring viii, 217): "Of this work the parent hints were drawn from the logic of Aristotle, viz. from Bishop Sanderson's compend of it in the years 1760 or 1761 to 1762 or 1764 when the author was a youth, or rather a child, at College: at Queen's College in the University of Oxford. Of the notions therein delivered, some he found continually applicable, and applicable with advantage to ordinary practice. These treasured themselves up in his mind." Moreover, in a letter addressed to his father Jeremiah (12 June 1761), Bentham wrote that "we are just gone through the Logic Compend" (see *Correspondence* i, 45–7; the quotation is taken from p. 47).

16 On the Aristotelian tradition handed down by Sanderson's *Logicae Artis Compendium* see Ashworth's *Introduction* to Sanderson, *Logicae Artis Compendium*, xi–lv; Sgarbi 2013, 152–7.

17 *Appendix. Logical Arrangements or Instruments of Invention and Discovery*, in *Nomography; or the Art of Inditing Laws*, Bowring iii, 286.

18 *Chrestomathia*, 257.

namely in the very first period of his career as a philosopher: "C'est de vous que je tiens le fil du labyrinth des connoissances humaines."[19]

The difference between a real entity and a fictitious entity seems to refer to and recast the difference worked out in the Scholastic tradition between *ens reale*, existing independently of the human mind, and *ens rationis*, existing in dependence on the human mind. Nominalists, in particular, regarded logical universals as *entia ficta*, namely intellectual constructions without correspondence to real objects. Henry of Harclay considered concepts as figments and William of Ockham, his pupil, claimed the fictitious character of mental notions. According to Murphy, Hobbes, who mentions the notion of *ficta* in his *Computatio sive Logica*, could have contributed to the circulation of the nominalist approach and its transmission to Bentham.[20]

Murphy minimizes the originality of Bentham's notion of fictitious entity, since it is imported from other thinkers as Bentham himself acknowledges. In fact, Bentham's original contribution in the history of fictionalism does not lie in the discovery of fictitious entities, but in conceiving of the distinction between real and fictitious entities as the general framework of the various domains of knowledge and especially ethics. Bentham's theory of real and fictitious entities is a powerful instrument to interpret our representation of reality as it is constructed by the activity of the human mind.

We can conclude, with De Champs' words, that "in the case of real and fictitious entities, Bentham's references reveal a complex network of inspiration and invention."[21] From this point of view, to the three above mentioned main sources of Bentham's theory of real and fictitious entities we could also add British empiricism, especially Locke and Hume's approach, which largely influenced Bentham's epistemology and, thus, his understanding of the role of sensibility in the construction of reality as we think about it. Properly speaking, although the idea of fictitious entity does not belong to this tradition, empiricism provided Bentham with the theoretical instruments to disentangle the metaphysical complexities of the fields of ethics and jurisprudence, which are made up by abstract entities.

The study of Bentham's application of his metaphysical distinction between real and fictitious entities in the different fields of knowledge, such as physics, mathematics, and then ethics, including morality and law, is a work preliminary to the exploration of his construction of the notion of obligation. Bentham's theory of real and fictitious entities provides an interdisciplinary approach to understanding the foundations and the constitution of theoretical and practical knowledge, thereby challenging both a realist and an antirealist perspective and inviting us to adopt a critical view of the notions we are familiar with.

19 *Correspondence* ii, 115–8 (the quotation in the text is taken from p. 117). The correspondence between Bentham and D'Alembert is commented on by De Champs 2015, 45–9.

20 On D'Alembert and the scholastic tradition as the historical sources of Bentham's theory of real and fictitious entities, see Murphy 2014, 61–7, in part. 62–3.

21 De Champs 2015, 49.

The objective of the first part of my book, *The Ontology of Fiction*, is to afford a general and comprehensive reconstruction and assessment of Bentham's treatment of the ontological and epistemological nature of the multiplicity and variety of the objects making up reality as we think about it. The first part of my book aims to investigate Bentham's fictionalism in order to understand better the philosophical foundations of the way in which we constitute and structure the world in which we live and interact. This examination is preparatory to the second part of my book, *The Normativity of Fiction*, which is devoted to the exploration of the normative and motivational character of ethical concepts as fictitious entities. The activity of the human mind basically consists in creating an artificial framework, without which knowledge and action, and more generally social life, would be impossible. The originality, importance and contribution of Bentham's fictionalism to our ideas of reality and society can scarcely be overstated. Nonetheless, his theory of real and fictitious entities still remains largely unexplored and requires much more attention and analysis.

Before starting the exploration of Bentham's ontology, it is important to make a terminological clarification concerning the terms *fiction* and *fictitious entity* in his vocabulary. It is worth noting the confusion of *fictions* with *fictitious entities* in much of the literature. Schofield has recently stressed their difference: *fiction* denotes an "erroneous proposition," while *fictitious entity* points out "an entity which [does] not have a physical existence." In other words, *fictions* are lies, untruths. Consequently, Schofield warns against the adoption of the expression *theory of fictions*, introduced by Ogden, which is "potentially confusing," when accounting for Bentham's treatment of real and fictitious entities.[22]

Schofield relates the notion of *fiction* to that of "falsehood" and the notion of *fictitious entity* to "an abstract term," having meaning because of its connection with the physical world, and thus susceptible to being true or false. As a support for his interpretation, Schofield refers to a passage contained in *First Principles Preparatory to Constitutional Code*, in which Bentham makes "a plain statement [. . .] that a fiction [is] a falsehood."[23]

Schofield admits that "very occasionally" the words *fiction* and *fictitious entity* are interchangeably employed. Indeed, Bentham adopts the notion of *fiction* to identify "abstract entities" (*Essay on Language*),[24] and maintains that "the idea of fiction" is free from blame and beneficial to the development of human language (*Chrestomathia*).[25] These two passages are taken from writings dealing

22 Schofield 2006, 2 n. 14.

23 Schofield 2015, 1128 and the related note 19. As Schofield notes, that passage is contained in *First Principles Preparatory to Constitutional Code*, 267.

24 *Essay on Language*, Bowring viii, 334: "Abstract entities can no otherwise be expressed than by fiction."

25 *Chrestomathia*, 258: "Strict, to the highest pitch of strictness, as is the property with which the *entities* here called *fictitious* are thus denominated, in no instance can the idea of *fiction* be freer from all tincture of blame: in no other instance can it ever be equally beneficial; since, but for such fiction, the language of *man* could not have risen above the language of *brutes*."

with logical matters, in which a higher level of semantic accuracy is expected in the usage of the philosophical vocabulary. Furthermore, in *Of Ontology* Bentham characterizes *fiction* as "the mode of representation by which the fictitious entities [. . .] are dressed up in the garb, and placed upon the level, of real ones."[26] Here *fiction* appears to be the way of being of fictitious entities.

Bentham does not always adhere to a standard usage of *fiction* and *fictitious entity* and, probably by virtue of this, commentators often use indiscriminately these two notions, as noted by Schofield too.[27] For example, in *Deontology* Bentham denominates virtue and vice both as fictitious entities and fictions.[28] Therefore, any semantic difference between *fiction* and *fictitious entity* may only indirectly be deduced from their usage in Bentham's texts, in which he seems to show a preference for the notion of *fictitious entity* when denoting intellectual objects, but also to make use of the notion of *fiction* for the same purpose. So, one might acknowledge a prevailing but not an exclusive meaning of the words *fiction* and *fictitious entity*. The understanding of the particular conceptual context in which they occur can solve the difficulty of interpreting their meaning.

Bearing in mind Schofield's observations and in accordance with Bentham's vocabulary, I generally adopt the expression *fictitious entity* to identify a single linguistic or mental object; however, on occasion I continue to use the term *fiction* with this same meaning in conformity with Bentham's linguistic choices. Furthermore, I employ the notion of *fiction* also to point out the way of being of fictitious entities as an alternative to the notion of reality, understood as the way of being of real entities. In this sense, *fiction* can identify the area or domain of fictitious entities as opposed to and distinguished from the area or domain of reality, made up by single real entities. This highly abstract usage of the term *fiction* enables us to account for the whole of fictitious entities, without adulterating Bentham's thought. So, one might talk of *area* or *domain of fiction*, *ontology of fiction*, *normativity of fiction*, and so on, *fiction* meaning, in these cases, the field of fictitious entities as a whole and not a single item of it.

26 *De l'ontologie*, 84 (Bowring viii, 198).
27 Schofield 2015, 1128 n. 19.
28 *Deontology*, 126 n. a.

1 The distinction between reality and fiction

1.1 Real entities

The map of entities

Any investigation into particular aspects of Bentham's thought, including his reflections on the normative grounds of human action, cannot leave his treatment of fictitious entities out of consideration. The distinction between real and fictitious entities is the general and basic tenet of Bentham's account of the physical and practical domain. According to Bentham, our understanding of the natural world and the foundation of a science of morality and law depend on the relation between reality and fiction.

Bentham devoted a number of his manuscripts to the treatment of ontological issues. Most of these manuscripts are now collected in *Of Ontology*, published under the French title *De l'ontologie et autres textes sur les fictions.* This text, in which the grounds of the theory of real and fictitious entities are laid down, is substantially different from Bowring's edition of *A Fragment on Ontology.* The first sections of the text *Of Ontology* and its appendix deal with the general characterization of the status of a real and a fictitious entity. In addition, a long essay included in *Chrestomathia*, corresponding to Appendix iv *Nomenclature and Classification*, is concerned with the same subject. In order to provide a comprehensive and quite consistent reconstruction of Bentham's distinction between real and fictitious entities, the following examination has been conducted on certain parts of the book *Of Ontology* by integrating them with some information contained in the above-mentioned excerpt from *Chrestomathia.*

Bentham demarcates the boundaries of the discipline called ontology, by identifying generality and abstractness as its distinctive features.[1] Before examining the field of ontology, Bentham makes a methodological statement. He will account for the general and abstract entities which are the subject matter of ontology according to their increasing level of complexity, that is, from elementary notions to composite ideas.[2] The most basic starting notion is that of *entity*, the nature of the existence of which is central to Bentham's concern.

1 Cf. *De l'ontologie*, 78–80, 162 (Bowring viii, 195).
2 Cf. *De l'ontologie*, 78–80 (Bowring viii, 195).

> An entity is a denomination in the import of which every subject matter of discourse, for the designation of which the grammatical part of speech called a noun-substantive is employed, may be comprised.[3]

An entity is identified as a "denomination," corresponding, from a syntactical point of view, to the "subject matter of discourse," i.e. the subject of a sentence, and, from a grammatical point of view, to a "noun-substantive." Bentham seems to restrict the existence of an entity within a linguistic and logic horizon by tracing ontology back to language.

Since the order of exposition of the text *Of Ontology* might create some misunderstanding,[4] I take into consideration and follow Bentham's map of real entities, briefly outlined in *Chrestomathia.*

> According to that conception of the matter, which is here alluded to and assumed, entities are either *real* or *fictitious*: real, either *perceptible* or *inferential*: perceptible, either *impressions* or *ideas*: inferential, either *material*, i.e. *corporeal* or *immaterial*, i.e. *spiritual*. Material are those of which the principal divisions are exhibited in the *Ramean* tree: of such inferential real entities as are immaterial, examples may be seen in the Almighty Being, and in the human soul, considered in a state of separation from the body.[5]

Because of its intelligibility, this passage can be schematized in a diagram, as shown in Figure 1.1.

As Bentham sees it, the field of reality stretches from sensorial and mental representations of corporeal objects, acquired by means of perception or inference, to few spiritual elements, derived through an inference. Nevertheless, Bentham's view of real entities is far from being clear. When we compare the treatments of real entities provided in *Chrestomathia* and *Of Ontology*, some substantial differences arise. For the sake of clarity, let us also schematize Bentham's map of real entities taken from *Of Ontology* (Figure 1.2).

3 *De l'ontologie*, 162 (Bowring viii, 195).

4 The classification of entities included in *A Fragment on Ontology* (Bowring viii, 195–7) and in *Appendix B* of the text *Of Ontology* (*De l'ontologie*, 164) seems to be misleading, because it postpones the distinction between real and fictitious to the distinction between perceptible and inferential. More reasonably, in *Chrestomathia* Bentham assumes the qualifications of perceptible and inferential as specifications of a real entity. Because of this inexplicable postponement, Bentham is forced to conclude that "An entity, whether perceptible or inferential, is either real or fictitious", entailing the possibility of perceptible or inferential fictitious entities, along with perceptible or inferential real entities. Actually, the distinction between perceptible and inferential should be applicable without contradiction only to real entities. Tyler (2004, 698), too, acknowledges the contradictory character of this statement made by Bentham; it appears to be scarcely justifiable: "Perceptible entities can be either real or fictitious, as can inferential entities. It is tempting to reject this proposition as it stands, on the grounds that a perceptible fictitious entity seems to be a contradiction in terms. Certainly there is a problem with perceptible fictitious entities." It is meaningless to qualify as perceptible a fictitious entity, which, by being immaterial and incorporeal, cannot be perceived. Moreover, the notion of reality is required when depicting the perceptual or inferential character of an entity.

5 *Chrestomathia*, 271 n. a.

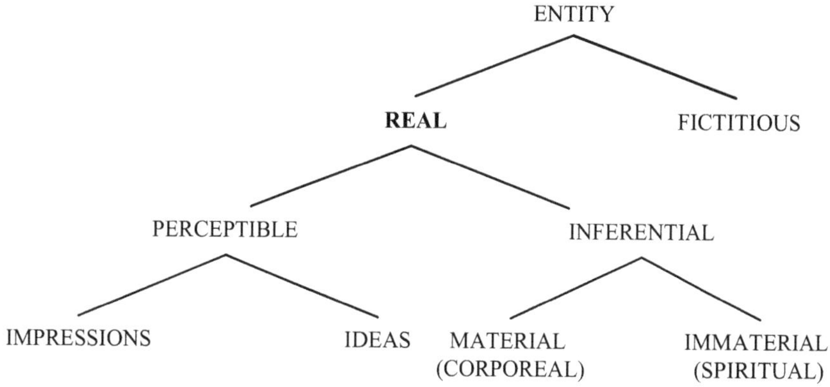

Figure 1.1 Real entities *Chrestomathia*

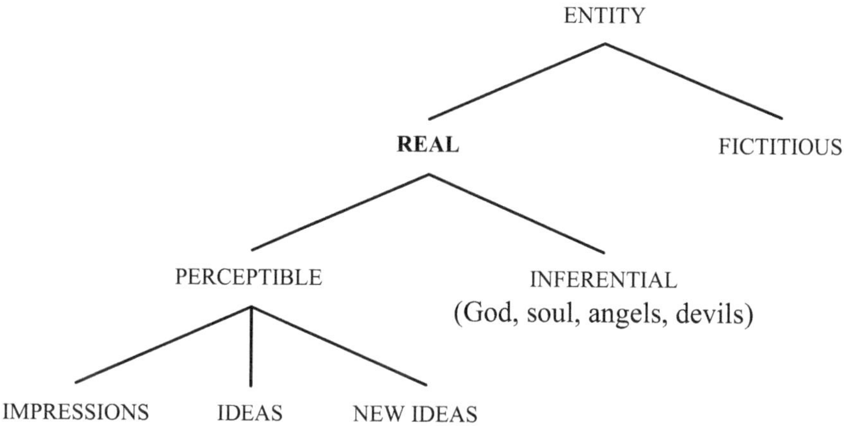

Figure 1.2 Real entities *Of Ontology*

At a first glance, we can acknowledge two main differences between the two treatments of real entities: the introduction of new ideas as specification of perceptible entities in *Of Ontology*; the distinction between material and immaterial inferential entities in *Chrestomathia*. Let us analyse Bentham's definitions of the various species of real entities, following not their order of exposition in *Of Ontology* and *Chrestomathia*, but their ontological order.

Bentham understands the notion of real entity in terms of existence, which is regarded, in this context, as a property bestowed by language:

> A real entity is an entity to which, on the occasion and for the purpose of discourse, existence is really meant to be ascribed.[6]

The reality of an entity consists in its existence. According to Bentham's above definition, the kind of existence ascribed to a real entity does not belong to it as

6 *De l'ontologie*, 164 (Bowring viii, 196).

one of its constitutive properties. On the contrary, existence is conferred on a real entity by language and, thus, it would be an external property attached to it. Bentham's choice of the verb *to ascribe* does not seem equivocal: it means the attribution or assignment of something as a quality. Existence, as a quality, is attributed to a real entity and this attribution is made by language. An entity is said to be real to the extent that its existence is assigned to it by language for the need for communication.

Perceptible entities

Bentham's statement about the existence-conferring ability of language apparently conflicts with another of his pivotal statements about perceptible entities, whose existence is testified by sense-organs. This empirical meaning of existence is accounted for by Bentham as follows:

> A perceptible entity is every entity the existence of which is made known to human and other beings by the immediate testimony of one or more of their senses.[7]

> *Perceptible and inferential*: under one or other of these denominations may be reduced all *real* entities: *perceptible* those of the existence of which the persuasion is produced by sense without reasoning, i.e. without reflection.[8]

The existence of a perceptible entity is immediately apprehended through physical sensibility, without the intervention of rational faculties. Bentham identifies a perceptible real entity with "a body," which is the *genus generalissimum* of the whole class of real entities.[9]

While in the definition of a real entity existence is given by language, in the definition of a perceptible real entity existence has a material import: it inheres in a real entity, that is, in a corporeal substance, and it is experienced through sensibility. Existence is approached, on the one hand, as a linguistic notion and, on the other, as a perceptual notion. These two meanings of existence seem incompatible because, in the first case, existence is regarded as a property assigned to an object by the human mind and, in the latter, as a property intrinsically characterizing an object and made known by sensibility. The notion of existence in Bentham's lexicon needs to be clarified and circumscribed.

A possible attempt to solve this interpretative difficulty might consist in acknowledging that Bentham does not employ a uniform notion of existence. In other words, linguistic existence and empirical existence should be conceived as two different modes of existence, belonging to different areas, i.e. the human

7 *De l'ontologie*, 164.
8 *De l'ontologie*, 170–2.
9 Cf. *De l'ontologie*, 168 (Bowring viii, 195 and n. ‡) (Note: Here and hereafter I reproduce the symbols which Bowring used to identify the footnotes in his edition).

mind and sensibility. So, there is no conflict between linguistic and empirical existence, because they pertain to different planes of reality. An entity can have both an empirical and a linguistic existence and another entity can have either an empirical or a linguistic existence, namely, an existence either experienced by the senses or acknowledged within a sentence.

With this distinction in mind, one may admit without contradiction the existence-conferring ability of language and the independent prerogative of existence of empirical entities. More specifically, language ascribes existence to a name, i.e. a noun-substantive, denoting a real entity. The kind of existence provided by language is nominal, that is, referring to names, and, by virtue of this, it is different from the existence belonging to empirical objects. Language does not bring into existence an entity, but rather its corresponding denomination. Thus, when Bentham argues that "a real entity is an entity to which [. . .] existence is really meant to be ascribed" by language, he means not directly a real entity but the name signifying a real entity. Indeed, by being real, i.e. perceptible or inferential, an entity is already existent. The context of Bentham's definition of real entity, as well as its attribution of existence, is purely linguistic.

Within a sentence, a real entity corresponds to a subject or a noun-substantive, which is treated as existent because of its nominal nature. A name is conceived as real and existent because of the internal needs for language or, as Bentham explicitly states, "on the occasion and for the purpose of discourse." From a linguistic point of view, existence is conferred on a name designating a real entity only by virtue of its being a name, without considering the nature of the object denoted by it and its type of existence. Thus, in the case of a real entity, language ascribes a verbal existence to a name corresponding to an entity having empirical existence. If language were to give existence and reality to a real entity and not merely to its denomination, there would be a conflict between the verbal existence, assigned by language to it, and the empirical existence, pertaining to it.

The activity of language, however, should not be regarded as an acknowledgement, on the level of discourse, of the empirical existence of an entity. Language is not able to give an account of the materiality of the entities denoted by names. The kind of existence provided by language is completely different from the empirical existence of an object and it is the outcome of an autonomous constructive process. The quality of existence is not discovered but ascribed by language. The separation between perception and language is clear. With reference to the notion of existence Bentham adopts two different approaches: on the one hand, a form of empirical realism and, on the other, a form of linguistic constructivism.

In *Of Ontology*, Bentham shows an extensive interpretation of the area of reality, incorporating in it abstractions and generalizations of bodies, which thus are saved from the area of fiction, namely, of nothing. As instances of fictitious entities, Bentham does not mention ideas of material objects such as the apple or the animal, but rather notions such as "faculties, powers of mind, dispositions," which have no empirical counterpart.

Bentham accounts for the notion of idea as a perceptual entity, acknowledging to it an empirical nature.[10] Ideas are included in the set of "perceptible real entities," in which Bentham gathers "individual perceptions of all sorts." These perceptions are distinguished in impressions, which are "produced in groups by the application of sensible objects to the organs of sense"; in ideas, which are "brought to view by the recollection of those same objects"; and in new ideas, which are "produced by the action of the imagination, by the decomposition and recomposition of those groups."[11] Bentham concludes that "to none of these [. . .] can the character, the denomination, of *real* entities be refused."[12]

Bentham's collection of real entities is not confined only to actual corporeal perceptions, acquired by the faculty of sensibility in the form of impressions, but also encompasses ideas and new ideas: they are produced through the intervention of mental faculties, i.e. memory and imagination which perform reflective activities on sense-data, namely recollection, decomposition and recomposition. Thus, ideas maintain a constitutive relation with experience and, because of this relation, they can be considered as perceptions in a derivative and mediate form.

Elsewhere Bentham gives Hume credit for the discovery of the distinction between impressions and ideas.[13] However, Bentham's understanding of this distinction is dissimilar from Hume's. Unlike Bentham, Hume holds that the difference between impressions and ideas "consists in the degrees of force and liveliness, with which they strike upon the mind, and make their way into our thought or consciousness." Thus, impressions, including "all our sensations, passions and emotions" are stronger than ideas, which are "the faint images" of impressions "in thinking and reasoning."[14]

Instead, for Bentham, impressions and ideas do not correspond to different degrees of perception, but they stand out because of the type: impressions are immediate perceptions acquired through the senses; ideas are mediate perceptions, worked out by the intellectual faculties which operate on impressions.

10 The empirical origin of ideas is remarked on by Bentham in *Of the Limits of the Penal Branch of Jurisprudence*, 172–3, n. c: "Our ideas originate all from the senses: our ideas of mischief and the causes of it, as well as any other. Imagination may do something: but it must always have experience or observation or report, that is it must have sense, as a ground to work upon."

11 More information on Bentham's distinction between impressions and ideas is contained in his unpublished manuscripts (UC 101.408): "In the case where the perception is ab extra so long as the organ of sense is acted upon by the external object, the result belongs to the original or primitive faculty of perception, and has been distinguished by the appellation of an *impression*"; "Where the organ of sense is no longer thus acted upon, if any effect remains in the mind, it belongs to the faculty of *derivative* perception, i.e. the *memory*: and has been distinguished by the appellation of *an idea*." (These quotations are taken from Tyler 2004, 697 n. 54.)

12 Cf. *De l'ontologie*, 172 (Bowring viii, 196).

13 *A Table of the Springs of Action*, 350: "Hume made a most important distinction between impressions and ideas. I do not know what people did before this distinction. It was a great discovery. My impression of you is from seeing; my idea I have when, after seeing you, I shut my eyes."

14 Cf. Hume, *A Treatise of Human Nature*, i.i.1. For a comparison between Hume and Bentham's account of impressions and ideas, see Schofield 2006, 16.

Moreover, contrary to Hume, the belief in the existence of ideas is superior to the belief in the existence of impressions.

In line with its widespread usage in the eighteenth century, under the influence of Locke's *Essay Concerning Human Understanding*, the term idea has a very broad meaning in Bentham's vocabulary.[15] He says that "The several objects we are said to have in our mind when we are thinking, we call *ideas.*"[16] The notion of idea generally denotes any mental representation which has the form of a recollection of experience or of a reflection on experience. In both cases, experience is the source of ideas. Ideas basically have an empirical nature, because they correspond to recollected impressions or to concepts developed from impressions.

Bentham adopts the notion of idea in a similar way to Locke, who defines it as "Whatsoever the mind perceives in itself, or is the immediate object of perception, thought, or understanding."[17] Yet Bentham excludes actual perceptions from the notion of idea, identifying them as impressions. Impressions are direct perceptions while ideas are derivative perceptions, that is, perceptions resulting from the mental operations carried out on empirical phenomena.[18]

Inferential entities

In *Of Ontology*, in parallel to the definition of a perceptible real entity, Bentham characterizes the notion of an inferential real entity. *Perceptible* and *inferential*

15 The widespread eighteenth-century usage of the notion of idea is testified to in the *Encyclopédie ou Dictionnaire raisonné des sciences, des arts et des métiers* viii, 489 (*sub vocem*): "idée: [. . .] nous trouvons en nous la faculté de recevoir des idées, d'appercevoir les choses, de se les représenter. L'idée ou la perception est le sentiment qu'a l'ame de l'état où elle se trouve."

16 Cf. *Preparatory Principles*, 382. The passage continues as follows: "Ideas have been very usefully distinguished into ideas properly so called, and impressions. It is an impression | |. Of Ideas, some are exact, unvarying, literal copies of impressions, others not. To take an example from the sense of sight. An impression of the object is that we have present to our mind when we see the object: a mere idea, when, without seeing it, we think of it, or remember to have seen it." Bentham (*Preparatory Principles*, 382–3) mentions as examples of ideas extension, figure, void, space, time, colour, tangible quality, odorous quality, impenetrability, heat and cold. As we will see, these examples are regarded as fictitious entities in *Of Ontology*, which was written many years after *Preparatory Principles.*

17 Locke, *An Essay concerning Human Understanding*, ii.viii.8.

18 It is hard to identify a consistent meaning and a uniform usage of the notion of idea in Bentham's vocabulary. In *Of Ontology*, when articulating the notion of idea from an ontological point of view, Bentham seems to adopt it in different and contradictory ways: on the one hand, specifically in the context of the characterizations of real entities, he employs idea to identify a kind of real entity, by meaning with it a recollection and a manipulation of impressions (see, for example, *De l'ontologie*, 172; Bowring viii, 196); on the other hand, he calls ideas the notions of matter and form, that is, two fictitious entities, which are "fractional results, produced from the decomposition of the idea belonging to the word *substance*" (*De l'ontologie*, 90; Bowring viii, 201). Because of this inclusion of fictitious entities, the meaning of idea in *Of Ontology* might sometimes appear confusing. Moreover, in *Chrestomathia* (398–9) he makes a lexical disambiguation of the word idea, by reducing it to two heads: the idea of subject, that is, of a real or a fictitious entity regarded as subject; and the idea of the relation between two or more subjects. In this case, Bentham defines the notion of the idea from a linguistic standpoint, by referring it to all syntactic units corresponding to the subject of a sentence and to the relation among such subjects.

are, indeed, the divisions of the genus *real entity*. Also, in the case of the inferential entities, the quality of existence is a distinctive mark which takes on a specific rational form.

> An inferential entity is an entity which at this time of day at least is not made known to human beings in general, by the testimony of sense, but is inferred from a chain of reasoning.[19]

> *Perceptible and inferential*: under one or other of these denominations may be reduced all *real* entities: [. . .] inferential those of the existence of which the persuasion, in as far as it has place, is produced by reason, by reflection.[20]

Unlike the existence of a perceptual entity, the existence of an inferential real entity is the product of a reflective process carried out by the human mind. In this process sense-perception plays no role. Such entities are inferential insofar as their existence is the outcome of a chain of reasoning. The existence of an inferential entity is a persuasion which is not derived from sense-data but is produced by reflection. At the origin of inferential entities there is a rational operation that results in the belief in their existence.

Bentham distinguishes inferential entities into human and superhuman. As an instance of a human inferential entity Bentham brings up the human soul, "considered as existing in a state of separation from the body." It is an entity of which "no man living will [. . .] be found ready to aver himself to have had perception of any individual example."[21] Bentham distinguishes further a superhuman entity into supreme and subordinate. As an instance of a superhuman entity Bentham cites God, whom no man has ever seen, according to Christian tradition. A supreme inferential entity such as God is not "capable of being referred to the class of perceptible real entities" because of the limits of the human senses. As instances of subordinate superhuman entities, Bentham mentions an angel and a devil.[22]

Entities such as a soul, God, an angel and a devil are inferential because they are logically derived from certain premises or suppositions. Bentham does not withhold reality and existence to inferential entities, which however are not experienced through the senses, but only derived by reasoning: "Of this description of beings, the reality, not being in any instance, attested by *perception*, can not therefore be considered any otherwise than as matter of *inference*."[23] Thus, inferential entities exist outside the human mind, though their existence is not perceived but inferred.

Bentham specifies that former logicians adopted the notion of substance "to comprise perceptible and inferential real entities." In particular, with the

19 *De l'ontologie*, 164 (Bowring viii, 195).
20 *De l'ontologie*, 170–2.
21 *De l'ontologie*, 174 (Bowring viii, 196).
22 Cf. *De l'ontologie*, 164, 174–82 (Bowring viii, 195–6).
23 *De l'ontologie*, 176 (Bowring viii, 196).

appellation of substance they designated "Souls, God, Angels, Devils,"[24] which are the same entities that Bentham regards as inferential and real. One might suppose that Bentham is attempting to give an account of real entities which is in line with the long-standing ontological and metaphysical tradition preceding him. Hence, he is persuaded to include such metaphysical elements in the area of reality, in agreement with their mainstream treatment. Their specification as inferential could derive from Bentham's need to stress their non-perceptible or unempirical character.

It is worth noting that the number of inferential entities is so limited and uninfluential that Bentham himself acknowledges that "all these subjects of *ontology*, may, without much detriment (it is believed), either to any other useful *art*, or any other useful Science, be left in the places in which they are found."[25] Bentham does not appear to be very interested in deepening the ontological status of metaphysical and spiritual entities. In these passages from *Of Ontology* he is rather more concerned with perceptual entities, although he does not intend to provide an account of reality in conflict with the previous ontological and metaphysical tradition.

In conclusion, the area of reality appears to be well-defined: it is composed by impressions, ideas of material bodies and a few metaphysical creatures. If we consider the negligibility of these metaphysical creatures in Bentham's account, we might, by and large, trace the area of reality back to perceptions, that is, to elements related to the senses both in a direct way, as in the case of impressions, and in an indirect way, as in the case of ideas and new ideas. Consequently, experience is the cognitive source of reality to the extent that reality basically has an empirical nature.

Unlike *Of Ontology*, in the above schematized passage from *Chrestomathia*, Bentham extends the class of inferential objects, composed by immaterial, i.e. spiritual, entities such as the Almighty Being and the human soul, to material, i.e. corporeal, entities "of which the principal divisions are exhibited in the *Ramean* tree."[26] The Ramean or Porphyrian tree is a classification of predications according to the distinction between *genus* and *species*, provided by the application of the method of dichotomy.

The Porphyrian tree shows a series of divisions, by means of *differentiae*, from the most general predicament, for example substance, having no prior genus, to the most special predicament, for example a particular man, having no posterior species. The intermediate predicaments, contained in the Porphyrian tree, are related to one another in a hierarchical order, according to which each one is both the species of its superordinate predicament and the genus of its subordinate predicament. So, starting from the genus *substance*, the deriving divisions are *body* and *soul*; then, from *body* derive *animate body* and *inanimate body*; from *animate*

24 Cf. *De l'ontologie*, 168 (Bowring viii, 195 n. ‡).
25 *De l'ontologie*, 180 (Bowring viii, 196).
26 Cf. *Chrestomathia*, 271 n. a.

body, *animal* and *vegetable* (*plant*); from *animal*, *rational animal* (*man*) and *irrational animal*.[27]

Bentham labels as material, inferential and real the entities corresponding to the branches of the Porphyrian tree. Their inferential character might lie in their being the outcome of a rational process consisting either in a division from general to particular or in a generalization from individuals.[28] In spite of the deductive structure of the Porphyrian tree, Bentham stresses the perceptual origin from which its entities derive, that is, from which they are inferred.

According to Bentham's map of ontology, the distinctive mark of the elements set out in the Porphyrian tree is materiality. Probably the relation these entities have with empirical individualities or particularities could have persuaded Bentham to differentiate them as material or corporeal. The branches of the Porphyrian tree are characterized by Bentham as generalizations or abstractions of material instantiations, as in the case of the entity *animal*, which is the general or abstract form of particular material animals.[29]

Bentham employs the notion of materiality with a broad meaning in mind. He includes in it not merely corporeal elements but also their generalizations. Actually, a generalization or abstraction has a material nature not in a direct but in a derivative form, by virtue of its close reference to matter, from which it arises by means of the intervention of the intellectual faculties such as imagination. The Porphyrian tree is thus, in Bentham's view, a rational construction aimed at the reproduction of the order of reality, that is, more specifically, of empirical reality, according to different levels of generality and inclusion of its elements. Bodies, corresponding to abstractions of corporeal objects, are organized and coordinated in a deductive scheme mirroring the structure of material reality.

Again in *Chrestomathia*, Bentham asserts that "The names, by which the branches of the *Porphyrian* or *Ramean* tree are designated, are names of *real* entities." Generalizations of empirical bodies are incorporated in the field of reality, while the field of fiction is confined to "The names of the branches of the Encyclopædical tree" devised by D'Alembert, which are, for example, understanding, memory, history, reason, imagination. All of them have manifestly no empirical instantiation, namely, no individual element to which they can be associated. In brief, "Names of *bodies* [. . .] are names of *real entities*; names of qualities and relations, names of fictitious entities."[30]

27 In outlining the Porphyrian Tree, I follow diagram no. ii, provided by Bentham in *Chrestomathia*, table iv. The passage from which the construction of the diagram called Porphyrian Tree originated is contained in Porphyry, *Introduction*, 5–6. However, Bentham's knowledge of the Porphyrian Tree is due to Sanderson's *Logic*, as he himself admits in *Chrestomathia*, 239–40. Bentham devotes some sections of his writings included in *Chrestomathia* (239–42) and *Essay on Logic* (UC 101.336–9; Bowring viii, 266–7) to the treatment of the Porphyrian Tree.

28 See *Essay on Logic*, UC 101.336 (Bowring viii, 266): "The process or course by which, setting out from *individuals* and those *determinate*, men arrived at the seat of [the] most extensive aggregates has received the name of *generalization*: it has *division* – logical or psychical *division* – for its *converse*."

29 See *Essay on Logic*, UC 101.336–8 (Bowring viii, 266).

30 *Chrestomathia*, 257–8.

The clarification of the notion of body, equivalent to that of real entity, enables us to set the boundaries of the field of reality. By *body* Bentham seems to mean not only particular corporeal elements, but also their abstractions and generalizations, corresponding to the branches of the Porphyrian tree. The title of body is attributed, for example, to an individual living animal and to the idea of animal, which is the generalization of particular animals. So, the demarcation between reality and fiction depends on the semantic area of the notion of body, whether it is restricted to material objects or whether it includes immaterial entity. No doubt, the notion of body, if meant to denote merely something corporeal, would be unable to embrace the variety of entities listed by Bentham under the class of real.[31]

The belief in the existence of real entities

It is worth stressing that, save for metaphysical creatures, whose importance in Bentham's ontology is very limited, real entities are perceptions, namely impressions and ideas of material bodies, to which inferential corporeal entities are added in *Chrestomathia*. This fact is implicitly acknowledged in a passage from *Of Ontology*, in which Bentham observes that under the denominations of real and fictitious entity "may be comprehended every object that ever was or ever can be present to any faculty of the human frame – to perception, memory, or imagination."[32] In other words, the knowledge of the existence of something depends on the human sensory and cognitive structures.

Human beings become aware of the world external to their mind by means of the manifold perceptions that that world produces in their sense-organs.[33] Bentham credits the title of real entities to these sensory elements and not to the objects occasioning them, the ontological character of which remains enigmatical. Reality would seem to consist of beliefs about external objects and not directly of objects. Indeed, when accounting for the existence of real and fictitious entities, Bentham expresses himself in terms of "persuasion."[34]

31 The relation between ideas and material inferential real entities is particularly problematic, because both entities, despite their different character, perceptual and inferential, seem to some extent to identify the same contents, that is, conceptual objects related to empirical instantiations. It is no coincidence that Bentham characterizes material inferential entities as ideas. Unfortunately, in *Of Ontology* Bentham does not give an example of the notion of ideas and especially new ideas, which could have helped us to have a clearer understanding of his outlook of reality and, in particular, of the relation between new ideas and the inferential material of real entities outlined in *Chrestomathia*. So, the analogies and differences between these two species of real entities, one perceptual and the other inferential, are unexplored and thus blurred. May inferential material objects be regarded as ideas just as certain perceptual objects? Or, to put it differently, may the branches of the Porphyrian tree, which are inferential, be identified as ideas without contradiction? These questions remain unresolved.

32 *De l'ontologie*, 80.

33 A similar position is expressed by Hume, *A Treatise of Human Nature*, i.ii.5.

34 See for example *Essay on Language*, UC 102.300 (Bowing viii, 300): "It is only through some *sense* or *senses*, *external* or *internal* – i.e. *physical* or *psychical* – that any thing can be *known* to a man; or (to speak more correctly) that, concerning any object or aggregate of objects, any *persuasion* can be obtained."

These considerations lead us to a vexed issue, recently raised again by Tyler, concerning the kind of existence affecting real entities according to Bentham. In his provocative article, Tyler challenges the prevailing realist interpretation, which asserts the physical existence of corporeal objects, and endorses, radicalizing it, the minority anti-realist interpretation, which traces the existence of real entities back to a subjective belief.[35] With reference to Bentham's manuscripts dating back to 1813–16, Tyler argues that "a real entity has a purely conceptual structure" and, thus, its ontological status, i.e. its existence, is not objective but depends on a person's belief, that is, on a person's persuasion.[36]

Bentham's characterization of existence in terms of persuasion, that is, of subjective belief, is the main textual and theoretical support on which Tyler bases his contention. No doubt, in Bentham's view, the consideration of existence as a persuasion is an essential cognitive element in the representation of reality. However, understanding existence as a belief does not entail a denial of materiality, that is, more specifically, of the mind-independent existence of the physical world. Knowledge basically consists in beliefs, having a subjective nature, which mediate between external reality and the human mind. Belief or persuasion has a crucial role in Bentham's ontology and epistemology, as also remarked by Schofield, who admits that a statement about the existence of something physical is tantamount to a statement about what is believed to exist.[37]

In his text on ontology, Bentham acknowledges without contradiction both the objective reality of corporeal objects and the subjective belief in their existence. He reconciles these two dimensions by claiming a correspondence between the contents of the mind, i.e. ideas, and material reality. The conclusions gained by the human mind in the form of beliefs are consistent with the structure of the physical world. Consequently, Bentham rejects mere immaterialism, as for example that advocated by Berkeley: he does not reduce reality, and thus matter, exclusively to perception.[38] Mental representations, encompassing any kind of

35 Tyler 2004, 687: "I will argue that in the 1813–16 manuscripts, Bentham operated within a paradigm that subsequently and very famously (and without reference to Bentham) Dummett has called 'anti-realism'. My interpretation stands in opposition to the prevalent tradition that sees Bentham as being engaged in a 'realist' project throughout his life." On the same question regarding the status of real entities in Bentham's thought, see Cléro 2007, 81: "Bentham a reproduit cette analyse un nombre incalculable de fois avec, pour seules variations, des flottements, en particulier sur la question de savoir si les entités réelles sont *existantes* ou si leur réalité ne consiste qu'en ce qu'on les *tient pour* réelles afin de satisfaire les besoins d'un discours."

36 Cf. Tyler 2004, 693–5; on p. 695: "It has been has indicated so far that, at least between 1813 and 1816, Bentham adopted an anti-realist metaphysics in which he rested his distinction between real entities and fictitious entities not on a claim about the object's ontological status, but on the agent's belief about its ontological status."

37 Schofield 2006, 18: "It should be emphasized that Bentham recognized that persuasion or belief had a crucial role to play. A statement about what existed in the physical world could not be separated from a statement about what was believed to exist." Schofield (2006, 22) explicitly maintains Bentham's endorsement of physical realism: "Bentham accepted that the physical world had an existence which was independent of the human mind."

38 Berkeley lays the foundations for his ontology and epistemology in *A Treatise Concerning the Principles of Human Knowledge*, i.1–7.

perception, are regarded as real insofar as they enable a subject to grasp the reality external to his/her mind.

Bentham's realist position plainly emerges from his frequent attacks on Berkeley's immaterialism. By distancing himself from Berkeley, Bentham vindicates the existence of matter. His argument, supporting a realist view as an alternative to Berkeley's anti-realism, is based on physical, and thus perceptual, evidence, as the following quotation from *Essay on Language* illustrates.

> *This pen exists*, – meaning the pen employed in the tracing of these characters. This pen exists, *i.e.* my opinion is that this pen exists. Such is very decidedly and firmly my own opinion. But of no pen with which he ever wrote would any such opinion have been entertained by Bishop Berkeley.[39]

In Bentham's account of the physical world, empiricism and realism coexist, without being in conflict by virtue of their substantial conformity. The contents of the mind, originated by perception, reflect the structure of the world. My belief in the existence of the pen I am using finds correspondence in the fact that this pen has its own existence. So, the subjective process of knowledge is in harmony with materiality. In this way, Bentham implicitly also disagrees with scepticism about the existence of matter, which is championed for example by Hume.[40] In Bentham's account, the autonomy of the human mind in representing reality does not involve questioning or refusing materiality; on the contrary, cognitive activity brings individuals to the acknowledgment of the external existence of objects.

Bentham's junction of empiricism and materialism could have been inspired by Locke's claim of the independent existence of substances, notwithstanding their being complex ideas. According to Locke, "the ideas of substances are such combinations of simple ideas as are taken to represent distinct particular things subsisting by themselves."[41] Locke regards the existence of a substance, on the one hand, as the product of the cognitive activity performed on experience-data and, on the other, as an autonomous property. One would not expect any discrepancy to be found between the two natures, mind-dependent and mind-independent, shown by the notion of existence belonging to substances. Indeed, the ideas of substances, unlike the ideas of modes, "carry with them the supposition of some real being, from which they are taken, and to which they are conformable."[42]

Similarly, Bentham supposes the correspondence between the subjective belief in the existence of an object and the objective existence inhering in that object. Put differently, ideas bridge the human minds and objects. Our knowledge of the world is not direct and immediate but is a mediate process in which the world is represented in the form of impressions and ideas, that is, of sensory

39 *Essay on Language*, Bowring viii, 321.
40 Hume, *A Treatise of Human Nature*, i.iii.1.
41 Locke, *An Essay concerning Human Understanding*, ii.xii.6.
42 Locke, *An Essay concerning Human Understanding*, iii.v.3. Cf. Fuller, Stecker & Wright 2000, 7.

and intellectual contents. The human mind perceives material objects indirectly, that is, by means of ideas representing these material objects, which have an independent existence. Our image of external reality is a representation of it through ideas. This is the reason why Bentham speaks of perception of ideas and not of perception of things. Ideas, which are subjective entities, connect the human mind to the world.

Bentham rejects any criticism of the reality of perceptions, which, according to a philosophical tradition going back to ancient times, have not "solidity or permanence," i.e. the stability necessary to exist. Human beings are aware of the existence of corporeal objects by means of perceptions, the reality of which, however, is superior in the degree of evidence to the reality of such objects.

> Whatsoever claim an object belonging to the class of bodies may be considered as possessing to the attribute of reality, i.e. of existence, every object belonging to the class of *perceptions* will be found to possess a still better title – a title established by still more immediate evidence. Of the reality of perceptions, they are themselves their own evidence: it is only by the evidence afforded by perceptions that the reality of a body of any kind can be established.[43]

Bentham makes it clear that the attribute of reality coincides with the attribute of existence: they belong both to objects and perceptions, though in different degrees of evidence. The reality and existence of perceptions is directly and immediately experienced, whereas the reality and existence of objects is proved on the basis of perceptions.

Bentham specifies that our perception of ideas is "still more direct and immediate than that which we have of corporeal substances." As a consequence, with regard to the existence of ideas our persuasion "is more intense and irresistible than that which we have of the existence of corporeal substances."[44] Bentham does not deny the existence of corporeal substances but recognizes the superiority of our beliefs in the existence of ideas, whose contents should represent corporeal substances.

Bentham's empirical realism consists in the acknowledgment of an empirical meaning of existence, which is a persuasion of the human mind concerning the reality of the perceptions of material entities. The sensory faculties lead the individual to the knowledge of the world. By virtue of their immediacy and strength, ideas might be regarded as "the *sole perceptible*" entities, while, as opposed to them, the substances of the corporeal class would be "no other than *inferential*" entities.[45]

Bentham exhibits a chain of logical deductions, which I try to outline hereafter: (1) from corporeal entities (i.e. bodies) derive perceptions; (2) from the existence

43 *De l'ontologie*, 174 (Bowring viii, 196).

44 *De l'ontologie*, 180 (Bowring viii, 196).

45 Cf. *De l'ontologie*, 180 (Bowring viii, 196–7). In this passage, however, Bentham clarifies that the attribution of inferential is employed to designate only incorporeal substances and thus corporeal substances are perceptible too.

of perceptions (i.e. sensible perceptions) derives the existence of corporeal entities (i.e. bodies); and (3) from the existence of perceptible entities (i.e. corporeal substances, bodies) derives the existence of incorporeal entities (i.e. souls and gods). According to Bentham, the second inference is "much stronger and more irresistible" than the third.[46] Human beings are made aware of the existence of physical bodies by means of reasoning, whose conclusions are not in contradiction with materiality. The existence of physical bodies is not directly discerned by the senses but is supposed by the mind and corroborated by the senses.

Bentham concludes his reflection by stating the existence of corporeal substances with a proof by contradiction. If you deny the existence of bodies and act with this supposition in mind, "pain, the perception of pain, will at once bear witness against you, and be your punishment, your condign punishment."[47] Bentham's proof of the existence of corporeal substances can be further clarified by physical evidence: "if of the wall opposite me, I infer the non-existence, and run that way as if there were no wall, the erroneousness of the inference will be but too plainly perceptible on my forehead."[48] The existence of corporeal objects is undeniable: when we move, we cannot leave the reality of bodies out of our consideration on pain of physical suffering. The case of "inferential incorporeal substances" is completely different, because the supposition that they exist cannot be proved by physical evidence as in the case of corporeal substance; from a material point of view, it is not possible to ascertain whether this supposition is "conformable or not conformable to the truth of the case."[49]

Elsewhere Bentham makes an unequivocal statement on the existence of the material world; he supports this statement by the consideration that it, unlike its reverse, does not bring about any negative consequence.

> I assume, in a word, the existence of what is called the material world. [. . .] I assume it boldly for this reason; because in point of practice, no bad consequences can, as every one is ready to acknowledge, possibly arise from supposing it to be true; and the worst consequences can not but arise from supposing it to be false.[50]

46 Cf. *De l'ontologie*, 180–2 (Bowring viii, 197).

47 Cf. *De l'ontologie*, 182 (Bowring viii, 197).

48 Here the whole passage from *Chrestomathia*, 402 n. a: "According to those who agree with Bishop Berkeley, matter belongs to the class of those entities of which the existence is inferential; impressions and ideas being, in that case, the only perceptible entities. But, in the case of matter, the justness of the inference is determinable, at all times determinable by experimental proof: if of the wall opposite me, I infer the non-existence, and run that way as if there were no wall, the erroneousness of the inference will be but too plainly perceptible on my forehead; which is not the case in any one of these other instances."

49 Cf. *De l'ontologie*, 182 (Bowring viii, 197).

50 This quotation of Bentham's text is taken from Quinn 2012, 8. On p. 9 note 28, Quinn mentions the source of this passage, which is the section entitled "Key. What things exist" of the manuscript UC clix. 52. As a commentary to this passage Quinn notes that "Bentham assumes at the outset not only that the world which we perceive exists, but that sense experience is capable of delivering accurate information about it."

The existence of the material world has a hypothetical character and that is as far as it goes. The assumption of the existence of the material world is fruitful, though it cannot be ascertained beyond bodily experience. It cannot be more than a persuasion of the human mind, supported by sensory data. The passage just quoted sketches out a practical proof: the consequences drawn by the assumption of the existence of the material world are not bad; on the contrary, the denial of the existence of the material world entails negative consequences, such as hurting oneself when moving. These consequences are verified by experience; thus, this proof is empirical, notwithstanding its inferential nature.

1.2 Fictitious entities

Empirical ontology and linguistic ontology

The notion of fictitious entity is defined by Bentham in *Of Ontology* by making clear the type of existence which characterizes and identifies it. No doubt, if real and fictitious entities are both existent, the type of existence affecting each of them should be different, not in the degree but in the kind. Thus, the notion of existence is central to the understanding of a fictitious entity and of its difference with a real entity.

> By this term [= fictitious entity] is here meant to be designated one of those sorts of objects which, in every language, must for the purpose of discourse be spoken of as existing, – be spoken of in the same manner as those objects which really have existence, and to which existence is seriously meant to be ascribed, are spoken of – objects of the existence of which a serious persuasion is seriously intended to be produced – but without any such design as that of producing any such persuasion as that of their possessing each for itself any separate, or strictly speaking any real existence.[51]

> A fictitious entity is an entity to which, though by the grammatical form of the discourse employed in speaking of it existence be ascribed, yet in truth and reality existence is not meant to be ascribed.[52]

Apparently, Bentham's above definitions would seem contradictory, because, first, they acknowledge existence to fictitious entities, although only from a grammatical or linguistic point of view, but, then, they deny this attribution according to reality and truth. It is not yet clear whether a fictitious entity exists or does not exist or, at least, whether it has some form of existence. This contradiction lies

51 *De l'ontologie*, 86 (Bowring viii, 198).

52 *De l'ontologie*, 164 (Bowring viii, 197). Bentham's concern with the existence of fictitious entities is clear also in his definition of them in *Preparatory Principles*, 387: "By fictitious entities, such as, without being represented seriously as existing, are feigned and endued with names that in strictness are proper only for real beings, viz: substantives, merely for the purpose of discourse. Such are Liberty, Right, Condition, Quality, disposition &c."

in the fact that the way in which an entity can exist is not univocal, but one may identify, by and large, two forms of existence, one linguistic or mental and the other empirical. Bentham articulates the definition of fictitious entities by making reference to both kinds of existence.

While employing the notion of existence, Bentham seems to distinguish between the area of language, which is fictitious, and the area of perception, which is real and true: the former is purely mental and includes conceptual objects; the latter is purely empirical and includes corporeal objects. The concept of existence, concerning these two different and conflicting areas, has a double meaning, one linguistic and the other empirical. Bentham seems to presuppose a separation between a mental kind of existence, created and assigned by language, and an empirical kind of existence, inherent in the materiality of objects as they are apprehended by the human senses.

Rightly speaking, a real entity is an object having both an empirical existence, by virtue of its perceptual character, and a mental existence, by virtue of its nominal character, namely of its being a noun-substantive in a sentence. A fictitious entity is an object having no empirical existence because of its imperceptibility, but rather having a mental existence conferred on it by language. Therefore, from an empirical point of view, only real entities exist, because experience is the only source of reality and existence; from a mental point of view, both real and fictitious entities exist because language assigns reality and existence to them. Perception and language correspond to two different human faculties, sometimes leading to the same results, as in the case of the existence of empirical objects, sometimes producing conflicting results, as in the case of the existence of conceptual objects.

Real entities and fictitious entities involve different conceptions of existence. However, according to Bentham, only perceptions are real and existent. As a consequence, the area of fiction is the realm of non-existent objects because it is made up by fictitious entities whose existence and reality, even though necessary for us, are not true. The existence and reality of fictitious entities are not apprehended through perception as properties affecting these entities but are constructed by mental faculties by means of language. Thus, fictitious entities, including their existence and reality, are mere artefacts, i.e. creations of the human mind, "feigned in virtue of an irresistible demand, for the purposes of discourse."[53] It is, in other words, language itself which needs to construct fictitious entities for the sake of communication.

The real or fictitious character of an entity depends on the kind of existence inhering in it. Existence is conferred by language upon fictitious entities, although empirically this feature does not belong to them. Language plays the same existential function with both a real and a fictitious entity. In the case of a real entity, language ascribes mental existence and reality to a name designating an object which has empirical existence and reality. The existence provided by

53 *Essay on Logic*, UC 101.116 (Bowring viii, 223).

language finds correspondence in the perceptual nature of a real entity. In the case of a fictitious entity, language bestows mental existence and reality upon a name denoting an object which has no empirical existence and reality, that is, which is nothing in perceptual terms. Language brings this perceptual nothing to existence, by ascribing to it a form of reality insofar as it is a nominal entity, that is, a noun-substantive.

So, in the two above-quoted passages from *Of Ontology* Bentham highlights the ambiguous status of fictitious entities: they are mentally but not empirically existent. Fictitious entities exist, though they are not perceived by the senses. They owe their existence to language, to which they are necessary for the construction of the discourse. Within a sentence, fictitious entities are employed as if they really exist, without differentiating them by perceptual entities, which however have a real existence.

The type of existence of fictitious entities is different from the type of existence of real entities: in the case of fictitious entities the attribution of existence is provided by the language, in the case of real entities the acknowledgment of their existence is made by sensibility. The existence that characterizes fictitious entities is not a weak or faded form of empirical existence, which properly pertains to perceptual objects. On the contrary, it belongs to another kind, which may be regarded as linguistic insofar as it results from mental activities such as imagination and communication. Although employed in a sentence in the same manner of real entities, fictitious entities should not produce the belief that they possess a "separate existence," namely an existence independent of a mental source. Indeed, fictitious entities cannot be conceived without the intervention of the human mind. Thus, real entities are perceived, whereas fictitious entities need to be created.

Real and fictitious entities are equally designated by names: they correspond to *names of real entities* and *names of fictitious entities*. Despite the different nature, i.e. empirical and mental, of the objects signified by them, both are merely names and only with this denominative function are they taken into account by language. The distinction between real and fictitious entities is thus specified as distinction between names of real and names of fictitious entities.[54] The common verbal nature of real and fictitious objects is clarified by Bentham in the following excerpt from *Essay on Logic*.

> Like the names of real and those of fabulous entities, all these words, it will be seen, are, in the language of Grammarians, *noun substantives*. All these fictitious entities are accordingly so many fictitious substances. The properties which for the purposes of discourse are attributed to them are so many properties of substances – so many properties of all substances.[55]

54 *De l'ontologie*, 84 (Bowring viii, 198): "In language, the words which present themselves and are employed in the character of *names* are some of them names of real entities, other names of fictitious entities: and to one or other of these classes may all words which are employed in the character of *names* be referred."

55 *Essay on Logic*, UC 101.322 (Bowring viii, 263).

From a grammatical and a syntactical point of view, there is no substantial difference between names of real entities and names of fictitious entities: both are indistinctly identified as nouns or subjects. A noun-substantive can signify something real, something fictitious or something unreal, without distinguishing these things and, thus, designating each of them in a uniform way. Denominations of real, fictitious and unreal entities share the same nominal or verbal form.

In the context of a sentence, a name is regarded as if it signifies a real and existent object, even if this object is not actually perceived by the senses. By virtue of its being a noun-substantive or a subject of a clause, a name denoting a fictitious entity is considered on an equal footing with a name denoting a real entity. Indeed, "To be spoken of at all, every fictitious entity must be spoken of as if it were real."[56] Within a sentence the names either of real or of fictitious entities are affected by the same kind of reality, namely a conceptual kind of reality provided by language.[57]

The nominal indistinction between what is real and what is fictitious reveals the incapacity of language to illuminate and account for the difference between sense perception and the human mind. Language is not able to identify and distinguish real and fictitious entities, because in a clause both are merely denominations, which, despite their purely nominal character, are regarded as signifying existent and real objects. The linguistic dimension is completely separate from the empirical dimension. The equal consideration of objects as names, notwithstanding their actual nature, is at the origin of an error, namely of the mistaken belief that every noun, including those designating fictitious entities, denotes a substance, i.e. a real object having a perceptual nature. Instead fictitious entities are "fictitious substances," which, because of their conceptual nature, are not sensorially experienced.

On the one hand, Bentham states the need for fictitious entities, namely for mental constructions, for the purpose of communication; on the other, he acknowledges the misunderstanding of fictitious entities as if they were real entities, namely empirical objects. The linguistic inability to make a difference between real and fictitious entities has consequences on the ontological level, by inducing the human mind to believe that what is treated as a noun or a subject in a sentence is an entity that has the features of reality and existence. This misunderstanding, derived from a limitation of language, i.e. its inability to differentiate between names of real entities and names of fictitious entities, is at the origin of a process of "substantification":[58] language ascribes an ontological nature, that is, reality and existence, to fictitious entities, although, properly speaking, they

56 *De l'ontologie*, 166 (Bowring viii, 197).

57 About the meaning of the locution *as if* see Vaihinger 2001, 93: "This formula, then, states that reality as given, the particular, is ***compared*** with something whose impossibility and unreality is at the same time admitted."

58 See *Preparatory Principles*, 401: "By the same rule, a more general mode of speech might be laid down by which sounds are made to represent beings by those motions or situations being attributed to them which in reality are to be met with only in the things signified by the names of real substances: and one might call it *Substantification*."

should not be regarded as substances, that is, as "objects that really exist" from an empirical point of view.[59]

The act of denomination has an ontological import. The attribution of existence and reality to a name is made regardless of the concrete ontological nature of the object designated by that name. In a sentence language cannot reproduce the distinction between empirical and mental entities, that is, between real and fictitious entities. Bentham acknowledges to language the ability to confer reality and existence or, more precisely, a kind of reality and existence that is not material but mental. Therefore, in Bentham's metaphysics one may recognize at least two ontologies: an ontology of real entities, that is empirical, and an ontology of fictitious entities, that is mental or linguistic.

The area of reality and the area of fiction

In *Of Ontology* Bentham defines the area of fiction in a quite generic way. It is identified as opposed to the area of reality. Indeed, as Bentham claims, "Every noun-substantive which is not the name of [a] real entity, perceptible or inferential, is the name of a fictitious entity."[60] It is, thus, important to provide a more detailed clarification of the contents of the area of fiction, in order to precisely identify and separate it from the bordering area of reality.

A fuller treatment is provided in *Chrestomathia*, where Bentham lists a number of "*undefinable* fictitious entities" and distinguishes them into physical fictitious entities, such as motion, rest and quality, ethical fictitious entities, such as obligation, right and power, and ontological fictitious entities, such as condition, certainty and impossibility.[61] Again in *Chrestomathia* Bentham puts forward a similar classification of fictitious entities, by distributing them "according to the branch of Art and Science for the purpose of which the names of them require to be employed." Thus, Bentham identifies somatic or somatological fictitious entities; noological fictitious entities; ethical fictitious entities.[62] Probably, by somatic or somatological, i.e. corporeal, Bentham intends physical entities and by noological he means mental entities.

59 See *Preparatory Principles*, 424: "The only objects that really exist are *substances*: they are the only real entities. To convey any notion by words which are the names of any objects [other] than substances, we are obliged to attribute to such objects what in truth is attributable only to substances: in a word, we are obliged to feign them to be substances. Those others, in short, are only fictitious entities."

60 *De l'ontologie*, 164 (Bowring viii, 197).

61 *Chrestomathia*, 259 n. a.

62 *Chrestomathia*, 398. About ethical fictitious entities Bentham observes: "Ethical will be those belonging to the æsthetically or pathically passive faculty. The Ethical fictitious entities will be obligation, right, power, &c: distinguishable according to the *sanction* from which the good and evil is considered as flowing, viz. 1. physical, 2. popular, 3. legal, 4. religious. *Sanction* – a source of good and evil" (*Essay on Logic*, UC 101.347; Bowring viii, 267 n. *). George Bentham, who was Jeremy's nephew, supplies a list of ethical fictitious entities in a document published in Ogden 1932, 156.

Generally speaking, the distinction between sense-perception and the human mind seems to give a satisfactory account of the distinction between the realm of reality and the realm of fiction. One may suppose that in the realm of reality Bentham encompasses abstract and general ideas strictly corresponding to empirical material objects, such as the apple, the book and the pen. These sorts of ideas could be qualified as material and thus perceptual because of their closeness or reference to particular empirical bodies. Bentham seems to endorse an extensive interpretation of real entities. Other kinds of ideas, having no empirical direct correspondence, even though affecting materiality, such as roundness, ripeness and hardness, are, without difficulty, included in the area of fictitious entities or, more precisely, of physical or somatic fictitious entities. Contrary to the idea of the apple, the idea of ripeness has no corresponding material object existing as a particular ripeness. It is rather an empirical aspect, the reality of which is given by the human mind through a process of abstraction and generalization of the perceptions of *ripe* affecting material substances such as fruits.

Despite their strict separation, reality and fiction are not two unrelated areas. On the contrary, Bentham underlines the constitutive relation of dependence of fictitious entities on real entities, on which the nature of a fictitious entity is based.

> Every fictitious entity bears some relation to some real entity: and can no otherwise be understood than in so far as that relation is perceived, – a conception of that relation is obtained.[63]

The relation that fictitious entities maintains with real entities is characterized by different "removes," that is, by different degrees of distance of a fictitious entity from a real entity.[64] One may distinguish a fictitious entity "of the first remove," a fictitious entity "of the second remove" and so forth, according to the vicinity of that fictitious entity to its corresponding real entity. A fictitious entity of the first remove has a direct relation with a real entity, without the mediation of another fictitious entity.[65] A fictitious entity of the second remove has a relation

63 *De l'ontologie*, 164 (Bowring viii, 197).

64 According to Cléro (1993, 54) the word *remove* "indique une idée de '*passage*' et de '*transition*' à un ordre supérieur", probably to a superior order of complexity. Cléro (1993, 55) supposes that Bentham's principle of classification of fictitious entities would have been inspired by Newton's method of fluxions. Evidences of the application of the Newtonian method to psychological entities can be found in the work of Hume and Burke, who both were Bentham's predecessors. In Harrison's opinion (1983, 83) "although these fictitious entities vary in degree of distance from real, and although this can lead Bentham to talk of one being 'so to speak, a still more fictitious fiction' than another (viii 200), his general attitude to the whole lot is that of acceptance or approval."

65 See *De l'ontologie*, 164–6 (Bowring viii, 197): "A fictitious entity of the first remove is a fictitious entity a conception of which may be obtained by the consideration of the relation borne by it to a real entity without need of considering the relation borne by it to any other fictitious entity."

with a real entity by means of a fictitious entity of the first remove.[66] The closer is the connection with a real entity, the lesser is the remove at which the fictitious entity lies. Thus, fictitious entities "may be classed in different ranks or orders" with reference to the relation they have with reality.[67]

The connection that a fictitious entity has with a real entity is essential to understand it: the meaning and truth of a fictitious entity are enlightened by its reference to a real entity. As instances of fictitious entities Bentham mentions motion and rest, belonging to the first remove, and quality, belonging to the second remove. Bentham, however, specifies that a quality can affect both a real entity directly and a fictitious entity of the first remove, as in the case of motion whose qualities, for example, can be rectilinearity or curvilinearity and slowness or quickness. In his writings Bentham insists considerably on the real roots of fictitious entities and, consequently, commentators highlight the relation which a fictitious entity has with a real entity as the key to interpreting his ontological theory.[68] The exploration of this relation uncovers that fictitious entities are not purely human inventions, but they have empirical roots from which they take shape. To put it differently, perceptions are the foundations of fictitious entities, that is, the elements on the basis of which the human mind carries out its constructive activity in order to create new entities.

From a logical point of view fictions have the aim to carry on human converse, that is, the communication and the exchange of thought. Generally speaking, Bentham distinguishes four different types of fiction: the logical, the literary, the religious and the political. The fiction examined by the logician, which is bred for the needs of human intercourse, differs deeply from the fiction of the poet, the purpose of which is to amuse,[69] and from the fiction of the priest and the lawyer, the purpose of which is to deceive and then govern.[70]

Logical fictions derive from the need to think and communicate. In the context of logic, the notion of fiction or fictitious loses its etymological pejorative

66 See *De l'ontologie*, 166 (Bowring viii, 197): "A fictitious entity of the second remove is a fictitious entity for obtaining a conception of which it is necessary to take into consideration some fictitious entity of the first remove."

67 See *Essay on Language*, Bowring viii, 325: "These sorts of fictitious entities may be classed in different ranks or orders, distinguished by their respective degrees of vicinity to the real one."

68 See, for example, Harrison 1983, 83–4; Cléro 1993, 54: "Comprendre une fiction, c'est savoir la rattacher – certes pas l'identifier – à une entité réelle. Une fiction qui serait dépourvue de telles attaches serait en même temps dépourvue de sens"; Schofield 2006, 8: "fictitious entities only existed in real entities, and it was only from real entities that the idea of fictitious entities could be derived."

69 In *The Rationale of Reward*, Bowring ii, 253–4, Bentham makes some remarks about the fictions used by poets. For an investigation of fiction in literature and law with reference to Dickens and Bentham's work, see Stone 1985.

70 More generally, oratory or rhetoric, as the discipline employed by priests and lawyer, is regarded by Bentham as "the art of misrepresentation–the art of misdirecting the judgment by agitating and inflaming the passions" (*Memoirs of Jeremy Bentham*, Bowring x, 510). For an analysis of the role of fictions in law according to Bentham see Bozzo-Rey 2008, 2009b; Harrison 1983, 24–46; Korošec 1994, 163–8; Tusseau 2011, 2011a.

nuance, consisting in its deceptive or misleading purpose, but keeps its constructive meaning, by signifying something that is artificially fabricated. By designating the constructions of language, the words fiction and fictitious entity are adopted by Bentham in a morally neutral sense, that is, as a technical notion without any evaluative import.[71] The case of literature and especially religion and law, in which the notion of fiction or fictitious ambiguously keeps its double meaning of human artefact and device to deceive, is different.[72]

Bentham shows a double attitude to words designating fictitious entities. On the one hand, he wants to bring out and fight their deceptive usage in politics and law; this is the *pars destruens* of his work of reform. On the other, Bentham acknowledges that ethics, including politics and law, is necessarily built through fictitious words, which are human artefacts enabling individuals to communicate and thus to interact. The social reform, to which the *pars construens* of Bentham's work is devoted, requires first and foremost a linguistic reform, aimed at reconnecting the ethical vocabulary, on which a society is framed, to its proper empirical bases.[73]

The unempirical character of a fictitious entity depends on its artificial nature; indeed, a fictitious entity is invented by the human mind and is not already existent. A fictitious entity is still defined as an *entity* and with the term *entity* Bentham identifies a being, namely something having its own existence and reality. Consequently, the expression *fictitious entities* appears to be contradictory: it denotes an existent and real element, i.e. an entity, which is non-existent and unreal, i.e. fictitious.

> Fictitious entity says some one, – of such a locution where can be the sense or use? By the word *entity* cannot but be represented something that has existence, – apply to the same subject the adjunct *fictitious*, the effect is to give instruction that it has not any existence. This, then, is a contradiction in terms, a species of locution from which, in proportion as it has any employment, confusion, and that alone, cannot but be the effect.[74]

The notion *entity* amounts to what exists, to what is to some extent real, whereas the attribute *fictitious* amounts to what does not exist, to what is not real. The adoption of the expression *fictitious entity* could create confusion because of its supposed incongruous sense. This locution seems to put together a reference to existence, i.e. to the area of being, and a reference to

71 According to Harrison (1983, 84) "'Fictitious entity' has now, however, become a technical term; the pejorative implication has disappeared, and the names have the force and use in the language that the names of real entities have."

72 Tusseau (2011a, 38–44) points out "the ambiguity of the status of fiction", especially from a political point of view: on the one hand, fiction is or should be the object of criticism; on the other, it is the means for a new foundation of politics and society.

73 Bentham's double attitude towards fiction is examined at length by Tusseau 2011a.

74 *De l'ontologie*, 80 (Bowring viii, 198).

non-existence, i.e. the area of non-being, of nothing. Fictitious entities appear to be in an intermediate state between an entity and a non-entity, between a being and nothing, only partly identifying with each one of them, without being completely one of them. Bentham is thus driven to state the question on the ontological status of a fictitious entity and to try to formulate an answer so as to throw light on the particular nature of this entity.

> Entities are either real or fictitious, what can that mean? What? but that of entities there are two species or sorts: viz. one which is itself, and another which is neither itself nor anything else? Instead of fictitious entity – or as synonymous with fictitious entity, why not here say, non-entity?
>
> *Answer.* Altogether inevitable will this seeming contradiction, it is believed, be found. The root of it is in the nature of language: that instrument without which, though of itself it is nothing, nothing can be said, and scarce any thing be done.[75]

Bentham wonders whether a fictitious entity is a kind of being, different from a real entity, or a mere nothing, i.e. a non-entity. The question is crucial and requires the clarification of the ontological nature of fictitious entities.[76] In his answer Bentham acknowledges the inner contradiction of fictitious entities, wavering between being and not-being in an undefined intermediate state. He traces back this contradiction to the ambiguous nature of language, which, on the one hand, is nothing from an empirical point of view, but, on the other, is the indispensable condition to say or do anything. Language itself is depicted in fictitious terms, namely as a fictitious entity.

In order to understand the ontological status of a fictitious entity, the realist contraposition between perceptibility and imperceptibility seems no longer adequate. Because of its incorporeal nature, a fictitious entity would be nothing, that is, unreal and inexistent, a mere non-entity. However, Bentham refuses to identify a fictitious entity with a non-entity, that is, to make an identification between fiction and nothing, which instead would be natural in an empirical and realist perspective. Though it is undeniable that fictitious entities have no empirical existence, they still exist as a condition for human intercourse. Bentham needs to select a different form of existence and reality to be ascribed to fictitious entities, that is, a form of existence that escapes the sharp identification between perceptibility and reality. He seems to find a kind of existence and reality apt for fictitious entities in language itself: "To language, then – to language alone – it is that fictitious entities owe their existence – their impossible, yet indispensable, existence."[77]

75 *De l'ontologie*, 80–2 (Bowring viii, 198).

76 About Bentham's consideration of fictitious entities as having "no properties", i.e. as "a mere nothing", Rosen (2005, 49) holds: "But this is puzzling and Bentham knows it. If there are fictitious entities, surely they must at least possess the property of being fictional, and if there are many of them they must presumably differ from one another in various respects."

77 *De l'ontologie*, 84 (Bowring viii, 198).

Bentham assumes a constructivist perspective in outlining the type of existence of fictitious entities, which is qualified both as impossible and indispensable. It is impossible because real existence belongs only to perceptions and fictitious entities are manifestly imperceptible. It is, however, indispensable, because if fictitious entities were nothing, i.e. inexistent and unreal, it would not possible to think and communicate. Language provides this special or, tautologically speaking, fictitious form of existence and reality to fictitious entities. By means of this linguistic existence, communication and human interrelations can take place.

The kind of existence in which fictitious entities participate is linguistic, because it is the product of the human mind. It cannot be perceived in the same way in which the existence of an apple is perceived by sight. And yet the existence of fictitious entities is recognized by the human mind, which, by means of language, creates new entities. Along with an empirical form of reality and existence there is a linguistic form of reality and existence. The existence and reality of both real and fictitious entities can be predicated without contradiction. However, real entities are characterized by an empirical existence and fictitious entities by a linguistic existence. With this linguistic approach to existence and reality in mind, the expression fictitious entity is no longer contradictory. Fictitious entities are objects created by the imaginative and communicative faculties. Through his fictionalism Bentham outlines a sort of linguistic ontology, which, unlike empirical ontology, is not grasped by the senses but is constructed by the human mind.

Unreal or fabulous entities

Bentham outlines the nature of a fictitious entity and distinguishes it not only from a real entity but also and especially from a non-entity. More specifically, he intends to clarify the difference between the import of the words *fictitious entity* and *non-entity*,[78] which seemingly might be identified as non-being, i.e. nothing, without making a distinction between them. In *Of Ontology* Bentham confines himself to merely taking as an instance of non-entity "the Devil" and formulating a sentence in which its fabulous figure is described. In this case, the Devil is regarded as a denomination included in an averment, the purpose of which is "to produce in the minds to which communication is thus made, a serious persuasion of the existence of an object, conformable to the description thus expressed."[79] Despite it being plain that a devil is a non-entity, the sentence including its name aims to persuade the mind of the hearer about its existence.

A definition of unreal or fabulous entity is formulated by Bentham in *Essay on Logic*.

> Fabulous entities are either fabulous persons or fabulous things.
>
> *Fabulous entities*, whether persons or things, are supposed material objects of which the separate existence is capable of becoming a subject of belief: and

78 Cf. *De l'ontologie*, 84 (Bowring viii, 198).
79 *De l'ontologie*, p. 84 (Bowring viii, 198).

> of which accordingly the same sort of picture is capable of being drawn in and preserved in the mind as of any really existent object.[80]

It is also useful quoting Bentham's characterization of fabulous entities in *Preparatory Principles*, as it contains interesting elements which completes their definition.

> Names of fabulous entities are words which serve to exhibit to the mind assemblages of simple ideas which, though no where co-existing in any real subject, are manifest and determinate.
>
> Names of fabulous entities are words which of themselves exhibit no idea at all, but which, by means of other terms they are combined with, are seen to be destined to represent an indefinite something as if it were in some of those situations which real beings are liable to be in, and by that contrivance, and that alone, to be raised to the class of beings.[81]

As examples of fabulous entities, Bentham points out "such beings as, in the fables of the Poets [. . .], have been represented and spoken of as really existing"[82], namely imaginary divinities, persons, things or places: "Gods of different dynasties," "Kings, such as Brute and Fergus," "Animals, such as Dragons and Chimæras," "Countries, such as El Dorado," "Seas, such as the Straights of Anian," and "Fountains, such as the fountain of Jouvence."[83] Bentham seems to characterize a non-entity in the same terms as a fictitious entity, namely from a mental and linguistic point of view. As names, i.e. nouns, they are mistakenly considered as real objects, i.e. corporeal, because of the inability of language to account for their imaginary and thus unreal nature. Although Bentham does not intend to equate fictitious entities with non-entities, his short treatment of non-entities does not make clear their difference with fictitious entities. The belief in the existence of a non-entity and the belief in the existence of a fictitious entity are both the result of the same constructive process of substantiation carried out by language.

Bentham himself is urged to demarcate the area of fictitious entities and the area of fabulous entities in order to avoid their overlap. According to him, fictitious entities do not "raise up in the mind any correspondent images," as the above-mentioned names of fabulous entities do.[84] Fictitious entities are not

80 *Essay on Logic*, UC 101.342 (Bowring viii, 262).

81 *Preparatory Principles*, 387. See also *Preparatory Principles*, 409: "Entities I call fabulous are fictitious entities personalized."

82 *Preparatory Principles*, 386.

83 For the examples of fabulous entities cf. *Essay on Logic*, UC 101.342 (Bowring viii, 262 n. †); *Preparatory Principles*, 386. See also *Chrestomathia*, 271 n. a: "By *fictitious entities* are here meant, not any of those which will be presented by the name of *fabulous*, i.e. imaginary *persons*, such as *Heathen Gods*, *Genii*, and *Fairies*, but such as *quality-property*, (in the sense in which it is nearly synonymous to *quality*) *relation*, *power*, *obligation*, *duty*, *right*, and so forth."

84 Cf. *Essay on Logic*, UC 101.322 (Bowring viii, 263).

linked to images: a quality, a quantity, a relation and an obligation cannot be portrayed, but only symbolized. Instead, the name and the description of a fabulous object, both in the case of a person and a thing, give rise to an idea, i.e. an image, in the mind.[85] Fabulous entities have a visual character which is not shared with fictitious entities. Bentham specifies the difference between unreal and fictitious entities not in terms of existence, but in terms of graphic representation. However, as with fictitious entities, fabulous entities are subject, within a sentence, to process of reification, which makes them "material objects," even though they actually have no corporeal nature. Thus, we still need to investigate the ontological difference between fictitious and unreal objects.

If language confers the same conceptual kind of existence and reality to any entity denoted by a name, it is difficult to make explicit the distinction between a name corresponding to a non-entity such as the Devil and a name corresponding to a fictitious entity such as motion. From a conceptual point of view, a fictitious entity and a non-entity participate in the same sort of linguistic existence; from an empirical point of view, they are both immaterial and, thus, do not exist.

Bentham seems to leave to the reader's insight the understanding of the difference between fictitious entities and non-entities. If one compares the objects exemplifying these kinds of entities, for example the Devil in the case of non-entities and a motion or a quality in the case of fictitious entities, one may notice that, contrary to a fictitious entity, a non-entity is simply the product of the human mind, probably of the faculties of imagination and invention, without any type of connection with reality. Indeed, the Devil, along with other fantastic creatures, has no relation with a real object.[86] Bentham qualifies unreal entities as "fabulous"[87] presumably with the purpose of stressing their complete independence from reality. Instead, by definition, a fictitious entity maintains a relation with reality according to a variety of degrees or removes. The connection to reality is thus the crucial element that distinguishes a fictitious entity from a non-entity.

1.3 Language and imagination

Verbal reality

The kind of existence owned by a fictitious entity has a linguistic nature, lying in its nominal function as a noun contained in a sentence. This linguistic typology of existence also concerns empirical bodies, insofar as they are susceptible to being denoted by nouns. Bentham himself identifies this form of existence or reality as

85 Cf. *Essay on Logic*, UC 101.342 (Bowring viii, 262).

86 It is baffling that in *Of Ontology* Bentham adopts the same example, i.e. the Devil, to illustrate two ontologically completely different objects such as a non-entity and an inferential real entity. The characterization of the Devil as a fabulous creature shows how problematic for Bentham is the notion of inferential entity, whose exemplifications, such as the soul, God, the angel and the Devil, appear more similar to fabulous than to real entities.

87 *De l'ontologie*, 86 (Bowring viii, 199).

nominal or verbal, laying the foundations for an ontology of language in order to characterize the status of fictitious entities. This way of existence peculiar to fictitious entities, but also characterizing real entities, is denominated "verbal reality" by Bentham in the following passage from *Chrestomathia*.

> Incorrect as it would be, if the entities in question were considered as being, in point of reality, upon a footing with *real* entities, as above distinguished, the supposition of a sort of *verbal* reality, so to speak, as belonging to these fictitious entities, is a supposition, without which the matter of language could never have been formed, nor between man and man any converse carried on other than such as hath place between brute and brute.[88]

The supposition that fictitious entities have a verbal reality is a necessary condition for the development of language. It is indeed the language that by itself ascribes a form of existence or reality to the names of fictitious entities. This form of existence is qualified as "verbal" because of its linguistic nature. Verbal existence, having a conceptual character as a product of the human mind, has to be distinguished from empirical existence, inhering in physical bodies of which human beings are made aware through their senses.

Fictitious entities, such as relation, situation, faculty and power,[89] have no real existence but merely a linguistic existence to the extent that they are identified by words. To put it another way, fictitious entities exist only on a linguistic level, namely as names in a sentence, but not on an empirical level, namely as perceptions of corporeal objects. As a consequence, the notion of reality or existence can no longer be uniformly conceived as empirical, because it can also be mental or, more precisely, linguistic. Sensibility is not able to grasp all the forms of reality and existence. Along with a perceptual kind of reality, affecting physical bodies, there is a mental or linguistic kind of reality, affecting conceptual entities. Language or, more generally, the human mind is thus the source of verbal existence just as sensibility is the source of empirical existence.

In the construction of fictitious entities language plays a constitutive function. Fictitious entities have a mental form of existence and reality, ascribed to them by language, because of their being denoted by names included in a sentence. The clarification of the nature and structure of language is thus pivotal to the account of fictitious entities. According to Bentham, language is made up by a "collection of signs";[90] "Words are the signs of ideas" and "To render a word understood, is to point out the idea of which it is a sign."[91] Yet words are not independent units without a context, but their meaning and their intelligibility depend on the assertion or sentence in which they are contained. Bentham claims that "Every

88 *Chrestomathia*, 271 n. a.
89 Cf. *De l'ontologie*, 86 (Bowring viii, 198). The fictitious character of the notion of power is remarked in *Preparatory Principles*, 150.
90 *Essay on Language*, UC 102.471 (Bowring viii, 332).
91 *Essay on Language*, Bowring viii, 333 n. *.

word to be made intelligible, must be represented as part of some assertion or proposition."[92] When Bentham refers to words, he means words included in a propositional context.[93] Words correspond to parts of a sentence and, consequently, they are enlightened by the whole in which they participate.

The names employed in a sentence can signify either a real or a fictitious entity.[94] This operation of denotation has an ontological value, because it assigns a mental form of existence and reality, which is different and parallel to the empirical existence and reality belonging to corporeal objects. Thus, real entities have both a material and mental reality whereas fictitious entities have only a mental reality. Fictitious entities exist insofar as they are the products of the human mind.

> What will, moreover be seen is, that the fiction – the mode of representation by which the fictitious entities thus created, in so far as fictitious entities can be created, are dressed up in the garb, and placed upon the level, of real ones – is a contrivance but for which language – or at any rate language in any form superior to that of the language of the brute creation – could not have existence.[95]

Bentham's usage of a constructivist terminology in the treatment of fictitious entities does not appear to be random. He clearly speaks of "mode of representation" and "creation" of fictitious entities, which are "dressed up in the garb" and "placed upon the level" of real entities. Bentham outlines the process of construction of fictitious reality, which is shaped by imagination and reified by language. Fictitious entities are regarded as if they were real objects; this is the only way in which they can be thought and communicated. The reification of fictitious entities within language is an indispensable condition for social intercourse. Hence, by means of mental faculties, and in particular by means of the cooperation of imagination and language, fictitious entities are susceptible of being considered as having a form of existence or reality, although it itself is fictitious.

The constructive activity of the human mind, consisting in giving existence to new objects, is not only the result of a misunderstanding due to the inability of language to mark a distinction between names of real entities and names of fictitious entities. The creation of new entities endowed with existence and reality is

92 *Essay on Language*, Bowring viii, 333.

93 Beginning with Quine (1981, 69–70) scholars unanimously underline Bentham's originality in connecting the meaning of a word to the sentence including it; consequently, sentences have a "semantic primacy" over words. On this constitutive propositional aspect of words in Bentham's approach see, for example, Bouveresse 1993. See also Tyler 2003, 13–7.

94 *Essay on Language*, UC 102.462 (Bowring viii, 331): "Coæval with the very first steps that can be taken in the endeavour to give a clear explanation of the true nature of language must be the intimation given of the distinction between real and fictitious entities, and the correspondent distinction between names of real and names of fictitious entities."

95 *De l'ontologie*, 84 (Bowring viii, 198).

an internal need for language or, as Bentham says, "a contrivance" which allows language to be structured and articulated in a form superior to a very elemental level, exclusively limited to the denotation of single corporeal objects. The existential relation between language and fiction is reciprocal, because, on the one hand, fictitious entities could not exist without language and, on the other, language could not exist without fictitious entities. As Bentham claims it, fiction is "a necessary resource" of language, already at its very first step and in its simplest case.[96]

The linguistic process of substantiation

Bentham specifies the uses of language by separating a "purely self-regarding" or "*solitary* use" and an "extra-regarding" or "*social* use." The former has as its object "the *improvement* of thought" and the latter mainly "the *communication* of thought." According to Bentham, the existence of language is due to the extra-regarding or social use. With reference to language, a "comparatively mature" "state of *society*" has been characterized by the development in human beings of "The practice of applying the mind [. . .] to look at its own ideas, by means of the words to which they stand associated." The establishment of a connection between the signs composing language and the contents of the mind distinguishes a more advanced cognitive level in human evolution.[97]

Bentham sketches out a short *genealogy* of fictitious entities, which basically derive from the human propensity to associate "the idea of a name" and the idea "of the reality of the object to which it was applied." Fictitious entities are the outcome of the evolution of the earlier human habit to relate a word to a material object, which is empirically existent. Fictitious entities belong to a more complex phase of the development of the human cognitive, including communicative, faculties.

The activity of denomination, at the beginning limited to corporeal entities, extends to incorporeal entities, which do not exist independently of the human mind. Bentham himself notes that from the intimate connection, originally established between a denomination and the reality of the body denominated, sprang a very natural propensity to attribute, that is, to ascribe reality to any object designated by names, without considering if these names refer to fictitious entities, as in most cases a proper examination discloses.[98] The process of substantiation performed by language by means of its activity of denomination rests on the human propensity and disposition to regard words, adopted with the function

96 Cf. *Essay on Language*, UC 102.462 (Bowring viii, 331).

97 Cf. *Essay on Language*, Bowring viii, 301.

98 Cf. *De l'ontologie*, 86 (Bowring viii, 199): "from a connexion thus intimate sprung a very natural propensity, viz. that of ascribing reality to every object thus designated: in a word, of ascribing reality to the objects designated by words which, upon due examination, would be found to be nothing but so many names of so many fictitious entities."

of names, as if they signify objects having a real existence,[99] despite their actual, often imaginary, nature.

By being imperceptible, fictitious entities are nothing but name. Bentham specifies several times that the expression *fictitious entity* is the shortened form of the locution *name of a fictitious entity*, i.e. name having no empirical but rather a conceptual reference. Outside the human mind, including language as one of its faculties, fictitious entities do not exist. The import of fictitious entities is simply linguistic, since they are "introduced for the common purposes of every discourse"[100] and, thus, substantiated within a sentence in which they play the role of nouns.

Bentham warns against the identification of the linguistic act of nominalization with an ontological act of substantiation. The propensity to consider the names of fictitious entities as denoting really existent objects is "a frequent source of confusion: of temporary confusion and perplexity: and not only so, but even of persisting error."[101] It is, therefore, important to have clear the linguistic nature of fictitious entities and its difference from the empirical nature of real entities.

The realist disposition to denominate corporeal entities evolves in a constructivist disposition to create, i.e. to give shape and meaning to conceptual entities, whose kind of existence has a linguistic, and not an empirical, value. Intellectual creations, moulded by imagination, are identified by words, as their stamp, without which they could not exist. Bentham's empirical realism, pertaining to bodies, is enriched by a form of constructivism, which finds expression in language.

The operations of the human mind

The collaboration between language and thought is constitutive of fictitious entities or, to be more precise, of the substantiality of fictitious entities. Bentham never separates language from thought and never minimizes the role of thought in the production of fictitious entities. Language and thought are instrumentally interconnected. Generally speaking, "the faculty of *discourse*, including the faculty of *speech*" is the "Grand instrument of thought."[102] Language has a double instrumental value in the activity of mind. It does not only enable the transmission of perceptions and ideas, but also the creation of ideas. In other words,

99 Cf. *Essay on Logic*, UC 101.341 (Bowring viii, 262): "hence, wheresoever a word is seen which to appearance is employed in the character of a *name*, a natural and abundantly extensive consequence is – a disposition and propensity to suppose the existence, the real existence, of a correspondent object – of a correspondent thing – of a thing to which it ministers in the character of a name."

100 See *Essay on Logic*, UC 101.322 (Bowring viii, 263). It is worth underlining that this expression occurs several times in Bentham's writings on fictitious entities.

101 *Essay on Logic*, UC 101.341 (Bowring viii, 262).

102 *Essay on Logic*, UC 101.143 (Bowring viii, 230). Language is characterized as an "instrument" by Bentham also in *De l'ontologie*, 82 (Bowring viii, 198).

language is, on the one hand, "the sign of thought," the vehicle through which thought is made manifest and interchanged,[103] and, on the other, the framework adopted by thought for its articulation and deployment.

> That language is an instrument of discourse – of communication between one mind and another – that it is the product of the sort [of] operation called *Expression*, *Discourse*, *Converse* – the work of the correspondent faculty – to speak of it in any such way is but tautology. But, as hath been observed already, it is an instrument not only of *discourse*, but of *thought* itself: an instrument, by which not only are perceptions and ideas *communicated*, but ideas *formed*.[104]

Bentham identifies two correlate functions of language, which are communication and thought. The former consists in the transmission of specific contents, i.e. perceptions and ideas, from one mind to another. The latter corresponds to the ability to structure and organize the contents of the mind, i.e. ideas. This prerogative of language finds expression in the formation of ideas whereby the human mind can think and interact. Language and thought are intimately and reciprocally related, so that one shapes the other.

The instrumentality of the faculty of discourse in thought is affirmed several times by Bentham, whose purpose is to highlight the cooperation between language and thought in our understanding of the world. The communicative and the reflective spheres of the human mind are consequently closely connected: as an "instrument of discourse," language expresses the contents of thought through words; as an "instrument of thought," language builds the ideas of the mind. Language is not merely in the service of thought, because thought itself is articulated and structured by language.

> Language being not merely the instrument of discourse but, moreover, the instrument of thought, the stock of a man's ideas is limited and determined by the stock of the words which he finds at his command for giving expression to those ideas.[105]

An examination of the ontological nature of fictitious entities has to throw light on the human cognitive frame, on which the existence and reality of fictitious entities depend. The intimate and reciprocal relation between language and thought is argued by Bentham also in *Chrestomathia*. On the one hand, the primary function of language is "to make communication of thought"; it is, indeed,

103 In *Essay on Language* (UC 102.456; Bowring viii, 329), language is depicted as "the sign of thought – an instrument for the communication of thought from one mind to another." Again, it is "the sign of the thought: of some thought which is in the mind of him by whom the discourse is uttered."

104 *Essay on Logic*, UC 101.144 (Bowring viii, 231). Schofield annotates that the above quoted passage, "which appears in the text at this point, has been cancelled by Bentham."

105 *Essay on Language*, Bowring viii, 319.

for the need for communication that language has been created. On the other hand, "Of the nature of language no clear, correct, and instructive account can be given but with reference to thought."[106]

Language and thought, especially imagination, work together in the process aimed at the creation of fictitious entities. It is no surprise that Bentham, in his study of fictitious entities, investigates human faculties. Generally speaking, Bentham defines a faculty as a nominal and, thus, fictitious entity "framed for the purpose of holding up to view the imaginary cause or productive instrument of some real effect." The word faculty "is not indicative of any thing but the *operations* which, when called into exercise, it performs if it be an *active* faculty, or the impressions which, if it be a passive faculty, it receives."[107]

By taking inspiration from D'Alembert's *Table*, in *Chrestomathia* Bentham enumerates the mental faculties which cooperate to understand and represent the world. According to the order given by Bentham, they are 1. perception; 2. judgment; 3. memory; 4. deduction; 5. abstraction; 6. synthesis; 7. imagination; 8. invention; 9. attention; 10. observation; 11. comparison; 12. generalization; 13. induction; 14. analysis; 15. methodization; 16. distribution; 17. communication.[108]

As the names employed reveal, the faculties listed correspond to specific operations carried out by the human mind. Mental faculties are nothing but names of fictitious entities, which denominate particular activities characterizing the receptive and constructive functions of the human mind. When outlining the process of the creation of fictitious entities, Bentham often takes into special consideration, among the above-mentioned faculties, imagination, "or say *imaginative faculty*, whereby a number of *abstracted ideas* – results, or products of the exercise of the *abstractive faculty* – are combined, compounded, put together as it were, into one *image*." The activity of imagination is subsequent to the activity of abstraction, on which it relies. Hence, abstraction and imagination correspond to different faculties, which interact in the formation or production of fictitious entities.[109]

Subsequent to imagination, the faculty of invention is accounted for in practical terms, namely as "*imagination*, directed in its exercise to the attainment of some particular *end*." This faculty contributes to the creation of fictitious and also fabulous entity, since it forms new compounds "out of a number of the products of the *abstractive* faculty."[110]

106 *Chrestomathia*, 397. In the same place, Bentham again points out that "The origin of language" lies in "the need men found themselves under of making communication of their thoughts."

107 *Essay on Logic*, UC 101.116 (Bowring viii, 224).

108 Cf. *Chrestomathia*, 163–6 n. a.

109 *Chrestomathia*, 163 n. a.

110 *Chrestomathia*, 163 n. a. For the sake of shortness, Bentham habitually refers to the imaginative faculty also the activities of abstraction and invention, which, strictly speaking, correspond to two distinct faculties. This is quite frequent in contexts in which it is not necessary to give a detailed specification of the human operations involved in the creation of fictitious entities. Thus, when Bentham says that fictitious entities are the product of language and imagination, he probably means imagination in a broader sense, by including in it also abstraction and invention. See *Essay on Logic*, UC 101.373 (Bowring viii, 272): "That without impropriety every instance of abstraction and every instance of invention are capable of being referred to the imaginative faculty has been seen already."

Presumably, abstraction is carried out on perceptions of physical objects gathered by sense-organs; consequently, fictitious entities are the outcome of an advanced elaboration, made by imagination, on sensory phenomena. In the creation process of fictitious entities there are, on the one hand, perceptual data, and, on the other, a series of human operations performed on them. Receptive and active faculties contribute to the process of the production of fictitious entities: the former perceive, store and arrange empirical elements; the latter disassemble, abstract and then assemble the material provided by receptive faculties.

A subsequent operation in the fiction-creating process is communication, "a faculty which may have for its *subject*, the results or products of the exercise of any one or more of the several faculties above-mentioned."[111] Therefore, in the construction of fictitious entities, language is connected with the perceptive, abstractive and imaginative faculties. The activity of denomination, whereby human beings are able to communicate in different forms such as speaking, writing and pantomiming, concurs to the linguistic and the alleged ontological characterization of an entity, the nature of which is fictitious, inasmuch as it is the result of several mental operations performed by the human mind on the perceptions of the physical world.

A slightly different and more detailed presentation of the mental operations is provided in a series of manuscripts included in *Essay of Logic* (UC 101.118–34; Bowring viii, 224–9). Here Bentham groups the various faculties in six classes.

- *Class i*: 1. Perception, Conception, Apprehension; 2. Attention.
- *Class ii*: 1. Remembrance; 2. Retention; 3. Recollection; 4. Revocation, viz. to memory; 5. Reminiscence.
- *Class iii*: 1. Judication; 2. Decision; 3. Determination; 4. Comparison; 5. Examination.
- *Class iv*: 1. Abstraction; 2. Imagination; 3. Invention.
- *Class v*: 1. Designation; 2. Denomination; 3. Methodization or Arrangement.
- *Class vi*: 1. Discourse or discoursing.

Among the above-listed mental operations Bentham acknowledges perception, recollection, attention, abstraction (whence imagination and invention), judication, designation, and converse or communication of ideas as "instrumental and subservient" to the performance of language.[112]

Bentham implicitly outlines the several phases that characterize the construction of fictitious entities, which is part of the general process of human knowledge. In the beginning of this process there is the perception of a material body, which, when applied to sense-organs, produces certain impressions. In other words, a corporeal entity, i.e. "an individual portion of matter," is the source of impressions on the faculty of sensibility. The awareness of the existence of that corporeal

111 *Chrestomathia*, 165 n. a.

112 Cf. *Essay on Logic*, UC 101.424 (Bowring viii, 229).

entity is "in a secondary and comparatively remote way" the object of perception or rather, rightly speaking, of inference, which, unlike direct impressions, is susceptible to error.[113] The subject of perceptions unifies the different impressions grasped by sensibility in an entire and single substance.[114]

The faculties of the second class, regarding past time, correspond to mnemonic operations, which still have a perceptual import. Memory is "a kind of *receptacle*" in which "perceptions of all sorts" and "whatsoever thoughts have by composition or decomposition been formed out of these materials" are placed.[115] Then, the third class brings together a series of judicial operations, in which "objects or subjects more than one are considered as being at the same time present to the mind."[116] These operations involve examination and comparison, as in the case of judgment whereby an inference or a conclusion concerning two or more entities is obtained.

The creative abilities are encompassed in the fourth class and basically consist in three main operations: decomposition of a number of actual or collected perceptions, i.e. impressions and ideas, received by the subject as conjoined in a unity; separation and consideration of one or more component parts of such grouped perceptions; composition of the selected elements "in an order and mode of conjunction different" from the original perceived unity. The first two operations characterize particularly abstraction, in which "the mind by its apprehensive faculty lays hold of" some impressions or ideas, corresponding to distinct aspects of the whole, "leaving the rest unnoticed and unheeded."

Bentham illustrates the activity of abstraction applied to an apple, which is a unity, composed by certain features grasped by perception in the form of impressions and ideas. An apple, when applied to the different sense-organs, gives birth to various impressions pertaining to its external configuration (smoothness or roughness, hardness or softness), shape, colour, odour and flavour.[117]

> In so far as any one of these impressions or ideas is rendered present to the mind and becomes a subject or object of perception or thought or attention without being accompanied with the rest, the mental operation called *abstraction* has place.[118]

113 Cf. *Essay on Logic*, UC 101.118 (Bowring viii, 224).

114 Elsewhere, in his writings devoted to language, Bentham regards the existence of a real entity, i.e. of a substance, knowable to us through our senses: it is not the result of an inference but is a direct impression. See, for example, *Essay on Language*, Bowring viii, 325: "By a real entity, understand a substance, – an object, the existence of which is made known to us by one or more of our five senses. A real entity is either a person or a thing, a substance rational, or a substance not rational." Contrary to Hume, in Bentham's approach perceptions are not only colours, sounds, tastes and so on as separate aspects, but are subsequently assembled by the human imagination to form a substance. Within perceptions Bentham also includes the ideas of physical individual bodies, consisting in aggregates of properties. Even though it is the product of an inference, the substantiality of a body is not a creation of human imagination. See Hume, *A Treatise of Human Nature*, i.i.6.

115 Cf. *Essay on Logic*, UC 101.121 (Bowring viii, 224–5).

116 Cf. *Essay on Logic*, UC 101.122 (Bowring viii, 225).

117 Cf. *Essay on Logic*, UC 101.124 (Bowing viii, 225).

118 *Essay on Logic*, UC 101.124 (Bowing viii, 225).

A specific impression, such as smoothness, is separate from the perceived whole, consisting in the apple, and is taken into consideration as an independent object by the mind. The concept of smoothness is the outcome of the abstractive process. Instead imagination, which is usually mentioned by Bentham together with language in the creation of fictitious entities, is more related to the third activity, corresponding to the original conjunction of the decomposed perceptions. Bentham defines the faculty of imagination in the following terms.

> In so far as a number of these fragmentitious ideas formed by abstraction are put together by the mind and formed into new compounds – into compounds which either do not exist in nature, or have not as yet presented themselves to the mind of the person in question, as it were, in and by the hands of a body already existing in nature, the operation whereby this effect is produced is stiled *imagination.*[119]

Imagination is a constructive operation based on the combination of the abstractions of sensory experience and aimed at the creation of new entities which have no empirical corresponding object. These new compounds do not exist in nature as perceptual elements, but only in the human mind as conceptual elements; so, they owe their existence and reality to the human mind. Bentham exemplifies this creative process, performed by the human mind, as an assemblage of certain abstracted properties originally joined to material objects. For instance, the idea of *shape*, which is separate from the perceived apple-tree, and the ideas of *weight*, *colour* and *consistency*, which are separate from perceived gold, are gathered together in order to form the new entity of *the golden apple*, a fruit grown in Hesperides' garden, according to Greek mythology.

Although a fictitious entity is a mental compound, its creation is not from scratch, *ex nihilo*, but is the outcome of a process carried out on sensory data. The imaginative component in the construction of fictitious entities lies in the original assemblage of the features abstracted from perceptual aggregates. The last creative mental operation, called invention, is very close to imagination: it has mostly a practical purpose, concerning objects which serve as a guide for action or for the accomplishment of an end.

The linguistic mental operations, belonging to the fifth class, are distinguished by Bentham in two groups, the former pertaining to the denotative function and the latter to the communicative function. In the former group Bentham differentiates designation and denomination. The operation of designation is individual and consists in associating an object "to which a name is to be attached" to a name "which is [. . .] to be attached" to that object; a specific object is thus designated by a proper name, which is fixed on it.[120] The operation of denomination, instead, is collective, because a name designates a number of individual objects; indeed, a common name is the outcome of a generalization of particular

119 *Essay on Logic*, UC 101.125 (Bowing viii, 225).
120 Cf. *Essay on Logic*, UC 101.126 (Bowing viii, 226).

instances. The last operation of the fifth class is methodization or arrangement, which is related to the operation of denomination: it essentially consists in systematizing a multitude of groups or collections of general ideas.[121]

The sixth class encompasses the mental operations, which, by means of designation and expression, consist in the communication or transfer of the ideas formed in one mind into another mind. Discourse is performed by signs which give expression to objects and ideas, and which are recognised by the mind of the hearer.

Along with this communicative function, discourse also has a formative function. To be precise, language has two interrelated uses, a "transitive" and "intransitive," i.e. a designative and a discursive: on the one hand, it is a "vehicle of thought" by means of a collection of signs, and, on the other, "it is an instrument employed in the creation and fixation of thought itself." Metaphorically speaking, "Uncloathed as yet in words, or stript of them, thoughts are but dreams: as the clouds in the sky, they float in the mind one moment and vanish out of it the next."[122] Discourse or language does not only convey thoughts, by denoting them with signs, from a mind to another, but contributes to increasing the stock of ideas and to giving meaning to them.[123] By virtue of this formative or constructive aspect, language is actively involved in the shaping of fictitious entities and not merely in their transmission.

The whole structure of the human mind, examined at length in its various faculties, is generally divided by Bentham into two broad areas, that is, the perceptive and the appetitive. To the former belong the passive or receptive faculties, concerning "mental experiences," which consist in receiving perceptions; to the latter belong the active or concupiscible faculties, concerning "all mental operations and their results."[124] Bentham distinguishes the faculties also in "intellectual" and "volitional."[125] He does not confine the intellectual sphere only to conceptual activities but also to sensorial operations.

> On this occasion and for this purpose, the whole of the mind of man may be considered as distinguishable into two parts – the purely *passive* and the *active*. In the passive is included the intellectual: the active may also be stiled the concupiscible. The passive, the seat of *perception*, memory, even judgment in so far as it is, as in *seeing*, capable of being exercised without any consciousness of the intervention of the *will*: the active, the seat of desire, and thence of volition, and thence of external action.[126]

121 Cf. *Essay on Logic*, UC 101.127–9 (Bowing viii, 226–7).

122 Cf. *Essay on Logic*, UC 101–423 (Bowing viii, 228).

123 See *Essay on Logic*, UC 101–423 (Bowring viii, 229): "Without language, not only would men have been incapable of communicating each man his own thoughts to other men, but compared with what in the existing state of things he possesses, the stock of his own ideas would in point of number have been as nothing: while each of them taken by itself would have been indeterminate and flitting."

124 *Essay on Logic*, UC 101.406 (Bowring viii, 279). See also *Essay on Logic*, UC 101.138 (Bowring viii, 229): "*Passive* and *active* – in one or other of these two divisions may every distinguishable faculty appertaining to the human frame be considered as included."

125 See for example *Essay on Language*, UC 102.332 (Bowring viii, 307).

126 *Essay on Language*, UC 102.456 (Bowring viii, 329).

The operations of perception, memory and judgment of perceptions are included in the passive part of the mind. The act of designation of objects by means of words is a kind of modification carried out by the active or concupiscible part of mind.[127] Put differently, a linguistic act is an act of the will. Consequently, by virtue of their nominal import, fictitious entities are the product of volitional faculties; an act of the mind is at the basis of their creation.

Because of their mental nature, fictitious entities cannot be discerned by passive faculties. However, the perception of material bodies as aggregates of a number of features is essential for the construction of fictitious entities. The active faculties, namely abstraction, imagination and invention, operate on the accumulated sense-data, by separating certain features and generalizing them in the form of concepts, as in the case of the quality yellow which is considered apart from the aggregate apple and substantialized as an individual entity, having an independent mental nature.

Every thought corresponds to a state or an act of mind belonging either to the intellectual or to the volitional department of the mind, that is, the understanding and the will.[128] Most probably, thoughts pertaining to the intellectual part are different from thoughts pertaining to the volitional part. The mind has an active role in the creation of fictitious entities, which are nothing but linguistic products. By giving verbal expression to the contents of the mind, language contributes to this creative act not merely by assigning a denomination to fictitious entities, just as in the case of real entities, but also shaping their ontological nature.

127 Cf. *Essay on Language*, UC 102.457 (Bowring viii, 329).

128 *Essay on Language*, Bowring viii, 320: "Of language, the primary and only original use is the communication of thought, the conveyance of thought from mind to mind, from the mind of a speaker to the mind of a hearer. All thought belongs either to the intellectual or to the volitional department of the mind – to the *understanding* or the *will*."

2 The representation of the physical world

2.1 The epistemology of physics

The fictitious framework of reality

The operations which mental faculties carry out on perceptions are constitutive of our understanding of the world as a whole. Human beings have a natural propensity to create fictitious entities, which have a mental, i.e. linguistic and imaginative, character. Although Bentham is accurate when separating the classes of entities into real and fictitious on the basis of their empirical or mental nature, he acknowledges to fictitious entities a general influence in our representation of the world, which is not merely perceptual. Despite the apparent superiority of perceptions as regards reality and existence, our way to know the world, even the physical world, is largely determined by fictitious entities or, more precisely, by our constructive abilities in thinking objects and their connections and in communicating them.[1]

Paradoxical as it is, the framework of reality is fictitious. Our representation of reality depends on our cognitive structures, which consider objects as filling a portion of space, formed by a portion of matter, being at rest or in movement, and so forth. Basic concepts such as space, matter, form, rest and movement, which are constitutive of our understanding of the world, are nothing but fictitious entities, that is, products of the mind. As mental creations, space, matter, time, rest and movement do not exist as autonomous entities outside the human mind but are constructed and employed to arrange impressions and ideas of physical bodies.[2] We might say that they are created by the human mind with the purpose of saving perceptual phenomena.

1 On this point see also Postema 2002a, 418.

2 In a following passage Bentham contradicts himself by attributing to the notion of space no longer the status "fictitious entity" but the intermediate status of "semi-real entity." He justifies it because of the fact that real and fictitious entities are in part and not entirely applicable to the notion of space; consequently, "space may be regarded and spoken of as a semi-real entity" (*De l'ontologie*, 96; Bowring viii, 202). The particular notion of "semi-real entity" is also considered in *Essay on Logic*, UC 102.039 (Bowring viii, 223).

Let us take into consideration the notions of matter and form: they belong to the class of fictitious entities and are opposed to substance, namely "the only class which has in it any corporeal entities." According to Bentham, matter and form spring from the real entity linguistically identified as substance. Both are "fractional results, produced from the decomposition of the word *substance*": matter is the corporeal part of a substance and form identifies its figure, configuration or shape. Although matter and form are fictitious entities, we have to acknowledge that "every physical real entity, every corporeal substance, every sort of body, has its matter and form." In spite of their immateriality, the concepts of matter and form determine our understanding of material substances by intervening in their composition or, more precisely, in their mental representation. Our knowledge of a physical body is shaped by notions which are the product of our analytical and synthetic abilities, i.e. decompositional and compositional abilities, aimed at constructing our image of the world on the basis of sense-data and by means of language.[3]

Fictitious entities not only orient us in the network of the interrelations which underpin reality but contribute to their shaping in our mind. Sensibility, instead, is unable to systematically organize empirical elements and to make the mind aware of their connections. Our apprehension of the physical world is moulded by fictitious categories which have the function to arrange in an orderly way the perceptual material gathered by the senses. Fictitious entities regulate our grasping of materiality: they manipulate and combine impressions with the purpose of giving them organic and coherent structure, i.e. of building a suitable representation of reality.

> On pain of having some of the most interesting subjects of thought, discourse, and action undiscoursed of, and even unthought of, we set to work the powers of our imaginations in the creation, as it were, of a multitude of imaginary beings, all spoken of as if they belonged to the class of bodies or substances; and on the occasion, and for the purpose of this creation, we attach to them a name or sign, called a part of speech: viz., a species of word, termed a noun substantive; the same species of word as that of which, in the character of a common name, we make use for the designation of real entities, appertaining strictly and properly to the class of substances.[4]

Consequently, nature, or more precisely our representation of nature, is fictitious, since it is the outcome of an organizational process in which imaginary objects intervene. Human cognitive faculties do not confine themselves to reflect the natural order, but they are actively involved in its construction. Bentham does not specify whether, outside the human mind, nature has its own organization, which is different from that represented by mental faculties, or whether our image of nature corresponds to nature itself. What is certain is that fundamental notions such as space and matter, which are intimately connected to our representation of

3 Cf. *De l'ontologie*, 88–90 (Bowring viii, 201).

4 *Chrestomathia*, 277 n. a.

physical world, are nothing but fictitious entities. Without these notions, nature, at least as we know it, should be unthinkable and uncommunicable.

The Ten Predicaments

The regulative function of sensory perceptions is played not only by basic fictitious concepts such as space and matter, but also by other fundamental notions through which human beings *think of* the world. For the purpose of classifying the names of physical fictitious entities, Bentham resumes and readapts Aristotle's list of *Ten Predicaments.* Just as Aristotle, in Bentham's approach categories have a logical and linguistic value: they are the conditions for thinking and communicating what it is, namely reality.

Except for the first category, corresponding to substance, which is a real entity, the other nine categories, i.e. quantity, quality, place, time, motion, rest, action, passion and relation, are fictitious entities. These nine categories are susceptible to being divided in two subsets, according to their increasing level of complexity. In *Of Ontology* Bentham distinguishes a group of absolute fictitious entities of the first order, which is composed by matter, form, quantity and space, and a group of absolute fictitious entities of the second order, which is composed by quality and modification.[5] In *Essay on Logic* Bentham puts forward a different subdivision of the fictitious predicaments: to the first group belong quantity and quality, which are "affections of *substance*, i.e. of substances of bodies," whose existence "is made [known] to us by our senses"; to the second group belong the remaining seven predicaments, which are all "species of *relation.*"[6]

The notion of substance is central in establishing the import of fictitious entities; a clear understanding of it provides a sound account of the distinction and connection between real and fictitious entities. Theoretically, substance should designate perceptions of material entities; however, in the manuscripts included in *Of Ontology*, Bentham's adoption of the term substance is not always uniform, as it identifies empirical and certain non-empirical objects, not without ambiguity.[7] Most of the time, substance is employed to denote only perceptions of corporeal bodies, that is, real entities,[8] but sometimes it also refers to particular fictitious entities, such as motion and matter.[9]

5 Cf. *De l'ontologie*, 88–100 (Bowring viii, 201–3).
6 Cf. *Essay on Logic*, UC 101.164–5 (Bowring viii, 234–5).
7 Sometimes in Bentham's vocabulary the notion of substance encompasses both the area of materiality and the area of immateriality. As an example, see *De l'ontologie*, 88 (Bowring viii, 201): "By the word *substance*, substances incorporeal as well as corporeal are wont to be designated."
8 See for example *De l'ontologie*, 90 (Bowring viii, 201): "The word substance is the name of a class of real entities, of the only class which has in it any corporeal entities"; *De l'ontologie*, 96 (Bowring viii, 202): "Substances being real physical entities, matter, form, quantity, and so on, so many fictitious entities"; and also *Essay on Logic*, UC 101.164 (Bowring viii, 235): "Substance, the first upon the list, is the name of a real entity – of a species of real entity: the only species of real entity, as hath already been observed, that belongs to the class of perceptible ones."
9 In *Of Ontology* (*De l'ontologie*, 188; Bowring viii, 200), the notion of substance is used also to denote fictional entities in a very few cases. For example, Bentham qualifies motion, a fictitious entity, as "a thing, a momentarily imagined substance, within which the body is conceived as being placed."

Moreover, it is not rare, in Bentham's writing, to find some fictitious entities labelled as fictitious substances. In *Essay on Language*, for example, words such as largeness, smallness, length, shortness, thickness and thinness are instances of fictitious substances. Their substantial import is a consequence of their linguistic treatment: each one of them is regarded as a "*substantival name* of quality," i.e. as "a complete idea, conceivable of itself." Instead, when used with their "adjectival denomination," that is, large, small, long, etc., each of these entities is "an incomplete idea" which requires for its completion the idea of a certain substance in which to inhere.[10] By and large, substance has two main meanings: an empirical meaning, when it corresponds to the perception of a corporeal body, and a mental meaning, when it is linguistically understood as a noun. Only in this latter case may we talk of fictitious substance, because, from an empirical point of view, fictitious entities have no substantiality.

In the section of the text *Of Ontology* pertaining to the ten predicaments, Bentham seems to have in mind an empirical notion of substance. Indeed, the characterization of fictitious entities is based on a clear and close reference to physical bodies, understood as substances. Bentham asserts that "Quantity cannot exist without some substance of which it is the quantity" and "Quality cannot exist without some substance of which it is the quality." In the same way, "Of place, the notion can not be entertained without the notion of some substance considered as *placed*, or capable of existing, or, as we say being *placed*, in it."[11] Time is "a still more fictitious fiction, leaning upon nothing more substantial than the fiction of place."[12] Time is a fictitious entity of the second remove, related to substance by means of the fictitious entity of place. Bentham goes on to define other categories, again underlining the connection they maintain with substance.[13]

10 Cf. *Essay on Language*, Bowring viii, 326.

11 *De l'ontologie*, 184 (Bowring viii, 199). Bentham regards space and place as fictitious entities, which do not exist if the notion of substance is left out of consideration: "Compared with substance, and in particular with body, place is, as hath been [seen], a fictitious entity. Without some body placed in it, or considered as being capable of being placed in it, place would either not have existence, or what with reference to use would amount to the same thing, there could be no purpose for which, no occasion on which, it would be considered as having existence" (*De l'ontologie*, 184; Bowring viii, 200).

12 *De l'ontologie*, 186 (Bowring viii, 200). Bentham (*De l'ontologie*, 188; Bowring viii, 200) remarks that "To be capable of being spoken of, time itself must be – can not but be – spoken of as a species of space."

13 See, for example, the definition of motion (*De l'ontologie*, 188; Bowring viii, 200), which is "a thing, a momentarily imagined substance, within which the body is conceived as being placed." In some cases, when referring to corporeal objects, Bentham identifies the notion of substance, which is a real entity, with the notion of matter, which is a fictitious entity. See *De l'ontologie*, 88 (Bowring viii, 201): "Matter. At first view the word matter may naturally enough be considered as exactly synonymous to the word substance. It may undoubtedly be with propriety employed instead of *substance* on many of the occasions on which the word substance may, with equal propriety, be employed. But there are occasions on which, while substance may, matter cannot, with propriety be employed. By the word *substance*, substances incorporeal as well as corporeal are wont to be designated; the word matter is wont to be employed to designate corporeal, to the exclusion of incorporeal substances."

The subject of predications is thus substance, in which the other categories inhere and participate. Fictitious entities, classified as quantity, quality, place, time, motion, rest, action, passion and relation, depend upon real entities, i.e. substances. Bentham explains the relation of inherence and participation which links a predicament to its corresponding substance, by comparing that substance to the fictitious image of a "receptacle" in which the several fictitious attributions are contained or lodged. By means of prepositions designative of place, such as *in*, the names of fictitious entities "are connected with the name of real entity substance."[14] We say "*In* that substance exists such and such matter." In this case, matter, a fictitious entity, is regarded "as if it were a real entity contained *within* that receptacle" corresponding to a substance.[15]

A more specific example of the relation between a substance and its predicaments is provided by the inherence of the quality of ripeness, a fictitious entity, to the substance apple, a real entity. When pronouncing the sentence *that apple is ripe*, we claim the existence of the apple and of ripeness. However, the quality of ripeness does not exist in a form separate from that apple, the reality of which is experienced by my mouth when tasting it. By virtue of its non-empirical character, ripeness is a linguistic entity, created by the human mind on the basis of the perceptions of objects susceptible to being ripe. Without these objects, such as an apple, ripeness would not exist. By saying that "this apple is ripe," we affirm that "*in* this apple is the quality of ripeness" and, with this assertion, we bring to view the image of the apple as a receptacle in which the quality of ripeness is lodged.[16]

> *Fictitious* as they are, entities of this description could not be spoken of at all, if they were not spoken of as *real* ones. Thus a *quality* is spoken of as being *in* a thing or a person: i.e. the thing or the person is spoken of as being a *receptacle*, and the *quality* as being something that is contained *in* it.[17]

Another instance of the creative ability of human beings in conceiving of the physical world is provided by the predicament of motion. It is feigned and usually adopted as an imaginary cause to account for the distance between bodies. By means of language, motion is considered "as a sort of receptacle in which bodies are lodged," so that "they are accordingly said to be *in* motion, as a man is said

14 *De l'ontologie*, 90 (Bowring viii, 201): "These names of entities possess both of them the characteristic properties of fictitious entities. It is by means of propositions designative of place, and by that means of a fictitious material image, that the names of them are connected with the name of the real entity substance."

15 See *De l'ontologie*, 90 (Bowring viii, 201). Bentham also takes into consideration the cases in which matter is regarded as deriving from a substance, as when we say, "behold the matter *of* that substance," "behold all this matter from that substance."

16 *Essay on Language*, UC 102.461–2 (Bowring viii, 330–1).

17 *Chrestomathia*, 271 n. a.

to be *in* a house."[18] As shown in this case, the notion of *receptacle* is also used by Bentham to qualify some fictitious entities, such as motion, and not only substances: "motion is a receptacle, in which the body is considered as stationed."[19]

In order to illustrate the participation of a predicament in its substance Bentham also employs the metaphorical image of two bodies placed one inside the other. So, the fictitious notion of quantity is depicted like "a smaller body which is *in* some substance in question, or a larger body in which the substance in question is." In the same way, a quality is represented "as it were, a small body *in* which the substance in question is: or it is a sort of object *of*, i.e. from which the substance of which it is the affection is considered as issuing"; a man, for example, "is said to be *of* a quality."[20]

The relation between a substance and its predicaments is reciprocal because if it is plain that substances enable fictitious entities to be thought, it is also true that substances cannot be thought without fictitious entities. Our understanding of substances depends on fictitious entities, since no substance, in its general or individual form, can exist "without existing in some certain quantity," "without being of some quality" or "of a multitude of qualities," without being "considered as placed," without being "itself matter," without being "of a certain determinate form," without being in a time and without being related to other substances through identity or alterity and action or passion.[21]

The notions of relation and causality

An important contribution to our representation of the world is provided by another predicament, that is, relation. Bentham defines it as "a fictitious entity, which is produced and takes place as often as the mind, having perception of any one entity, obtains at the same or at any immediately succeeding instant

18 Cf. *Chrestomathia*, 279: "To account for the difference of bodies in point of distance, a sort of nominal entity is feigned, to represent the cause of it, and Motion is the name by which this imaginary cause is designated. Motion is thereupon considered (for such are the shifts that language is reduced to) as a sort of receptacle in which bodies are lodged; they are accordingly said to be *in* motion, as a man is said to be *in* a house." See also *Chrestomathia*, 278: "In the *Attraction of Gravity* may be seen one of the fictitious entities, to the operation of which, in the character of causes or sources, the birth of motion, howsoever modified, may, as far as we are acquainted with it, be referred."

19 See *De l'ontologie*, 108 (Bowring viii, 204).

20 Cf. *Essay on Logic*, UC 101.164 (Bowring viii, 235).

21 See *De l'ontologie*, 184 (Bowring viii, 199): "Of substance, no species, no individual, can exist, without existing in some certain quantity"; "Of substance, no species can exist without being of some quality: of a multitude of qualities"; "Of place, the notion cannot be entertained without the notion of some substance considered as *placed*, or capable of existing, or, as we say, being *placed* in it." See *De l'ontologie*, 88 (Bowring viii, 201): "No substance can exist but it must be itself matter – be of a certain determinate *form* – be or exist in a certain determinate quantity: and were there but one substance in existence, all these three attributes would belong to it."

perception of any other entity, or even of that same object."[22] Subsequent to the attribution of a denomination, i.e. to the ascription of nominal existence to two entities, real or fictitious, there is the category of relation, which metaphorically is the third entity. Indeed, the perception of the two entities is followed by the perception of their relation of difference or identity. This relation, by means of abstraction and denomination, acquires a nominal existence in which its fictitious nature lies.[23]

By virtue of its generality and indispensability, the notion of relation "Once introduced upon the carpet [. . .] swells into an extent such as to swallow up all the others." According to Bentham, any other fictitious entity can be conceived as a mode of relation. Along with identity and diversity, types of relation are place, time, motion, rest, action, passion, subalternation, opposition, connection, cause and effect, and existence.[24] The notion of relation is an essential condition for thinking and communicating the connections between entities, real or fictitious, making up the physical world. Notwithstanding its influence on our representation of reality, relation is still a fictitious entity, that is, a product of the human cognitive faculties, created with the purpose of enabling human beings to coordinate perceptions.

Among the modes of relation, causality has particular importance in the scientific explanation of physical phenomena. Two events or objects are bound together by a fictitious relation of causality, according to which one is the cause and the other the effect.

> For the purpose of rendering, in the best manner in which we are able, an account of the motion of such bodies as are in motion, and of the rest of such as are at rest, certain fictitious entities are, by a sort of innocent falsehood, the utterance of which is necessary to the purpose of discourse, feigned to exist and operate in the character of causes, equally real with, and distinct from, the perceptible and perceived effects, in relation to which they are considered in the character of causes.[25]

The relation of causality is a conceptual device of the human mind, which allows it to explain physical phenomena such as the movement or the rest of material bodies. Thus, two events experienced through the senses are associated

22 *De l'ontologie*, 100 (Bowring viii, 203). For another definition of the notion of relation see *Preparatory Principles*, 356 and in part, the following lines: "We see thus what relation is; it is nothing more than the condition any two objects are said to be in, in virtue of the mind's being determined to pass from the consideration of the one of them to that of the other." See also *Preparatory Principles*, 382–3: "One may say that Relations do not exist: since they have not any separate existence from the things that are related: from the things *between* which the Relation is said to subsist."

23 Cf. *De l'ontologie*, 100–2 (Bowring viii, 203).

24 Cf. *De l'ontologie*, 100–2 (Bowring viii, 203).

25 *Chrestomathia*, 277.

as the cause to its effect by the human mind. By virtue of language, the relation of causality between those events is regarded as real, despite its imaginary nature.

The image of the physical world

A peculiar prerogative of the human mind is the creation of a special kind of fictitious entity, resulting from the logical processes of aggregation and division and of subalternation.[26] These entities are called by Bentham "fictitious unities"; instances of them are mineral, vegetable and animal. They consist in an assemblage or aggregate of a number of individuals, which are selected and kept together by virtue of a quality that they have in common and that distinguishes them from others. These "boxes" or, in a more detailed way, "fictitious receptacles" are usually designated as kingdom, class, order, genus, species and variety. Fictitious unities, made up by individuals sharing the same property, are identified by a common denomination. They are susceptible of being divided by imagination "into lesser component aggregates or units" or sub-aggregates on the basis of a more particular quality belonging only to certain individuals included in the larger group.

The image of the physical world in the human mind consists of a series of inclusive and exclusive aggregates or units, the nature of which is clearly fictitious, although they were "mistaken for realities" in the past. From the largest all-comprehensive group to single individuals, the entities composing reality can be collected and separated. The human mind, by means of imagination and language, that is, of creative powers, carries out an analytical and synthetic activity on objects, by assembling and dissembling them, in order to organize the whole of reality into a general fictitious classification.

The division between genus and species, on which dialectic is grounded, is no longer a typical feature of reality, of which the human mind becomes aware. Genus and species are regarded by Bentham as "phantoms," to which ancient philosophers such as Plato and Aristotle mistakenly attributed a real existence.[27] Actually, genus and species are mere creations of the mind. In Bentham's view, dialectic, understood as the device to account for reality according to the distinction between genus and species, is no longer aimed at exploring the order of reality, but rather at giving it an order and thus a sense, by organizing the bundle of perceptions received from the external world.

The representation of reality is a fictitious construction made by the mind on the basis of empirical data. Fictitious entities, such as form, matter, substance and the other nine categories, numerical system, genus, species and so forth, are nothing but devices created by the human mind to think of the world. The structure of

26 This topic is examined in chapter 7 of the text *Of Ontology*, 118–9 (Bowring viii, 206).
27 See, for example, *Chrestomathia*, 259.

reality is not properly discovered but conceived of by human beings, who are able to construct new entities aimed at representing it.[28]

Although Bentham is an empirical realist, who never denies the reality of impressions made on us by external objects, he acknowledges that our image of the physical world is a combination of perceptual and mental elements. Therefore, there might be a discrepancy between the physical world as it is and our representation of it.

Our mind is not merely a mirror of material nature, which reflects the state of affairs as it is or might be. The peculiar creative power of our faculties intervenes in the representation of nature, in which real and fictitious objects are so closely intertwined that it is not possible to separate them. Without fictitious entities we could not conceive of reality, because fictitious entities themselves become a part of reality, enabling us to understand it. Our image of the world is influenced by our mind, which has not innate contents but cognitive abilities that makes it actively involved in the construction of that image. Hence, Bentham's approach to the physical world attempts, not without difficulty, to harmoniously combine empirical realism with constructivism.

A basic tenet of Bentham's fictionalism is the connection of fictitious entities to perceptual reality. Through his theory of real and fictitious entities Bentham aims not only to make thought and communication possible, but also to save the phenomena, i.e. perceptual reality, which, by taking part in the general representation of the world, makes sense. In other words, the human mind throws light on perceptions, by interpreting them as fundamental part of a wider intellectual construction.

2.2 The double meaning of existence

An empirical account of existence

Bentham understands the property of existence in terms of reality. This is commonplace in seventeenth- and eighteenth-century British philosophers' writings and also in Kant. Locke, Berkeley and Hume adopt the expression "real existence," by making explicit the harmony between the meaning of existent and real. Existence appears to be a prerogative of reality, even though British philosophers disagree on what reality is, contending whether reality and, thus, its existence are independent of or dependent on the human mind. Locke, for example, claims that

28 Another case of the influence of fictitious entities in shaping our image of the world is provided in *Of Ontology* (*De l'ontologie*, 156; Bowring viii, 211): "It is impossible that among a multitude of bodies all equal to one another, four taken together should not be greater than two taken together: – why? – because by the word *four* has by every person been designated a number greater than by the word two." Bentham takes into consideration numbers as a fictitious system of measurement, which determines our perception of material things. Indeed, "the human mind having it in its power to apply [itself] to any object or to forbear to apply [itself] at pleasure, the person in question has exercised this power in relation to the import of the words in question."

real beings have "a steady existence,"[29] whereas Berkeley alleges that the existence, i.e. the reality, of things consists in their being perceived, so that reality does not have an existence distinct from human sensibility.[30] More sceptically, Hume argues that one cannot ascertain the origin of our sensible impressions from which our representation of reality derives, that is, "whether they arise immediately from the object, or are produced by the creative power of the mind, or are derived from the author of our being."[31]

The concept of existence holds a pivotal position in Bentham's philosophy and, particularly, in his distinction between real and fictitious entities. It should demarcate the boundaries of the field of reality, by separating it from the field of fiction. Existence is a constitutive and distinctive feature of reality and should not be attributed to or predicated on what is fictitious. However, far from being uniformly understood, in Bentham's manuscripts the notion of existence appears to be employed in a controversial way. Its ambiguous adoption gives birth to certain contradictions which seem to undermine the fundamental distinction between reality and fiction, by acknowledging a form of existence to fictitious entities.

A clear realist account of the notion of existence is provided by Bentham in a passage of *Essay on Language*. Also in this case, language, with its name-giving activity, plays a decisive role in conferring existence and reality to empirical objects.

> By this name an existence is ascribed to the individual object, or sort of object, of which it is the name. In the case where to the object thus spoken of, existence is actually an object of one of the five senses, and in particular of the sense of touch or feeling, – the only one without which man cannot exist, say, in a word, where the object is a tangible one; here there is no fiction, – as this man, this beast, this bird, this fish, this star; – or this sort of man, this sort of beast, this sort of bird, this sort of fish, this sort of star, – the object spoken of may be termed a real entity.[32]

The existence of the perceived material thing is not a fictitious construction of the human mind, but the "object of one of the five senses, and in particular of the sense of touch or feeling." In other words, existence is a real entity that is as tangible as the body to which it belongs. The particular empirical bodies, such as this man, this beast, this bird, this fish and this star, are real and existent objects. Their reality and existence are persuasions based on our sense-perception. Our belief in their existence finds correspondence in their materiality, which is not denied by Bentham.

29 Locke, *An Essay concerning Human Understanding*, ii.xxii.1.
30 See, for example, Berkeley, *A Treatise Concerning the Principles of Human Knowledge*, sections 1–7.
31 Hume, *A Treatise of Human Nature*, i.iii.1.
32 *Essay on Language*, Bowring viii, 327.

The reality and existence of corporeal bodies, along with their actual materiality, are discerned by human beings. Bentham's ontological realism is grounded on sensory experience, which is the criterion for the identification of real entities and their distinction from fictitious entities. The existence of a corporeal object is "tangible," that is, real, to the extent that it is perceived by the senses and particularly by touch.

Bentham claims the superiority or priority of sensibility over the human mind. The human mind is subordinate to sensibility because, from an empirical point of view, sensibility is the first and only source of reality, that is, of existence. The ascription of existence to a real entity by means of its denomination is not merely the attribution of a fictitious property: the linguistic existence of a real entity finds correspondence in the empirical existence of that entity, namely in its being perceived. Language makes intelligible, from a verbal point of view, the existence and reality of an empirical entity. In the case of perceptions, language is not detached from ontology, but gives it verbal expression.

A linguistic account of existence

The case is different when a noun denotes an intangible object, namely an imperceptible and non-empirical entity.

> On the other hand, in the case in which the object is not a tangible one, the object, the existence of which is thus asserted, not being a real existing one, the object, if it must be termed an entity, as on pain of universal and perpetual non-intercourse between man and man, it must be, – it may, for distinction's sake, be termed a fictitious entity. Take, for example, this motion, this operation, this quality, this obligation, this right. Thus then we have two sorts of names, with two corresponding sorts of entities. Names of real entities, – names of fictitious entities.[33]

The attribution of a name to a fictitious object entails ascribing existence and reality to it, and yet these properties cannot be perceived by the senses because of their origin and nature, which are exclusively mental. When we designate some objects that are purely imaginary with names such as motion, operation, quality, obligation and right, we ascribe existence and reality to them. From a linguistic point of view, that is, in the context of a proposition, there is no difference in terms of existence and reality between names of real entities such as fish and names of fictitious entities such as obligation. Both are noun-substantives and, by virtue of their propositional function, are characterized as existent and real. However, these names designate entities belonging to two different areas, namely reality, the contents of which are empirical, and fiction, the contents of

33 *Essay on Language*, Bowring viii, 327.

which are mental or linguistic. Real entities have both an empirical and a linguistic existence whereas fictitious entities have only a linguistic existence, which is bestowed upon them by the human mind.

Bentham's form of constructivism can be specified as linguistic. Language associates, in the minds of the interlocutors, a name with an entity, which is "apt to be taken for a real one" notwithstanding its actual nature. Thus, "To speak of an object by its name, its universally known name, is to ascribe existence to it."[34] Generally speaking, from an empirical point of view, existence and reality should belong only to perceptions. However, if there were only perceptions and if knowledge were reduced only to sensibility, human beings would not be able to communicate and establish a social order with its values and norms. Then, the human mind fills this gap, by creating, through language, new entities which have an imaginary nature. Despite their fictitious character, these entities are treated as if they were as existent and real as perceptible objects. In other words, paradoxical as it is, they have a fictitious existence and a fictitious reality.

Bentham would seem to contradict himself when he outlines existence, on the one hand, as a property experienced by the senses and, on the other, as a property artificially assigned by language. In short, should existence be depicted in empirical or conceptual terms, viz. in realist or constructivist terms? More fundamentally, is existence a real or a fictitious notion? Bentham does not solve this ambiguity and, in a seemingly contradictory manner, he embraces these two different views on the notion of existence, one empirical and the other mental, one realist and the other fictitious or constructivist.

Surprisingly, in *Of Ontology* Bentham accounts for the notion of existence as a fictitious entity. Existence, along with its modifications and its corresponding fictitious entities, such as "non-existence, futurity, actuality, potentiality, necessity, possibility, and impossibility," is subordinate to the fictitious predicament of relation. Although all these notions are more extensive than the notion of relation, it has priority over them in the logical order of presentation. The wide extension of existence and of its corresponding notions depends on their applicability "to relations of all sorts, and in a word to entities, fictitious as well as real, of all sorts."[35]

It seems equivocal to consider the notion of existence, coinciding with reality, a fiction. This contradiction might lie in an unresolved tension, in Bentham's writings, between a realist and a constructivist approach to reality. By ascribing existence to fictitious entities, Bentham seems to introduce a constructivist perspective on reality, contradictorily joined with a realist perspective. Even existence, i.e. reality itself, would not escape the process of human creation and nominalization of entities. Ontology seems also to derive from the activity of the human constructive faculties such as imagination and communication. If the property of existence is not only a feature of empirical real entities, but can be

34 *Essay on Language*, Bowring viii, 328.
35 Cf. *De l'ontologie*, 102 (Bowring viii, 203).

extended to intellectual fictitious entities, then the attribution of existence is a prerogative exercised by both sense-perception and the human mind.

Bentham offers a more detailed account of the concept of existence in section 10 of the text *Of Ontology*, entitled *Existence, and the classes of fictitious Entities related to it.*

> Existence is a quality that is the most extensively applicable, and at the same time the simplest of all qualities, actual or imaginable. Take away all other qualities, this remains: to speak more strictly, take any entity whatsoever, real or fictitious, abstract the attention from whatsoever other qualities may have been found belonging to it, this will still be left. *Existence* is predicable of naked *substance.*[36]

Bentham regards the notion of existence as a transcendental property: it is a very general concept coextensive to being and thus belonging to any entity, real or fictitious. We cannot think of an object without thinking of it as existent. The possibility of understanding reality depends upon the notion of existence. Among all qualities, existence is both the most extensive, as it pertains to all objects, and the simplest, as it is the first and basic attribute inherent in all entities. No object, no entity can be grasped or thought without considering it as characterized somehow by the feature of existence, or also by its opposite of non-existence. The quality of existence shapes our idea of any individual substance. Paradoxically, this implies that a fictitious entity, namely existence, determines our understanding of reality as a whole.

> Of every other entity, real or fictitious, either *existence* or *non-existence* is at all times predicable. Whether such other entity be real or fictitious, its existence is of course a fictitious entity: i.e. the word existence is in all cases the name of a fictitious entity.[37]

Bentham asserts the fictitious nature of the notion of existence and its opposite of non-existence, meaning by it "the negation of existence," i.e. "the idea of *absence* extended."[38] Bentham maintains that the attributes of existence and non-existence can be alternatively predicated on any entity, either real or fictitious. So, it is possible to identify both an existing real entity and an existing fictitious entity and both a non-existing real entity and a non-existing fictitious entity. Bentham's empirical realism seems to be put seriously to the test by the acknowledgment that existence is a fictitious property attributed to things by the creative ability of the human mind and not a real property belonging to perceptions and experienced by sensibility.

36 *De l'ontologie*, 150 (Bowring viii, 210).

37 *De l'ontologie*, 150 (Bowring viii, 210).

38 In this context Bentham means non-existence in absolute terms and not in relative terms, that is, as absence in any place and not in a place. Consequently, existence may be understood in terms of presence. See *De l'ontologie*, 152 (Bowring viii, 210): "The idea of *non-existence* is the idea of *absence* extended. Take any *place,* and therewith, any real entity – any body – existing in that place: suppose it no longer existing in that place, you suppose its *absence,* its *relative* non-existence: expell it in like manner from every, you suppose its *absolute* non-existence."

Bentham's statement about the general inherence and predicability of the notion of existence is not free from ambiguities. The universality acknowledged to the concept of existence, in particular, arises some difficulties. First, if the character of existence is applicable to real and fictitious entities, considered as different categories, the notion of reality is not tantamount to the notion of existence. Bentham, however, never introduces a division between what is real and what is existent: according to him existence and reality coincide.

Second, the kind of existence of a real entity should be distinguished from the kind of existence of a fictitious entity, otherwise the separation between reality and fiction, sharply drawn by Bentham, is doomed to failure. Similarly, the notion of non-existence cannot be ascribed in the same form to real and fictitious entities. Nevertheless, Bentham assumes the notions of existence and non-existence in a uniform way: the same quality of existence or non-existence which is predicated on a real entity is also predicated on a fictitious entity. Third, if existence is a fictitious notion, one needs to explain how it is possible to predicate it on what is real, or, put differently, how reality can be fictitious without contradiction.

The questions raised by Bentham's outline of the notion of existence reveal their centrality in the interpretation of the distinction between real and fictitious entities, which underpins our conception of the world. The empirical notion of existence is incapable of giving an account of the constructive ability of the human mind, which is the source not merely of fictitious entities but also of our understanding of reality.

> Being as above a species of quality, *existence* itself is a fictitious entity: it is *in* every real entity: every real entity is *in* it.[39]

Bentham does not hesitate to compare the core notion of existence with "nothing,"[40] notwithstanding its importance in the constitution of the world. Existence is a fictitious entity or, more precisely, a type of quality, i.e. a fictitious entity of the second remove depending on another fictitious entity in its relation to reality. By virtue of its generality and import, the notion of existence cannot be put on the same footing of other qualities. Unlike ripeness, sweetness and goodness, existence is not merely one of the various attributes with which a substance can be endowed. On the quality of existence depends the ontological status of anything and, more generally, the nature itself of reality, to the extent that what is real is existent.

On the one hand, Bentham's ontology appears to be consistent with a long-standing metaphysical tradition which treats the notion of existence as a transcendental or universal attribution, i.e. an accident predicable of everything. On the other hand, Bentham's ontology deals with existence in an original way,

39 *De l'ontologie*, 152 (Bowring viii, 210).

40 *De l'ontologie*, 152 (Bowring viii, 210): "In it [= existence], the man the object of whose appetite is the sublime, and he the object of whose appetite is the ridiculous, may here find matter for their respective banquets. *Nothing* has been laughed at to satiety: the punster who has played with *nothing* till he is tired may renew the game with existence and non-existence."

by depicting it as a fictitious entity, that is, as a quality created by the human mind for the need for communication. The above passages from *Of Ontology* testify to a shift, in the history of ontology, of the source of existence from a metaphysical creature such as God to the human mind. The existence of any substance, fictitious or real, is a belief.

Bentham outlines not only the notion of existence but also the group of fictitious entities associated with it in purely constructivist terms.

> *Necessity*, *Impossibility*; *Certainty*, *uncertainty*; *Probability*, *improbability*; *actuality*, *potentiality*; – whatsoever there is of reality correspondent to any of these names is neither more nor less than a disposition, a persuasion of the mind, on the part of him by whom these words are employed, in relation to the state of things or the event or events to which these *qualities* are ascribed.[41]

The degree of reality affecting fictitious entities such as existence and its cognates is reduced by Bentham to "neither more nor less than a disposition, a persuasion of the mind." Nevertheless, fictitious entities have reality, although Bentham does not specify how this kind of reality differs from the reality of empirical objects. Existence and its related notions are words ascribed in the form of qualities to an object or an event. The process of ascription of existence, as well as of other less fundamental properties, to something is carried out by the human mind by means of language. This ontological ability to ascribe existence makes the human mind a source of being.[42]

Bentham's challenge to a realist position becomes far stronger when he introduces a further problematic distinction, within the category of quality, between "real qualities" and "fictitious qualities." The former group is made up by qualities that "belong to the objects themselves to which they are ascribed," namely that belong "in the character of attributes of the objects to which they are ascribed." As examples of real qualities Bentham mentions physical properties such as gravity, solidity, roundness and hardness.[43] In this case, the human activity of ascription of these qualities is not a mere creation of the mind but a conceptual and linguistic acknowledgement of a state of affairs. The physical qualities expressed by language find correspondence in material objects as their own properties. Even though the idea of solidity is an abstraction, the particular solidity of an object in front of me can easily be perceived by my sense-organs. Despite their generality, real qualities have empirical references.

The group of fictitious qualities includes certain metaphysical entities corresponding to the above-mentioned concepts related to that of existence such as

41 *De l'ontologie*, 152 (Bowring viii, 210–1).

42 Bentham's usage of the verb *to ascribe* is not random but seems to point out a specific constructive human ability.

43 Cf. *De l'ontologie*, 154 (Bowring viii, 211).

necessity, impossibility, certainty, uncertainty, probability, improbability, actuality and potentiality. In Bentham's opinion, fictitious qualities "are mere chimeras, mere creatures of the imagination," that is, "nonentities."[44] Contrary to real qualities, they have no empirical instantiation which can be experienced. Sense-organs are unable, for instance, to perceive the probability of a state of affairs. Fictitious qualities are imaginary notions without an empirical basis from which they can be abstracted or derived. For this reason, they are pure creations of the human mind.

The subdivision of the wide class of qualities, operated by Bentham, seems to be motivated by the need to provide a clear specification of the notion of quality, which encompasses a rich variety of ontologically different properties. However, this subdivision appears to be far more problematic than its uniform treatment. Bentham adopts categories such as "real quality" and "fictitious quality" which are manifestly contradictory or redundant: literally speaking, if we consider that quality is a fiction, they mean *real fiction* and *fictitious fiction*. In the former case, a fiction cannot be real by definition and, in the latter, it is pleonastic to specify a fiction as fictitious.

Bentham's distinction between real and fictitious qualities might be understood as a rough attempt to separate empirical elements from mental notions.[45] We may suppose that empirical qualities are real because of their perceptibility whereas conceptual qualities are fictitious insofar as they are mere products of imagination without particular perceptible instances. If we can see and touch the roundness of an object, we cannot experience the necessity or actuality of a state of affairs.

Besides these difficulties, the treatment of the notion of existence appears still more controversial because of this subdivision of the notion of quality into real and fictitious. As a metaphysical property, existence belongs to the group of fictitious qualities. By virtue of this status, existence should not be accounted for as a property already belonging to empirical aggregates, as a property which the mind can abstract from those aggregates and then substantialize. Existence is a pure invention of the mind, along with core metaphysical concepts such as necessity, certainty, potentiality and actuality. Notwithstanding the imaginary nature of these concepts, their mischievous effects are however "too real," as Bentham ironically says by making reference to the strong influence they, and in particular necessity, have on our understanding of reality and on our planning and performance of action.

In Bentham's view, properties such as roundness and hardness are real qualities while existence is a fictitious quality. No doubt, this is a paradox which cannot be

44 *De l'ontologie*, 154 (Bowring viii, 210–1). On Bentham's notion of probability, especially from a mathematical point of view, see Cléro 2004, 203–31.

45 In this context it might be useful to quote Bentham's definition of metaphysics (*Essay on Logic*, UC 101.099; Bowring viii, 220): "the branch of art or science upon which the mind will not in any natural course have entered until it has touched upon that which is called physics: nor indeed without having [past] over, or at least past *through*, that branch." As examples of metaphysical terms Bentham mentions existence, contingency, possibility and necessity, which are the most general, i.e. the most extensive, in any language.

explained simply by assuming the real character of the elements belonging to the empirical domain as opposed to the fictitious character of the elements belonging to the mental domain. More than gravity, solidity and other physical properties, which are all real qualities, existence, despite its fictitious nature, is a necessary condition for the reality of the empirical and the mental world. By putting aside the notion of existence or reducing it to a nonentity, reality itself is destined to be unreal, namely it could not exist.

A general constructivist reading of Bentham's treatment of existence as a fictitious entity risks neglecting the basic tenet of Bentham's thought, that is, the distinction between reality and fiction. If existence is reduced to a fictitious entity, the natural consequence is that the whole of reality is a fiction too: the separation between real and fictitious entities does not make sense any more.[46]

The reconciliation between realism and constructivism

When examining the passages in which Bentham deals with the notion of existence, the interpreter is faced with the problem of explaining the presence of a realist and a constructivist approach. Bentham wavers between an empirical and a mental account of the notion of existence, whose adoption seems to document an unsolved tension between realism and constructivism in his writings. The main difficulty lies in reconciling the acknowledgement of the notion of existence as a perceptual feature with the idea of existence as a fictitious creation.

Empirical realism and constructivism seemingly conflict in Bentham's thought. His understanding of existence as a perception appears to be scarcely consistent with his conception of existence as a mental entity. Is existence a property experienced by sensibility or is existence a property created and ascribed by the human mind? To what extent may existence be predicated both on real and fictitious entities?

As regards existence, Bentham does not set the realist view against the constructivist view, but rather attempts to make them compatible with each other, though they are alternative. Bentham takes into consideration two distinct notions of existence and thus of reality, one empirical and the other mental: the empirical existence concerns the entities perceived by the senses; the mental existence concerns the imaginary creations of the human mind. Sensibility is the source of empirical existence: the perception of a material body is accompanied by the belief in its existence. The human mind, with particular reference to its faculties of imagination and communication, is the source of mental existence: an imaginary entity, treated in the form of a noun-substantive, is regarded as existent.

Much of the confusion about the notion of existence probably depends on the lack of a clear distinction between the two accounts of it provided by Bentham.

46 The difficulty of combining a fictionalist approach with an autonomous conception of reality is also expressed by Cléro 2014, 109–10.

We may identify two types of existence and, consequently, two types of reality, which diverge without conflicting. The difference between an empirical and a linguistic existence is not in the degree but in the kind. Linguistic existence is not weaker than empirical existence or vice versa: both forms of existence are on the same footing, as Bentham does not admit a medium between existence and non-existence.[47] However, empirical existence and linguistic existence do not come into opposition because they belong to two different domains of the world, that is, materiality and immateriality.

Bentham's account of existence is double: he provides, on the one hand, a realist treatment of empirical objects and, on the other, a constructivist treatment of mental objects. He identifies two sources of existence, namely sensibility, with reference to the existence of perceptual entities, and the human mind with reference to linguistic entities.

Bentham does not attempt to merge these two perspectives but makes them suitable to his pivotal distinction between reality and fiction. Thus, the two accounts of the notion of existence are not competing since each one pertains to a specific area, viz. perception or the human mind. The problem of this double approach lies in finding a relation between these two areas, corresponding to reality and fiction, which risk remaining unrelated.

2.3 The connection between reality and fiction

Empirical realism and constructivism

The adoption of the interpretative categories of realism and constructivism appears to be adequate to approach Bentham's distinction between real and fictitious entities. However, the meaning of realism and constructivism needs to be contextualized in and fitted to Bentham's thought. Realism and constructivism are broad historiographical categories, generally adopted to identify and label a variety of positions concerning the nature of the physical and the practical world. Consequently, there are different versions of realism and constructivism in metaphysics and metaethics.

Basically, as its denomination suggests, any type of realism admits the reality of certain entities, which are independent of the human faculties which grasp them. Bentham embraces a particular form of realism. His claim of reality is restricted to all kinds of perceptions and to several negligible spiritual entities. By and large, we might say that Bentham puts forward a type of realism which

47 See *Fragments on Universal Grammar*, UC 102.558 n. a (Bowring viii, 348–9 n. †): "Take any conceivable state of things at pleasure: either it exists or it does not exist—between existence and non-existence there is no medium." The possibility of a medium is also denied in the case of a relative notion of existence (i.e. relative to a place), as stated in *De l'ontologie*, 152 (Bowring viii, 210): "At any point of time, take any entity – any real entity – whatsoever, between its existence in that place and its non-existence in that same place, there is not any *alternative* – there is not any *medium* – whatsoever."

is purely empirical to the extent that it mainly pertains to sensory elements. Bentham's realism does not concern material bodies in themselves, but material bodies as they are discerned by the perceptual faculties.

Constructivism has a more recent history than realism. Generally speaking, it consists in the idea that beliefs about the world are produced, i.e. literally constructed, by the activity of certain faculties of the mind. Knowledge corresponds to a representation of reality, which is, to some extent, a creation of the human mind. No doubt there are different degrees of constructivism, according to the powers assigned to the human mind for the representation of reality and to the role that perceptions are acknowledged as playing.

In Bentham's philosophy constructivism is originally joined with fictionalism and has a linguistic form. Constructivism and fictionalism concern the creation, by means of language, of notions, which, by virtue of their conceptual nature, are nothing but fictitious entities. Scholars such as Cléro and Tusseau interpret Bentham's treatment of fictitious entities as a constructivist stance on reality, to the extent that the entities produced by language and imagination contribute to building the human system of truths and values.[48]

Bentham seems to combine elements belonging both to the realist and constructivist traditions. He sets forth a realist approach to the empirical phenomena, which are experienced by the sensory faculties, and a constructivist approach to the mental objects, which are creations of the intellectual faculties. Although sensibility and the human mind and, consequently, reality and fiction are clearly distinguished, they are not separate, but are in a relation of subordination. Just as the mind depends on sensibility in its constructive activity, so fictitious entities depend on real entities as regards their import and truth. Bentham grounds his constructivism on his empirical realism: the creative ability of the human mind makes sense when rooted in the empirical world. Bentham's ontology appears to be a network of connections between perceptual and conceptual elements, that is, between real and fictitious entities.

Sense-perception and the human mind

A fictitious entity is a creation of the mind and has meaning and truth by virtue of the relation it maintains with a real entity. The dependence of the field of fictitious entities on the field of real entities underlies the human representation of the structure of the world. Real entities are the foundations of the fictitious construction of the world carried out by the human mind. The exploration of the network of the ontological connections between real and fictitious entities brings to the fore Bentham's attempt to link empirical realism and constructivism.

In an original way, Bentham's trust in the truth of perceptions underpins his constructivism. "Simple perception," he maintains, "is not capable of erring, no,

48 See Cléro 2006, 37–58, in part. 47–8; Tusseau 2011a, 107. See also Cléro 2000, 446; Tusseau 2009, 247 and 249.

nor sensation neither"; instead, "judgment is, on the part of every person, and on almost every occasion exposed to error."[49] Bentham's constructivism does not challenge the veracity of simple perceptions and sensations, i.e. perceptions accompanied by pleasure or pain,[50] but assumes them as the fundamentals on which the human cognitive faculties exercise their creative ability.

Bentham questions the reliability of the human mind, even in its operations which are closer to perceptions, as in the case of judgment, when for example a man believes that he sees a hill and instead the cause of his perception is a cloud or when he believes that he hears the rain falling while "the cause of his perception is not rain, but the wind whistling through certain trees." To avoid possible confusion, Bentham specifies that "judgment is continually included" in the states of mind exemplified, i.e. the sight of a tree and the hearing of the rain, which usually are considered as instances of mere perceptions.[51]

Bentham's realist account of perceptions allows him to ground his fictionalist system on the truth, that is, on empirical bases. Hence, the construction of concepts from sensory elements is not a false and meaningless process. The creation of new fictitious entities makes sense because these entities are the outcome of the activity of assembling and dissembling performed on real perceptual elements.

The relation between fictitious entities and their corresponding real sources is examined in depth by Bentham in a manuscript, included in his *Essay on Language*, stating the "*necessity of names of material objects for the designation of pneumatic or immaterial objects*" (Bowring viii, 327–9). In this manuscript too, the constitutive connection between real and fictitious entities is accounted for from a linguistic viewpoint: it is reframed as a connection between names of material objects and names of immaterial objects. This section of his work allows us to recapitulate Bentham's main achievements about the distinction between real and fictitious entities in the light of the interpretative categories of realism and constructivism.

> All our psychological ideas are derived from physical ones, – all mental from corporeal ones. When spoken of, mental ideas are spoken of as if they were corporeal ones. In no other manner can they be spoken of. But thus to speak of them is to give an erroneous, a false account of them, an account that agrees not with their nature, – it is to misrepresent them. But very different from what it is in most other cases, in this case misrepresentation is not matter of blame. By it no deception is intended [. . .]. From what there is of falsehood not only is pure good the result, but it is the work of invincible necessity, – on no other terms can discourse be carried on.[52]

49 *Essay on Language*, Bowring viii, 320. According to Bentham, simple perceptions, sensations, "i.e. perceptions attended with pain or pleasure," and judgments or opinions concerning similitudes and causal connections among objects are all "Acts of the intellectual department or faculty."

50 Cf. *Essay on Language*, Bowring viii, 320.

51 These examples are provided by Bentham in *Essay on Language*, Bowring viii, 320–1.

52 *Essay on Language*, Bowring viii, 327.

Bentham understands the relation between real and fictitious entities in terms of derivation. The process of derivation of psychological ideas from physical, i.e. corporeal, ideas is not internal to the nature of things but involves the intervention of mental faculties such as abstraction, imagination, communication and so forth. Fictitious objects are constructed through a series of operations performed by the human mind, which shapes those fictitious objects as if they were real entities. Mistakenly, two entities such as rain and roundness are put on the same footing from a linguistic point of view. Both are nouns or subjects in the context of a sentence and indicate an individual object. Language is not able to account for their constitutive difference, lying in their nature, which is empirical in the case of real entities and mental in the case of fictitious entities. This treatment of mental objects, as if they were material, is still necessary for the formulation of discourse and, more generally, for the human communication of thoughts.

Notwithstanding the misrepresentation of fictitious entities as real, the constructive activity of the human mind, performed by means of language, is not condemned by Bentham as a deception, a blame.[53] Bentham admits the limit of language, that is, the "imperfection of the instrument for the purposes of discourse," but he is also aware of "the necessity of mixing falsehood with truth, on pain of being without ideas, as well as without conversation."[54] Without the creation of new verbal entities, any form of interaction and even solitary reflection would not be possible.

In spite of their clarity, sense-data are not sufficient to the exercise of the highest mental operations, namely thought and communication. The human mind needs to construct concepts, i.e. imaginary entities, to orientate itself in the world. Therefore, reality, at least as we grasp it, is the product of the cooperation between sense-perception and the human mind. In particular, the operations of the human mind make both theoretical and practical reasoning possible.

In Bentham's approach, both the receptive activity of sensibility and the constructive activity of the human mind are necessary for our understanding of the world. Receptive and imaginative faculties work together when accounting for the world where human beings live and act. In the Benthamite perspective, our representation of the external world is a network of connections between real and fictitious entities, which are so deeply interrelated that they reciprocally depend on each other. From an ontological point of view we may distinguish, on the one hand, empirical objects, the existence of which consists in their perceptibility, and, on the other, mental objects, i.e. concepts, endowed with a form of existence conferred by the human mind through language.

53 See also *Essay on Language*, Bowring viii, 327–8: "Unfortunate it is, howsoever necessary and indispensable, that for speaking of fictitious entities, there is no other possible mode than that of speaking of them as if they were so many real entities. This blameless falsehood being universally uttered, and remaining universally uncontradicted, is, to a considerable extent, taken for truth."

54 *Chrestomathia*, 277 n. a. Bentham also adds that this necessity "is productive but too abundantly of misconception and false reasoning; and this not only in the physical department of the field of thought, discourse, and action, but also in every other."

The ontological function of language

A denotative relation characterizes a material thing and the name or sign referring to it: "the sign is presented to the sense of the addressee, the individuality of the object, the idea of which is, by that sign, presented to notice, is continually established." When saying "Bring hither that loaf" and "behold that apple," we use a denomination such as loaf or apple to designate a portion of matter and this denomination is shared by the addresser and the addressee of the communication. Consequently, "the import of the word loaf or apple is [. . .] fixed, readily fixed, and beyond danger of mistake."[55]

The relation between immaterial things and their denominations has a different character.

> Objects of a corporeal nature may be designated and denominated in a direct way.
>
> Not so in the case of an object of which the seat lies in the mind; – not so in the case of an immaterial being. For producing in any other mind any conception whatsoever of an object of this class, a man has absolutely but one means, and that is to speak of it as if it belonged to the other class, – to speak of it as if it were a material object.[56]

When referring to immaterial entities, whose "seat lies in the mind," the act of denomination has not merely a denotative but also a constructive import. By receiving a name, immaterial objects are treated in the same way as material objects, though they have no empirical nature insofar as they are products of the mind. The denomination of an immaterial entity, however, does not refer to an entity perceived by the senses, and thus actually existent, such as the loaf or the apple in front of me. Giving a name to an immaterial object means giving linguistic existence to that which does not exist in the material world but exists in the human mind as the outcome of its operations. So, the name of an immaterial entity is an artefact brought into existence by language.

Bentham distinguishes between "discourse having matter for its subject," consisting in material language, and "discourse having mind for its subject," consisting in immaterial language. When saying *bring me that loaf of bread, it's in that pan* in the presence of an existent loaf in an existent pan, the speaker gives rise to the ideas of a pan and a loaf in the hearer's mind. In a metaphorical manner the speaker places the ideas of a pan and a loaf *in* the hearer's mind. In this context, the preposition *in*, indicating a place, is employed in an immaterial sense, though it actually has a material sense. The hearer's mind is similar to "a receptacle, in which the idea has been made to have place, *as* in the material pan the material loaf is deposited."[57]

55 *Essay on Language*, Bowring viii, 328.
56 *Essay on Language*, Bowring viii, 328.
57 Cf. *Essay on Language*, Bowring viii, 328–9.

Immaterial names are treated as if they correspond to material things. The linguistic and thus ontological analogy between names signifying material objects and names signifying immaterial objects makes communication of immaterial objects possible. The materialization of immaterial objects is a requirement of human communication.

If in the case of material entities the nominalization has only a communicative function, in the case of immaterial entities the nominalization has both a communicative and ontological function. Language gives birth to immaterial objects, enabling them to be considered just as existent as material objects. Thus, ripeness, i.e. an immaterial entity, and the apple in front of me, which is a material entity, have both reality and existence because of their common nominalization in a substantive form. The ontological gap between immateriality and materiality is filled by language. This double role, communicative and ontological, of the denomination act makes Bentham's fictionalism a form of linguistic constructivism: "To speak of an object by its name, its universally known name, is to ascribe existence to it."[58] By means of language the human mind has the prerogative to materialize immaterial things, that is, to give them reality.[59]

> Applied to the designation of any class of material objects, a sign is, or may be, the sign of a *real entity,* applied to the purpose of designating any object of the class of immaterial objects, a sign cannot, in that respect, be the sign of anything but a fictitious entity. The entity of which the sign in question is given as a sign, – your mind, as in the above example, shall in the character of an immaterial substance, have whatsoever reality it may be your pleasure to see ascribed to it.[60]

In Bentham's approach realism and constructivism do not conflict, because they concern two different areas, that is, materiality and immateriality. The area of materiality has reality and existence insofar as it is empirically experienced; the area of immateriality is endowed with reality and existence by human faculties, which create it. Language mirrors this strict division between materiality and immateriality but is incapable of expressing it in a sentence: language treats any name as a noun, without distinguishing the class to which it belongs.

The risk of a similar view is a breaking of the conception of the world into two parts. Bentham, however, rejects a dualistic view, characterized by a sharp separation between materiality and immateriality, sense-perception and the human mind, reality and fiction. Bentham's theoretical efforts are devoted to highlighting the connection of immateriality to materiality. Bentham attempts to throw light on this connection from a linguistic, or more precisely etymological, point of view.

58 *Essay on Language*, Bowring viii, 328.

59 This power of materializing immaterial things by means of language is clarified by Bentham in a passage of *Chrestomathia*, 371–2.

60 *Essay on Language*, Bowring viii, 328.

Bentham alleges the material origin of the names employed to designate immaterial things. In order to be understood and communicated, immaterial objects have been denominated with certain signs, which in the beginning were adopted to identify material objects. By virtue of the nominal "resemblance" or "analogy" between the originally denoted material object and the currently denoted immaterial object, the sign, i.e. the name, is capable to excite in the hearer's mind "the idea of the immaterial object."[61]

Bentham, however, admits that "in some instances" the original materiality of the import of a sign denoting an immaterial thing is no longer discernible. He takes as examples of immaterial words the mind, the will, the understanding, conception and imagination; they have in common the fact that their material root is mislaid. An exception is the name adopted to denote the mind in French language, that is, *esprit*, whose material origin is manifest. In the beginning, *esprit*, deriving from the Latin word *spiritus*, was employed to mean breath, "*i.e.* air discharged out of the lungs."[62]

According to Bentham, the meaning of the words designating immaterial objects is disclosed by their corresponding material roots. Consequently, the immaterial language depends on the material language as regards its meaning and then usage: "In so far as any origin at all can be found for it, it is in a material import that the origin of the import of every word possessing an immaterial import is to be found."[63]

Immaterial language has a symmetrical but not reciprocal relation with material language, by running in parallel to it. Indeed, "to every word that has an immaterial import there belongs, or at least did belong, a material one," whereas "to every word that has a material import" there does not belong "also an immaterial one."[64] To each word denoting an immaterial object corresponds a word denoting a material object: immaterial language is subordinate to material language.

The transition of names from the denotation of material things to the denotation of immaterial things testifies to the foundational relation between immateriality and materiality. Bentham concludes that by virtue of "the numerous instances in which both sorts of imports are attached to the same word," the rule, according to which the origin of the immaterial import is to be found in the material import, is verified.[65]

61 Cf. *Essay on Language*, Bowring viii, 328.
62 Cf. *Essay on Language*, Bowring viii, 328–9.
63 *Essay on Language*, Bowring viii, 329.
64 *Essay on Language*, Bowring viii, 329. See also *Chrestomathia*, 398: "Throughout the whole field of language, two languages, as it were, run all along in a state of parallelism to each other, – the one *material*, the other *immaterial*; – the material all along the basis of the immaterial. The same stock of words serves for each, – each word serving, or being capable of serving, in both senses; – at any rate, every word originally employed in a material sense, is capable of being employed in an immaterial sense."
65 *Essay on Language*, Bowring viii, 329.

Nonetheless, the linguistic and ontological relation between materiality and immateriality still needs to be more fully explained. In particular, the examples, selected by Bentham, of words signifying immaterial objects and having a material origin appear to be weak. Bentham prefers to mention words whose material origin is mysterious rather than exemplifying cases in which the relation between immateriality and materiality is ascertainable. It is, moreover, baffling that Bentham adduces as sole actual example of that relation a word, *esprit*, which does not even belong to his native language.

Bentham's conception of language is fundamentally materialistic and empirical. Language is grounded on experience. A certain portion of matter produces in the speaker and hearer's minds certain impressions and ideas, which are identified by means of words. Matter is a non-verbal channel of communication which connects human beings. Language aims to verbalize this channel by giving names to these empirical perceptions.[66] Because of its empirical origin, language, even in its fiction-creating and existence-providing functions, should maintain a relation with matter.

An interesting example of the semantic connection that words denoting immaterial objects have with words denoting material objects is provided in *An Introduction to the Principles of Morals and Legislation* and concerns the notion of sanction. On the basis of the testimony of the Latin grammarian Servius, the meaning of the word *sanctio* (sanction) is related to the meaning of the word *sanguinis* (blood). This relation is brought to light through a "far-fetched process," according to which "intellectual ideas are derived from sensible ones." Bentham clarifies this semantic relation between *sanctio* and *sanguinis* by making clear their historical connection: Roman priests used the blood of victims during certain ceremonies, in order to persuade people that a mode of conduct was rendered obligatory by means of the force of the religious sanction, consisting in a divine intervention aimed at punishing the individual who failed to conform to such a mode of conduct.[67]

The connection between the names of real entities, designating material objects, and the names of fictitious entities, designating immaterial objects, is deepened by Bentham in certain passages of *Chrestomathia*. His proposal is not merely to look for the material import of the words signifying immaterial elements, but to substitute the name of the corresponding real entity for the name of the fictitious entity. So, in order to throw light on the notion of causality, we should replace the word *cause* with the word *author* or *instrument*.[68]

Bentham's basic claims concerning the relation between real, i.e. material or empirical, entities and fictitious, i.e. immaterial or mental, entities are the

66 *Essay on Language*, Bowring viii, 329.

67 *An Introduction to the Principles of Morals and Legislation*, 34 n. a.

68 *Chrestomathia*, 279–80. See also *Preparatory Principles*, 118: "A Cause is an instrument in action. An instrument is a Substance; a Cause, a Mode of that substance. The word Cause is in general promiscuously bestow'd on the substance and the mode: but as we have another name full as expressive for the *Substance*, for precision's sake, it is better to confine it to the mode."

following two: "it is from our corporeal ideas that all our mental ideas are derived"; consequent to it, "all words now employed in giving expression to incorporeal ideas, were originally employed in giving expression to corporeal ideas."[69] The linguistic and ontological dependence of immateriality on materiality is stated by Bentham several times.[70]

By mixing truth with falsehood, the construction of a fictitious language[71] has produced confusion and darkness. The names of fictitious entities have been considered as denoting real entities. Without minimizing the contribution that the creation of fictitious entities gives to the development of human thought, Bentham points out the need to clearly distinguish fictitious entities from real entities. The identification of the real, i.e. empirical, sources of fictitious entities could help to avoid misunderstanding and erroneous reasoning.[72] Bentham stresses the importance of discovering the perceptual or corporeal origin of the words currently adopted to designate immaterial, i.e. mental, objects.

Notwithstanding his distinction between material language and immaterial language, referring to empirical ontology and mental ontology, Bentham aims to give a unified and consistent account of the world, by tracing fictitious entities, produced by the human mind, back to perceptions, i.e. real entities, which are the sources of their truth and meaning. In this way, Bentham harmonizes empirical realism, asserting the veracity of experience, with constructivism, maintaining the imaginary nature of the immaterial entities created for the intelligibility and communicability of the contents of the world.

Bentham overcomes linguistic and ontological dualism, which consists in a complete division of the world in two unrelated domains, i.e. reality and fiction. He intimately connects these two dimensions, identifying the foundations of fictitious entities in real entities. Just as material language underlies immaterial language, so the real ontology of perceptions underlies the fictitious ontology of the human mind, which receives its meaning and truth from it. Bentham establishes a linguistic and ontological dependence of immateriality on materiality, that is, of the human mind on sensibility, but without undermining the autonomy of the human mind in thinking and constructing the external world.

69 *Chrestomathia*, 323. With reference to the issue treated in this passage, Bentham praises Locke's work in the field of psychology.

70 See, for example, *Chrestomathia*, 259: "Almost all names, employed in speaking of the phenomena of the mind, are names of fictitious entities. In speaking of any *pneumatic* (or say *immaterial* or *spiritual*) object, no name has ever been employed, that had not first been employed as the name of some *material* (or say *corporeal*) one. Lamentable have been the confusion and darkness, produced by taking the names of *fictitious* for the names of *real* entities."

71 Bentham himself adopts the locution "fictitious language," probably as opposite to "real language." For an instance of this, see *Chrestomathia*, 373.

72 See also *Chrestomathia*, 370: "For the explanation of these fictions, and, indeed, for the justification of the use so copiously made of them, two operations would, it should seem, require to be performed. One is, the indication of the really exemplified state of things, to which the fiction is now wont to be applied, or is considered as applicable, the other is the indication of the advantage derived from the use of this the fictitious language, in contradistinction to the language by which the state of things in question would be expressed plainly and clearly without having recourse to fiction."

The normativity of fiction

The evolution of the theory of real and fictitious entities

Bentham's idea of fictitious entity first appeared and was shaped in his very early writings, dating back to the early 1770s; they were devoted to mathematics and particularly to geometry. These as yet unpublished manuscripts are addressed to his brother Samuel in order to introduce him to certain elemental notions of Euclidean mathematics and thus improve his education.[1] Along with the technical explanation of some portions of Euclid's *Elements*, these texts offered Bentham the opportunity to outline his view on the ontological and epistemological nature of mathematical objects and properties according to the general distinction between real and fictitious entities.[2]

Bentham understands mathematical notions as fictitious, that is, as intellectual constructions, which, however, need to be rooted in real entities, such as bodies or substances perceived by the senses, in order to be made intelligible. Bentham is aware of the interrelation between fictitious properties and real objects, from which the former are conceived to derive, and, by virtue of this, he adopts specific expository strategies aimed at disclosing the meaning and truth of fictitious entities. This view of mathematics is later put forward again in an educational context, in *Appendix viii* of his book *Chrestomathia*. The high level of abstraction and the unempirical character of mathematical concepts probably attracted Bentham and allowed him to put to the test his insight into the fictitious character of certain entities which are not susceptible to being experienced by perceptive faculties.

The chronological order of Bentham's writings seems to suggest an important element in understanding the origin and evolution of his theory of real and fictitious entities. At the beginning of his career as a writer, Bentham's interests were mainly focused on law or, more generally, on ethics. In that time, roughly between 1774 and 1789, he did not produce a separate treatment of the distinction

1 For an overview of the contents of Bentham's manuscripts on mathematics see Schofield 2006, 7–8, on which the short account given here is based.

2 Unfortunately, there is so far no comprehensive investigation devoted to Bentham's view on mathematical entities. A first attempt to explore Bentham's conception of mathematical notions as fictitious is provided by Cléro (1998; 2004, 203–31, 436–7 and 445–53) within his general analysis of fictionalism in mathematics. Cléro's examination is mostly based on *Rationale of Judicial Evidence* and *Chrestomathia*.

between real and fictitious entities, even though he used to regard the main political and legal notions as fictitious entities.

The adjective *fictitious* and the noun *fiction* occur many times in the works belonging to the first phase of Bentham's production, such as *Preparatory Principles*, *An Introduction to the Principles of Morals and Legislation*, *A Comment on the Commentaries*, *A Fragment on Government*, and *Of the Limits of the Penal Branch of Jurisprudence*. When employing the words *fictitious* and *fiction*, Bentham was aware of the particular status characterizing certain entities. As a legal scholar, he was mostly concerned with the examination of central elements of law and also ethics, thereby revealing their fictitious nature, which was usually misconceived.

The paragraphs collected in *Preparatory Principles* show Bentham's involvement in ontology, logic, language and grammar. In these texts he sketches out the foundations of his theory of real and fictitious entities, but without giving it a sort of unity. In particular, Bentham sets out his ideas concerning the nature of fictitious entities and their difference from real and fabulous entities, the importance of definition and of the method of exposition, the concept of substance, and the notions of cause, relation, motion and rest.[3]

The material contained in *Preparatory Principles* throws light on the metaphysical and epistemological background of Bentham's conception of ethics and law; it may be regarded as preliminary to his specific treatment of ontological, logical, linguistic and grammatical issues. Bentham's concern with these issues, thus, is intimately related to his reflections regarding human behaviour and the organization of the State. Indeed, he maintained a lifelong committment to working out the theoretical foundations of the practical domains.

Bentham's long-standing interests in ontology and metaphysics derived from his belief that the various subsets of ethics have a linguistic structure underpinning them. The linguistic clarification of the ideas, namely of the words, employed in a particular area of knowledge is a crucial task belonging to metaphysics.[4] Exploring the empirical roots of ideas such as obligation, right, good, virtue and so on enables us to understand the meaning and the truth of these notions along with their distinctive normative claim. In Bentham's view, metaphysics consists in an analysis of the language we use. This metaphysical analysis illuminates the structure of ethics and, therefore, should precede and underlie any attempt to examine the moral and legal regulation of human behaviour.

Therefore, the distinction between real and fictitious entities, although not yet systematically formulated, was initially adopted by Bentham to account for the ethical and especially the legal field. Bentham aimed at the clarification of the structure of ethics and law, understanding each ethical and legal notion within

3 See, for example, *Preparatory Principles: Inserenda*, paras. 1–2, 39, 259, 324, 533–4, 539, 584, 627, 708, 726, 774, 787, 792–4, 863, 1011, 1127–8, 1153–6, 1168, 1176, 1179, 1205, 1234–5, 1253–5, 1266, 1271–2, 1287–8 and 1323; *Preparatory Principles: Introduction*, para. 21.

4 Cf. *Preparatory Principles*, 196–7.

the larger framework of the interrelations between real and fictitious entities. His doctrine of real and fictitious entities served as a basis for the investigation of the practical branches of knowledge, with particular regard to law.

Only in a subsequent phase of his production, dating back to the years 1813–15, did Bentham's theory of real and fictitious entities received an independent theoretical formulation. His manuscripts on ontology, logic, language and grammar testify to a systematic attempt to theorize the status of a fictitious entity, along with its relation to reality, and to explore its usage no longer only in the practical domain, but also in the physical domain. The theory of real and fictitious entities began to provide the general framework to explain the world as a whole.

In this later period Bentham lays the ontological and logical foundations for his treatment of ethics. Bentham's concern with ontology, namely the study of being or "an account of *being* in general,"[5] is chiefly motivated by his interest in the study of well-being. Insofar as well-being is a type of being, eudæmonics, i.e. the science of well-being, may be regarded as depending on ontology. An examination of well-being implies the knowledge of being in general because, from a cognitive point of view, eudemonics is subordinate to ontology: "Eudæmonics is the art of *well-being*. Necessary for *well-being* is *being*. In every part, therefore, of the common field, concomitant and correspondent to *Eudæmonics* considered as an *art*, runs *Ontology*."[6]

In line with the tradition, Bentham considers ontology as the most basic and general discipline, which investigates being in general. Each discipline focuses on a type of being as its own object of research. For example, eudemonics or ethics investigates well-being, physics material being and, we may suppose, arithmetic numerical entities. All these objects are particular forms of being, which is, in its generality, scrutinized by ontology.

The ethical dimension of life depends on ontology. Insofar as ethical notions such as happiness, goodness and rightness are entities, that is, types of being, they fall within the domain of ontology. Thus, ontology deals with the characterization of an entity in general and eudemonics examines its ethical characterization as well-being, namely happiness. However, the exploration of the practical component of human life seems to have a priority over Bentham's theoretical interests: the main purpose of his treatment of ontology is the clarification of the concept of well-being or happiness. Indeed, "Directly or indirectly, *well-being*, in some shape or other, or in several shapes, or all shapes taken together, is the subject of every thought, and object of every action, on the part of every known *Being*, who is, at the same time a sensitive and thinking Being."[7]

Similarly, Bentham's practical interests influence his conception of logic, "the art of thinking."[8] This discipline is not merely a working instrument to offer to the various branches of knowledge in order to help them to carry out their

5 *Chrestomathia*, 181 n. a.
6 *Chrestomathia*, 181; see also 208.
7 *Chrestomathia*, 179.
8 *Chrestomathia*, table v, 198.

particular investigations. Logic contributes to the accomplishment of the end at which each discipline aims. Bentham defines logic as "the art, which has for its object or end in view, the giving to the best advantage, direction to the human mind and thence to the whole human frame, in its pursuit of any object or purpose, to the attainment of which it is capable of being applied."[9]

Logic reveals a practical finality: it directs the human mind to the achievement of the main and general end of human life, namely well-being or happiness, in any fields of knowledge. Well-being is not simply "the end in view, the ultimate as well as direct and immediate object" of ethics, but also and especially the "ultimate object" of any action, the "common result" pursued by any action.[10]

By being aimed at the pursuit of well-being, ethics is not, or at least not only, a descriptive but most of all a prescriptive discipline, which claims to direct human conduct. In this task ethics is guided by logic. The relation between logic and ethics is compared by Bentham to the relation between a commander-in-chief and the generals under him. In this way, he expresses the directive or guiding function played by logic over ethics. Indeed, logic has the task to "to take the command and give direction to the course of Ethics itself" in the pursuit of well-being.[11]

Logic, like any other branch of human knowledge, is a discipline "capable of being, of *use*." The utility of logic lies in its ability to be "conducive to the diminution of pain in some shape or other or to the encrease of pleasure."[12] The notion of utility is central to the working of the human mind, in its theoretical and practical divisions: any thought concerns the attainment of an end, generally corresponding to well-being or, in its ultimate form, to pleasure or exemption from pain. The principle of utility, worked out by Bentham, acknowledges such a teleological constitution of the human mind.

Along with the theorization of the ontological and logical bases for its treatment of ethics, Bentham, in his years of maturity, was committed to the generalization of his theory of real and fictitious entities and to its application to the field of physics. Bentham extended the interpretative categories of reality and fiction from the domain of ethics and law to the domain of physics. Just as ethical and legal elements, so natural elements were handled according to the distinction between real and fictitious entities.

Bentham pursued the objective of giving a comprehensive doctrine of real and fictitious entities, making it suitable to the treatment of each area of human knowledge, including physics. As the theoretical bases of law and morality have already been identified with the elemental feelings of pleasure and pain, Bentham focused on laying the foundation for physics: he worked out a theory of knowledge with the purpose of clarifying the human representation of the

9 *Essay on Logic*, UC 101.092 (Bowring viii, 219). Another similar definition is provided in *Essay on Logic*, UC 101.106 (Bowring viii, 222).
10 *Essay on Logic*, UC 101.108 (Bowring viii, 222).
11 Cf. *Essay on Logic*, UC 101.108 (Bowring viii, 222).
12 Cf. *Essay on Logic*, UC 101.108 (Bowring viii, 222).

material world in the light of the distinction between reality and fiction. Such a distinction was already providing a successful and fruitful comprehension of ethical and legal concepts.

Bentham tried to export the interpretative model based on the relation between real and fictitious entities from ethics to physics. He generalized the connection between reality and fiction by making it an overall explanatory principle. After having adopted this model in ethics, he implanted it in physics: he attempted to track down the connection that physical fictitious entities have with reality. First, he separated the elements making up the physical domain into fictitious and real entities and, then, he coordinated them by virtue of the relation of derivation operated by the human mind. In Bentham's view, the phenomena of the natural world could be expounded and justified by qualifying them as real and fictitious and by relating them according to the general principle which grounds fiction in reality.

Bentham establishes an ontological and epistemological parallelism between ethics and physics. He is firmly persuaded that the world, as it is represented by the human mind, is made up of a network of interrelations between real and fictitious entities. The understanding of such a particular interrelated structure provides the key to explaining the phenomena of the world, regardless of their specifications, namely, their being ethical or physical elements.

Just as pleasure and pain are at the basis of ethics, due to their giving a foundation to ethical notions, so too are perceptions at the basis of physics and play the same foundational function. Bentham transplanted from ethics to physics the view that fictitious entities have empirical roots, on which they depend as regards their meaning and truth. The comparison between the practical and the physical area enables us to better outline Bentham's strategy in accounting for natural events.

The idea of a connection between real and fictitious entities, which is constitutive of the human representation of the world, is the basic theoretical and operative principle of Bentham's philosophy. In order to classify the variety of ethical and physical elements, Bentham identifies which of them are fictitious and then traces such fictitious objects back to their empirical sources.

The theory of real and fictitious entities, developed for the sake of clarifying the nature of legal and moral elements, is adapted to the field of physics. In this case, such a theory aims to give an explanation of the states of affairs by relating them to perceptual elements, corresponding to their ontological and epistemological bases. Bentham's picture of the physical world, characterized by a series of interconnections between real and fictitious entities, appears to be moulded to his previously conceived picture of ethics and law.

The successful examination of ethical and legal elements in terms of real and fictitious entities provides Bentham with a model to investigate various branches of knowledge. Bentham's fictionalism is then reworked in a general form and made suitable to be employed in the domain of physics. So, in his manuscripts on ontology, logic, language and grammar Bentham supplies a general and comprehensive theory of real and fictitious entities, the intuition of which goes back to the early period of his reflection, when it was largely devoted to the investigation of ethics and especially law.

Bentham's account of the physical world appears to be moulded to his account of the practical world. While looking for methodological uniformity between ethics and physics, Bentham puts forward the empirical foundation of any mental construction. The analogy between the physical and the ethical dimension of the world is guaranteed by the principle of the dependence of fictitious entities upon real entities; such a principle is at the basis of Bentham's representation of the physical and the ethical world.

Bentham has the systematic ambition to reduce the variety of natural and ethical elements to a uniform model, namely to reduce the complexity of the world to a general explanatory and justificatory principle consisting in the distinction and relation between real and fictitious entities. He pursues the reconnection of fictitious entities to their foundations, distinguished as real and thus having an existence independent of the human mind, though subject to sensory interpretation.

Finally, in his endeavour to supply a new treatment of physics on the basis of the distinction between reality and fiction, Bentham found inspiration in the work of some leading philosophers of his age, such as Locke, Hume and, to a lesser extent, Berkeley. Bentham borrowed and put together various elements from their theories, notwithstanding their divergences, as in the case of the question pertaining to the existence of matter. Without underrating Bentham's originality in outlining his ontology and epistemology, there is no denying that his account of physics evinces traces, sometimes conflicting, of the influences of the approaches produced by other empiricist thinkers contemporary to him. The difficulty of harmonizing these influences could be at the origin of some discrepancies in his treatment of physics.

3 Ethical fictitious entities

3.1 The problem of definition

The import and truth of real entities and fictitious entities

The path that leads us from the general treatment of fictitious entities to their ethical specification is sketched out in two similar passages of *A Table of the Springs of Action*,[1] the reading of which enables us to outline an overall picture of the ontological status of ethical notions. Basically, Bentham states that both real and fictitious entities correspond to noun-substantives in a propositional context.[2] Then, he marks the difference between the area of reality and the area of fiction by means of the notion of truth. Two pivotal points articulate this distinction: "Real entities alone can be subjects of strictly true propositions"; "Abstractedly from all relations to real entities, a proposition having for its subject a fictitious entity has neither truth nor meaning."[3] The notion of truth belongs to real objects by nature; however, fictitious entities can also participate in that notion, inasmuch as they maintain a connection with reality.

The separation between reality and fiction and the dependence of fiction on reality as regards the notion of truth are tackled again by Bentham in the following excerpt from *A Table of the Springs of Action.*

> By every name of a real entity, in so far as the import of the word is understood, is held up to view an object really existing, an object in relation to which assertions, grammatical propositions having more or less in them not only of meaning but of truth, are incapable of being advanced.
>
> Taken by itself and apart from any relation which it may be understood to bear to some proposition which has for its subject a real entity, a proposition which has for its subject no other than a fictitious entity has neither truth nor meaning: it is no better than a heap of nonsense.[4]

1 See *A Table of the Springs of Action*, 5–9 and 74–9.
2 Indeed, "Every noun substantive is the name of a real or fictitious entity" (*A Table of the Springs of Action*, 5).
3 *A Table of the Springs of Action*, 5.
4 *A Table of the Springs of Action*, 74.

The relation that a fictitious entity has with a real entity is constitutive of its sense and of its truth. Divorced from reality, fiction is nothing but "falsehood or nonsense"[5] or, metaphorically, "a heap of nonsense."[6] On the basis of these observations Bentham makes two important remarks, characterized as axioms, pertaining to the meaning of fictitious entities. First, the name of a fictitious entity is understood through the relation which its import has with the import of the corresponding name of a real entity. Second, the relation between the import of a fictitious entity and the import of its corresponding real entity is understood and made manifest through a proposition which has the name of that real entity as its subject; this proposition has the same signification, namely is the exact equivalent of the proposition having the name of that fictitious entity for its subject.[7]

> Shortly, thus: any name of a fictitious entity can no otherwise be made clearly intelligible than by means of some relation which the import of it bears to some word which is the name of a real entity.
>
> Any proposition having for its subject a fictitious entity can no otherwise be made clearly intelligible than by means of some relation which the import of it can be shewn to have to a correspondent proposition having for its subject the name of some real entity.[8]

Bentham understands the notion of truth as synonymous to reality: what is real is also true. Consequently, real entities, basically corresponding to perceptions, are the only sources of truth. Instead, a fictitious entity is not true in itself, but can be regarded as true to the extent that it is connected to a real entity. This connection between a fictitious entity and a real entity enables the former to obtain truth and meaning from the latter. A proposition having for its subject the name of a fictitious entity has to be interpreted through another proposition having for its subject the name of the corresponding real entity. This latter proposition clarifies the meaning of the former proposition and consequently throws light on the connection between their subjects or, more precisely, on the connection that the subject corresponding to the name of a fictitious entity has with the subject corresponding to a real entity.

> Nothing has no properties. A fictitious entity, being as this its name imports – being, by the very supposition, a mere nothing, can not of itself have any properties: no proposition by which any property is ascribed to it can,

5 *A Table of the Springs of Action*, 5: "Setting aside its relation to a proposition having for its subject a real entity, a ditto having for ditto a fictitious ditto is but falsehood or nonsense."

6 *A Table of the Springs of Action*, 74: "Taken by itself and apart from any relation which it may be understood to bear to some proposition which has for its subject a real entity, a proposition which has for its subject no other than a fictitious entity has neither truth nor meaning: it is no better than a heap of nonsense."

7 See *A Table of the Springs of Action*, 5 and 74.

8 *A Table of the Springs of Action*, 74–5.

> therefore, be in itself and of itself a true one, nor therefore an instructive one: whatsoever of truth is capable of belonging to it can not belong to it in any other character than that of the representative of – the intended and supposed equivalent and adequate succedaneum of – some proposition having for its subject some real entity.[9]

Thus, fictitious entities cannot exist independently of reality on pain of falsehood or nonsense. The dependence of fictitious entities on real entities as regards their truth does not involve a debasement of fictitious entities, the need for which – for the purpose of communication and thought – is instead reaffirmed by Bentham. No imputation can be made against anyone who resorts to fictitious entities in formulating a proposition:[10] "in no instance can the idea of *fiction* be freer from all tincture of blame: in no other instance can it ever be equally beneficial; since, but for such fiction, the language of *man* could not have risen above the language of *brutes*." The field of fictitious entities has not to be depicted with "the repulsive character of an absolutely dark spot."[11]

> For discourse having for its subject the state or any operations of the mind, fictitious entity discourse is necessary, real entity discourse being inapplicable.[12]

> By one short howsoever comprehensive observation, the necessity of the language of fictitious entity to every purpose of rational discourse will be rendered sufficiently apparent. As to the greatest part of it, to all discourse having for its subject the state of the human mind, the operations which it is in the habit of performing, the distinguishable parts into which it is capable of being represented as divisible, and the modifications of which it is susceptible, names of fictitious entities – in a word, fictitious entity language – are essentially and indispensably necessary.[13]

The need for fictitious entities to denote the states and operations of the human mind should be accompanied by the awareness of the connection that these fictitious entities maintain with reality. In order to give meaning and truth to the act of nominalization, the names of fictitious entities have to be related to their real roots. By means of this relation between fiction and reality "the import of divers fictitious entities will be made perceptible."[14]

As Bentham clarifies in a passage from *Chrestomathia*, the relation that the import of a word denoting a fictitious object has with the import of a word denoting a real object discloses "the nature and origin of the idea attached to

9 *Essay on Logic*, UC 101.217 (Bowring viii, 246).
10 *A Table of the Springs of Action*, 75.
11 Cf. *Chrestomathia*, 258.
12 *A Table of the Springs of Action*, 5.
13 *A Table of the Springs of Action*, 75.
14 *A Table of the Springs of Action*, 6.

the name of a *fictitious* entity." The pointing out of this relation is necessary for the explanation of the import of the word designing a fictitious object. Such an operation to trace a fictitious name back to its original real name, from which it receives its import and its truth, is called by Bentham "genealogy" or "genesis" of a fictitious entity.[15] Thus, the human mind is based on sensibility. Without understanding the relation that a fictitious entity has with a real entity, the fictitious entity is upon the same footing of a fabulous entity, which is a purely fantastic invention of the human mind, dissociated by reality.

In *A Table of the Springs of Action*, as instances of fictitious entities Bentham lists desires and aversions, wants, hopes and fears, motives and interests along with their respective synonyms.[16] All the fictitious entities mentioned have in common an ethical character, since they pertain particularly to human behaviour and have no general meaning such as the notions of quantity, quality, relation and so on. In *A Table of the Springs of Action* Bentham's concern is the constitution of agency and not, as in the logical writings, the structure of the human understanding.

Bentham specifies that the above-listed names of ethical fictitious entities are related to two names of real entities, that is, pleasure and pain, which are their empirical sources.[17] In other words, the import and truth of ethical fictitious entities depend on the perceptions of pleasure and pain. Bentham characterizes pleasure and pain as individual sensations: they are "doubtless real entities," "the only immediately perceptible entities" together with all neutral or uninteresting perceptions; the evidence of their existence is still more immediate than that of the body or of the mind "in which they have respectively their seats."[18]

15 Cf. *Chrestomathia*, 271 n. a: "As in the case of all words, which have an immaterial, as well as a material, the root of the *immaterial* will be found in the *material* import; so, to explain the nature and origin of the idea attached to the name of a *fictitious* entity, it will be necessary to point out the *relation*, which the import of that word bears to the import of one or more names of *real* entities: i.e. to show the *genealogy*, or (to borrow an expression from the mathematicians) the *genesis* of the fictitious entity."

16 See *A Table of the Springs of Action*, 6 and 75–6.

17 See, for example, Bentham, *A Table of the Springs of Action*, 6: "Correspondent real entities in which these fictitious entities have their root: *Pleasures* and *Pains.*" *A Table of the Springs of Action*, 76: "The name of the real entities, in which these fictitious entities have their root, are 'Pleasure' and 'Pain', with their synonyms and the specific names contained within and under them, of which the significations respectively are subordinate to theirs."

18 Cf. *A Table of the Springs of Action*, 6: "Of their existence, the evidence is more immediate than that of bodies or of mind. Sensation with or without pleasure or pain are the only immediately *perceptible* entities. All other are but *inferential.*" *A Table of the Springs of Action*, 76: "That Pleasure and Pain (understand always individual pleasures and individual pains) are real entities – [and] that consequently the words 'Pleasure' and 'Pain' are respectively names of real entities – no man, it is believed, will feel disposed to doubt. Of their existence the evidence which we have is still more immediate than any that we have of the existence either of the body or of the mind in which they have respectively their seats. Pain and pleasure, together with all sensations of the neutral or uninteresting classes (for by these names may be designated and distinguished all sensations or perceptions other than those of pain and pleasure), are to us the only immediately perceptible entities."

The method of paraphrasis

In order to illuminate the distinction between real and fictitious entities along with their connections, Bentham focuses on certain central ethical fictitious concepts, namely right and obligation, which are his favourite examples. Bentham states that the traditional method of definition, consisting in an exposition *per genus et differentiam*, cannot work as an instrument for explaining the meaning of a fictitious notion. It is incapable of making a fictitious entity intelligible.

When applied to a name of a fictitious entity, this ordinary method can at best provide merely a synonym of that name, without adding more information and thus without disclosing its import. The operation of definition is applicable only to notions having a superior genus, by reference to which the definition of those notions can be formulated. Instead, the name of a fictitious entity does not often correspond to the species of a superior genus but can be regarded in itself as a "*genus generalissimum.*"[19] Surely, there are a few cases of ethical fictitious notions having a superior genus, such as privilege and exemption, which are species of right, and yet they usually have no more than one superior genus. So, the large majority of fictitious entities are independent notions, as in the case of right, the "genus it distinguishes has none above it."[20]

In order to explain fictitious entities, we need a method different from the traditional strategy of definition, a method suitable to their special nature. The definition of right "in the ordinary sense is impossible," but "It is, notwithstanding, susceptible of *exposition.*" Bentham identifies this method fitting the nature of fictitious entities as *paraphrasis*, which is the "*substitute to definition.*" As we have seen, definition is more appropriately employed for real entities, which can be arranged according to the Porphyrian Tree.[21] Instead, paraphrasis performs "the function of a *definition*, but in its *form* not coinciding with any proposition to which that name is commonly attached."[22] Actually, it is the expository strategy apt for fictitious entities.

A detailed account of paraphrasis is contained in *Chrestomathia*.

> The *paraphrasis* consists in taking the word that requires to be expounded – viz. the name of a *fictitious* entity – and, after making it up into a *phrase*, applying to it another phrase, which, being of the same import, shall have for its principal and characteristic word the name of the corresponding *real* entity. In a *definition*, a phrase is employed for the exposition of a single word: in a *paraphrasis*, a phrase is employed for the exposition of an entire phrase, of which

19 For the identification of fictitious entities with the notion of *genus generalissimum* see *Chrestomathia*, 259: "Of these fictitious entities, many will be found, of which, they being, each of them, a *genus generalissimus.*"

20 *A Table of the Springs of Action*, 7.

21 *A Table of the Springs of Action*, 7.

22 *Chrestomathia*, 272 n. a.

> the word, proposed to be expounded, is made to constitute the principal or characteristic word.[23]

While definition, which is applicable to real entities, is a nominal method explaining a single term by means of a phrase, paraphrasis, which is applicable to fictitious entities, is a propositional method explaining an entire phrase.[24] Before making a paraphrasis, one has, first, to select the name of the fictitious entity to be expounded and, then, to formulate a phrase having it for its subject. This latter operation is called phraseoplerosis by Bentham. The strategy of paraphrasis entails recasting that phrase in another phrase, containing as its subject the name of the real entity, which is thus corresponding to the name of the fictitious entity to be elucidated.

> Improper substantives, names of fictitious entities, are unfit to serve as titles of Divisions. A proper substantive, the name of a real entity, is understood immediately and of itself it offers a certain image to the conception. An improper substantive offers no such image. Of itself it has no meaning. It means nothing till, with other words, it be compounded into some sentence. It then is seen to have a meaning, which is the clearer, the more clearly it is seen to be equivalent to some sentence the terms of which are names of real entities.[25]

The validity of the application of the method of paraphrasis to fictitious entities rests on the fact that fictitious entities maintain a constitutive relation with real entities, on which their import and truth depend. A real entity has an expository function in relation to a fictitious entity, when, by virtue of being its empirical foundation, it makes that fictitious entity intelligible.[26] Contrary to the traditional method of definition, the advantage of paraphrasis when applied to a sentence containinga fictitious entity is that it makes explicit the reference to its constitutive or causal real entity.

23 *Chrestomathia*, 272 n. a. For another definition of paraphrasis, provided by Bentham, see *Essay on Logic*, UC 101.217 (Bowring viii, 246): "By the word paraphrasis may be designated that sort of exposition which may be afforded by transmuting into a proposition having for its subject some real entity, a proposition which has not for its subject any other than a fictitious entity." See also *Preparatory Principles*, 386: "To expound an improper substantive by Paraphrasis is to compleat it into a sentence, and for that sentence to find an equivalent sentence consisting of words significative of real entities."

24 Quine (1981, 67 and 69–70) acknowledges Bentham's doctrine of paraphrasis as the second of five milestones "where empiricism has taken a turn for the better." Bentham's contribution basically consists in "the shift of semantic focus from terms to sentences." Quine states that "contextual definition precipitated a revolution in semantics [. . .]. The primary vehicle of meaning is seen no longer as the word, but as the sentence."

25 *Preparatory Principles*, 401.

26 Cf. *A Table of the Springs of Action*, 7: "The mode of exposition suited to the case is *paraphrasis*: the name of the fictitious entity in question is made parcel of a *phrase*, which contains in it the correspondent and *expository* real entity." In the following lines Bentham adds that "Form of such a paraphrasis in the case of a *right*: 'A man is said to have a right when, etc.' In this place, no room for completing the exposition. Of right, there are many species, some of them requiring different paraphrases."

The method of paraphrasis is based on the theoretical assumptions that "our ideas are derived all of them from our senses" and that "the only way of rendering any of our ideas clear and determinate is to trace it up to the sensible objects in which it originates."[27] Rather than connecting a fictitious entity to a superior genus, presupposing a "scale of logical subalternation,"[28] as the method of definition does, paraphrasis is a sort of tracing back the fictitious entity to a real entity, regardless of any linguistic or ontological taxonomy.

Paraphrasis has an explanatory purpose, because it reconnects a fictitious term to the real term from which it derives and, by doing so, it highlights the particular relation which links a fictitious entity to a real entity. A real entity is "the *real source*, *efficient cause*, or *connecting principle*" of a fictitious entity; indeed, from its corresponding real entity a fictitious entity obtains its meaning and truth.[29] Thus, the relation that a fictitious entity has with a real entity is clarified in terms of meaning and truth.

Along with the method of paraphrasis Bentham introduces that of archetypation. Both are aimed at "the explanation of a fictitious entity."[30] Archetypation "consists in indicating the *material image*, of which the word, taken in its primæval sense, contains the expression."[31] The difference between paraphrasis and archetypation lies in the distinction between "the *root* of the *idea*" and "the *root* of the *word*," namely of the idea and the word corresponding to a fictitious entity. Paraphrasis aims to discover the root of the fictitious idea, whereas archetypation aims to discover the root of the fictitious word. This latter operation is more visual and maybe also etymological, to the extent that etymology is usually related to an archetype or pattern.[32] Because of the common enquiry on roots of fictitious entities, paraphrasis and archetypation are also generically identified as *Rhizophantia*.[33]

Bentham exemplifies this methodological difference by means of the fictitious notion of obligation.

> Thus, in the case of *obligation*, if the above conception be correct, the root of the *idea* is in the ideas of pain and pleasure. But the root of the *word*, employed as a sign for the designation of that idea, is altogether different.

27 *Of the Limits of the Penal Branch of Jurisprudence*, 317.
28 *Essay on Logic*, UC 101.217 (Bowring viii, 246).
29 Cf. *Essay on Logic*, UC 101.218 (Bowring viii, 246): "Of any such fictitious entity or fictitious entities, the real entity with which the import of their respective appellatives is connected, and on which their import depends, may be termed the *real source*, *efficient cause*, or *connecting principle*."
30 *Chrestomathia*, 272 n. a.
31 *Chrestomathia*, 272 n. a. For another definition of archetypation see *Preparatory Principles*, 386: "The word *archetypus*, a Latin word of Greek extraction, signifies a pattern. By Archetypation, then, I mean the finding of the real appearance of real entities that served as a pattern for the appearance suggested by any of those sentences of which an improper substantive makes a part."
32 See, for example, the case of the expression *cardinal virtue*, in which the term *cardinal* derives from the Latin *cardo* and means *a hinge*: cardinal virtues in fact are "the virtues on which, as doors on hinges, all other virtues were said to turn" (*Deontology*, 180).
33 See *Chrestomathia*, 272 n. a.

> It lies in a material image, employed as an ***archetype*** or ***emblem***: viz. the image of a ***cord***, or any other ***tie*** or ***band***, (from the Latin *ligo*, to bind,) by which the object in question is ***bound*** or fastened to any other, the person in question bound to a certain course of practice.[34]

The image of a cord corresponds to the root of the word obligation.[35] Thus, the archetype is "an ***index*** and a *holdfast* to the sense" of a name pointing to an immaterial object.[36] However, in the case of a name denoting a fictitious entity, "the only sure test of intellection is ***paraphrasis***."[37] The method of paraphrasis has the advantage of relating a fictitious entity to its corresponding real entity, on which its import and truth depend. In such a way, paraphrasis contributes to the intelligibility of the fictitious entity. Therefore, it is an expository method, having as its "subsidiary operations" archetypation and also phraseoplerosis, i.e. "a filling up the phrase."[38]

The definition of obligation

Bentham's focus shifts onto the notion of obligation, which needs to be exposed through the method of paraphrasis because of its fictitious nature. Generally speaking, this definitional strategy requires the identification of the real entity corresponding to the fictitious entity to be explained. It is important to discover the empirical sources of obligation, i.e. the foundations giving to the fictitious entity of obligation its import and truth.

> For exposition of obligation, ***convenience*** might recommend the bringing to view its connection with expressions of ***will*** and ***command***: necessity requires ditto as to pleasures and pains.
>
> General Rule. Sources or modes of obligation, as many as sources of pain and pleasure, thence of motives.
>
> [Sanctions] sources of ***pain*** and ***pleasure***, thence of ***motives***: 1. Political, including legal; 2. Popular or moral; 3. Religious; 4. Sympathetic; 5. Physical.[39]

As the sources of obligation, Bentham identities pain and pleasure, two real entities experienced through sensibility. Pain and pleasure usually derive from several sanctions, which can be political or legal, popular or moral, religious, sympathetic and physical, according to their issuing authority. Consequently, there are

34 *Chrestomathia*, 272 n. a.
35 See also *Essay on Logic*, UC 101.218 (Bowring viii, 246).
36 In *Of the Limits of the Penal Branch of Jurisprudence*, 67 n. a, Bentham makes the Archetypation of the words *circumstance* and *case*. See also 247–8 n. a.
37 *Chrestomathia*, 274 n. a.
38 Cf. *Essay on Logic*, UC 101.217 (Bowring viii, 246).
39 *A Table of the Springs of Action*, 7–8.

different types of obligation related to different types of sanction. In spite of their specifications, all the forms of obligation share the same normative foundations, corresponding to pleasure and pain, as Bentham reiterates in the conclusion of the introductory marginal of *A Table of the Springs of Action*, devoted to the distinction between real and fictitious.

> On the above grounds might be constructed paraphrastic expositions of "right" and "obligation": whereby, in a form as precise as definitive, the import of "right" and "obligation," of "right" through "obligation," might be explained, viz. by indications of the connections which import of these fictitious entities has with that of the corresponding real ones, viz. "pleasure" and "pain."[40]

The application of the method of paraphrasis to the notion of obligation is examined at length in a section of the *Essay on Logic*. Bentham's special concern for ethics in his account of fictionalism and in particular of paraphrasis, as a strategy to disentangle it, is not random. The group of ethical fictitious entities, made up by obligation, right and "other advantages dependent on obligation," provides the most instructive exemplification of paraphrasis. By illustrating the method of paraphrasis, Bentham throws light on the particular nature of fictitious entities belonging to the area of ethics. First of all, obligation is the core notion in the understanding and assessment of ethical fictionalism, because all ethical fictitious elements involve it.

> The fictitious entities which compose this groupe have all of them for their *real source* one and the same sort of real entity, viz. *sensation*: the word being taken in that sense in which it is significative not merely of perception, but of perception considered as productive either of pain, of pleasure, or of both.[41]

The sensations of pleasure and pain underlie the system of ethics worked out by Bentham. He also specifies that pain and pleasure can be considered as equivalent to "loss of pleasure" and "exemption from pain." Pleasure and pain are the only real entities from which ethical fictitious entities receive their meaning and truth. All ethical notions are thus traced back to the same normative source, lying in experience. Because of this constitutive relation between psychical and physical entities, one may say that ethics, as a product of the human mind, depends on sensibility or, more precisely, on the physiological structure of human beings.

Bentham provides a naturalistic foundation for ethics, which still remains a human artefact. In the connection between sense-perception and the human mind, realism and constructivism, Bentham sees neither contradiction nor conflict. Ethics is an artificial construction of the human mind, based on empirical elements, which, by being real, are its sources.

40 *A Table of the Springs of Action*, 8–9.

41 *Essay on Logic*, UC 101.221 (Bowring viii, 247).

Bentham clarifies the relation that joins the fictitious entity of obligation to the real entities of pleasure or pain.

> An obligation (viz. the obligation of conducting himself in a certain manner) is incumbent on a man (i.e. is spoken of as incumbent on a man), in so far as, in the event of his failing to conduct himself in that same manner, pain or loss of pleasure is considered as about to be experienced by him.[42]

Pain is connected to obligation as a consequence that the obliged can experience in case he/she does not act in the prescribed way. Thus, the force of an obligation corresponds to the intensity of the pain which is expected to be felt by the agent in case of non-compliance with that obligation. The stronger the pain, the more binding the related obligation. The strength of the constraint exerted by an obligation is determined by the strength of the painful sensation resulting from disregarding that obligation. The source of an obligation is a certain quantity of pain to which the obliged is exposed when failing to conform to the dictate in which that obligation consists. To be under an obligation means to be under the risk of being punished for disobeying a command.

Bentham gives a telling example of paraphrasis by applying it to the core notion of obligation. In this way, he illustrates and throws light on the phases of the process of paraphrasis. First of all, "the word to be expounded," i.e. "the exponend," is "*an obligation.*" Because of its fictional nature, it is "not susceptible of a definition in the ordinary shape," which requires the reference to a superior genus. The only sound way of definition or exposition for the notion of obligation then is paraphrasis.

In order to apply this method, one needs to formulate a fictitious phrase. This phrase should contain as its subject the notion to be expounded, i.e. *obligation*, the corresponding predicate, i.e. *incumbent on a man*, and the copula which connects both. The fictitious phrase *An obligation is incumbent on a man* is thus composed. The operation performed, aimed at completing a phrase, is called by Bentham phraseoplerosis.

As a subsidiary operation, concurring in the formulation of the fictitious sentence, Bentham adverts to the process of archetypation: it consists in indicating "the emblematical, or archetypal image" of the fictitious entity which constitutes the subject of the fictitious phrase. Bentham here identifies as archetypal image of the notion of obligation

> [t]hat of a man lying down, with a heavy body pressing upon him, to wit in such sort as either to prevent him from acting at all, or so ordering matters that if so it be that he does act, it can not be in any other direction or manner than the direction or manner in question – the direction or manner requisite.[43]

42 *Essay on Logic*, UC 101.222 (Bowring viii, 247).
43 *Essay on Logic*, UC 101.223 (Bowring viii, 247).

The archetypal image of the fictitious entity of obligation metaphorically expresses the idea of a constraint or the idea of putting a constraint on someone. The archetypal operation proves to be useful to compose the fictitious sentence which has to be paraphrased and, in particular, to select the predicate of the fictitious subject. Indeed, the archetype of "a man lying down, with a heavy body pressing upon him" visually shows the idea of something "incumbent on a man."

Paraphrasis can be now applied to the completed fictitious sentence *An obligation is incumbent on a man*.

> The source of the explanation thus given by paraphrasis is the idea of eventual sensation, as expressed by the names of the different and opposite modes of sensation, viz. pain and pleasure with their respective equivalents, and the designation of the event on the happening of which such sensation is considered as being about to take place.[44]

The method of paraphrasis aims to recast the phrase having a fictitious entity as its subject in a new phrase including the real entity corresponding to that fictitious entity as its subject. The real entity is indeed the source of explanation which the paraphrasis has to provide. In order to formulate a new sentence in such a way, one needs to discover the real entity corresponding to the fictitious entity under scrutiny. In this case, "the idea of eventual sensation," basically consisting in the expectation of pleasure or pain, is explanatory of the notion of obligation. However, as a source of explanation Bentham adds the specification of the event whose occurrence involves the experience of that sensation. With reference to the notion of obligation, we may suppose that this event is the failure to conform to a prescription.

Unfortunately, Bentham does not finish completing his paraphrasis; he does not formulate the paraphrased sentence as a conclusion of his methodological considerations. This gap might be filled by paraphrasing the sentence *An obligation is incumbent on a man* with *Pain is incumbent on a man if he does not act in compliance with an obligation*.[45] Pain is causative of an obligation, that is, of the binding power in which it consists.

In Bentham's approach, pain and pleasure are "constitutive" of obligation. They are expected to stem from several sanctions, viz. the physical, the moral, the political, the religious and also the sympathetic. In brief, the physical sensations of pain

44 *Essay on Logic*, UC 101.222 (Bowring viii, 247).

45 Rosen (2005, 55) suggests a similar solution: "The paraphrase of 'M is under an obligation to do A', viz., 'M will suffer pain or loss of pleasure unless he does A' is a reasonable candidate for the literal meaning." About Bentham's method of paraphrasis for the explanation of the notion of obligation see also Hart 1982, 127–32. Hart (1982, 132–8) interprets Bentham's theory of obligation as mixed, since it combines an imperative and a probabilistic element: the imperative element is "a principal law requiring the act which is obligatory" whereas the probabilistic element depends on "a subsidiary law requiring or permitting punishment for breach of the former" (134); in other words, the probabilistic element lies in "a punishment for failure to comply with the requirements of some principal law" (133).

and pleasure are "the only true and intelligible source of obligation," "the only true and intelligible explanation of its nature."[46] Finally, Bentham acknowledges that his exposition of the word *obligation* provides a sort of paradigm of the exposition to which other ethical fictitious entities such as rights are susceptible.[47] The notion of obligation is at the basis of Bentham's ethics inasmuch as ethical elements are connected with it to varying extents and depend on it for their definition.[48]

Bentham argues the empirical nature of the foundations of ethics: pleasure and pain are the real sources from which the human mind, by means of language, elaborates on the fictitious framework of practical principles, behavioural standards and moral values, in compliance with which action is performed. Divorced from these perceptual foundations, the practical domain has neither meaning nor truth. However, Bentham rejects reductionism when accounting for fictitious entities: he does not intend to challenge the autonomy of the human mind, including language, but rather to regulate it by maintaining fictitious entities related to their perceptual sources.[49]

Bentham's empirical foundationalism aims to explain the constructions of the human mind through their connection to experience. The language of fiction, created by human imagination for the need for communication, is made intelligible by the language of reality, denoting pure and simple sensory elements, endowed with meaning and truth. So, the obscure fictitious notion of obligation is enlightened when it is related to the real sensations of pleasure and pain.

> The word obligation may be employed in an abstract sense: it may, for the convenience of discourse, be spoken of as a fictitious entity; but it ought to be possible to decipher such language into the language of pure and simple truth – into that of fact. To understand abstract terms, is to know how to translate figurative language into language without figure.[50]

46 *Essay on Logic*, UC 101.224 (Bowring viii, 248).

47 Cf. *Essay on Logic*, UC 101.224 (Bowring viii, 248): "On the exposition thus given of the term obligation, may be built those other expositions of which it will form the basis, viz. of *rights*, and their respective modifications, as well as of the several modifications of which the fictitious entity *obligation* is itself susceptible." See also *Essay on Logic*, UC 101.221 (Bowring viii, 247): "For exposition and explanation of Paraphrasis, and of the other modes of exposition connected with it and subsidiary to it, that which presents itself as the most instructive of all examples which the nature of the case affords is that which is afforded by the groupe of Ethical fictitious entities, viz. *Obligations*, rights, and other *advantages* dependent on obligation."

48 With particular reference to the area of law Bentham (*Of the Limits of the Penal Branch of Jurisprudence*, 317) states: "What is that every article of law has in common with the rest? It issues commands, and by doing so it creates *duties*: or, what is another word for the same thing, *obligations*. The idea of duty is concerned in every thing that belongs to law."

49 As Postema (2002, vol. i, xii) observes, "The aim of paraphrasis is not to reduce all fictitious entities to real ones, but rather to subject our necessary use of language apparently referring to entities beyond sensory experience to a salutary discipline." See also Postema 1986, 297: "The aim of the theory of fictions was not to provide a rationale for the elimination of entities from our folk ontology or their concepts from our conceptual scheme, but rather to *regiment* this essential intellectual device: to define a method whereby the range of legitimate application and use of the concepts could be precisely determined."

50 *General View of a Complete Code of Laws*, Bowring iii, 181.

Paraphrasis proves to be an interpretative strategy, which consists in turning non-figurative terms into figurative terms and in pointing out the representational content underlying fictitious names. Bentham clarifies the crucial distinction and relation between fictitious language and real language in *General View of a Complete Code of Laws*, when examining the case of the notion of *title*, a fictitious entity largely employed in the legal field.[51] Like obligation, the word *title* cannot be expounded through the application of the classical method of definition. Its "logical ramification is stopped at the first step: there are no species of titles; it is an absolutely barren trunk." Consequently, the word "title" remains "obscure," because "it does not exhibit things as they are," that is, it does not denote a real event and then does not produce an image or picture of it in a hearer's mind.

Bentham sets "the language of simple truth" against "the language of fiction." The former announces "a fact which presents an image to the mind," i.e. provides "a picture which could be painted," whereas the latter utters "sounds which do not present any image." Fictitious language distinguishes itself from real language because of its non-figurative character, that is, because of its inability to give rise to a material representation in the mind. In order to be meaningful and true, fictitious language needs to be translated into real language, which deciphers it by giving it a representational content. This transition from non-figurative to figurative vocabulary, made possible through the strategy of paraphrasis, is necessary for explaining fictitious entities.

The fictitious utterance *to possess or have a title* can be enlightened by means of the less fictitious utterance *to possess a right over a thing*, which refers to the fact of possessing a thing in a legal sense. Indeed, the verbs to possess and to have, when understood in a physical sense, mean a real fact, consisting in occupying or being able to occupy a thing. So, the real notion of possession discloses the meaning of right and, by means of it, of title. Bentham concludes by stating that the word title is not a "fundamental term," but, "once translated from the language of fiction into the language of reality," that is, more specifically, when resolved as "a dispositive event," it can be employed without hesitation. The word title "is not luminous in itself, but when it has received light, if it be properly placed, it may serve either to reflect or to transmit it."

It remains baffling why Bentham's technique of paraphrasis is not exemplified by physical elements but is exclusively illustrated by ethical elements, even though it is a method suited to the treatment of all fictitious entities. This fact perhaps depends on Bentham's main interest in ethics, and especially in law, the explanatory model for which, based on the connection between real and fictitious entities, can be exported and applied to the other branches of knowledge such as physics.

Probably, in Bentham's opinion, the paraphrasis of obligation provides a leading example of the methodology which each discipline can adopt when dealing with the elements pertaining to it. In the same way that ethical fictitious entities

51 *General View of a Complete Code of Laws*, Bowring iii, 189. The entire passage concerning the paraphrasis of *title* is also quoted by Ogden 1932, cxxxii–cxxxiii.

are based on pleasure and pain, so physical fictitious entities should be based on sensory perceptions: ethical constructivism and physical constructivism find their natural roots in empirical reality. Bentham's preference for ethical and legal notions when expounding his theory of real and fictitious entities could provide an indirect support to the hypothesis that his representation of the physical world is moulded to his view on ethics.

Bentham's generalization of the explanatory method of ethics and its transplantation to physics is probably at the origin of certain conceptual ambiguities and discrepancies in his examination of material phenomena. Such ambiguities and discrepancies implicitly evince the difficulty of adapting a model aimed at accounting for ethics to different areas of knowledge. From a conceptual and a methodological point of view, Bentham's physics appears to be not so consistent and linear when compared with his ethics. His physics shows some critical points, probably consequent on his attempt to make an external explanatory method suitable to it.

As an example of Bentham's difficulty in generalizing his ontological and epistemological model, centred on the relation between real and fictitious entities, we can take into consideration the impracticability of inferential entities, such as the soul, God and the Devil, to be treated as real entities to which to relate fictitious entities and into which to translate them. Inferential entities cannot fulfil the explanatory function which by definition should characterize all real entities.

In summary, Bentham's approach consists in explaining and justifying fictitious entities by tracing them back to their respective real entities. So, from a linguistic point of view, sentences having a fictitious name as their subject should be paraphrased into sentences having a real name as its subject. The meaning and the truth of fictitious entities depend, indeed, on real entities.

Bentham identifies pleasure and pain as the foundations of ethics and law: any ethical and legal element may be referred to them for its justification and explanation. When theorizing his doctrine of real and fictitious entities, Bentham enlarges the set of real entities to impressions and ideas, which have a perceptual character, and to inferential objects, which are derived from a chain of reasoning. By being real, inferential entities should provide the foundations for certain fictitious notions just as perceptual entities do. However, inferential entities prove to be unable to supply ontological justification and linguistic explanation for any fictitious element. They cannot play the foundational function to which they are entitled as real entities.

The impracticability of inferential entities to give a foundation to mental representations might be motivated by Bentham's tension in reconciling a traditional ontological view, maintaining the real existence of certain immaterial or spiritual substances, such as the soul, God and the Devil, with his theory of meaning, relating names of fictitious entities to names of real entities. As a consequence, Bentham is forced to save the reality of those spiritual substances, despite their inability to serve as a basis for linguistic constructions. Though inferential entities have a marginal or even insignificant role, their presence is still problematic for the overall consistency of Bentham's ontology.

The notions of right and power

Along with the notion of obligation, which is at the heart of ethics, Bentham usually mentions the notion of right, as a typical instance of an ethical fictitious notions. Just as in the case of obligation, a right obtains its meaning and truth from its corresponding empirical roots, identified with pleasure and pain. When defining the concept of right, Bentham underlines the relation that it maintains with sensation.

> A right then to a thing, is, as I understand it, the relation a man is in with respect to a thing, which that man is left free to convert to the purposes of his own pleasure, punishment being denounced against any other man who shall impede him from so doing, or does the like as the first man with respect to that thing, without his consent.[52]

A right is the possibility of doing a thing or performing an act. An agent who has a right has the prerogative to enforce it for his own pleasure. The issuing of a right for an agent entails the obligation for another agent to acknowledge that right and not to ascribe it to himself/herself. A punishment is indeed envisaged for those who prevent the agent entitled from asserting his/her right or for those who assert that right without the consent of the agent entitled.[53] Right and obligation are linked by a reciprocal relation, which basically is constitutive of the general fictitious framework regulating intercourse among human beings.

As Bentham alleges, "A right is another fictitious entity, a kind of a secondary fictitious entity, resulting out of a duty."[54] In order to be expounded, the notion of right, just as any ethical element, has to be related to the notion of obligation or duty, which is in turn directly related to the notions of pleasure and pain.[55] We might say that a right is a fictitious entity of the second remove, insofar as it needs a fictitious entity of the first remove, namely obligation, to make its meaning and truth intelligible. In fact, the notion of obligation connects the fictitious entity of right with the real entities of pleasure and pain.

In *Preparatory Principles*, Bentham ironically observes that those who attempted to formulate a definition of "right" in the traditional way, namely according to the distinction between *genus* and *species*, filled "a barrel without a bottom." Indeed, the word right, cannot be defined in such a way, as if it were a real entity. The notion of right is a fictitious entity and, thus, it can be understood only by applying the method of paraphrasis: "The way to enable us to form

52 *A Comment on the Commentaries*, 87.

53 See also *Preparatory Principles*, 247 and 334.

54 *Of the Limits of the Penal Branch of Jurisprudence*, 316.

55 In *Preparatory Principles*, 247, Bentham observes that "Those who have been attempting to give a Definition of the word right, have been filling a barrel without a bottom. Of the word right, no definition is to be given. The way to enable us to form an idea upon the mention of it is to bring it with others into a sentence: and then expound that sentence by such another sentence as contains in it words that *are* capable of being defined."

an idea upon the mention of it is to bring it with others into a sentence: and then expound that sentence by such another sentence as contains in it words that *are* capable of being defined."[56]

In the explanation of the notion of right, Bentham specifies the role of obligation as an efficient cause.[57] In a passage from *Pannomial Fragments*, he holds that "Otherwise than from the idea of obligation, no clear idea can be attached to the word right"; indeed, "Absence of correspondent obligation" and "presence of correspondent obligation" are the two joined efficient causes for the existence of a right. The former cause consists in the fact that the agent is not under an obligation to abstain from performing a thing; this is "a naked kind of right," that is, a right positively granted to the agent. The latter cause consists in the fact that one or more people are under an obligation to refrain from disturbing the agent in the exercise of his/her right; this is "a vested or established right," that is, a right negatively acknowledged by the imposition of an obligation on the part of the people which are not invested of it.[58]

The right of the agent to do something corresponds to the obligation for other agents to leave him/her free to enforce that right. The acknowledgment of the agent's right to do something requires the imposition, on other agents related to him/her, of an obligation not to do the same thing and not to impede him/her in doing it. A right for someone entails a duty for someone else. As Bentham makes clear in *Preparatory Principles*, "*Right* and *Duty*, as also *Right* and *Restraint*, are, therefore, *relatives*: the existence of the one supposes that of the other."[59] Thus, the notion of right is explainable in terms of pain or, more rarely, pleasure by means of the notion of obligation. Pain, in the form of a punishment, is indeed imposed on the agent if he/she does not conform to the obligation to forbear interfering in another agent's exercise of the right with which he/she is invested.

The reciprocity between right and obligation is remarked upon by Bentham in a long and rich note in *A Fragment on Government*, devoted to some metaphysical considerations on ethical and legal concepts. In particular, this section of the book focuses on the notion of duty and, at the beginning, illustrates the relation between a political duty and a right. I have a political duty to do something when you have a right to have me be made to do it. Just as I have a duty towards you, so too you have a right over me. More specifically, to say that you have a political right consisting in having me be made to do something means that I am liable, from a legal point of view, to be punished when disregarding it. The punishment, i.e. a type of pain, is in fact attached to an act diverging from that required by an obligation. Thus, Bentham concludes, without a punishment there is neither a right nor a duty.[60]

56 See also *Preparatory Principles*, 249.

57 By efficient cause Bentham (*Preparatory Principles*, 61) means "the person or thing that has acted upon it [the thing or portion of matter] to make it what it is."

58 *Pannomial Fragments*, Bowring viii, 217–8.

59 *Preparatory Principles*, 334.

60 *A Fragment on Government*, 494–5 n. b. Some interpretative remarks on this passage are provided by Schofield 2009, 53.

Bentham connects the ideas of duty and right to that of punishment or, more basically, to that of pain from which they derive their meaning and truth. He traces the notions of duty and right back to the simple notion of punishment, i.e. of pain.[61] The expectation of a punishment, i.e. pain, in consequence of non-compliance with the obligation to allow someone to do something is the source of a right. The idea of right refers to the idea of obligation, which enables it to be connected to its empirical basis. These interrelations between duties and rights structure ethics, the intelligibility of which depends on the connection its components have with the perceptions of pleasure and pain.

Similarly to the notion of right, the notion of power, another ethical fictitious entity which is often mentioned by Bentham as an example, is related to the notion of obligation and, then, to punishment, i.e. pain. In *Preparatory Principles: Inserenda*[62] Bentham makes it clear that the notion of power cannot be defined, because it has no genus to which it can be referred. Indeed, powers are not the names of substances or modes and, thus, "they are not names of any thing[s] that exist." As a consequence, "To define the single word Power is impossible," at least if one means as definition the classical method of tracing a substance back to its genus and then of specifying its difference.

Bentham applies the strategy of paraphrasis to the notion of power, since this strategy turns out to be suitable to fictitious entities. Bentham suggests working out a sentence in which the word "power" is preceded by the verb "create." Then, "This proposition may be translated into another proposition that is equivalent."

> To create a power in a person over a thing, or what is shorter and more familiar, to give a person a power over a thing, is to restrain another person from meddling with that thing, the first person being left unrestrained.
>
> To say, then, that you have a power given you over your Coat is only another way of saying, that I am restrained from meddling with it, you being left unrestrained.[63]

The ascription of a power over something to someone implies the obligation for someone else not to interfere in this exercise of power. In the above-mentioned paragraph from *Preparatory Principles* Bentham does not make explicit reference to the punishment envisaged for the one who does not comply with the duty not to impede an individual from exercising a particular power, which is, for example, acknowledged by law. It is plain, however, that the idea of power, by means of that of obligation, derives its normative force from the idea of punishment or,

61 See also *Preparatory Principles*, 70: "The Substantives *Power*, *Right*, *Title*, *Duty*, *Obligation*, with their conjugates, whether Particles, Verbs, or Adjectives, also the Verbs *may* and *can*, which are quasi-conjugates to some of them, refer to punishment, and to Law, real or fictitious, by which punishment is appointed. By punishment they may be explained, and by nothing else. Wherever these words occur, take away the idea of punishment, and you leave nothing."

62 *Preparatory Principles*, 380.

63 *Preparatory Principles*, 380.

more basically, pain, which is its real source. Hence, as in the case of right, the notion of power is indirectly explainable in terms of pain.

Bentham makes clear the foundations of ethics through an analytical process of resolution of its complex ideas, such as "*duty, right, power, title*"[64] and so forth, into the simple ideas of pain and, to a lesser extent, pleasure.[65]

> Now the idea belonging to the word *pain* is a simple one. To *define* or rather (to speak more generally) to *expound* a word, is to resolve, or to make a progress towards resolving, the idea belonging to it into simple ones.[66]

This process of tracing back a complex entity to a simple entity has a linguistic and an ontological value. It is suitable to the conceptual framework of ethics, which is the outcome of the mental activity of creating verbal objects from empirical elements. Thus, the understanding of ethical notions involves their reconnection to their perceptual foundations, the simplicity and clarity of which contribute to illuminating ethics as a whole.

Real and fictitious entities require different expository methods, which reflect distinct relations between *definiendum* and *definiens*. On the one hand, real entities are explained by means of a sort of theoretical ascent in the hierarchy of reality, namely of an ascending movement from a *definiendum*, i.e. a species, to an acknowledged *definiens*, i.e. its genus. On the other hand, fictitious entities do not presuppose a hierarchy to which they can be referred for their explanation; they are derivative elements which need to be related to their original elements. The *definiendum*, as a complex notion, has to be resolved in its *definiens*, corresponding to a simple notion.

> To the words Pain, Pleasure, Volition, Motion, Rest, the ideas that are annexed are simple ones. These nobody defines, or if any one defines, nobody makes clearer by defining. They need not be defined, they can not. For to define a word is to point out, in some way or other the simple ideas that go to the composing of the more complex idea of which usage has made that word the sign. But of these, each is the sign of one simple idea, and no more.
>
> With these words, therefore, we set out, supposing the meaning of them understood.[67]

By not being a descending process, the definitional method for fictitious entities is not the reverse of the definitional method for real entities. It presupposes a

64 *A Fragment on Government*, 495 n. b.

65 See *Preparatory Principles*, 71, in part. para. 68 ("We all know but too well what pain is. It is a simple idea. It is felt: it is not to be defined") and para. 71 ("We all know, it is to be hoped, what *Pleasure* is: it is to be felt: it is not to be defined").

66 *A Fragment on Government*, 495 n. b. See also *Preparatory Principles*, 189: "a Definition is but a progress made towards the resolution of the complex idea signified by the word defined into it's [sic] component simple ones."

67 *Preparatory Principles*, 102–3.

different ontological order and, consequently, adopts a different logical strategy. Hence, the definitions of real and fictitious entities belong to two distinct logics. Since in his works Bentham generally distinguishes between a logic of the understanding and a logic of the will,[68] one could be inclined to suppose that the former deals with real entities and the latter deals with fictitious entities. Despite appearances, the connection between the logic of the understanding and real entities, on the one hand, and the logic of the will and fictitious entities, on the other, is never explicitly stated by Bentham.[69]

The usage of the notion of *simple idea* to identify the entity of pain has induced some readers to argue the influence of Locke's basic distinction between simple and complex ideas on Bentham's ontology and epistemology. A similarity, at least in the linguistic choices, between these two approaches seems to be undeniable. Locke regards certain notions such as obligation as "complex ideas," which he denominates "mixed modes" because they consist "of several combinations of simple ideas of different kinds." He further specifies that "These mixed modes [. . .] are not looked upon to be characteristical marks of any real beings that have a steady existence, but scattered and independent ideas put together by the mind."[70]

Roughly speaking, according to Locke, simple ideas are directly received by sensation, whereas complex ideas are the product of the combination of simple ideas, carried out by the human mind.[71] Locke and Bentham both distinguish between simple and complex ideas, along with the acknowledgment of mental activity in the construction of complex ideas. However, this distinction is worked out by them in different ways. Locke adopts an atomistic and combinatory view of the world, based on the composition and decomposition, the assembling and disassembling of ideas, performed by the human mind. Instead, Bentham does not consider complex ideas as the outcome of the aggregation of simple ideas and, thus, he is committed to a creative and non-combinatory view of the world.

According to Bentham, complex ideas such as obligation and right are not composed by a number of simple ideas, but are creations of the human mind, invented for the purpose of communication and thought. They are based on simple entities, to which they are related for their meaning and truth. Complex ideas exist or, better, are supposed to exist to the extent that they are connected with real entities, whose simplicity consists in their empirical clarity. So, Bentham appropriates the Lockean terminology, but he reworks and adapts it for his philosophical system, which is centred on the fundamental distinction between real and fictitious entities.

68 See, for example, *An Introduction to the Principles of Morals and Legislation*, 8.

69 Moreover, Schofield (2015, 1128 n. 19) has recently warned against the interpretative hypothesis, labelled as an "error," according to which "Bentham's logic of the will is concerned with fictions."

70 Locke, *An Essay concerning Human Understanding*, ii.xxii.1. Bentham makes an explicit reference to Locke's distinction between simple and mixed modes in *A Fragment on Government*, 495 n. b.

71 Cf. Locke, *An Essay concerning Human Understanding*, ii.ii.12.

If we pay attention to its historical sources, we may note that Bentham's approach to fictitious entities appears to be more similar to Hartley's method, developed in *Observations on Man, His Frame, His Duty and His Expectations*, than to Locke's conception of simple and complex ideas. As Bentham acknowledges in *An Article on Utilitarianism*, Hartley gives in his book "an intimation [. . .] of the connection of the import of the word 'happiness' with that of the word 'pain' and that of the word 'pleasure'" and, in addition, he makes "a translation [. . .] of the language (so to speak) of happiness into the language of pain and pleasure." However, Bentham complains that Hartley, when assuming the notion of happiness or utility as a principle, makes no broad hint about its "character of an all-directing guide in the walks of the public as well as private life."[72]

3.2 Moral qualities

Good versus bad or evil

Another instance revealing the common sensible roots of ethical fictitious entities is that of good and its opposite bad or evil. Both receive their import and truth from pleasure and pain in a positive or negative way, that is, in a direct or indirect way. The relation between good and evil, on the one hand, and pain and pleasure, on the other, consists either in an identification or in a causal connection. Positive good is either pleasure itself or a cause and an instrument of pleasure; negative good is either exemption from pain or a cause and an instrument of this exemption. Positive evil is either pain itself or a cause and an instrument of pain; negative evil is either loss of pleasure or a cause and an instrument of this loss.[73]

Physical sensations are subject to a moral evaluation: what is identified with or is causative of pleasure, in a positive or negative form, is good; what is identified with or is causative of pain, in a positive or negative form, is bad or evil. The meaning and truth of moral distinctions, such as good and evil, is disclosed by pleasure and pain, which are the foundations of ethics.

> Strictly speaking, nothing can be said to be good or bad, but either in itself; which is the case only with pain or pleasure: or on account of its effects; which is the case only with things that are the causes or preventives of pain and pleasure. But in a figurative and less proper way of speech, a thing may also be styled good or bad, in consideration of its cause.[74]

> *Good* is a word employed to denote either pleasure, or exemption from pain – and the cause efficient, and more or less effective, of either.
>
> *Evil* is a word employed to denote either pain or loss of pleasure, or a cause efficient, and more or less effective, of either.[75]

72 *Article on Utilitarianism*, 324.
73 Cf. *A Table of the Springs of Action*, 89; "*Legislator of the World*": *Writings on Codification, Law and Education*, 256.
74 *An Introduction to the Principles of Morals and Legislation*, 88–9.
75 Bowring iii, 214.

Good and evil are not natural properties which need to be discovered by the human mind. They are artificial notions, constructed by the human mind in relation to the perceptions of pleasure and pain which are experienced or are expected to be experienced. As qualities characterizing an object or an act, good and evil make explicit the agent's state of mind about that object or that act. If an object or an act consists of or is conducive to pleasure, it is termed good; if an object or an act consists or is conducive to pain, it is termed evil.

In his writings on codification Bentham further clarifies the notions of good and evil: he relates them to the greatest happiness principle, meaning by happiness "the sum of pleasures, deduction made or not made of the sum of pains." This principle, which is at the basis of Bentham's utilitarian approach, asserts that the pursuit of happiness, understood as desire for pleasure and aversion to pain, is the standard for practical decision at both an individual and a community level. Happiness is a fictitious entity, which is resolvable, as all ethical fictitious entities, in terms of pleasure or exemption from pain.

> No otherwise than by reference to the *greatest happiness* principle, can epithets such as *good* and *evil*, or *good* and *bad*, be expressive of any quality in the *act* or other *object* to which they are applied: say an act of an individual: say an act of government: a *law*, a *measure* of government, a *system* of government, a *form* of government. But for this reference, all they designate is – the *state of mind* on the part of him in whose discourse they are employed.[76]

Good and bad express the quality of the thing on which they are predicated. They are attributed to an object or an act on the basis of the greatest happiness principle, that is, on the basis of the pleasure or pain of which that object or that act consists or is causative. The ascription of good and bad reflects the state of mind of the speaker employing them. Good and bad have thus a subjective component, relying on the subjective character of pleasure and pain, in accordance with which they are determined and predicated.

Good and bad or evil do not correspond to objective qualities which inhere in a substance as its own properties, independently of the sensory and intellectual faculties. They are states of mind of the agent who ascribes them to something on the basis of their identification with or conduciveness to his/her individual happiness, that is, with more basic terms, to his/her individual pleasure or exemption from pain.

As Bentham acknowledges in *Of Ontology*, among all qualities good and bad "are the very first that would present themselves to notice, these are the very first that would obtain names." They are the most frequent moral distinctions adopted by humankind, as testified by the common habit of regarding something as good or bad. However, the meaning of these qualifications remains obscure, if they are not connected to their empirical roots.[77]

76 *"Legislator of the World": Writings on Codification, Law and Education*, 256.

77 A direct relation between goodness and pleasure is stated in *Deontology*, 150: "Every act by which pleasure is reaped is good, if either no pain at all is the result of it, or if, pain being among its consequences, the magnitude of the sum of pain is less than that of the sum of pleasure: and the converse is true in regard to pain."

In order to illuminate the dependence of good and bad on pleasure and pain, Bentham introduces the notion of interest, characterized as desire for pleasure and for exemption from pain. As it consists in the pursuit of pleasure and aversion to pain, interest can be regarded as "the source of every thought, as well as the cause of every action."[78] Good and bad make explicit the relation that the thing to which they are attributed, i.e. an object or an action, has with the agent's interest, by disclosing the pleasurable or painful character of that thing. An action, which is qualified as good, is related to the agent's pleasure and then is worth performing from his/her point of view; on the contrary, an action, which is qualified as bad, is connected to the agent's pain and then is not worth performing from his/her point of view.

Bentham's adoption of the notion of interest in the characterization of ethical values has the advantage of stressing their subjective character. The attribution of the moral qualities of good, bad, evil, right, wrong and so forth to an object or an action is established by the agent's interest, that is, by his/her consideration of the relation that that object or action has with his/her individual perception of pleasure and pain. The subjective sensibility to pleasure and pain, which arouses an individual's interest, guides him/her in the construction of the ethical world. Something is good for an individual inasmuch as it consists of or leads to what is regarded by him/her as pleasurable. Hence, the agent's sensory constitution provides the only and universal standard for the assessment of ethical elements.

The opportunity to perform or not to perform an act is marked out by the qualification of good or bad as well as right or wrong, which thus have a binding and a motivational character. Insofar as an act is considered good and right or bad and wrong by an agent, he/she has a duty to perform or not to perform it. The goodness or rightness of an act lies in its identification with or conduciveness to pleasure, to the achievement of which the agent is prompted; the badness or wrongness of an act lies in its identification with or conduciveness to pain, which the agent is urged to avoid.

Good and bad, right and wrong, along with other moral distinctions, acquire a normative feature, corresponding to their guidance claim or binding force, by virtue of the relation they have with pleasure and pain, which are the only original sources of normativity in Bentham's ethical system. When an agent acknowledges that an action is good or right, because it exempts him/her from a type of pain, he/she is compelled to perform that action if he/she wants to avoid that pain.

The notion of obligation shows a sort of primacy or centrality in the constitution of ethics. As Bentham clearly alleges, "*Obligation* is the root out of which all these other fictitious entities spring."[79] Ethical fictitious entities evince

78 *Pannomial Fragments*, Bowring viii, 203.
79 *De l'ontologie*, 158 (Bowring viii, 206).

a connection with obligation.[80] This is plain in the case of the idea of right, which is defined as the reverse of the idea of obligation, and can also be seen in the case of the moral distinctions of good, evil, right and wrong. Qualifying an object or an action as good or right means recommending its adoption or performance; qualifying an object or an action as evil or wrong means advising against its adoption or performance. The primacy or centrality of obligation is also indirectly corroborated by Bentham's choice to employ it to instance his method of paraphrasis and, more generally, the relation between ethical fictitious entities and the empirical real entities of pain and pleasure.

Right and wrong

In the group of ethical fictitious entities, Bentham often takes into consideration the opposite attributes of right and wrong. In *A Comment on the Commentaries* Bentham analyses at length these two qualifications, comparing his view with Blackstone's; the latter supports a realist perspective on moral and legal values. The matter of contention is the relation between the law and the notions of right and wrong. Bentham and Blackstone disagree on the nature of what is right and what is wrong and, consequently, on the function of law as an expression of rightness.[81]

Bentham summarizes and criticizes Blackstone's position, quoting certain sentences from his *Commentaries on the Laws of England*, which was an influential and leading work belonging to the common law tradition. Blackstone's book may be regarded as one of the most powerful instance of the mainstream Natural Law Theory in the early modern period. Throughout his reflections on law and morality, Bentham faced with Blackstone's thought, which represents an alternative view to his utilitarian account of law.[82]

One of Blackstone's basic assumptions is that the law should command what is right and prohibit what is wrong. According to him, what the law "commands must be a *right* action" and what the law "prohibits a *wrong* action." So, a law is a rule "commanding what is *right*" and "prohibiting what *is* wrong." The nature of right and wrong is still vague until Blackstone makes his statement on the realism of moral and legal values in the following passage.

80 Cf. *Essay on Logic*, UC 101.221 (Bowring viii, 247): "For exposition and explanation of Paraphrasis, and of the other modes of exposition connected with it and subsidiary to it, that which presents itself as the most instructive of all examples which the nature of the case affords is that which is afforded by the groupe of Ethical fictitious entities, viz. *Obligations*, rights, and other *advantages* dependent on obligation." *Essay on Logic*, UC 101.224 (Bowring viii, 248): "On the exposition thus given of the term obligation, may be built those other expositions of which it will form the basis, viz. of *rights*, and their respective modifications, as well as of the several modifications of which the fictitious entity *obligation* is itself susceptible."

81 On Bentham and Blackstone, and their dispute concerning natural rights and law, see Burns 1989; Lieberman 1989, 219–40 and 257–76; Posner 1976; Schofield 2006, 51–77.

82 On Bentham's legal positivism see Niesen 2014, 37–62.

> That the action it commands must be something that *is* right *already*, the action it prohibits something that *is* wrong *already*, that is, before the Law in question goes to work upon it, else on this account it is no Law.[83]

Right and wrong are already existent and real properties: their existence and reality are prior to and independent of the human mind both from an ontological and an epistemological point of view. The law of a State should conform to the eternal moral values of right and wrong, giving expression to them. The legislator should acknowledge and take into account these standards in working out a legal system. The human law should be a sort of verbal transcription of existent and real ethical values. The task of a legislator is to command what is right and prohibit what is wrong in conformity with "the Law of Nature" and "the Law of Revelation."

According to Bentham's words, adopted to summarize Blackstone's position, "Municipal Law issues commands and prohibitions: however to be a municipal Law those commands and prohibitions must be such commands and prohibitions as are already issued by the Law of Nature."[84] God, the natural law-Maker, operates as a legislator, whereas the human legislator transcribes his law. This purely realist approach is sharply criticized and opposed by Bentham, who sets forth an original criterion for the attribution of moral qualities.

> Were I to be asked what it is I mean when I call an action a *right* one, I should answer very readily: neither more nor less than, an action I *approve* of: and so of a *wrong* action, an action I *disapprove* of.[85]

Subjective approbation and its opposite, subjective disapprobation, are the criteria for the establishment and the evaluation of the rightness and the wrongness of something. Bentham's approach is alternative to Blackstone's: rather than looking for an external and objective standard, such as the natural law issued by God,[86] Bentham introduces an internal and subjective standard, which relates ethics and law to the agent's constitution. In the above-mentioned passage Bentham champions a manifestly constructivist perspective on ethical and legal values and norms.

Bentham's constructivism in ethics, as well as in physics, is not disjoined from empirical realism, because it acknowledges the existence of perceptual reality. Approbation and disapprobation are the agent's states of mind intimately depending on pleasure and pain, which are the only sources from which practical standards receive their normativity, that is, their power to influence and guide the agent's will in choosing a course of action.

83 *A Comment on the Commentaries*, 53.
84 *A Comment on the Commentaries*, 54.
85 *A Comment on the Commentaries*, 53.
86 Bentham criticizes the idea of God as a foundation of morality in *Preparatory Principles*, 153–4 and 167–8.

This aspect is elucidated in another passage of *A Commentary on the Commentaries*,[87] in which Bentham takes into consideration again Blackstone's claim about the law as a rule that commands what is right and forbids what is wrong. According to Blackstone, the qualifications of right and wrong are written in the nature of things by their Maker. The rules of conduct are not created or established by human beings themselves but are directly dictated to them. A legal system should mirror the natural system, so that what the law prescribes is absolutely right and what the law forbids is absolutely wrong. The work of the legislator consists in discovering, and not in constructing, the framework of ethics and law and then in making it intelligible to his/her subjects by issuing legal norms consistent with the natural order.

Blackstone's standpoint on ethics and law is in the tradition of theological voluntarism, which is based on the idea that obligations derive from the will of a superior being, namely God. Law binds its subjects because it is the direct expression of a divine authority. The natural law conceived by God is revealed by right reason: what the natural law commands corresponds to what best fits the most rational nature of creatures.

According to Blackstone's realist epistemology, creatures intuitively grasp the eternally existent standards of good and right, which are independent of their minds and have an autonomous ontological structure. After having grasped these standards, creatures ought to act in accordance with them, by virtue of their normative force. The conformity of individuals to the will of the Supreme Being is a requirement of human rationality, insofar as individuals are creations of the Supreme Being.[88]

Rather than accounting for ethics as a system of values and rules consistent with an alleged natural order, Bentham relativizes, and thus internalizes, the concepts of rightness and wrongness. He connects the ascription of right and wrong to something with the individual agreement or disagreement with that thing, which is liable to moral evaluation.

> Right, and wrong are relative terms and signify merely the agreement, or disagreement of a thing with some given rule. Our Author therefore would have spoken more intelligibly, had he laid down the rule itself, and instead of "right or wrong," had used the term "useful, or hurtful to Community": for the End of all Legislation is, or ought to be, to promote the happiness of the Community.[89]

Agreement and disagreement are nothing but approbation and disapprobation of something, i.e. an object or an action, on the basis of its utility to the individual

87 See *A Comment on the Commentaries*, 383–4.

88 For an overview of Blackstone's approach to moral distinctions, see his *Introduction* to *Commentaries on the Laws of England*, vol. i, in part. section 2, entitled *Of the Nature of Laws in General.*

89 *A Comment on the Commentaries*, 384.

and his/her community. Something is useful to the extent that it promotes pleasure or exempts from pain. In Bentham's view, pleasure and pain are the ontological and normative foundations of ethics, including its concepts such as obligation, right, wrong, good, bad or evil, virtues and vices. While Blackstone advocates a type of realism, according to which ethics and law reflect an eternal and divine natural order, Bentham puts forward an original form of empirical constructivism in ethics and law.

Bentham's constructivism manifestly has an empirical basis: the system of ethical and legal values and rules of conduct, which is a creation of the mental faculties, especially of imagination and communication, is grounded on pleasure and pain. Consequently, right and wrong, along with other moral qualities, are "relative terms," that is, notions depending on the principle of utility. When an agent characterizes something as right or wrong, he/she means that that thing is useful or pernicious to him/her, namely, that it consists of or tends to his/her pleasure or pain. Right and wrong are related to the agent's cognitive structures and, from this point of view, are not neutral.

Bentham's account of ethics and law is agent-centred and is alternative to Blackstone's nature-centred and agent-independent account. In Bentham's view, the ontology of normativity, underpinning the whole system of moral values, legal norms and social standards, is agent-relative: it depends on the agent's experience and judgement. The fictitious domains of ethics and law take shape from the cooperation between the agent's sensibility and mind.

Bentham rejects the idea of the existence of natural rights and natural law: as he famously states, "Natural rights is simple nonsense: natural and imprescriptible rights, rhetorical nonsense, – nonsense upon stilts."[90] Nevertheless, this position does not lead him to deny the physical roots of ethics and law. Even though he is not a natural law theorist, he strongly maintains the naturalistic foundations of the practical domains. His constructivist conception of ethics and law, regarded as human artefacts, is based on the acknowledgment of the perceptual character of their sources. Humankind builds the normative orders of ethics and law by taking into account the sensations of pleasure and pain.

Ethical and legal elements are established not by an external authority, but rather by the agent's cognitive faculties. Despite the mind-dependent and agent-relative character of ethics and law, Bentham dismisses radical constructivism, which is completely separate from experience. He assumes the objectivity and reality of pleasure and pain, which are the yardstick of ethical and legal notions and consequently the guide of human action. Bentham joins an empirical, and for him realist, view to a constructivist, i.e. linguistic, view of the practical domains. When dealing with ethics and law, Bentham embraces an empirical and constructivist stance, which finds its ontological form in the linguistic distinction between real and fictitious entities.

90 *Rights, Representation, and Reform: Nonsense Upon Stilts and Other Writings on the French Revolution*, 330. For an examination of Bentham's criticism of natural rights and natural law, see Schofield 2014a; Tusseau 2002; Waldron 1987.

By empirical constructivism in ethics one might define an approach focused on the activity of the human mind, which is devoted to the creation of certain patterns to understand the world; this creative activity has its roots in perception, insofar as the elements on which it is carried out are discerned by the sensory faculties. The representation or interpretation of the world requires empirical adequacy, because its meaning and truth stem from the feelings of pleasure and pain.

Fictitious entities, invented by the human mind, should be consistent and not contradictory with the perceived phenomena. So, for instance, the creation of an obligation, if it purports to be effective, needs to be based on a type of pleasure or pain. The pleasurable or painful component takes part in the definition of an obligation as its constitutive element.

Fictionalism turns out to be not a form of intuitionism, consisting in grasping certain truths, but rather a form of constructivism, committed to the creation of entities, regarded as true, which contribute to the shaping of the world. Bentham intends to save the phenomena by incorporating them in a fictitious framework which enables human beings to develop thoughts, communicate them and orient action. An ethical or legal notion has meaning and truth and thus can be normative if and only if it refers to perceptions as its sources.

The theory of virtue

A pivotal moral distinction in ethics is that between virtue and vice, which fully shows Bentham's empirical constructivism at work. Bentham develops at length his theory of virtue in his late treatise *Deontology*, devoted to the investigation of the branch of private ethics.[91] Bentham's treatment of virtue and vice is consistent with his approach based on the naturalistic foundation of the system of human values; thus, it contributes to giving a comprehensive overview of his axiology and, more generally, of his ontology of normativity.

According to Bentham, virtue and vice are:

> [t]wo fictitious entities, imagined and spoken of as real for the purposes of discourse. [. . .] Fictions as they are, deception is not in the use made of them either an object or an effect. Without fictions of this nature, and those in considerable abundance, discourse on subjects such as this could not be carried on.[92]

Unlike other fictitious words, virtue and vice alike have a double usage, being employed "sometimes as a generic, sometimes as a specific name." As generic names they designate all or any of the several entities denominated virtue or vice;

91 According to Goldworth (*Deontology together with A Table of the Springs of Action and Article on Utilitarianism*, xix), the purpose of *Deontology* is "to provide both a theoretical foundation and a practical guidance for behaviour along these lines." For a study of Bentham's treatment of virtue, see Parekh 1993a.

92 *Deontology*, 126 n. a.

in other words, they indicate "an aggregate composed of all the virtues" or of all vices.[93] As a specific name, virtue and vice designate a particular entity embodied in that aggregate.

Virtue is not merely the name of a fictitious entity; as Bentham alleges, "that fictitious entity is a fictitious personage," which is "a member of a sort of fictitious family." Though singular, the term virtue encompasses in itself a plurality, made up by the several virtues, to which it refers. Therefore, this sort of family is composed by a parent, i.e. the general virtue, and a number of children, i.e. the particular virtues. Since the appellative of virtue, in its original Latin version, belongs to the feminine gender, such a family might be imagined as composed by a mother surrounded by her daughters.[94]

Bentham clears up the misunderstanding of the notion of virtue as a real entity; according to him, such a misunderstanding is due to "the unavoidable and almost incurable imperfections of the instrument called language." However, the consideration of virtue as a fiction does not mean that the existence of virtue is denied or that virtue is an empty name. More radically, the disclosure of the fictitious character of virtue does not entail its identification with its opposite vice, another fictitious entity, because of their common nature, namely of their being "Both alike creatures of the imagination, alike objects of indifference." In spite of their fictitious and thus linguistic nature, virtue and vice are not on the same level, as expressions of nothing.[95]

Bentham warns against a form of moral relativism, consisting in neglecting the distinctions of morality, when their fictitious ontological structure is revealed. Though different from empirical reality, morality has a specific and peculiar form of existence, which is the outcome of the constructive process of the human mind, involving language and imagination; this process is carried out on the basis of perceptual experience, consisting in feeling pleasure and pain.

As Bentham explicitly states, moral elements, including virtue and vice, are characterized by a linguistic ontology: "Of virtuous acts, habits, dispositions, propensities, the existence, in so far as such entities are in any case susceptible of existence, is admitted, and for all practical purposes, namely for the purpose of discourse, assumed."[96]

When a man speaks of an act, a habit, a disposition or a propensity as being virtuous, he means by it "that in his mind a sentiment of approbation is associated with the idea of it" and, consequently "at the same time that, to the act, habit, disposition or propensity in question, a degree of importance not altogether inconsiderable belongs." So, Bentham puts a foundational question, which may be labelled in today's language as the normative question: "of the sentiment of approbation thus connected with the idea of the object in question, what is the efficient cause, or, in one word, what is the ground?"[97]

93 *Deontology*, 126–7.
94 *Deontology*, 208.
95 *Deontology*, 208–9.
96 *Deontology*, 209.
97 *Deontology*, 209.

> In the present instance, this exclusively true answer will be given without difficulty. The efficient cause, or say ground, for whatever sentiment of approbation stands in any mind associated with the idea of any act, habit, disposition, or propensity, is its tendency to give a net increase to the quantity of happiness in all its shapes taken together, about to have place in the community, whatsoever it be, that is in question. Thence, if it be of the human species, of the whole human species, this effect is produced on the part of any one individual, without the production of an equal quantity of unhappiness in any other.[98]

The ground of the individual sentiment of approbation of something, approbation which makes it virtuous, is the tendency of that thing to augment the amount of happiness in all its shapes, that is, with regard to the individual himself/herself and other people. The acknowledgment of the ability of an act, a habit, a disposition or a propensity to bring about happiness is causative of their approbation on the part of an individual and then of their entitlement as virtuous. Such a sentiment of approbation is linked to the enjoyment of pleasure or exemption from pain to which something such as an action is conducive.

Likewise, one may suppose, the acknowledgment of the ability to bring about unhappiness or to diminish the quantity of happiness to something leads to its disapproval from an individual viewpoint and then its consideration as vicious. So, "Destitute of reference to the ideas of *pain* and *pleasure*, whatever ideas are annexed to the words *virtue* and *vice*, amount to nothing more than that of groundless *approbation* or *disapprobation*."[99]

An agent approves of and performs an action not because it is virtuous in itself, but because, first and foremost, it promotes his/her happiness and, for this reason, it can be assessed as virtuous. The acknowledgement of a thing as virtuous or vicious is consequent to the acknowledgment of its beneficial or detrimental contribution to happiness. The standard and the test to regard "with property and consistency" something "as entitled to the name of virtue" is its "subservience to well-being."[100] In short, "the conduciveness to happiness is the test of virtue."[101] An act deserves the agent's approval and then his/her acknowledgement as virtuous when "in its tendency it is conducive to the augmentation of the sum of happiness." The notion of happiness or well-being shows its centrality in Bentham's axiology: "For that, on this occasion, all that is ultimately and for its own sake worth regard is happiness."[102]

The above passage expresses a conception of particular or individual happiness which is inclusive of a general and plural dimension. The notion of happiness provides each human being with guidance, by being the ultimate goal

98 *Deontology*, 209–10.
99 *A Table of the Springs of Action*, 99.
100 *Deontology*, 210.
101 *Deontology*, 180.
102 *Deontology*, 122.

to the achievement of which his/her action is pursued. First and last, the idea of happiness is agent-relative as it corresponds to the agent's desires and needs. Yet it takes into account "the happiness of others" inasmuch as the agent's happiness "is promoted by promoting theirs" and his/her "interest coincides with theirs."[103] Certain feelings are sympathetic to the extent that the happiness of others is a motive for my happiness.

Bentham puts forward a basically selfish notion of happiness which, however, is not in conflict with an altruistic view, depending on it for its fulfilment. Indeed, "each man's happiness is ultimately promoted by an intermediate regard shewn in practice for the happiness of others."[104] By encompassing extra-regarding happiness, self-regarding happiness is plural in itself.[105] The promotion of one's well-being entails to some extent the promotion of the well-being of others: "though self-regard, the desire in man to feel himself happy, is in every situation the predominant desire and propensity in human nature, neither is social regard, sympathetic regard, the desire to see others happy, less extensively inherent in it."[106]

As Bentham plainly states, "the essence of virtue consists in its being in its general nature conducive in some shape or other to well-being."[107] Virtuousness and viciousness are not properties belonging to something in itself, independently of the agent's cognitive and volitional structures. Virtue and vice are states of mind referring to happiness and unhappiness or, more basically, to the feelings of pleasure and pain experienced by the agent. Virtue and vice indicate the tendency to pleasure and pain: they express the ability or propensity of something, on which they are predicated, to cause pleasure and avert pain. Hence, virtue and vice have an inherently subjective constitution, indicating the conduciveness of something to individual pleasure and individual pain.

Bentham applies the method of paraphrasis to the notions of virtue and vice: his theory of meaning underpins their examination throughout.[108] Bentham

103 *Deontology*, 122–3: "For its ultimate and practical result, this work has for its object the pointing out to each man on each occasion what course of conduct promises to be in the highest degree conducive to his happiness: to his own happiness, first and last; to the happiness of others, no farther than in so far as his happiness is promoted by promoting theirs, than his interest coincides with theirs."

104 *Deontology*, 123.

105 See also *A Table of the Springs of Action*, 56: "The principle of the greatest happiness to the greatest numbers is opposite to selfishness."

106 *First Principles Preparatory to Constitutional Code*, 14. See also p. 233: "In the general tenor of human life, in every human breast, self-regarding interest is predominant over all other interests put together. More shortly thus, self-regard is predominant: or thus, self-regarding interest is predominant over all other interests put together: or thus, self-preference has place every where."

107 *Deontology*, 160.

108 By being fictitious entities, virtue and vice cannot be defined in the traditional way. Cf. Deontology, 208: "Virtue is an appellative by which a fictitious entity is wont to be designated. The entity signified by it having no superior genus, the term is not susceptible of what is commonly meant by a definition." Cf. *A Fragment on Government*, 495 n. b: "'Fortitude is a virtue:' – Very well: – but what is a virtue? 'A virtue is a disposition:' – Good again: – but what is a disposition? 'A disposition is a. . .;' and there we stop. The fact is, a disposition has no superior genus: a disposition is not a. . ., any thing: – this is not the way to give us any notion of what is meant by it." See also *Preparatory Principles*, 248.

explicitly connects virtue to happiness or well-being insofar as virtue is referred to something that tends to produce happiness or well-being. Vice also is linked to happiness, though in a reverse manner, as it characterizes something that averts from happiness or directly leads to unhappiness. Therefore, the relation with happiness is constitutive of the import and truth of each single virtue and, in a negative form, of each single vice.

It might seem that, from a linguistic point of view, Bentham regards the notion of happiness and well-being alike as *primitive terms* in respect of which virtue and vice are *derivative terms*. Bentham does not explicitly clarify the relation between happiness and pleasure, that is, whether happiness is a fictitious entity originated by pleasure or whether happiness is a real entity like pleasure or even coinciding with pleasure. Bentham's texts sometimes lead the reader to believe that happiness or well-being and the notions of goodness and rightness are on the same plane as pleasure.[109]

A similar difficulty, concerning the interpretation of the relation between goodness and pleasure, is raised by Goldworth, who states that there is no identification of goodness with pleasure; consequently, to say that good is a kind of pleasure is not tautologically equivalent to saying that pleasure is pleasure: "There is no passage in Bentham's writings where he expresses the view that pleasure is good or good is pleasure, in the sense of defining the terms 'pleasure' and 'good'." Goldworth concludes that "Appearances to the contrary notwithstanding, whenever Bentham asserts or expresses the view that good is pleasure or that good is the maximum surplus of pleasure over pain, he is not providing definitions but paraphrases of the term 'good'."[110]

The same interpretation might be adopted in the case of the relation between happiness and pleasure. Bentham defines happiness in terms of pleasure, suggesting the idea that it consists of or amounts to pleasure: "What happiness is has also been seen: any pleasure or combination of contemporary pleasures, considered as existing at an elevated point, though without the possibility of marking it in the scale of intensity."[111] Similarly, Bentham resolves the notion of well-being in terms of pleasure and pain: "a man's well-being will be at the higher pitch, at the higher degree of the scale, the greater the quantity of pleasure and the less the quantity of pain which for and during that length of time he has experienced."[112] Bentham's approach is unequivocal on this point and is based on the principle according to which only perceptions are real entities.

Happiness is not a sensation such as pleasure, but, more properly, is a fictitious construction, the import of which consists in a type of experienced pleasure.

109 See, for example, the following passage from *Deontology*, 127: "Considered with relation to happiness, every human act is either indifferent or important: indifferent when not considered as producing an effect of one or other of the two opposite sorts, to wit encrease or decrease (or a tendency to the one or the other). In so far as it is considered as productive of an encrease to happiness it is termed 'good' or 'beneficial' or 'salutary': in so far as it is considered as productive of decrease, [it is termed] 'evil,' 'mischievous' or 'pernicious'."

110 Goldworth 1972, 335 and 343.

111 *Deontology*, 135.

112 *Deontology*, 250.

The notion of happiness is a product of human language, rather than a simple perception. When explaining virtue, the notion of happiness mediates between virtue and pleasure because it relates virtue to the basic feeling of pleasure. In this case, virtue is like a fictitious entity of the second remove, which is linked with a real entity, i.e. pleasure, by means of a fictitious entity of the first remove, i.e. happiness, in order to be expounded.

> In this way and this way alone – namely by indication of the relation borne to happiness, that is to pleasures and pains – can any clear conception be attached to the words "virtue" and "virtues," "vice" and "vices." Were it not for this principle of order, not one of these names, familiar as they are, [has a] meaning which is not confused, unsettled and indeterminate.[113]

Bentham's theory of virtue is modelled on his basic idea of the connection between fiction and reality. Virtues are fictitious entities, the meaning and truth of which is disclosed by referring them to their physical roots, namely pleasure and pain. Bentham repeatedly states that "Virtue for its very existence depends upon pain and pleasure."[114] He ultimately understands the notions of virtue and vice in terms of pleasure and pain, specifying that "Whatsoever may [. . .] be predicated of Virtue, the reverse of it may with equal truth be predicated of vice."[115]

Virtue indicates the tendency of a thing to bring about pleasure and avert pain; so, to say that something is virtuous means that it is instrumental in the achievement of happiness, namely pleasure, or in the exemption from unhappiness, namely pain. On the contrary, vice indicates the tendency of a thing to produce pain; in this sense, a thing is regarded as vicious when it keeps an agent away from happiness, i.e. pleasure, or conducts him/her to unhappiness, i.e. pain.

Bentham plainly uncovers the relation between virtue, on the one hand, and pleasure and pain, on the other, making clear the dependence of the former on the latter.

> The existence of virtue depends upon the existence of pain and pleasure.
>
> It is only in proportion as it is productive of pleasure or preventive of pain that it is promotive of well-being, possessed of any positive value, or entitled to any regard.
>
> Its dependence on pleasure is altogether as close and necessary as any dependence it has on pain.
>
> In respect of whatever tendency it has to promote pleasure in any shape and to any extent it is of exactly the same value and entitles to the same regard in respect of whatsoever equally strong and efficient tendency it has to avert pain in any shape to an amount corresponding and equal in value to such pleasure.[116]

113 *Deontology*, 180.
114 *Deontology*, 159 editor's note 3.
115 *Deontology*, 159 editor's note 4.
116 *Deontology*, 159.

Likewise, Bentham makes explicit the relation between vice, on the one hand, and pain and pleasure, on the other. Vice also is subordinate to pain and pleasure, but it differs from virtue because the terms of this relation are reversed. Vice aims to gain or increase pain and prevent or diminish pleasure. Consequently, an act which is regarded as vicious ought not to be performed since it is promotive of pain.[117] The human orientation to pleasure leads the agent to avoid pain and thus vice.

Bentham sets forth a taxonomy of moral values, by tracing "every known quality conducive to human happiness" or well-being, namely everything that bears or at least ought to bear the name of virtue, back to three denominations: prudence, probity and beneficence.[118] These objects may be designated as "'Primary virtues', 'principal virtues', 'virtues of the first rank', 'virtues of the first order'." Their primacy lies in the fact that they are "intrinsically useful virtues"; their utility consists in their tendency to pleasure and aversion to pain. The other remaining virtues, such as temperance, fortitude, justice and so on, may be designated as "'Secondary virtues', or 'virtues of the second order', or 'ancillary virtues'" since their value and utility, i.e. their conduciveness to pleasure, derive from and depend upon "their subserviency to these primarily and intrinsically useful virtues."[119]

The definitions of prudence, probity and beneficence are formulated by taking into account the relation they maintain with happiness. Prudence is a self-regarding virtue inasmuch as it denotes an act that is conducive to the happiness of the agent who performs it.[120] Probity and beneficence are extra-regarding virtues, inasmuch as they qualify an act that leads to the happiness of one or more people other than the agent performing that act. An act characterized by probity is included among "those acts which are considered as obligatory, i.e. as being rendered so by the force of one or more of the [. . .] four sanctions," namely the physical, the popular or moral, the political, including the legal, and the religious. On the contrary, an act characterized by beneficence or, more extensively, free beneficence is not considered included "within the field of any of those obligations."[121]

Dealing with virtue and vice in his treatise *Deontology*, Bentham intertwines his theory of meaning with his moral physiology. He aims to explore "the relation which Virtue and Vice, the Virtues and the Vices, bear to man's interests,

117 *Deontology*, 159.

118 Cf. *Deontology*, 190 and also 165.

119 Cf. *Deontology*, 211 and also 219.

120 However, in *Deontology*, 249, Bentham distinguishes between "purely self-regarding prudence" and "extra regarding-prudence." In the former case "the happiness a man is able to procure for himself may be procured independently of any relation he bears to others." In the latter case "a man's condition in respect of happiness is influenced by some relation that has place between himself and the others."

121 Cf. *Deontology*, 210–1. At the beginning of *Deontology* (122–3) Bentham, however, deems all virtues reducible only to prudence and benevolence, which are the "two leading terms," referring to self-regarding and extra-regarding happiness. Probably, probity and beneficence might be considered as sub-divisions of benevolence because of their common reference to extra-regarding happiness.

his happiness, and his duties."[122] More generally, Bentham attempts to show the intimate connection between ontology, epistemology, motivation and normativity. This connection is constitutive of the ethical domain, including the notions of virtue and vice. The normative character of moral entities such as virtue and vice, which have a linguistic nature, depends on their ability to influence an agent's behaviour, inducing him/her to choose a specific conduct. Virtue provides the agents with a dictate,[123] i.e. with a duty or reason to perform an action or to adopt a habit or a disposition; this duty or reason has both motivational and normative facets.

These motivational and normative characters are not intrinsic to moral values such as virtues: they derive from pleasure and pain, which thus are not merely primitive linguistic entities, but also constitutive ingredients of action. The enjoyment of pleasure and the exemption from pain are the ends, the achievement of which the agent's practical reasoning and conduct are aimed at. The agent's interest, consisting in the fulfilment of his desire for a type of pleasure, is the chief motive of his/her practical decision. Indeed, "to encrease the amount of his own well-being is actually the object of every man's wish – of every man's endeavour, from the beginning of his life to the end of it."[124] Happiness or well-being, basically referring to pleasure, has both a motivating and a normative force, prompting and directing the agent to choose a type of behaviour which is instrumental in its attainment.

The normativity of virtue stems from the human desire to increase well-being or, reversely, decrease ill-being. As Bentham holds, "*Prima facie*, and *pro tanto*, consequences apart, every species of pleasure, every individual pleasure to whatsoever species it belongs, is good and fit to be pursued."[125] Pleasure, as the general end of action, dictates the conditions for its achievement; in other words, it provides an agent with reasons for acting, having a binding character. If an agent wants to gain a kind of pleasure or to avoid a kind of pain, he/she ought to behave in a certain way. Pleasure and pain have a normative force, because they indicate the requirements for their enjoyment or exemption; in this way, they give direction to human reflection and conduct.

A certain form of conduct is considered virtuous when it is conducive to "the highest and most general end," namely happiness or well-being, consisting in "enjoyment of the several distinguishable pleasures and exemption from the several distinguishable pains." The agent who adopts such a form of conduct is considered virtuous; he may be said to be "a man of virtue." Instead a type of conduct "operating in an opposite direction" is liable to be regarded as vicious and the agent who endorses and performs it may be said to be "a man of vice."[126]

122 *Deontology*, 122.
123 See, for example, *Deontology*, 123, in which Bentham takes into consideration the "dictates of purely self-regarding prudence."
124 *Deontology*, 250.
125 *Deontology*, 150.
126 *Deontology*, 125–6.

Virtue and vice qualify the means for the accomplishment of a goal, that ultimately corresponds, in the case of virtue, to pleasure and, in the case of vice, to pain. Virtue and vice make explicit the instrumental nature of the action to which they are referred and, by doing so, they provide the moral agent with guidance. Virtue shows what is conducive to the enjoyment of a sort of pleasure, namely the condition for its achievement. This condition is a rational requirement for the agent who pursues that goal.

The directive aspect, springing from the pursuit of happiness, that is, of pleasure, distinguishes each virtue. Without neglecting a guidance function to all virtues, Bentham explicitly acknowledges the character of an obligation to probity and the secondary virtues related to it, such as justice. Probity requires conduct of a certain type; in other words, an agent is under the obligation to conduct himself/herself in such a way. The agent's obedience is obtained by means of a sanction,[127] which supplies a reason for compliance; this sanction can be pleasant as a reward or, in most cases, painful as a punishment. Similarly, "the dictates of justice may have place in respect of any act in so far as it is considered as being the subject of obligation: of obligation from any one of the sources of obligation, that is to say, from any one of the several sanctions."[128]

Understanding the ontological constitution of virtue and vice requires examination of their normative character, which is their fundamental ingredient. The existence of virtue and vice consists in their ability to guide people, that is, to make a claim on human behaviour, by recommending the adoption of a disposition or a habit and the performance of an action. Hence, the ontology of normativity intimately distinguishes ethics and its elements, including virtues and vices. The meaning and the truth of such a subjective ontology of normativity is disclosed by taking into account its foundations, namely pleasure and pain as individually experienced feelings. Virtues and vices are not inherently normative: their normativity, that is, their power to compel an agent's will, lies in their naturalistic grounds, corresponding to the sensations of pleasure and pain.

3.3 Pleasure and pain

Pathematic perceptions

The area of physics and the area of ethics both have their foundation in experience. However, the kind of experience at the basis of physics is different from the kind of experience at the basis of ethics. Physics is grounded on perceptions

127 The obligatory feature distinguishing probity from beneficence is also stated on p. 154 of *Deontology*: "Considered in an extra-regarding point of view, the maintenance of the conduct which it is considered as requiring at man's hands, and which, in so far as he is properly termed virtuous, he is considered as being, or as not being, under any obligation of maintaining: in the former of these two cases 'probity' is the appellation by which the virtue is wont to be designated; in the other case, 'beneficence'."

128 *Deontology*, 221.

that neither consist of nor are attended by pleasure or pain; these perceptions are called "apathematic." On the contrary, ethics is grounded on perceptions that consist of or are attended by pleasure and pain; these perceptions are called "pathematic."[129] Bentham draws a clear line of demarcation between physics and ethics by virtue of the emotional character of their empirical roots: knowledge in the field of physics has its sources in impressions and ideas which are not accompanied by the feelings of pleasure and pain and, therefore, are emotionally neutral; knowledge in the field of ethics has its sources in pleasure and pain, which affect the agent's psychological sphere.

The distinction between apathematic and pathematic perceptions is the key to understanding the separation between the physical and the practical field. Pathematic perceptions guide the agent into the planning and performance of an action. For example, when an agent is thirsty, the expected pleasure deriving from drinking water prompts him/her to perform such an action. The pathematic aspect of pleasure and pain lies in their influence on the human emotional sphere. Pleasure and pain exclusively characterize the practical field of knowledge and confer upon it its distinctive normative feature. Understanding the nature of pleasure and pain is thus crucial to the exploration of Bentham's ontology of normativity.

Pleasure and pain are objective sensations because they are not created, as in the case of abstract or imaginary entities, but are discerned by the agent through his/her sensibility, which is a purely passive physiological function. However, the perception of pleasure or pain is subject to be assessed, established and also mediated by the agent's sensibility. In other words, the ability to feel certain perceptions in a pleasurable or painful way depends on the particular structure of the sensibility, which is the human yardstick of reality. Sensibility is the cognitive function through which the agent perceives reality and becomes aware of it. Hence, pleasure and pain may be considered as agent-relative feelings: their pathematic aspect, namely their influence on the individual psychological structure, is experienced and thus determined by human beings. In this sense, pleasure and pain have a subjective character too.

While clarifying the distinction between pathematically passive and apathematically passive impressions, Bentham makes two examples that indirectly throw light on the subjective component of pleasure and pain. Pathematically passive are corporeal impressions joined to pleasure and pain. A certain action, such as drinking water, is not pleasurable or painful in itself, but according to the physiological structure and the state of mind of the individual performing it. When an agent is thirsty, drinking water is for him/her an action which brings a pleasurable sensation so long as his/her thirst is satisfied. When an agent, after the satisfaction of his/her thirst, is forced to keep drinking water for a further time,

129 Cf. *Essay on Logic*, UC 101.406 (Bowring viii, 279). See also *De l'ontologie*, 172 (Bowring viii, 196 n. ‡); *Essay on Logic*, UC 101.138–42 (Bowring viii, 229–30). However, Bentham also considers as pathematic and apathematic some "impressions made *immediately* on the mental part, without passing [. . .] through the corporeal part of the human frame" (*Essay on Logic*, UC 101.140; Bowring viii, 230).

this action becomes productive of painful sensation; it is no coincidence that, because of the pain it brings forth, drinking water was imposed as form of torture for the purpose of forcing a confession out of the tortured person.

Bentham's second example shows the different feelings produced by the same event, on the basis of its effect on the individual's psychological structure. By reading a newspaper, three people are made aware of the death of a person, with whom they were in a different relationship. To the mind of the first, who did not know the deceased, this news is indifferent, or, one might say, apathematic; to the mind of the second, who was a friend of the deceased, the event of his death brings forth a unpleasant sensation; in the mind of the third, who regarded the deceased as an enemy, the news of his death possibly provokes a pleasant feeling.[130] The death of that person is emotionally perceived in different ways by those three people. Pleasure or pain are not steadily attached to a thing but arise from the application of that thing to sensibility.

Sensations such as pleasure and pain are subjective or particular, namely agent-relative, inasmuch as they are perceived by the agent's sensibility, which feels the pleasurable or painful component of an object or an event affecting it. Bentham emphasizes several times the individuality of experiencing and evaluating pleasure and pain: "Every person is not only the most proper judge, but the only proper judge of what with reference to himself is pleasure: and so in regard to pain."[131] The existence of pleasure and pain depends on their being perceived by the agent's sensibility. Consequently, conceptual elements related to pleasure and pain, such as well-being, are susceptible of subjective assessment: "each man is the best judge of what is most conducive to his own well-being."[132]

> In the first place, it seems to be universally agreed, that in the original frame or texture of every man's body, there is a something which, independently of all subsequently intervening circumstances, renders him liable to be affected by causes producing bodily pleasure or pain, in a manner different from that in which another man would be affected by the same causes. To the catalogue of circumstances influencing a man's sensibility, we may therefore add his original or radical frame, texture, constitution, or temperament of body.[133]

> But in the same mind such and such causes of pain or pleasure will produce more pain or pleasure than such or such other causes of pain or pleasure, and this proportion will in different minds be different. The disposition which

130 Cf. *Essay on Logic*, UC 101.140 (Bowring viii, 230).
131 *Deontology*, 150.
132 *Deontology*, 251. A line of criticism, levelled by Rawls (1999, 24), maintains that utilitarianism, including thus indirectly Bentham, "does not take seriously the distinction between persons." This identification among people however does not seem to fit Bentham's approach, because, according to it, the individuality of the agent is constitutive of his/her being and acting in the world. The specificity of the single agent's physiology is plainly stated by Bentham when accounting for the motives that influence human action.
133 *An Introduction to the Principles of Morals and Legislation*, 61–2.

> any one has to have the proportion in which he is affected by two such causes, different from that in which another man is affected by the same two causes, may be termed the quality or *bias* of his sensibility.[134]

Pleasure and pain show a double opposite nature, i.e. objective and subjective. They are universally experienced by human beings and, thus, their existence lies in their empirical nature. Human sensibility perceives pleasure and pain as real entities. By acknowledging their intrinsic value, Bentham underlines the reality of pleasure and pain: they have their own nature, which is merely experienced and not created by human beings. The sensations of pleasure and pain are independent of the human mind, that is, independent of the active, i.e. constructive, abilities of the agent. Perceptions are merely discerned by sensibility, which has its own individual structure, characterizing each agent.

The causation of action

Perceptions, including pleasure and pain, are the elements on which the active faculties of the human mind, such as abstraction and imagination, operate in order to create new fictitious entities. Pleasure and pain have an ontological and practical character, because, on the one hand, they are the bases for the construction of the ethical domain and, on the other, they are the inescapable condition for agency, by providing agents with guidance. From a practical point of view, the feelings of pleasure and pain are the causes of action: they influence the agent's will and direct his/her behaviour.

Pleasure and pain can bring about action because they are the motivating causes of the agent's resolution to perform it. Thus, pleasure and pain have both a normative power and a motivational power, which are intimately intertwined. An action is produced only if the agent chooses to carry it out; consequently, pain and pleasure are causative of action since they can bind and exhort the agent's will to endorse a certain action.

One might say, in modern words, that pleasure and pain are normative because they influence and direct the agent's action by putting a constraint on his/her will. In this sense, Bentham ideally locates the source of normativity in empirical reality, which is independent of the agent's mind and has its intrinsic value. Pleasure and pain are causes of action: they affect the agent's states of mind referring to action and its production.

134 *An Introduction to the Principles of Morals and Legislation*, 51. In the same place see: "One man, for instance, may be most affected by the pleasures of the taste; another by those of the ear. So also, if there be a difference in the nature or proportion of two pains or pleasures which they respectively experience from the same cause; a case not so frequent as the former. From the same injury, for instance, one man may feel the same quantity of grief and resentment together as another man: but one of them shall feel a greater share of grief than of resentment: the other, a greater share of resentment than of grief." See also *A Table of the Springs of Action*, 61: "By shewing pleasures and pains to be their bases, shewing their dependence on ditto, i.e. on human feeling."

On the other hand, pleasure and pain are also motives for acting, which exert a pressure on the agent's will in order to influence his/her decision. A pleasurable thing, actual or anticipated, prompts the agent to perform the kind of behaviour aimed at its achievement or its maximization; a painful thing, actual or expected, urges the agent to choose the action aimed at avoiding its happening or at reducing it.

To say that an agent is under the obligation to behave in a certain way means that he/she has a reason to do this and this reason has an inherently motivational force. In Bentham's account of agency, a reason for action, having a causal nature, either corresponds to the pleasure which the agent feels or expects to feel because of his/her conformity to that obligation or corresponds to the pain which he/she experiences or will experience in the form of a punishment because of his/her disregard for what is prescribed to him/her. The rationality of action relies on naturalistic foundations, i.e. pleasure and pain, on the basis of which the will is exhorted to perform or to refrain from performing a type of conduct.

> A Reason, if it is any thing, for or against a point of conduct is the allegation of certain pains or pleasures to ensue from it. It is not necessary that it should name them: tho' perhaps it were always better. But it must point to them at least. To have any pretence to the name of reason, or any claim upon the attention, if not openly announce them, it must at least give some distant intimation of them. The word reason, to mean anything, applied to mere physical events and appearances is synonymous to cause: applied to moral actions, it is still synonymous to cause, by being synonymous to motive. And what is motive ever, but pain and pleasure? This seems to be the true test of what is genuine in reasons.[135]

Pleasure and pain operate in the form of final and efficient causes of action, that is, as ends or means, by giving direction to volition. They are causes of action, when the agent's desire for a kind of pleasure and his/her aversion to a kind of pain determine the will to adopt a specific course of action aimed at the achievement of that pleasure or at securing him/her from that pain. They are means to an end when they direct the agent to choose certain objects or actions which are instrumental in the accomplishment of an end, corresponding to another sort of pleasure to achieve or another sort of pain to avoid. In this sense, pleasure and pain, as motives, have a binding force on the human will: "It is the nature of the will (that is, of man in the business of volition) to be governed by motives and by nothing else but motives. Motives are the idea of pain and pleasure."[136]

Pain and pleasure, as the normative sources of the ethical fictitious domain, are constitutive of values, standards and norms which regulate behaviour: "Take

135 *Preparatory Principles*, 132–3. This paragraph ends as follows: "Let us conclude from hence, that the only firm foundations that Law can have must be a set of accurate speculations concerning pain and pleasure."

136 *A Comment on the Commentaries*, 83 and 86.

away *pleasures* and *pains*, not only *happiness*, but *justice*, and *duty*, and *obligation*, and *virtue* – all which have been so elaborately held up to view as independent of them – are so many empty sounds."[137] The essential role of pathematic perceptions in the construction of ethics is also rhetorically framed by Bentham in the following terms: "One question, however, may be ventured to be proposed for consideration, viz. whether, supposing no such sensations as *pleasure* or *pain*, *duties* would not be altogether without *force*, and *rights* altogether without *value*?"[138]

The feelings of pleasure and pain endow duties and rights with a normative force. Put differently, duties and rights can impose a constraint on the agent's will by virtue of the relation of derivation they maintain with pleasure and especially pain. Indeed, pleasure and pain are the sources of the normativity of the elements making up ethics and law: a duty is regarded as binding by the agent because disregarding it entails pain in the form of a punishment inflicted on that agent.

Pleasure and pain provide sound bases for ethics and law, which are created by the intellectual and volitional faculties performing certain operations, such as abstraction and imagination. Though ethics and law are fictitious fields of knowledge, their construction cannot disregard empirical reality, the perception of which guarantees to them meaning and truth. Like physical fictitious entities, ethical fictitious entities are the fruit of the creative activity carried out by the human mind on sensory elements, which are passively received by sensibility. The shaping of ethics is thus the result of the ability of the human mind to construct new entities on the basis of the sensations of pleasure and pain: without empirical grounds, ethics would have neither sense nor truth; without mental faculties, ethics would have neither existence nor form.

The normative force of ethical fictitious entities lies in their related sensations of pleasure and pain, which have the character of a praiseworthy or a blameworthy consequence ensuing from the performance of a certain mode of conduct. Normativity depends on the agent's expectation to be rewarded or punished, that is, to experience pleasure or pain. As Bentham clarifies with reference to obligation, ethical values and rules are not normative if the agent does not keep in mind the pleasurable or painful consequences deriving from his/her conformity or nonconformity to them: "It being at the same time understood that it is only in so far as he is aware of the probability that, in the event in question, the unpleasant consequence in question will befall him, that the obligation can possess the probability of proving an effective one."[139]

In this way, Bentham shows his agent-relative or agent-centred approach to ethics: standards of behaviour, norms and values are mere fictitious constructions of the human mind, which however have an actual influence on the agent's decision-making process because of their psychological nature. The subjectivity

137 *A Table of the Springs of Action*, 89.
138 *Chrestomathia*, 271–2 n. a.
139 *Essay on Logic*, UC 101.222 n. a (Bowring viii, 247 n. *).

of the ethical world, which is a product of human imagination aimed at regulating behaviour, is joined to the objectivity of its empirical sources.

The main feature of Bentham's ethics appears to be the combination of conflicting stances such as empiricism and constructivism, realism and fictionalism. Bentham originally attempts to reconcile them in the representation of the world as a whole. This syncretic perspective, labelled as empirical constructivism, combines, on the one hand, the prerogative of the human mind to create fictitious entities and, on the other, the awareness of the reality of the empirical bases from which these fictitious entities take their value. Bentham's fictionalism is therefore a form of constructivism which is grounded on the reality of perceptions.

Making a promise

As a consequence of Bentham's empirical constructivism, ethics is an artefact, whose elements have their seat in the human mind, which creates new entities from the perceived sensations. The human disposition to construct moral values on the basis of pathematic perceptions may be illustrated by the representative case of keeping a promise or, more precisely, of the obligation arising from making a promise. Bentham tackles this topic in *A Fragment on Government*, in the context of the discussion on the nature of the compact which binds a king to his people.[140] The promise is a form of compact, made between some people, which exerts an obligation on the contracting parties. In other words, by making a promise, the promise-maker places himself/herself under an obligation.

Bentham argues that the nature of this kind of obligation still remains vague, being generally considered a requirement or a command of justice, right reason or law of nature: "all which are but so many ways of intimating that a man is firmly persuaded of the truth of this or that moral proposition, though he either thinks he *need not*, or finds he *can't*, tell *why*."[141] Then, Bentham focuses on the source of the obligation characterizing a promise and contextualizes his analysis in the larger treatment of the social compact. He intends to investigate the nature of the duty of keeping a promise, by throwing light on the reason why it is binding, namely on the normative power that that duty has on the contracting parties or promise keepers.

> But, after all, for what *reason* is it, that men *ought* to keep their promises? The moment any intelligible reason is given, it is this: that it is for the *advantage* of society they should keep them; and if they do not, that as far as *punishment* will go, they should be *made* to keep them. It is for the advantage of the whole number that the promises of each individual should be kept: and, rather than they should not be kept, that such individuals as fail to keep them should be punished. If it be asked, how this appears? the answer is at

140 Cf. *A Fragment on Government*, 441–8.
141 *A Fragment on Government*, 442.

> hand: – Such is the benefit to gain, and mischief to avoid, by keeping them, as much more than compensates the mischief of so much punishment as is requisite to oblige men to it. Whether the dependence of *benefit* and *mischief* (that is, of *pleasure* and *pain*) upon men's conduct in this behalf, be as here stated, is a question of *fact*, to be decided, in the same manner that all other questions of fact are to be decided, by testimony, observation, and experience.[142]

The above passage clarifies the general process carried out by the human mind in the construction of moral values with reference to the instance of making a promise. Basically, the obligation to keep a promise is a fictitious entity, whose binding force depends on the real entities of pleasure and pain. In the particular case of a promise, pleasure takes the form of a general advantage for society and pain consists in punishment for the individual who disregards the obligation to fulfil the promise made. This pleasure and this pain are expected as consequences of compliance and non-compliance with the duty under which the promise keepers place themselves. Social profit and the risk of punishment, as types of pleasure and pain, give rise to and enforce the obligation to keep a promise. In other words, pleasure and pain extend and confer their inherent normative character to that obligation.

When deciding how to behave, the agent takes into consideration the utility of an act, that is, the consequences its performance is expected to bring about in terms of pleasure and pain. His/her desire for pleasure and aversion to pain influence his/her practical reflection. So, his/her desire for the general advantage of society and his/her aversion to a type of punishment bind and prompt the agent to keep his/her word.

There could also be other reasons to comply with the obligation springing from a promise and yet they are normative and motivating only if they consist of or are related to pleasure and pain. The pleasurable or painful consequence is not merely a support for the enforcement of an obligation, but is the reason why that obligation is normative, namely the reason why that obligation can require compliance. The empirical ascertainment of the benefit and mischief deriving from the fulfilment of a certain promise is crucial to the assessment of the binding force of that promise on the contracting parties.

The individuals making a promise commit themselves to keeping it. Each contracting party puts itself under the obligation not to break its word. When disregarding that obligation, each party risks losing its credibility. Such a punishment has an ontological and practical character, which are reciprocally connected. From an ontological point of view, by producing a type of pain, that punishment provides the foundation for the obligation to deliver on that promise. From a practical point of view, that punishment enforces obedience as a condition to prevent the happening of the expected pain.

142 *A Fragment on Government*, 444.

A promise in itself does not entail an intrinsic obligation to be kept. Its binding nature stems from the expectation of pleasure or pain. By making a promise, the agent commits himself/herself to honouring his/her word and then engages himself/herself to behave accordingly. The normative aspect of a promise does not lie in the promise itself or in an independent and general moral principle which prescribes to keep a promise. Rather, the prospect of a type of sanction applied when an individual fails to keep a specific promise endows that promise with a constraining force.

One painful consequence of breaking a promise consists in the moral sanction, which has a social character: the individual who goes back on a promise risks incurring the loss of reputation or friendship on the part of the other promise-keeper and his/her fellows. The promise-breaker is exposed to suffering the pain of dishonour or enmity, which could compromise his/her possibility of making a new promise in the future. Thus, the motives of the love of reputation and the desire for amity confer a normative character upon the act of keeping a promise. The individual is aware of the negative consequences of breaking that promise and, since he/she wants to avoid them, he/she is compelled to conform with the obligation under which he/she put himself/herself as a promise-keeper.

The fear of losing reputation and amity or, more generally, the fear of disgrace could discourage the agent from not fulfilling his/her promise, because the pain he/she is expected to suffer would be greater than the pleasure deriving from releasing himself/herself from that promise. The decision concerning the performance of a certain action involves a balance of the pain and the pleasure ensuing from that action. The normative feature of keeping a promise and also of any other ethical standard is given by the consideration of the consequences they bring about in case of compliance or non-compliance with them. The stronger the pain expected from breaking a promise, the stronger the normative force with which the obligation to keep that promise is endowed. In this way, Bentham joins consequentialism with particularism, because the ethical evaluation of a mode of conduct takes into account the particular consequences deriving from its performance.

The normativity of a standard of behaviour, such as keeping a promise, is bestowed by pleasure and pain in the form of sanctions backing it.[143] The acknowledgment of the utility of that standard of behaviour, namely of its conduciveness to pleasure or of its exemption from pain, makes its individual performance both binding and motivating. When its empirical foundations are disclaimed, ethics is "a mere nothing," "a heap of non-sense" and "an empty sound": it becomes a fabulous creation. On the contrary, when related to pleasure and pain, ethics acquires meaning and truth and can require compliance.

143 The nature of the obligation to keep a promise has been investigated from different philosophical perspectives. It is a special case that puts any ethical system to the test. Among the philosophers, in the early modern period, dealing with the duty generated by a promise, one might mention, along with Bentham, Hume (*A Treatise of Human Nature*, iii.ii.5) and Kant (*Groundwork of the Metaphysics of Morals*, Ak 4: 419).

An agent is duty-bound to keep a promise to the extent that it promotes his/her utility, that is, increases his/her pleasure and decreases his/her pain. By themselves moral values, legal norms and standards of behaviour have no normative force if they are not connected to their empirical sources. Hence, in Bentham's perspective human beings are committed to keeping a promise not by virtue of a moral sense or intuition making them aware of general normative principles, but by virtue of the particular utility, namely of individual pleasure or pain which is expected to result from that act. The obligation to keep a promise, as well as any other ethical fictitious concept, is thus a construction of the human mind carried out in relation to pleasure and pain.

The process that leads the agent from the awareness of pleasure and pain, as actual or expected perceptions, to the construction of ethical notions, which guide his/her behaviour, is directed by the human mind. It is able to create new entities, having a linguistic nature, on the basis of empirical entities, discerned by sensibility. Obligation in itself is a fictitious notion, that is, a linguistic creation of the human mind. An obligation receives its import and truth, consisting in its binding and motivating character, from pain or pleasure, which derive from a negative or positive sanction attached to that obligation. It is, in fact, the prospect of punishment or praise in case of non-conformity or conformity with something that makes that thing binding.

An obligation to perform or to refrain from performing an act affects the agent's practical reasoning and action by means of the pathematic perceptions of pain and pleasure, which occur as consequences of the compliance with or the disregard for that obligation. In this way, pleasure and pain suggest motives for complying with that obligation to the agent's understanding and will.[144] The fictitious entity of obligation is created by the human mind through a series of operations carried out on empirical elements. The expectation of a punishment, which is productive of pain, underlies the idea of obligation: "To appoint punishment for an act, is to impose a restraint. To appoint punishment for a forbearance, is to impose a duty."[145] So, the normative nature of an obligation depends on the relation it has particularly with pain and also with pleasure, which are its foundations.

Obligation is at the heart of the fictitious framework of ethics, inasmuch as each of its components have a binding feature. For example, the rightness and goodness of keeping a certain promise, which are established on the account of the balance of particular pleasurable and painful consequences, compels the agent not to break that promise. Just as obligation, ethical elements have their sources in experience. However, without the intervention of the human mind, empirical reality is unable to generate obligations and other notions associated with it. Through sensibility, the activity of the human mind can give rise to obligation or, more generally, to the ontology of normativity, characterizing the whole ethical domain.

144 Bentham states the constitutive relation between disregarding an obligation and its painful consequence in *De l'ontologie*, 160 (Bowring viii, 206).

145 *Preparatory Principles*, 139.

4 Normativity and motivation

4.1 The foundations of ethics

The principle of utility

According to Bentham, ethical entities, including obligation, are fictitious objects, i.e. names: they are worked out by the agent's mind on the basis of his/her experience of pleasure and pain, which give them meaning and truth. Like all fictitious entities, ethical notions have empirical bases. However, unlike physical and mathematical elements, ethical fictitious entities have a normative character which distinguishes them; indeed, duty, rightness, goodness, virtue and so on impose or recommend the adoption of standards of behaviour. In other words, ethical fictitious entities claim to guide human action. Their normative claim is bestowed on them by pleasure and pain or, more precisely, by the individual motivation to avoid a kind of pain and achieve a kind of pleasure.

Pain and pleasure have not only an ontological and epistemological function, by being the foundations of the linguistic or mental construction of ethics, but also a normative and motivational function, by giving a prescriptive and appealing force to values and standards of behaviour. As a consequence, the ontological and the epistemological aspect of ethical fictitious entities is closely related to their normative and their motivational aspect: all these aspects that intimately structure ethical fictitious entities depend on pain and pleasure.

Bentham's fictionalism in ethics cannot be limited to the definition of moral and legal objects, but it needs to explain how such objects can influence the agent's reasoning and action. Bentham's view of ethical notions, and especially obligation, as fictitious entities entails the examination of their effects on human behaviour or, more generally, on the constitution of the practical domain. In particular, it is important to clarify how the notion of obligation, despite its fictitious character, can place a constraint on an agent's will and obtain obedience.[1]

Understanding the normativity of an obligation first requires an investigation into the structure of human action, that is, into the process leading human beings

1 By obedience Bentham (*Preparatory Principles*, 437) means "the embracing that mode of conduct which is commanded; that is, which [is] the object of the Command."

to the planning and performance of a type of conduct. At the very basis of his theory of action, Bentham sets the principle of utility, whose meaning is disclosed by the elemental notions of pleasure and pain, which are the main real entities in ethics. Utility is a property ascribed to something by human beings, since this thing consists of or is conducive to a certain pleasure; likewise, something is regarded as useful when it averts from a certain pain.

The study of Bentham's theory of action and in particular of his view of human motivation is crucial to the explanation of normative phenomena. An agent is willing to act only if his/her will is urged to do so. What arouses no motivation in the agent has no normative power on him/her and thus cannot require compliance. The essence of an obligation lies in its ability to prompt the agent's will to conform to it. The so-called junction of interest and duty is the key to understanding Bentham's constructivist proposal on ethical values.

As a discipline, Bentham's ethics has a descriptive and a prescriptive facet. On the one hand, ethics examines the structure of rational agency, that is, how and according to which principles an agent acts; to this end, it incorporates the study of human psychology, consisting in an investigation of the motives that impel people to act. On the other hand, ethics aims to regulate human conduct, by intervening in individual practical reasoning and then in the production of action.[2] Both commitments, namely the description and the prescription of a kind of behaviour, require the identification and the exploration of the normative grounds which bring about human action. Such a project is embarked upon by Bentham in one of his most famous works, *An Introduction to the Principles of Morals and Legislation* (*IPML*), a book belonging to the first phase of his career, in which he lays the foundations for ethics, as a preparatory task "to a plan of a penal code."[3]

From the beginning of that book, Bentham makes it clear that human action is caused by pain and pleasure, which are thus the sources of normativity.

> Nature has placed mankind under the governance of two sovereign masters, *pain* and *pleasure*. It is for them alone to point out what we ought to do, as well as to determine what we shall do. On the one hand the standard of right and wrong, on the other the chain of causes and effects, are fastened to their throne. They govern us in all we do, in all we say, in all we think: every effort

2 Scholars identify two approaches in Bentham's treatment of action: Goldworth (*Deontology together with A Table of the Springs of Action and Article on Utilitarianism*, p. xi) acknowledges in Bentham's production a distinction between "a theory of human motivation" and "a theory of morals"; Mulgan (2007, 15) distinguishes between "*psychological hedonism*," lying in "the claim that people are *motivated* by pleasure and pain," and "*ethical hedonism*," lying in "the claim that morality is all about the promotion of pleasure and the reduction of pain"; Schofield (2009, 44–6 and 53–67) identifies a psychological theory, "determining what individuals actually did," and an ethical theory, "pointing out what they ought to do." See also Schofield 2006, 37: "The equating of 'force' with 'value' illustrated the connection between psychology and morality. The 'force' with which a pleasure operated was a matter of psychological fact, while the 'value' of that pleasure was a matter of moral worth, yet this was only to say the same thing from a different perspective."

3 *IPML*, 1.

> we can make to throw off our subjection, will serve but to demonstrate and confirm it. In words a man may pretend to abjure their empire: but in reality he will remain subject to it all the while. The *principle of utility* recognizes this subjection, and assumes it for the foundation of that system, the object of which is to rear the fabric of felicity by the hands of reason and of law.[4]

This opening sentence is one of the most quoted and commented upon passages of Bentham's texts, probably because it outlines with great clarity, though also with literary emphasis, the naturalistic foundations of Bentham's moral and legal system. Pain and pleasure are labelled as the "two sovereign masters," under the direction of which any human activity, including reflection and movement, takes place. Practical reasoning and the performance of a type of behaviour are regulated by pain and pleasure, which "point out what we ought to do," "determine what we shall do," establish "the standard of right and wrong" and decide "the chain of causes and effects."

Pleasure and pain or, more extensively, the desire for pleasure and the aversion to pain are the constitutive principles of practical reflection and, consequently, of action. When we think about how to behave, we are guided by the consideration of the pleasure or pain a certain action is expected to bring forth as a consequence of its performance. The human mind is by nature oriented to the pursuit of pleasure and to the avoidance of pain. This orientation is constitutive of human agency: it is not matter of choice, because it intimately structures rationality.

Bentham puts forward a deterministic or mechanical view of action, according to which an action is the result of a cause basically referring to pleasure and pain. An object or a way of conduct that is regarded as pleasurable, because it consists of or is conducive to a kind of pleasure, ought to be adopted or performed. Similarly, an object or a way of conduct that is regarded as painful, because it consists of or is conducive to a kind of pain, ought to be avoided. Practical causality arising from pain and pleasure is mandatory, because it requires conformity to the agent's will. Such a constraining character of pain and pleasure reveals their normativity, that is, their ability to provide the agent with reasons for action, which have an inherently motivational force.

These reasons, derived from the consideration of pleasure and pain, are motives for action for the agent.[5] The desirability of an end, consisting in a

4 *IPML*, 11.

5 Bentham makes explicit the motivational character of the principle of utility, i.e. of pleasure and pain, and the connection of this motivational character with normativity in the following statement (*IPML*, 16): "admitting (what is not true) that the word *right* can have a meaning without reference to utility, let him say whether there is any such thing as a *motive* that a man can have to pursue the dictates of it." This motivational aspect of the normative entities of pleasure and pain, to which the greatest happiness principle refers, is also captured by Schneewind (1998, 422–3) in the following lines: "The greatest happiness principle has another advantage. It is the only principle that people can be reliably motivated to follow [. . .]. Bentham holds that although language suggests that motives differ widely, the only facts behind language are pleasures and pains. Nothing moves us but anticipation of one or the other, as a consequence of action."

sort of pleasure, makes binding the performance of the action instrumental in the achievement of that end. The desire for pleasure and the aversion to pain have a causative power on action, because they dictate the condition for their fulfilment. Desires are normative as they create duties, compliance with which is supported by motivation. An agent who has the desire to enjoy a sort of pleasure has *ipso facto* an obligation to behave in a way that is aimed at the fulfilment of that desire. That behaviour is a necessary condition for the causation of the state of affairs regarded by the agent as desirable. The agent imposes on himself/herself duties that spring from his/her motivational structure, which is aroused by the attainment of pleasure and the avoidance of pain. Hence, Bentham delineates a self-governing or autonomous agent, who provides himself/herself with moral laws.

The connection between normativity and motivation, however, remains implicit in Bentham's opening sentence of *IPML*, whereas a deeper analysis of the relation between obligation and pathematic perception, i.e. pleasure and pain, will reveal the strategic function played by motives in the constitution of action. Here Bentham appears to be more interested in highlighting the normative feature of pain and pleasure and the recognition of this property by means of the principle of utility. Bentham himself is aware of the metaphorical and declamatory character of the very first lines of *IPML*, the purpose of which is probably to introduce the reader to his utilitarian system.[6]

Bentham specifies that the denomination of "*greatest happiness* or *greatest felicity* principle" was subsequently added or substituted for that of the principle of utility, in order to express the same content with the same concision but with more clarity. As Bentham observes, "the greatest happiness of all those whose interest is in question" is the "only right and proper and universally desirable, end [. . .] of human action in every situation," both in the case of a single agent reflecting on what to do and in the case of a functionary ruling on a plurality of agents. According to Bentham, "The word *utility* does not so clearly point to the ideas of *pleasure* and *pain* as the words *happiness* and *felicity* do."[7]

The principle of utility, namely the greatest happiness or greatest felicity principle, is a fictitious notion having an ethical nature and referring to pleasure and pain as its sources. Utility, happiness and felicity are complex ideas which derive their meaning and truth from the real entities of pleasure and pain. Yet the terms happiness and felicity suggest more clearly than the term utility a constitutive relation with physical sensations. So, Bentham alleges, the notion of utility has made the acceptance of that principle more difficult because of its opaque reference to pleasure.[8]

6 Some scholars have pointed out the metaphorical character of Bentham's statement in *IPML*, 11. They stress that this statement seems to be more an exaggeration than a scientific exposition of his thought. Actually, the above excerpt summarizes an elaborate argument concerning the connection between normativity and motivation springing from pain and pleasure.

7 Cf. *IPML*, 11 n. a; *A Fragment on Government*, 446 n. z.

8 Cf. *IPML*, 11 n. a.

Bentham was fully aware of the fictitious nature of ethical entities when writing *IPML*. He, for example, refers incidentally in a note to the particular character of the notion of interest, as "one of those words, which not having any superior *genus*, cannot in the ordinary way be defined."[9] This statement presupposes the awareness of the ontological and epistemological dependence of fictitious entities upon real entities. Moreover, Bentham employs the notion *fictitious* several times in *IPML* in order to characterize the products of the human mind.[10] However, the nature of fictitious entities remains quite vague because Bentham omits treating them and their related methods of exposition, especially paraphrasis, although he had already sketched out his fictionalist approach, as can be seen in his mathematical writings and in *Preparatory Principles*.

It is not putting it too strongly to say that Bentham's main concerns in *IPML* are not the ontology and epistemology of the practical domain, but its normativity and motivation. Yet these four dimensions cannot be separated in the examination of ethics, as they are deeply interrelated. Schofield rightly argues that "In his discussion of the principle of utility in *An Introduction to the Principles of Morals and Legislation*, Bentham did not explicitly refer to paraphrasis or his other methods of exposition, yet they form the foundation upon which the whole account is constructed."[11] So, the ontological structure of the fictitious realm of ethics cannot be left out of consideration when analysing the normative and motivational character of values, standards and norms regulating human behaviour. It is likely that the presence of fictitious entities was the "unsuspected corner of the metaphysical maze" in which Bentham "found himself unexpectedly entangled" when investigating some flaws he discovered in the preparation of his introduction to a penal code.[12]

The distinction between real and fictitious entities provides the framework for the foundation of ethics and, consequently, of its sub-disciplines such as morality, law and religion. The principle of utility or greatest happiness is nothing but a fictitious creation of the human mind grounded on the acknowledgment of the normative force of the empirical perceptions of pleasure and pain. A statement about the utility of something can be explained or, more precisely, paraphrased as a statement about the property of that thing to be instrumental in happiness, that is, to be conducive to pleasure or preventive of pain.

Bentham plainly states the relation between utilitarianism and fictionalism, when he connects the fictitious property of utility to happiness, which is another fictitious entity, explainable in the real terms of pleasure and pain: "Utility is the property of an action to encrease Happiness. Happiness is no otherwise encreased than by averting pains or increasing pleasures."[13] The property of utility is attributed to

9 *IPML*, 12 n. c.

10 See, for example, *IPML*, 12, 97 and 125.

11 Schofield 2006, 28–9. See also Schofield 2009, 44–6 and 53–67.

12 Cf. *IPML*, 1.

13 *Preparatory Principles*, 130. On the other hand, "Perniciousness is the property in an action to encrease Unhappiness: Unhappiness is no otherwise encreased than by averting pleasures and encreasing pains" (*Preparatory Principles*, 131).

something by the human mind according to the capacity of that thing to promote happiness, by leading to pleasure and averting pain. The constructive activity of the human mind in ethics consists in imagining and denominating concepts regarding human behaviour; this activity is based on experience, which provides ethics with its normative foundations. Bentham's theory of meaning is at the service of his utilitarian view on ethics.

The principle of utility, which underlies Bentham's philosophical system, is justifiable by means of the elemental terms of pain and pleasure. The explanatory ability of these perceptions depends on their being the empirical grounds from which the human mind creates the practical world and then coordinates actions. Hence, pleasure and pain, corresponding to real entities, are the ultimate foundations of ethics. Notwithstanding their linguistic nature, all ethical fictitious elements such as values, virtues and moral and legal considerations, including utility, can be traced back to pleasure and pain.

Bentham specifies that the word principle, when related to utility, "is conceived to serve as a foundation or beginning to any series of operation."

> The principle here in question may be taken for an act of the mind; a sentiment; a sentiment of approbation; a sentiment which, when applied to an action, approves of its utility, as that quality of it by which the measure of approbation or disapprobation bestowed upon it ought to be governed.[14]

The principle of utility has its real source in an agent's act of the mind, a sentiment of approbation. It is, in other words, the agent himself/herself who assesses the utility of something. According to Bentham, utility is the quality or property ascribed both to that which products benefit, advantage, good, happiness or, more basically, pleasure, and to that which prevents mischief, evil, unhappiness or, more basically, pain.[15] This ascription of utility to something is carried out from an individual and collective point of view, that is, from the point of view of the "party whose interest is considered."[16]

The normativity of pain and pleasure is acknowledged by the principle of utility, which is aimed at the explanation of the practical domain. The principle of utility has a double function: it describes the subjection of humankind to pain and pleasure and prescribes how to direct the behaviour of humankind in accordance

14 *IPML*, 12 note b.

15 Cf. *Preparatory Principles*, 449: "Utility is not a Law. For utility is but a quality, a property: a property an act has of encreasing happiness; that is of averting pains or encreasing pleasures. Utility is a quality of many kinds of acts."

16 *IPML*, 12. See also *Preparatory Principles*, 436: "A *Dictate of Utility* is not a Law: for a dictate of utility nothing but some one's *opinion* that such a mode of conduct tends to augment or to diminish the mass of happiness shared among [the] ranks of the persons it concerns." *Preparatory Principles*, 449–50: "A dictate of utility is not a Law. For a dictate of utility is but some one's opinion that there is utility in a certain mode of conduct; that is that the mode of conduct in question is likely upon the whole to be productive of more good than it is of evil. An opinion is an act of the understanding."

with its orientation to pleasure. In accounting for the principle of utility, Bentham provides a number of definitional remarks which make its understanding more difficult.[17] Indeed, Bentham's considerations on utility pertain to different aspects and levels, which need to be made explicit for the sake of clarity.

One may distinguish two aspects of the principle of utility, which are the expository and the censorial, namely the descriptive and the prescriptive,[18] and two levels of the principle of utility, which are the individual and the collective,[19] concerning the agent's practical reasoning and a number of people making up a political community. The two aspects characterize each one of the two levels, so that one may basically acknowledge four similar but different functions played by the principle of utility according to Bentham's view.

1. *Individual expository function*: the principle of utility outlines how the human mind works when making a practical decision;
2. *Individual censorial function*: the principle of utility directs the agent's deliberation to pursue pleasure and eschew pain;
3. *Collective expository function*: the principle of utility describes the general tendency of human beings to happiness when performing action;
4. *Collective censorial function*: the principle of utility guides the legislator to rule with the purpose of gaining the greatest happiness for the greatest number of the people subject to him/her.

These four functions are related to one another in the way of subordinate dependence. At the individual level, the knowledge of the machinery of practical reason is the condition for the authoritative imposition of duties over the agent; at the collective level, the knowledge of the rational activity of humankind is the condition for commanding and coordinating it.

The distinction between expository and censorial, which has a cardinal importance in Bentham's thought, seems to be moulded to the Humean distinction between *is* and *ought*,[20] namely to the so-called *Hume's law*. Both distinctions hint at a general separation between a factual and an evaluative level. Hume warns against the passage from a descriptive to prescriptive level, i.e. from *is* to *ought*, tacitly operated by moral theorists, when they derive obligations from mere states of affairs without any justification.

17 Lyons (1991, 19–49) interprets Bentham's principle of utility as entailing "a dual standard," because it concerns both self-interest and the community interest, corresponding to private ethics and public ethics. Though criticized, Lyons' interpretation has had the merit of sparking a lively debate on the scope and the function of the principle of utility. For an account of this debate see Dinwiddy 2004, 134–54.

18 Bentham's scholars acknowledge that the principle of utility wavers between a descriptive and a prescriptive function. See for example Cléro 2014, 53 n. 3. See also Bozzo-Rey 2007, 330–5; Cléro 2012, 86–92.

19 Postema (2002, vol. i, xii) identifies two basic tasks assigned by Bentham to the principle of utility: in the first case, it is "the fundamental principle of rational institutional design"; in the second case, it is "the ultimate principle of practical rationality."

20 See Hume, A *Treatise of Human Nature,* iii.i.1.

Bentham stresses the need to draw a distinction between *is* and *ought*, because, according to him, it provides a clue to the labyrinth of ethics; metaphors aside, it enlightens the whole field of ethics, identifying its descriptive and prescriptive facets.[21] Bentham claims to restore an appropriate distinction between to be and ought to be. This is made possible by the plain separation between an expository and a censorial level in ethics and law.[22]

In the following lines Bentham formulates a comprehensive definition of the principle of utility. This definition has the merit of emphasizing the two aspects, i.e. expository and censorial,[23] and the two levels, i.e. individual and collective, of the principle of utility.

> By the principle of utility is meant that principle which approves or disapproves of every action whatsoever, according to the tendency it appears to have to augment or diminish the happiness of the party whose interest is in question: or, what is the same thing in other words, to promote or to oppose that happiness. I say of every action whatsoever, and therefore not only of every action of a private individual, but of every measure of government.[24]

Generally speaking, the principle of utility is an evaluative standard, conforming to the pleasure-oriented nature of human beings. Indeed, it examines and then approves or disapproves of the tendency that an object or an action has to augment or to diminish the happiness of the people involved, namely "whose interest is in question."

> Of an action that is conformable to the principle of utility one may always say either that it is one that ought to be done, or at least that it is not one that ought not to be done. One may say also, that it is right it should be done; at least that it is not wrong it should be done: that it is a right action; at least that it is not a wrong action. When thus interpreted, the words *ought*, and *right* and *wrong* and others of that stamp, have a meaning: when otherwise, they have none.[25]

Duty, rightness and wrongness are derivative terms whose normative character depends on the property of utility, characterizing what produces pleasure and

21 Cf. *Chrestomathia*, 275–6 n. a.

22 Cf. *A Fragment on Government*, 397–8.

23 On the distinction between expository and censorial with reference to the principle of utility see also *A Table of the Springs of Action*, 9: "48. Principle of general utility the only trustworthy guide, but every where opposed. 49. Principles of utility two, or if but one, it is understood in two senses – viz. the *censorial* and the *expositive* or *exhibitive*"; *A Table of the Springs of Action*, 59: "655. Principle of Utility: 1. In its *censorial* sense, it holds up the greatest happiness of the greatest number as the only universally *desirable* end. 656. 2. In its *enunciative* sense, each man's own happiness, his only *actual* end. 657. Thence, for the influencing his conduct, influencing his happiness the only means."

24 *IPML*, 11–12.

25 *IPML*, 13.

prevents pain. An action that is considered as useful, i.e. consisting of or tending to pleasure, is an action that ought to be done; put differently, an agent who regards the performance of an action as useful has the duty to conform his/her behaviour to that action. Similarly, the quality of *rightness* is ascribed to something useful, i.e. pleasurable or which brings about pleasure; the quality of *wrongness* corresponds to something pernicious, i.e. painful or which brings about pain. Inasmuch as an action, a disposition or a habit is acknowledged as right, and thus useful, it has a binding force on the agent; in other words, it is worth being adopted because it is conducive to pleasure. Hence, the normative claim made by the concepts of duty, right and wrong stems from the real entities of pleasure and pain underlying them.

In *A Fragment on Government* Bentham regards the principle of "*the greatest happiness of the greatest number*" as the "fundamental axiom," which can lead us to a "reformation in the moral" world. It affords "*the measure of right and wrong*" and of other moral distinctions composing the practical domain.[26] Bentham makes a parallelism between the "discovery and improvement in the natural world" and "reformation in the moral": he intends to apply to morality the classificatory approach of natural sciences. Despite his usage of the language of axiomatization, Bentham does not intend to deductively derive moral properties, which rather need to be examined and selected according to their conformity to utility. Bentham's moral science is more similar to Newton's physics or even more to Linnaeus' botany than to Euclidean mathematics.[27] Unlike this latter discipline, natural sciences deal with particular phenomena, reconnecting them to a few grounding principles for their explication and justification. The reform of morality consists in identifying its foundations, i.e. pleasure and pain, and in tracing moral notions back to them.

The principle of utility approves of any action that maximizes and disapproves of any that minimizes individual and general happiness, i.e. pleasure. With reference to the collective level, "An action [. . .] may be said to be conformable to the principle of utility [. . .] when the tendency it has to augment the happiness of the community is greater than any it has to diminish it."[28]

The property of an action, which "is calculated so readily to engage, and so firmly to fix the attention of an observer," is the tendency to a common end or also its opposite, i.e. divergence. Bentham specifies this end as happiness. In the tendency to happiness consists the utility of an act and in the divergence

26 Cf. *Fragment on Government*, 393.

27 See the following two methodological statements, made by Bentham, on physics and botany: "The present work as well as any other work of mine that has been or will be published on the subject of legislation or any other branch of moral science is an attempt to extend the experimental method of reasoning from the physical branch to the moral. What Bacon was to the physical world, Helvétius was to the moral. The moral world has therefore had its Bacon, but its Newton is yet to come." (*Jeremy Bentham's Economic Writings*, vol. 1, 100–1). In *Deontology*, 219, Bentham states: "The Linnaeus of Natural History the world has had for some time past. The Linnaeus of Ethics is yet to come."

28 *IPML*, 12–13.

from happiness consists its mischievousness. This general practical principle, when applied to the arrangement of the field of law, should lead the legislator to point out the utility or the mischievousness of the action he intends to command or forbid.[29]

The tendency to happiness, namely the utility of a prescribed behaviour is the only property of the legal materials which any individual looks for. By enlightening the utility of the law, the legislator can fulfil his/her subjects' pursuit of happiness. A natural arrangement of law gives reason of its norms, namely it explains their utility, so that obedience to them is regarded by their subjects as a means to achieve happiness.[30]

Under the direction of utility the different modes of conduct would be identified and denominated according to their tendency to or, in the case of offences, their divergence from happiness.[31] That property is the reason that justifies the classification of actions from a legal and a moral point of view. The tendency characterizing an act, that is, its reason to be performable or avoidable, is acknowledged through experience.[32]

The principle of utility appears to be an evaluative and operative principle of the human mind: it has no specific content and shapes practical judgement. According to Bentham, the activity of rationality consists in a calculation made on the basis of the prediction of the consequences a type of conduct can bring forth in terms of pleasure and pain. In deliberating about how to behave, the individual is guided by the consideration of the utility of the action he/she plans to perform.

> When matters of such importance as pain and pleasure are at stake, and these in the highest degree (the only matters, in short, that can be of importance) who is there that does not calculate? Men calculate, some with less exactness, indeed, some with more: but all men calculate. I would not say, that even a madman does not calculate.[33]

Bentham places pleasure and pain at the foundation of ethics. They are labelled as "interesting perceptions"[34] to the extent that they are able to affect the agent's sensibility and to arouse his/her motivation. Pleasure and pain influence practical reasoning, which is committed to choosing the kind of behaviour more suitable to the fulfilment of desires, interests and needs. Humankind in fact pursues the enjoyment of pleasure and the prevention of pain; its reflection about what to do aims to the accomplishment of these ends. As Bentham argues, "The only right ground of action, that can possibly subsist, is, after all, the consideration of utility which, if it is a right principle of action, and of approbation, in any one case, is so

29 *A Fragment on Government*, 415–16.
30 *A Fragment on Government*, 416.
31 *A Fragment on Government*, 416.
32 *A Fragment on Government*, 416.
33 *IPML*, 173–4.
34 *IPML*, 42.

in every other."[35] The individual balance of the actions is based on the criterion of utility: the more a course of action is useful, because of its being conducive to pleasure, the more weight it has in the assessment about what to do.

> Now this other principle that still recurs upon us, what other can it be than the *principle of* utility? The principle which furnishes us with that *reason*, which alone depends not upon any higher *reason*, but which is itself the sole and all-sufficient reason for every point of practice whatsoever.[36]

The criterion of utility regulates the working of practical reasoning, pointing out what actions, and in what measure, enable an agent to gain pleasure and avoid pain. In such a way it provides a reason, that is, a justification for the agent's decision to endorse and perform a specific action. This reason essentially consists in the conduciveness to pleasure of the related action. The principle of utility reflects and is consistent with the structure of practical rationality, which is constitutively oriented to the pursuit of happiness, i.e. pleasure, and to the aversion to pain: "By the natural constitution of the human frame, on most occasions of their lives men in general embrace this principle, without thinking of it."[37]

As it is the fundamental tenet of practical rationality, the principle of utility cannot be proved. Its demonstration would be self-referential: "that which is used to prove every thing else, cannot itself be proved: a chain of proofs must have their commencement somewhere."[38] The demonstration of the principle of utility is a case of coincidence of *demostratum* and *demonstrandum*, requiring for the proof the same principle to be proved. The principle of utility is clear, primary and immediate like an axiom and it cannot be rejected without rejecting reason itself: "When a man attempts to combat the principle of utility, it is with reasons drawn, without his being aware of it, from that very principle itself."[39] Therefore, thinking and acting against utility might be regarded as a form of irrationality.

The criticism of asceticism and sympathy

As a strategy to defend the principle of utility, Bentham confutes the principles adverse to it, by showing that they are pointless. If we assume the rightness of utility, what diverges from it is consequently wrong. In particular, Bentham identifies two ways in which a principle can be different from utility: it can be either "constantly opposed to it" or "sometimes opposed to it, and sometimes not, as it may happen." By and large, the former case concerns what Bentham calls "the principle of *asceticism*," while the latter "the principle of *sympathy* and

35 *IPML*, 32.
36 *A Fragment on Government*, 446 and 448.
37 *IPML*, 13.
38 *IPML*, 13.
39 *IPML*, 14.

antipathy."[40] These principles could be considered as the main opponents to utility: their confutation strengthens the validity and veracity of utility as the only principle of practical reason. Moreover, Bentham's criticism allows one to gain an insight into the lively seventeenth- and eighteenth-century debates on the foundations of ethics.

Bentham goes on to analyse the principle of asceticism, whose origin dates back to some practices or exercises performed by monks. They tormented themselves in order to ingratiate themselves with the Deity in order to benefit from eternal happiness at his hand in a life to come. Their seeking of temporary earthly pain was aimed at the enjoyment of eternal celestial pleasure.[41]

> By the principle of asceticism I mean that principle, which, like the principle of utility, approves or disapproves of any action, according to the tendency which it appears to have to augment or diminish the happiness of the party whose interest is in question; but in an inverse manner: approving of actions in as far as they tend to diminish his happiness; disapproving of them in as far as they tend to augment it.[42]

Like utility, the principle of asceticism is related to pain and pleasure; however, it misunderstands the terms of this relation. The principle of asceticism approves of any action according to its tendency to minimize happiness, i.e. pleasure, and disapproves of any action according to its tendency to maximize unhappiness, i.e. pain. Whoever attacks pleasure in itself is thus a supporter of the principle of asceticism. Seemingly, it might be regarded as an appropriate standard of evaluation when it condemns "the most abominable pleasure which the vilest of malefactors ever reaped from his crime," if that kind of pleasure were to stand alone. Bentham, however, notes that the production of that abominable pleasure does not stand alone but is followed by a far greater quantity of pain, whose consideration would be sufficient to disapprove of the criminal act and thus to punish the offender. Hence, the principle of asceticism provides a shallow evaluation of facts, opposed to right reasoning, based on an overall utilitarian evaluation.

According to Bentham, the principle of asceticism has been championed by "a set of moralists" and "a set of religionists" with different motives: moralists have been animated by the prospect of pleasure, i.e. by the hope of honour and reputation given by people; religionists have been animated by the prospect of pain, i.e. by the fear of a future punishment inflicted by "a splenetic and revengeful Deity."[43] As we can see, in both cases, asceticism conforms to the principle of

40 *IPML*, 17. Bentham also mentions the theological principle: it is based on God's will, which provides the standard of right and wrong. As a consequence of the obscurity and difficulty in knowing God's will, people interpret what pleases God according to their own notion of pleasure. Therefore, the theological principle can be traced back to the cases of the principle of utility, asceticism or sympathy. Cf. *IPML*, 31 and n. g.

41 Cf. *IPML*, 17 n. a.

42 *IPML*, 17–18.

43 Cf. *IPML*, 18.

utility, by being motivated by the seeking of a kind of pleasure or the avoidance of a kind of pain. This reflects the fact that the human mind has an unavoidable utilitarian constitution, which is yet misunderstood by the supporters of the principle of asceticism. As Bentham observes, religionists have embraced asceticism "more consistently" than moralists, not only by reprobating pleasure, but also by making the seeking of pain "a matter of merit and of duty."[44]

Bentham points out that the principle of asceticism has been applied more to private conduct than to the business of government.[45] On the contrary, the principle of sympathy and antipathy "seems to have most influence in matters of government."[46]

> By the principle of sympathy and antipathy, I mean that principle which approves or disapproves of certain actions, not on account of their tending to augment the happiness, nor yet on account of their tending to diminish the happiness of the party whose interest is in question, but merely because a man finds himself disposed to approve or disapprove of them: holding up that approbation or disapprobation as a sufficient reason for itself, and disclaiming the necessity of looking out for any extrinsic ground.[47]

The principle of sympathy and antipathy does not justify the approbation and disapprobation of an action on the basis of an objective element, extrinsic to an agent, such as the utility that action produces, namely its tendency to augment happiness. So, the criterion of approbation and disapprobation remains ungrounded and provides by itself the reason for regarding an action as right or wrong, good or bad, praiseworthy or blameworthy and, consequently, for establishing the "*obligations* to be imposed."[48] In other words, moral considerations, values, virtues and duties spring from the feelings of sympathy and antipathy, which are affections of the agent's sensibility, without an external foundation. Likewise, in politics the principle of sympathy establishes the measure of punishment with reference to the individual "degree of disapprobation" of the corresponding crime.[49]

The principle of sympathy might also be denominated "the principle of caprice," because of its subjective and intrinsic character.[50] Whereas the principle of utility is based on both the acknowledgment of the existence of objective feelings, such as pleasure and pain, and their subjective perception, the principle of sympathy and antipathy makes moral distinctions exclusively dependent on the agent's sensory nature. Consequently, ethics has no longer stable and intersubjective foundations whereby it can be justified: it is related to the agent's individual dispositions, on which his/her approbation lies.

44 Cf. *IPML*, 18.
45 Cf. *IPML*, 19.
46 Cf. *IPML*, 21.
47 *IPML*, 21 and 25.
48 *IPML*, 21.
49 Cf. *IPML*, 25.
50 Cf. *IPML*, 21 n. c.

According to Bentham, the principle of sympathy cannot give a sure foundation to morality and law: "it is not a positive principle of itself" and aims only to deny all other principles. The principle of sympathy is at the basis of the relativist view in morality and law, because it assumes the sentiments of approbation and disapprobation as grounds and standards by themselves, without referring them to an independent and objective source.[51] On the contrary, Bentham alleges, "What one expects to find in a principle is something that points out some external consideration, as a means of warranting and guiding the internal sentiments of approbation and disapprobation."[52]

Although Bentham shares the need for an empirical foundation of morality, he does not acknowledge sympathy as a foundational principle, notwithstanding its emotional character. He prefers to ground morality on the external and objective perceptions of pleasure and pain; thus, he embraces the principle of utility, which acknowledges the human subjection to pleasure and pain.

Bentham, however, does not wholly reject the idea of sympathy as a guide for moral reasoning and action. He argues that our sentiment of approbation or disapprobation is pointless and remains ungrounded if taken in itself, that is, if cut off from its external physical roots. Instead, when connected to utility, that is, more realistically, to pleasure and pain, the sentiments of approbation and disapprobation disclose their meaning and truth and can provide human beings with guidance and motivation.[53]

> The only right ground of action, that can possibly subsist, is, after all, the consideration of utility which, if it is a right principle of action, and of approbation, in any one case, is so in every other. Other principles in abundance, that is, other motives, may be the reasons why such and such an act *has* been done: that is, the reasons or causes of its being done: but it is this alone that can be the reason why it might or ought to have been done. Antipathy or resentment requires always to be regulated, to prevent its doing mischief: to be regulated by what? always by the principle of utility. The principle of utility neither requires nor admits of any another regulator than itself.[54]

If divorced from pleasure and pain, our sentiment of approbation and disapprobation is meaningless and arouses moral caprice and political despotism.[55] Sympathy and antipathy make sense only when referred to pleasure and pain, that

51 Cf. *IPML*, 25.
52 *IPML*, 25.
53 Scholars agree about the fact that the objectivity and externality of the principle of utility lie in the relation of this principle with pleasure and pain. See Schofield 2006, 47; also Quinn 2012, 36.
54 *IPML*, 32–3.
55 Bentham reveals the political manipulation and distortion of the principle of sympathy. See *A Table of The Springs of Action*, 34: "Utilitarianism, working by calculation, is consistent and solicitous beneficence. Sentimentalism, in so far as independent of utilitarianism, is in effect a mask for selfisheness or malignity, or both for despotism, intolerance, tyranny."

are real entities, on which, notwithstanding their subjective perception, morality and law can be objectively grounded.

The individual sentiments of approbation or disapprobation of an action, characterizing it as beneficial or detrimental, need to be related to external grounds, which Bentham identifies with the real entities of pleasure and pain. An action which causes pleasure deserves to be approved of and then performed; an action which causes pain has to be disapproved of and then avoided. Pleasure and pain are objective because all humankind perceives them, along with their universal normative and motivational power. Humankind, indeed, is bound and prompted to act by pleasure and pain.

The foundations of Bentham's ethics are objective and extrinsic to the agent; by virtue of this, they can provide the agent with a sure standard of approbation and disapprobation whereby he/she can construct his/her moral domain and plan his/her action. Morality is empirically ascertainable, namely subject to objective verification, because it does not depend on an individual and thus inscrutable sense, but rather it is based on the universal and intersubjective criteria of the promotion of pleasure and the avoidance of pain.

> In morals, as in legislation, the *principle of utility* is that which holds up to view, as the only sources and tests of right and wrong, human suffering and enjoyment – pain and pleasure. It is by experience, and by that alone, that the tendency of human conduct, in all its modifications, to give birth to pain and pleasure, is brought to view, it is by reference to experience, and to that standard alone, that the tendency of any such modifications to produce more pleasure than pain, and consequently to be *right* – or more pain than pleasure, and consequently to be *wrong* – is made known and demonstrated. In this view of the matter, morality, as well as policy, is always matter of account.[56]

The principle of utility is the only test for the evaluation of moral distinctions, relating them to pleasure and pain as their proper source of both explanation and justification. The reference to experience provides the standard for the construction of moral reality. A thing is susceptible to being regarded as right when it consists of or tends to pleasure; on the contrary, a thing is susceptible to being regarded as wrong, when it consists of or tends to pain. Utility lies in the relation which that thing has with pleasure and pain. Morality and legislation are aimed at giving an account of states of affairs with reference to their utility, that is, with reference to the connection those states of affairs maintain with pleasure and pain.

56 *Rationale of Judicial Evidence*, Bowring vi, 238. The above-quoted passage goes on this way (238–9): "On each occasion, the task to be performed consists in collecting together the several items on both sides, and, in the instance of each item an estimate being formed of its value, regard being paid to the several elements of value, to determine on which side – on that of pleasure or pain, of profit or loss, the difference is to be found; in a word, to strike the balance."

The attack on the schools of thought adverse to utility

Bentham puts forward a reductionist view of the various philosophical positions alternative to his utilitarian approach, dealing with them in a uniform way, as if they all were based on the same principle of sympathy and antipathy: "They consist all of them in so many contrivances for avoiding the obligation of appealing to any external standard, and for prevailing upon the reader to accept of the author's sentiment or opinion as a reason for itself." According to Bentham, all these philosophical positions endorse the principle of sympathy, notwithstanding their different denominations.[57]

In a long note contained in *IPML*,[58] Bentham lists "the variety of inventions" and "the variety of phrases," sometimes very similar, sometimes different, which can be traced back to the principle of sympathy. These theories of right and wrong correspond to "one and the same method, couched in different forms of words."[59] The identification and generalization of these theories depend upon the fact that, when utility is put aside, "all notions are upon a level."[60]

Bentham explicitly mentions the following approaches:

- Shaftesbury, Hutcheson and Hume's moral sense, consisting in an internal affection which makes an agent aware of the distinction between right and wrong;
- Beattie's common sense, which is possessed by each agent and teaches him/her what is right and what is wrong;
- Price's understanding, which provides "the standard of right and wrong";
- "an eternal and immutable Rule of Right";
- Clarke's Fitness of Things, the conformity to which establishes the rightness of a kind of behaviour;
- the Law of Nature, to which "A great multitude of people" refer;
- certain views as embodied in expressions such as "Law of Reason, Right Reason, Natural Justice, Natural Equity, Good Order," which are sometimes employed in place of Law of Nature;
- Wollaston's relation between rightness and truth, on the one hand, and wrongness and falsehood, on the other;
- the opinion of God's Elect on what is right;
- the view asserting the unnatural character of some acts, which is manifest in their reprobation caused by the antipathy they arouse.[61]

Despite the differences among the various approaches, Bentham intends to provide a unified account of them, by regarding them as different expressions of

57 Cf. *IPML*, 25–6.
58 Cf. *IPML*, 26–9 n. d.
59 *IPML*, 28 n. d.
60 Cf. *A Table of the Springs of Action*, 42.
61 Cf. *IPML*, 26–9 n. d. See also *Preparatory Principles*, paras. 184–5.

the same principle, namely the principle of sympathy and antipathy. Bentham's criticism underlying his reconstruction of the sympathy-based theories is aimed at their subjective and internal interpretation of morality. Bentham complains that the above-mentioned thinkers adopt principles that conceal their real nature; indeed, these principles rely on sensibility and are nothing but manifestations of human sentiments.

Even when supporting an alleged realist view on moral values, centred for example on "an eternal and immutable Rule of Right," "the Fitness of Things" or "the Law of Nature," philosophers set forth their sentiments concerning what is right and what is wrong. On the basis of their subjective approbation or disapprobation they say which is the rule of right, the fitness of things, the law of nature and so on and then claim to guide human behaviour in accordance with their particular point of view.[62] Consequently, by words such as duty, right and wrong these philosophers mean what pleases them. Bentham exposes this fallacy, consisting in passing off individual sentiments or belief as objective grounds of morality.

As in the case of sympathy, Bentham allows that words such as "Natural Justice, Natural Equity, Good Order" should be employed in accounting for the foundations of morality and law, but he adds that they can play such a function only if they are connected to pleasure and pain. For this reason, the word utility is preferable to them, because it "is clearer, as referring more explicitly to pain and pleasure."[63] According to Bentham, sympathy cannot be by itself the source of morality and, thus, of its normativity. Moral judgment needs to be directed by an external and objective element; such features can be properly acknowledged to belong only to pleasure and pain.

By discarding and reprobating the calculation of pleasure and pain consequent to the performance of an action, the approaches alternative to utility, identified by Bentham as applications of the principle of sympathy, find their grounds in themselves and therefore they may be labelled as forms of ipsedixitism. They set up "*sense* or feeling, real or pretended, as a sufficient reason for [. . .] obligation to act in opposition to utilitarianism."[64]

In Bentham's perspective, an agent is duty-bound to keep a promise insofar as it is useful or beneficial to him/her, namely if it augments his/her pleasure

62 The supporter of the eternal and immutable Rule of Right gives "you his sentiments upon any thing that comes uppermost: and these sentiments (you are to take for granted) are so many branches of the eternal rule of right." Likewise, the supporter of the Fitness of Things "tells you, at his leisure, what practices are conformable and what repugnant: just as he happens to like a practice or dislike it." People endorsing the Nature Law Theory "go on giving you their sentiments about what is right and what is wrong: and these sentiments, you are to understand, are so many chapters and sections of the Law of Nature." In the same way, God's Elect says "If therefore a man wants to know what is right and what is wrong, he has nothing to do but to come to me" (Cf. *IPML*, 26–7 n. d).

63 *IPML*, 27 n. d.

64 *A Table of the Springs of Action*, 24. On Bentham's definition of *ipsedixitism* see also *A Table of the Springs of Action*, 24, 30, 42, 43, 47 and 58.

and diminishes his/her pain. Human beings are committed to keeping a promise not by virtue of a moral sense or intuition making them aware of the existence of binding standards of behaviour, but by virtue of the utility deriving from that specific behaviour. This approach has sometimes been defined as *act utilitarianism*, because it entails the evaluation of each single act with reference to its benefits in terms of promotion of pleasure and exemption from pain; it focuses on the consideration of the consequences of the performance of an action and it differs from *rule utilitarianism*, which evaluates each action not on the basis of its utility, but on the basis of its conformity to a previously selected set of rules, generally aimed at the maximization of utility.[65]

Bentham's criticism of the principles adverse to utility and, in particular, their identification with the principle of sympathy, are however quite controversial. From a careful reading of *IPML*, his interpretation appears to be misleading because it oversimplifies the terms of the early modern debates on the foundations of ethics, by reducing them to the correlated discrepancies between internalism and externalism and between subjectivism and objectivism. So, Bentham distinguishes the principle of utility as external and objective and all other principles as internal and subjective. This interpretative position, as conceived by Bentham in *IPML*, appears to be theoretically and historically barely defensible.[66]

From a theoretical point of view, there is no denying that Bentham's utilitarian theory reconciles objectivism and externalism with important elements of subjectivism and internalism. Indeed, the feelings of pleasure and pain, which universally direct human reflection and action, are individually experienced. The objective acknowledgment of the guidance function played by pleasure and pain on humankind depends on an agent's subjective physiological structure, which assesses the strength of these perceptions. Humankind is moved by the desire for pleasure and the aversion to pain and yet pleasure and pain are subjectively interpreted. Each moral agent is endowed with a particular perceptual faculty which differentiates him/her when feeling and evaluating pleasure and pain.

The agent's physical and psychical constitution specifies and individualizes the general desire for pleasure as a particular desire for a kind and a certain measure of pleasure. This kind and this measure are calibrated according to each agent's physiology. However, the subjectivity of sensibility in experiencing pleasure is

65 The definitions of act-utilitarianism and rule-utilitarianism are given by Smart 1973, 9: "Act-utilitarianism is to be contrasted with rule-utilitarianism. Act-utilitarianism is the view that the rightness or wrongness of an action is to be judged by the consequences, good or bad of the action itself. Rule-utilitarianism is the view that the rightness or wrongness of an action is to be judged by the goodness and badness of the consequences of a rule that everyone should perform the action in like circumstances." For a comparison between act-utilitarianism and rule-utilitarianism, see the whole paragraph devoted to it by Smart 1973, 9–12.

66 Parekh (1974, 114) holds that "Bentham's whole discussion of the principle of sympathy and antipathy is based on a confused and ultimately untenable distinction between 'internal' and 'external', and an equally muddled identification of the external with the objective and the internal with the subjective." So, the opposed interpretative categories of internal and external and of subjective and objective need to be reworked in order to better fit Bentham's empirical constructivism. On objectivity and subjectivity in Bentham's approach see Quinn 2014, 93–102.

only apparently opposed to the objectivity of the human orientation to pleasure, i.e. of the pursuit of happiness. Bentham attempts to make compatible these two dimensions, integrating the particularity or subjectivity of individual physiology into the universality or objectivity of the foundations of ethics.

From a historical point of view, if we consider certain ethical systems of Bentham's contemporaries, we can see that they are based on objective and external grounds, such as Clarke's fitness of things, Cudworth's eternal and immutable principles, Locke's right reason and Blackstone's law of nature. These approaches can hardly be traced back to the principle of sympathy and antipathy, which is intimately subjective and does take into account elements independent of the agent's mind.

In *Enquiry concerning the Principles of Morals*, Hume effectively summarizes the seventeenth- and eighteenth-century controversy between rationalism and sentimentalism about the sources of morality. He defines three aspects of this controversy: whether morality derives from reason or sentiment; whether moral notions are attained by "a chain of argument and induction" or by "an immediate feeling and finer internal sense"; whether moral distinctions "should be the same to every rational intelligent being" or should "be founded entirely on the particular fabric and constitution of the human species."[67] According to rationalists, human beings become aware of moral distinctions through a logical process of reason. According to sentimentalists, moral qualities depend on sentiment, namely on internal sense which perceives them.

This distinction between rationalism and sentimentalism, as portrayed by Hume, is generally accepted by historians of philosophy when reconstructing the early modern debate on the foundations of morality. They set an empirical view, championed by the so-called sentimentalists such as Shaftesbury, Hutcheson and Hume, against a rationalist view, supported by thinkers such as Cudworth, Clarke and Wollaston. Both views underlie a variety of ontological and epistemological approaches to moral normativity, which is difficult to account for in a few words.

Generally speaking, rationalists endorse a form of realism which basically maintains the objectivity of moral distinctions, in the sense that moral distinctions exist independently of the human mind which knows them. Clarke, for example, argues that there are "certain necessary and eternal differences of things, and certain consequent fitnesses or unfitnesses of the application of different things, or different relations one to another."[68] As a result, "necessary and eternal reason and proportions of things" give rise to "the original obligations of morality."[69]

On the contrary, empiricists refer the existence of morality to a person's states of mind, such as emotions, desires and needs. Despite their subjectivism, empiricists are not necessarily anti-realists; Shaftesbury and Hutcheson, for example,

67 Hume, *Enquiry concerning the Principles of Morals*, section i.

68 Clarke, *A Discourse Concerning the Being and Attributes of God, the Obligations of Natural Religion, and the Truth and Certainty of the Christian Revelation*, Proposition i, 165.

69 Clarke, *A Discourse Concerning the Being and Attributes of God, the Obligations of Natural Religion, and the Truth and Certainty of the Christian Revelation*, Proposition i, 203.

are realists on a sentimentalist and not rationalist basis, because they believe that a moral sense leads us to the discovery of rightness and wrongness. According to them, moral sense is a faculty that grasps or feels independent moral distinctions, which appear to us as natural affections. Shaftesbury argues that this sense "must consist in a real Antipathy or Aversion to *Injustice* or *Wrong*, and in a real Affection or Love towards *Equity* and *Right*."[70] Likewise Hutcheson defines moral sense as "a Determination of our Minds to receive amiable or disagreeable Ideas of Actions, when they occur to Observation, antecedent to any Opinions of Advantage or Loss to redound to our selves from them."[71]

Similarly, Hume maintains that "morality is determined by sentiment. It defines virtue to be *whatever mental action or quality gives to a spectator the pleasing sentiment of approbation*; and vice the contrary."[72] However, he does not refer to an external and objective distinction between right and wrong, but he makes it dependent on sentiment. The self-reflective activity of the agent leads him/her to the endorsement of the morality of a type of behaviour, which is grounded in human nature. The wrongness or viciousness of an action is not discovered "by demonstrative reasoning," but rather it is "felt by an internal sense, and by means of some sentiment, which the reflecting on such an action naturally occasions."[73] Hume concludes that "since vice and virtue are not discoverable merely by reason, or the comparison of ideas, it must be by means of some impression or sentiment they occasion, that we are able to mark the difference betwixt them." In short, "Morality [. . .] is more properly felt than judg'd of."[74]

Bentham's view scarcely fits comfortably in both categories of rationalism and empiricism or sentimentalism. On the one hand, Bentham rejects a merely rationalist approach to the knowledge of reality, though he does not neglect the contribution of the human mind in the construction of the moral domain; on the other hand, he stands in the empirical tradition and yet he is not a sentimentalist. Hence, Bentham appears to be committed to a constructivist view, which tends to assimilate some aspects pertaining to both the rationalist and the empiricist traditions.

Bentham's ontology of the ethical and the physical world reciprocally connects objectivism and subjectivism, so that one is constitutive of the other. The objectivity of real entities, which are experience-data, is linked to the subjectivity of their perception through the human sensory faculties. The subjectivity of fictitious entities, which are linguistic elements created by the human mind, is joined to the objectivity of their empirical grounds corresponding to real entities.

70 Shaftesbury, *Inquiry Concerning Virtue or Merit*, part iii, section i.
71 Hutcheson, *An Inquiry Into the Original of Our Ideas of Beauty and Virtue in Two Treatises*, ii.i.viii.
72 Hume, *Enquiry concerning the Principles of Morals*, appendix i.
73 Hume, *A Treatise of Human Nature*, iii.i.1.
74 Hume, *A Treatise of Human Nature*, iii.i.2. Bentham (*A Table of the Springs of Action*, 57) notes that "Hume acknowledges the dominion of utility but so he does of the moral sense: which is nothing more than a fiction of ipsedixitism."

The harmonization of subjectivism and objectivism, empiricism and rationalism, fictionalism and realism makes Bentham's strategy an original proposal to solve the question concerning the foundations of morality, that is, in modern words, the normative question. Because of its combinatory character, this proposal might properly be called *empirical constructivism.*

Empirical constructivism

Throughout his life, Bentham worked out an empirical version of constructivism, in the form of fictionalism, as the theoretical approach for his moral and legal doctrine. According to this approach, the elements of the natural and the ethical world are created by a mental process, but nevertheless such a process is based on perceptual experience, which is the foundation of the fictitious framework of physics and ethics.

After having mapped out Bentham's path from sensory perceptions to linguistic entities, we need to conceptualize his view in terms of empiricism, constructivism and fictionalism. Therefore, this section, *Empirical realism*, is devoted, first, to theorizing Bentham's connection between empiricism, which he understood as a sort of realism, and constructivism, which is based on the exercise of the human mind. The next section, *Constructivism and fictionalism*, which is closely related to this, is committed to explaining how Bentham's empirical and constructivist approach in metaphysics and metaethics can give expression to his fictionalism without contradiction.

Generally speaking, realism and constructivism both accept the truth of propositions concerning the natural and the practical world. Where they diverge is regarding the concept of truth: from a realist standpoint a proposition is true to the extent that it describes a state of affairs independent of the subject; from a constructivist standpoint a proposition is true to the extent that it expresses a state of mind. Realists and constructivists have different views on reality, considering it respectively either as an external state of affairs recognizable to the human mind or as an internal state of affairs produced by the human mind as its own creation.

Realism is usually associated with the idea of objectivity because it argues the mind-independency of physical and ethical elements. However, constructivism is not at all a subjective view, in the sense that it aims to save the requirements of objectivity, even though in a different way from the realist strategy. Constructivism claims that human practices and attitudes determine the structure of what is regarded as reality.

According to realists, moral facts are independent of the agent who discovers or knows them by means of reasoning or intuition. Constructivism, by contrast, countenances the view that moral reality is made by moral agents' thinking. Realism and constructivism entail different epistemologies: the former assumes that moral entities already exist and thus the human mind should discover them through various logical means such as intuition, deduction and induction; the latter alleges that moral entities are created through procedures employed by the human mind.

Bentham develops an empirical version of constructivism, in the form of fictionalism, according to which the contents of physics and ethics are established by the human mind and yet such an activity is oriented by perceptual experience, which is the fundamental ingredient of the representation of reality.

In contemporary debates, realism and constructivism are usually regarded as competitive theories to account for the practical domain.[75] According to a realist view, moral values and norms exist before and are independent of the judgment of individuals, which should take them into account in evaluating what to do. Realism is a form of ethical cognitivism: moral entities are knowable to the agent by means of his/her cognitive faculties. From a realist perspective, a proposition involving the notion of good is true because it concerns an ontologically autonomous entity of good.

Korsgaard articulates in the following terms a clear definition of moral realism, which can be soundly applied to the seventeenth- and eighteenth-century debates pertaining to the ontological status of moral entities: "Moral realism [. . .] is the view that propositions employing moral concepts may have truth values because moral concepts describe or refer to normative entities of facts that exist independently of those concepts themselves."[76]

Defining constructivism in general terms is a little harder than defining realism because of the variety of views that can be designated by this denomination.[77] Korsgaard again supplies a definition of constructivism, which, unlike that of realism, appears to reflect a more sophisticated level of philosophical development.

> So according to constructivism, normative concepts are not [. . .] the names of objects or of facts or of the components facts we encounter in the world. They are the names of the solutions of problems, problems to which we give names to mark them out as objects for practical thought. The role of the concept of the right, say, is to guide action: the role of the concept of the good might be to guide our choice among options, or of ends.[78]

75 In contemporary debates realism is usually opposed to constructivism, as Shafer-Landau (2011, cviii) observes: "One way to see the essence of constructivism is to consider its contrast with moral realism. Suppose again that the prohibition on gratuitous harm is a fundamental moral rule. Both realists and constructivists can agree that ideal observers will endorse this rule. But realists will say that ideal observers endorse the rule because it is correct. Being ideal, such observers will always land on the truth. But this truth, if realists are right, is antecedent to the endorsement of ideal observers. Constructivists disagree. They will say that the rule is correct only because ideal observer (or, on other version of constructivism, other appropriately positioned constructors) endorse it – prior to such endorsement nothing is right or wrong."

76 Korsgaard 2008, 302.

77 Lillehammer 2011, part. 66: "There is no simple formulation of moral constructivism that easily captures all the views that may be thought to deserve that name. Nevertheless, most forms of constructivism are committed to the following two theses. First, some moral claims are true; or if not robustly true, then objectively valid (I shall drop this qualification from now on). Second, the truth of moral claims is a function of what is either constitutive of, or what can be constructed in, moral reasoning or argument. Thus, insofar as it is acceptable to talk about moral facts or properties, these are facts or properties we, or some idealized version of us, have an essential role in constituting or creating."

78 Korsgaard 2008, 322.

Appearances notwithstanding, Korsgaard's general account of constructivism captures a central feature of Bentham's philosophical approach, namely the fact that normative concepts, such as good, right, virtue and so on, are created for the solution of theoretical and practical problems. More generally, as remarked by Bentham several times, the basic need for social intercourse, requiring the working out and the transmission of more complex notions than simple impressions received by our senses, may be regarded as the main problem to the resolution of which his constructivist procedure for creating fictitious entities is devoted.

Constructivism in Bentham's philosophy is essentially aimed at settling the problem of enabling human beings to think, communicate and act. It originates from the need to provide objective standards of thought which contribute to the full and consistent representation of the natural world and to the general regulation of individual behaviour in the wider framework of interpersonal relations. By means of these standards of thought, having a fictitious character, communication between people and, then, social life is made possible.

Constructivism turns out to be a form of fictionalism: it maintains the creations of certain entities which give sense and order to sensory perceptions and which establish values and norms guiding people's conduct. Consequently, the physical world and the ethical world are artefacts; their construction, however, is not a mere exercise in speculation, but has a theoretical and a practical purpose consisting in the development of society. Fictitious entities, therefore, are the constitutive elements of the ontology of the physical and the ethical domain, which is grounded on real entities, i.e. empirically experienced elements. This ontology is basically linguistic insofar as its elements are names, that is, names of real and fictitious entities.

The contrast between realism and constructivism in ethics can be vividly illustrated in the following alternative ontological and epistemological terms: are good, right and virtuous intrinsic or extrinsic qualities of things? Are they recognized or bestowed by the human mind?[79] The question on the nature of value is closely related to the question of normativity, which pertains to the foundations of the notion of obligation and, more generally, of the action-guiding character of ethical notions. Indeed, the value of ethical notions lies in their normativity, that is, in their prerogative to direct human behaviour. The question of normativity is at the heart of the controversy between realists and constructivists: their matter of contention concerns the foundations of ethics.

Moral constructivism, however, is not the opponent of or the alternative to moral realism. Moral constructivism requires more than an anti-realist position. Anti-realists could be sceptical about the existence of objective moral standards and values. Constructivists, instead, reject scepticism: moral entities such as good, evil, right and wrong exist as properties dependent on the agent's thinking and have an objective basis. The controversy between realism and constructivism is

79 The difference between a realist and a constructivist position is also briefly sketched out by Street 2008, 207: "Do valuable things possess their value independent of our valuing them? Or does their value always depend, at least ultimately, on our taking them to be valuable?"

not just an ontological question, since it involves the epistemological problem concerning the way in which human agents become aware of or construct physical and ethical concepts.

The mere opposition between realism and anti-realism falls short of giving an account of Bentham's original position. On the contrary, the alternative between realism and constructivism allows us to understand Bentham's attempt to make compatible the sensory faculty with the creative power of the human mind when accounting for the physical and the ethical domain. In this way, Bentham assimilates certain aspects of realism, such as the truth and objectivity of perceptual elements, and certain aspects of constructivism, such as the ability of the human mind to imagine new entities, i.e. values and virtues.

In Bentham's view, empiricism is reconciled with constructivism: sensibility receives perceptions, i.e. impressions and ideas, identified as real entities, on the basis of which the human mind creates new entities, which are fictitious. By being their grounds, sensory perceptions do not conflict with mental constructions. Surprisingly, Bentham's constructivism appears to be the natural consequence of his empiricism, which is restricted to perceptions and consequently cannot provide agents with a framework aimed at giving an image of nature and at orienting their decision on what to do. So, the creativity of the human mind fills this perceptual gap, shaping the physical and the practical subset of the world, without cutting off its connections with experience.[80]

Constructivism and fictionalism

The objective of this section is to examine, from a philosophical point of view, the plausibility of understanding Bentham's theory of real and fictitious entities in terms of empirical constructivism. Generally speaking, in metaphysics and metaethics a problem arises when we compare constructivism, which alleges the truth and objectivity of mental entities, to fictionalism, which maintains the falseness of the products of the mind. Consequently, how is it possible to regard empirical constructivism as an interpretative category for Bentham's theory of real and fictitious entities?

According to a generally shared view, "The simplest fictionalist approach to a discourse takes certain claims in that discourse to be literally false, but nevertheless worth uttering in certain contexts, since the pretence that such claims are true is worthwhile for various theoretical purposes."[81] More particularly, with reference to morality:

80 More generally, utilitarianism, and not only Bentham's approach, might be regarded as a form of constructivism. Bagnoli 2015, for example, notes that "While constructivism does not mandate any specific normative ethics and is often found combined with contractualism, as on the Scanlonian and Hobbesian models, some have suggested that Utilitarianism is a natural candidate for being paired with constructivism." In the following lines Bagnoli also mentions some studies of the relation between utilitarianism and constructivism.

81 Nolan, Restall & West 2005, 308.

> Fictionalism provides a way to deal with the distinctive nature of moral discourse. Moral discourse is useful in many ways, yet theories that attempt to give truth conditions for moral claims seem to founder. Fictionalism is well suited to these problems. Moral claims (at least positive ones – such as the claim that to cause suffering is morally wrong, in general) are, strictly speaking, false, just as claims about fictional characters (at least positive ones – such as the claim that Sherlock Holmes lived in Baker Street) are, strictly speaking, *false*. To state that Sherlock Holmes lived in Baker Street is to state that Holmes existed – but Holmes did not. To state that causing suffering is morally wrong is to ascribe a motivating objective property to a kind of action – and there is no such property. However, in the moral case, these falsehoods are *useful*.[82]

Along similar lines, though referring to law, Fuller identifies the two distinctive marks of fictionalism with the "consciousness of falsity" and "utility."[83] Fictionalism challenges the idea that moral beliefs correspond to objective moral truths.[84] Bentham, too, was convinced of the falseness of fictions. In *Chrestomathia*, for instance, he metaphorically compares a fictitious entity to "an automaton figure," "in the dress of a man, sitting and playing upon an organ," which is taken by mistake as "a real man," also by the most acute observer looking at it at a distance, while it is simply a "creature of human art."[85] So, Bentham understands a fiction as "an assumed fact notoriously false, which is reasoned upon as though it were true."[86]

As a result of Bentham's application of his theory of real and fictitious entities to ethics, moral and legal elements have no reality. A fictionalist stance seems to leave itself open to the attack of being a form of nihilism. This problem does not only concern the ontological and epistemological aspect of morality and law, but also involves the prerogative of morality and law to guide and direct human behaviour, namely to be normative. In brief, why should we be moral if morality is a fiction, that is, a construction of the human mind or, as Bentham states, a mere non-sense?

Replying to this criticism entails saving the demands that ethics makes on us from the realm of falsehood and also of nothingness. To this end, Bentham lays the theoretical foundation for ethics, so that its claims on us can be effective.

82 Nolan, Restall & West 2005, 308–9.

83 Fuller 1967, 9: "A fiction is either (1) a statement propounded with a complete or partial consciousness of its falsity, or (2) a false statement recognized as having utility."

84 On moral fictionalism see: Joyce 2001, part. 175–231; Joyce 2005; Nolan, Restall & West 2005; Kalderon 2005a; Kalderon 2008. On legal fictionalism see: Bouriau 2013; Del Mar & Twining 2015; Fuller 1967; Mathieu 2014; Olivier 1975. An overview of the current approaches to fictionalism is supplied by Kalderon 2005.

85 Cf. *Chrestomathia*, 277 n. a.

86 Cf. *Bentham's Theory of Legislation being Principes de législation and Traités de législation civile et pénale*, 93.

His strategy to ground morality and law on empirical reality escapes the risk of neglecting ascribing any import to moral and legal values. Morality and law remain fictitious constructions of the human mind and yet they can make claims on us by virtue of their constitutive relation with the real sources of pleasure and pain. So, Bentham does not advance a nihilist view on ethics, but acknowledges to ethics an agent-relative dimension which has an objective foundation and a justification in empirical reality. Without such a foundation, ethics, including morality and law, would be a meaningless and false invention, aimed only at deception.

Bentham would seem to be in a dilemma: as a fictionalist, he should allege the falseness or unreality of mental entities; as a constructivist, he should acknowledge the truth and reality of mental entities. This aporia, however, is only apparent because Bentham plainly ascribes a form of reality and existence also to fictitious constructions. From an empirical point of view, they are nothing and thus their claim on existence is false; instead, from a linguistic point of view, they are real and existent, inasmuch as they are products of the human mind. The human mind, including language, has an existence-providing ability: it creates objects which are not perceived but rather thought and expressed by words within a propositional context.

Bentham can combine, without ambiguity, two alternative views, i.e. empiricism, in which his realism consists, and constructivism, because he assumes two different but not conflicting notions of existence: on the one hand, an empirical existence, belonging to material things as they are perceived by the faculty of sensibility; on the other, a linguistic existence, belonging to conceptual, and thus fictitious, objects, which however are considered by the human mind as if they were real.

Fictitious as they are, linguistic constructions contribute, in the physical domain, to shaping the representation of the world and, in the practical domain, to providing guidance to moral agents. Fictitious entities have a form of existence conferred by the human mind – since it creates them – but depend on sensibility. Hence, from Bentham's perspective, fictionalism can find suitable expression in constructivism or, more precisely, in an empirical type of constructivism. Perception has indeed a regulative function, to the extent that the relation with it provides the distinguishing criterion for the creation and selection of fictitious constructions. The human mind builds the framework of the physical and the ethical domain on the basis of sensory elements.

The possibility of reconciling a fictionalist stance with a constructivist stance lies in the acknowledgment of the truth value of the propositions including names designating fictitious objects, which are the products of human language. Bentham ascribes to the names of fictitious entities a derivative form of import and truth, that is, a form of import and truth resulting from the names of real entities. Mental objects, considered fictitious, are related to empirical objects, considered real, as regards their import and truth.

Bentham makes use of the linguistic method of paraphrasis to throw light on the constitutive relation that a fictitious entity has with a real entity. On this relation depend the meaning and the truth of fictitious entities. The strategy of paraphrasis is aimed at understanding the meaning and ascertaining the truth of a certain fictitious entity, by connecting it to its empirical source, identified as a real entity. Paraphrasis consists in "transmuting" the proposition having for its subject the name of a fictitious entity, into a proposition having for its subject the name of the real entity corresponding to that fictitious entity.

A fictitious entity in itself is nothing and, consequently, has no properties. A proposition ascribing to a fictitious entity certain properties cannot be true unless this proposition is paraphrasable in an equivalent and adequate propositional substitute containing the name of a real entity as its subject.[87] Paraphrasis is thus not only the discriminating method for selecting fictitious entities and distinguishing them from non-entities, which have no connection with reality, but also and especially the method for expounding a fictitious entity, by tracing it back to its real root. The possibility of restating a fictitious proposition as a real proposition guarantees the meaning and the truth of that fictitious proposition, including its subject.

Human language, structured in propositions, creates new fictitious entities, whose meaning and truth derive from the relation they maintain with real entities, which have an empirical nature. Sensory experience provides the foundation from which the human mind constructs a meaningful and true ontology, made up by linguistic elements. By means of the constitutive relation between fictitious and real entities, disclosed by the method of paraphrasis, Bentham saves the requirement of truth, which is at the basis of any constructivist proposal.

Bentham's fictionalism entails, without contradiction, a form of empirical factualism or realism: the reality of fictitious entities can be claimed if they are connected to certain empirically ascertainable facts, which provide them with import and truth. However, Bentham rejects factualism or realism as a metaethical view maintaining the autonomous existence of moral notions such as good, right, virtues and duties. Moral qualities are created by the human mind which regards them as normative to the extent that they are conducive to individual pleasure or aversive to individual pain. Fictitious as they are, moral qualities make sense because they are grounded on perceived, and thus real, feelings.

Bentham's fictionalism may be regarded as a form of constructivism since it aims to found a verbal and thus mental ontology, which is separate from perceptual reality, but not in disagreement with it. So fictionalism moulds Bentham's ontology of normativity, whose elements, making up the practical domain, influence individual reflection and decision concerning action.

Surprisingly, in current debates fictionalism and constructivism run parallel: they appear as separate strategies in accounting for the variety of natural phenomena and ethical values. Bentham instead combines these seemingly distinct approaches. As a general basis for the explanation of the world Bentham adopts the distinction between real entities, experienced by the senses, and fictitious entities, invented by the human mind.

87 Cf. *Essay on Logic*, UC 101.217 (Bowring viii, 246).

The fictitious domain is not opposed to the real domain: the former derives from the latter and is complementary to it in the general representation of the world, which is produced by the interaction between the sensory and the intellectual faculties. Fictitious entities are constructed by taking into account experience-data. The physical world and the ethical world are ultimately made up by perceptions, which are their foundations. So, with reference to the ethical domain, pleasure and pain provide a clue to the labyrinth of morality and jurisprudence.

The invention of fictitious entities is a specific ability of the human mind that allows human beings to work out the physical and the ethical realm and consequently to act. Fictitious entities are contrivances with a guiding function: on the one hand, they are instrumental in our image of the world, giving an order to perceptions; on the other, they claim to orient and direct human behaviour.

Hence, in Bentham's approach, constructivism is not an alternative to realism, but rather it completes the elemental perception of the external world. Fictitious entities contribute to making sense of experience, by organizing and interpreting it in a composite fictitious framework, in which mental elements are interconnected with sensory elements. Constructivism throws light on the activity of the human mind which basically consists in creating new entities, without which knowledge and action would be impossible.

From Bentham's perspective, constructivism and fictionalism are strictly related. Constructivism consists in imagining and shaping fictitious entities, which, unlike real entities, do not have an empirical existence, but rather a verbal form of existence, inasmuch as they are produced by the human mind for the sake of communication. Bentham's constructivism is based on the capacity of the human mind to create fictitious entities, namely conceptual and linguistic objects. This capacity is necessary for the evolution of social life, because it enables the development of thought and language, which are at the basis of interpersonal relationships. Perceptual reality needs to be integrated with an artificial reality for the working of theoretical and practical rationality.

A fictitious entity is a mere nothing in terms of perceptions: it has neither a sensory nor an inferential character. A fictitious entity is not discerned by sensibility or derived from a logical process of generalization or abstraction. It is a pure creation of the human mind, which however maintains a constitutive relation with experience. So, Bentham outlines the world, including its natural and practical domains, as a harmonious combination of sensibility and the human mind, of perceptual reality and intellectual fiction, without discrepancies. The human mind, on the one hand, depends on sensibility, but, on the other, enriches it, by assimilating perceptions into a comprehensive representation of the world, which is not only restricted to empirical elements.

The complexity of the physical representation of reality cannot be reduced only to experience or to abstractions from experience but requires the intervention of mental faculties, which supply fictitious notions such as substance, movement, relation, causality and so forth; they are necessary to think of the natural world and to express the contents pertaining to it. Similarly, morality and law are not limited to pain and pleasure but result from the activity of imagination which the human mind carries out on these sensations. Moral qualities have no empirical existence, but nevertheless they exist to the extent that they have a special ontological nature ascribed by the human mind. Values and virtues are endowed with a form of reality, identifiable as linguistic, which is different but not inferior to the form of reality attested to by experience.

In Bentham's view, fictionalism and constructivism are consistently related to empirical realism. The faculty of sensibility does not afford moral and legal concepts or more complex notions than impressions or ideas. Fictionalism and constructivism prove to be the strategies aimed at overcoming the limits of empirical realism. In Bentham's account of the physical and the practical world, realism is not contrasted with constructivism or fictionalism. They concern different spheres, i.e. perception and the human mind, and perform complementary functions in giving a unitary representation of the physical and the ethical domain.

The distinction between realism and constructivism does not entail a sharp separation between real and fictitious elements in our mental image of the world. Bentham intimately connects fiction to reality, by deriving the import and the truth of the former from the latter. The dependence of the constructive, including volitional, on the perceptive abilities allows the human mind to create a linguistic ontology endowed with normativity. Bentham's empirical constructivism, in which his fictionalism consists, contributes to the shaping of the idea of cognitive and ethical self-determination, according to which individuals autonomously represent reality and decide how to behave.

4.2 The theory of action

Law and human behaviour

The intent of a general systematization of laws was pursued by Bentham throughout his life. The task of guiding human behaviour is the thread that ties the three theoretical cornerstones in which the project of codification was developed: first, the idea of a natural arrangement of laws, i.e. a systematization of legal elements consistent with the volitional nature of human beings;[88] second, the proposal to draft a *Pannomion*, "an all-comprehensive collection [. . .] of *rules*" expressing the will of the legislator of a community, "with whose will [. . .] all other members of that same community [. . .] are regarded as disposed to act in compliance";[89] and, third, the foundation of a new discipline, the *nomography*, i.e. the art of writing laws, "which is employed by a *superior*" with "the purpose of giving direction to the conduct of a corresponding inferior."[90]

88 Cf. *A Fragment on Government*, 415–16.

89 *Pannomial Fragments*, Bowring iii, 211.

90 *Nomography; or the Art of Inditing Laws*, Bowring iii, 233.

In underlining the novelty of his theoretical operation, Bentham explicitly relates the codification of law to the structure of human action. By aiming to influence people's conduct, a code of laws claims both to direct and motivate its subjects to act in accordance with it. The understanding of the machinery of practical rationality is not a subsidiary but a complementary commitment which, in Bentham's opinion, should accompany and, in a certain sense, orient legislative practice.

The study of practical reason is a constitutive part of codification, which cannot be conceived apart from it. Accurate knowledge of human action is the powerful instrument that Bentham wants to put in the hands of a legislator, who is setting up a legal order. In parallel to his efforts to theorize codification, Bentham is committed to the investigation of practical rationality.

The operation of codification steers Bentham towards two basic questions concerning obligation, which are in his view intimately connected. The first question pertains to normativity and consists in explaining how an obligation can bind the agent's will. The second question pertains to motivation and consists in explaining how an obligation can induce the agent's will to act in compliance with it. Answering these questions requires an exploration into the structure of practical rationality, in order to clarify the normative and the motivational features of the obligation deriving from a codified body of legal norms.

Bentham establishes a mutual relation between his project of codification and his examination of practical reason. Both are characterized by an underlying connection between obligation and motivation. Bentham lays at the basis of his codification proposal the idea of normative motivation, according to which something can be binding insofar as it prompts someone to behave in agreement with it. The shaping of this concept of normative motivation, that still requires elucidation, provides the theoretical framework for a new organization of legal elements and a particular treatment of action.

Despite its richness and complexity, Bentham's theory of practical reason and action is a much neglected topic in philosophical literature. To the best of my knowledge, only a few scholarly works tackle this issue and some of these are not recent, although there is now an increasing interest in it.[91] It is thus important to show the centrality of the principles of practical rationality to the project of codification; to this end, we need to outline Bentham's desire-based account of deliberation and to throw light on its underlying intimate relation between motives and duties.

From the beginning of his political reflections, as testified in the *Preface* to *A Fragment on Government*, Bentham embarks upon the task of a general

91 See for example Bozzo-Rey 2007, 349–66; 2012, 162–9 and 174–82 (here Bentham's treatment of practical reasoning is examined with reference to the idea of the legal panoptic paradigm); 2014, 338–57; Guidi 1987/8, 262–76; Hacker 1993; Samek Ludovici 2004, 41–58. The following studies, though more focused on motivation, may also be regarded as pertaining to the area of Bentham's philosophy of action: Dinwiddy 2004; Kelly 1990, 14–38; Leroy 2007; McReynolds 1993a; Pellegrino 2010, 69–138.

systematization of laws. In identifying the criteria that should underpin such a systematization, Bentham puts forward the idea of a "natural arrangement" of legal elements as an alternative to the "technical arrangement," championed by Blackstone. Bentham regards Blackstone's attempt to organize laws as "confused and unsatisfactory." A technical arrangement is unable to capture the character and the specificity of its components, which are human actions or more precisely – to use Bentham's words – "such actions as are the objects of what we call Laws or Institutions."[92]

An arrangement of laws that neglects the structure of human action is merely a technical or artificial exercise in speculation, which, even though "correct" and "elegant,"[93] fails to fulfil its function of guiding people's behaviour, by not giving adequate motives for abiding by the prescribed rules. Knowledge of the structure of human action, then, is not a collateral aspect in the organization of a system of law, but definitively contributes to its construction. In Bentham's view, the normativity of a legal order, that is, its binding feature, depends on the ability of that order to motivate its subjects to conform their behaviour to it. Without this ability, a system of law would lack effectiveness and would be doomed to failure, by not providing guidance.

According to Bentham, the property that should be held in view by the legislator in the arrangement of a corpus of norms is the tendency or divergence of an act from a common end, which is happiness. The utility of an act consists in its tendency to happiness, which it causes; on the other hand, the mischievousness of an act consists in its divergence from happiness.[94] This general practical principle should lead the legislator to point out the utility or the mischievousness of the action he/she intends to command or forbid.[95] Indeed, the tendency to happiness or, in other words, the utility of a type of conduct is the only property of the law which every human being seeks in deciding how to act.

By making the utility of a law explicit, a legislator can fulfil his/her subjects' primary need to pursue happiness or, more fundamentally, to attain pleasure and avoid pain. Hence, the naturalness of a legal arrangement displaying the utility of its norms does not consist in its reference to an alleged objective order of nature, which the legislator has to reproduce in a code, but relies on its correspondence to the structure of human action, teleologically oriented towards the pursuit of happiness.

By borrowing his own language, we might say that Bentham's examination of practical reason has both an expository and a censorial purpose: on the one hand, he aims to describe how deliberation works and how an agent acts; on the other,

92 Cf. *A Fragment on Government*, 415.

93 *A Fragment on Government*, 413.

94 *A Fragment on Government*, 415.

95 In *Preparatory Principles*, 403 (para. 1276), Bentham remarks: "I hope that nothing will be accepted, and therefore that nothing will be offer'd, under the name of a reason for a Law, but the indication of some utility, that is a tendency to procure some pleasure or avert some pain, as the result of it."

he intends to investigate how it is possible to intervene or interfere in the agent's decision-making process and thus influence it. The expository purpose, however, is subordinate to the censorial one: Bentham wants to enable the legislator to guide his/her subjects' behaviour by making it clear that obedience can be compelled by giving motives to their will. In practical reasoning the motivational aspect has priority over the binding aspect of an obligation, since the latter aspect depends on the former as regards its creation and force.

Bentham's commitment to the exploration of human action, while theorizing his codification proposal, also emerges from his actual attempts to draft a code, in which a particular concern for the motivational component of agency is evident. In *First Principles Preparatory to Constitutional Code*, Bentham conceives of "self-regarding interest," namely the general human tendency towards the realization of self-interest, as an axiom on which the work of codification should be grounded. Self-regarding interest is – in his words – one of the "first principles indicative of the foundation of this proposed constitutional code."[96] It may be specified as "the desire in man to feel himself happy," a desire or propensity that is predominant in human nature when planning and taking a course of action. As Bentham states, this desire should not necessarily be understood in selfish or solipsistic terms, because it also encompasses a social or sympathetic regard, consisting in "the desire to see others happy."[97]

The axiomatic character of the principles of practical reason in the context of codification is commented on in *Pannomial Fragments*, in which Bentham explicitly defines them as "a necessary ground for all legislative arrangements." More precisely, he suggests that one should understand "an axiom of mental pathology," namely a self-evident principle affecting the human mind, as "a proposition expressive of the consequences" resulting from the performance of an action "in respect of pleasure or pain."[98] As Bentham makes it clear in *Preparatory Principles*, the nature of an act, from a moral point of view, consists in its "pathological effects," that is, in the painful or pleasurable sensations which this act produces.[99] In this way Bentham underlines the relation between a course of action and the types of pleasure or pain to which it is conducive. This relation provides the general criterion on which all practical deliberation is based.

Motivational and normative elements of human behaviour, such as the tendency to happiness, the utility of an action, the desire to feel happy and self-regarding interest, contribute to the systematization of laws in a code. However, they remain vague and unintelligible until their grounds, which are the sensations of pleasure and pain, are uncovered. In a passage from *Traités de législation civile et pénale*, another text devoted to the drafting of a code, Bentham acknowledges the foundational role of pleasure and pain in practical reflection.

96 *First Principles Preparatory to Constitutional Code*, 229.
97 *First Principles Preparatory to Constitutional Code*, 14.
98 Cf. *Pannomial Fragments*, Bowring iii, 224.
99 Cf. *Preparatory Principles*, 402.

> The whole system of Morals, as well as Morals and any scheme of Legislation, rests upon this single foundation, the Knowledge of Pains and Pleasures. It is the groundwork of all clear ideas on these subjects. When we speak of vice or of virtue, of actions innocent or criminal, of a scheme of rewards and punishments, to what do we refer? Pains and Pleasures, and nothing else. Any reasoning in morals or legislation which cannot be translated into these simple terms, Pain and Pleasure, is obscure and sophistical reasoning, from which no conclusion can safely be drawn.[100]

Bentham intertwines the task of codification, consisting in a consistent and well-grounded arrangement of laws, with the examination of practical reason, namely of the individual capacity to think about how to behave, to balance alternative ways of conduct and to make a decision. If the codification of laws aims to be effective, that is, to direct and regulate human behaviour, it should affect and then modify individual judgment on what to do, by giving the agent reasons for action having a motivating force.

To this end, Bentham bases the work of codification on the same correlated principles which steer practical reasoning and behaviour: the seeking of pleasure and the avoidance of pain. A code of norms can guide the agent who is subject to it insofar as that code is able to lead him/her to the maximization of his/her pleasure and the minimization of his/her pain. In other words, a law, as a part of a codified system which claims to be normative, has to provide the agent with motivating reasons for acting.

The pursuit of pleasure and the aversion to pain underlie practical reason; by virtue of this, pleasure and pain are the foundations for the work of legislation and for the construction of morality. Any form of reasoning involving moral and legal content, such as virtue, vice, crime, reward, punishment and so on, should be traceable back to the elemental notions of pleasure and pain as regards its explanation. The explanatory character of pleasure and pain depends on their foundational character: pleasure and pain can give an account of law and morality because law and morality are grounded on them.

Practical reason

Bentham identifies the pillars of the practical domain with the feelings of pain and pleasure, regarded as the "productive instrument or cause" of action.[101] They are the sources both of motivation and normativity, as Bentham clarifies in the

100 *Bentham's Theory of Legislation being Principes de législation and Traités de législation civile et pénale*, 34–5.

101 *A Table of the Springs of Action*, 76. Pain and pleasure might be regarded as "moral causes." According to Bentham (*Preparatory Principles*, 365), "By a moral cause, when explained, is meant nothing more than some motive which, by it's [sic] influence on the will, gives movement to some or other of those animal organs, those *instruments*, the action of which, as masses of matter, comes back again into the class of physical causes."

first pages of *IPML*. On the one hand, the desire to enjoy pleasure or avert pain prompts an agent to behave with the purpose of fulfilling that desire.[102] On the other hand, the expectation of pain or pleasure creates deontological constraints, by pointing out what the agent ought to do in order to avoid that pain or achieve that pleasure. Motivation and obligation stem from the same empirical roots and thus are closely interrelated. The prospect of gaining pleasure or avoiding pain as a consequence of a kind of behaviour both impel and bind the agent's will to endorse and carry out that behaviour.

The fundamental tenets of practical rationality consist in attaining pleasure and averting pain. In deliberating how to behave, individuals are driven by the consideration of the utility of the action they intend to choose. That action is approved of inasmuch as it tends to the production of pleasure or to the avoidance of pain.[103] The conformity to the principle of utility makes that action binding: it is the necessary means to achieve a selected end. The dictates arising from utility, that is, from pleasure and pain, have a motivational force. The pursuit of pleasure and the aversion to pain are motives that generate in the agent a duty to carry out a specific kind of behaviour. So, pleasure and pain bestow a motivating and normative character upon an action. A type of conduct which aims to increase the happiness or reduce the uneasiness of an individual is right and good and, consequently, worth performing.

Bentham puts forward an account of practical reason which is pleasure-oriented or desire-based, with reference to the content, and which is calculative and predictive, with reference to the structure. Deliberation consists in balancing several courses of action in relation to sthe quantity of pleasure or pain their performance is expected to bring forth. The binding nature of an action depends on the desirability or undesirability of its expected pain or pleasure, the value of which is measurable in terms of intensity, duration, certainty, propinquity, fecundity, purity and extent.[104]

In Bentham's whole corpus we may acknowledge at least two separate treatments of practical reason and action, which, despite their basic similarity, are accounted for from two different points of view. The first treatment is contained in *IPML*, in particular in chapters i–xii, corresponding to the first half of the work. The second treatment is worked out in *A Table of the Springs of Action*, *Deontology* and certain passages of Bentham's writings on ontology, logic, language and grammar. These latter texts were written roughly between 1813 and 1815,[105] when Bentham's theory of real and fictitious entities was full-fledged, whereas the printing of *IPML* dates back to 1780 and then in 1789 when some bits were added, i.e. the "Preface" and a note.[106]

102 *IPML*, 11.
103 *IPML*, 12.
104 Cf. *IPML*, 39. See also *A Table of the Springs of Action*, 88–9.
105 For the dates of the draft and printing of *A Table of the Springs of Action* and *Deontology* see *Deontology together with A Table of the Springs of Action and Article on Utilitarianism*, xi–xii.
106 For the history of *IPML* see *IPML*, xxxvii–xxxix.

As we can see, a lapse of about twenty years divides these two treatments. According to Goldworth, the theory of human motivation and the theory of morals, which Bentham "did not present [. . .] in their final form" in *IPML*, were respectively "developed more fully" in *A Table of the Springs of Action* and "expounded further in" *Deontology*.[107] Goldworth suggests a continuity or, more precisely, a consistent evolution of Bentham's study of agency. There are not, indeed, particular theoretical contradictions between the two phases of Bentham's reflections on agency and yet their exposition is markedly different.

The examination of practical rationality in the first half of *IPML* is explicitly aimed at the construction of the theory of legislation. To this end, Bentham adopts the point of view of a legislator or a judge who bears in mind the structure of human practical thinking and action when enacting a law or deciding whether to inflict a punishment. As a consequence, both the ascertaining of the efficacy of a legal norm over a subject and the consideration of the individual responsibility in committing a crime contribute to Bentham's particular presentation of the elements making up the deliberation about what to do. The result is a quite long and complex causal chain of interconnected elements leading to the performance of behaviour.[108] Hence, in *IPML* the exploration of practical reasoning and action is instrumental in the purpose of legislation and adjudication.

In the second treatment of practical philosophy, Bentham's perspective noticeably changes. He does not investigate the structure of practical decision and action with the chief and explicit intent to provide a legislator and a judge with an instrument for guiding more effectively and soundly his/her legislative and judicial practice. Bentham adopts the point of view of the single agent reasoning about the action to perform and then performing it. So, his account of practical reason, belonging to this second phase, is more essential and simplified when compared with the account previously afforded in *IPML*. Certain elements, such as kinds of circumstances, i.e. aggravative or exculpative, or the types of intentionality producing an event, are no longer taken into consideration, because they are hardly influential or even uninfluential on the agent's decision on how to behave.

Practical judgment is reduced to its core elements of desire and belief, on the one hand, and means and end, on the other; they are plainly referred to the faculties of the understanding and the will, whose harmonious cooperation is decisive in the choice and production of an action. Bentham's theory of practical reason is no longer explicitly subservient to the reform of legislation, but receives an independent treatment, which makes it more similar to the traditional desire-based accounts, such as that provided by Hume.

107 *Deontology together with A Table of the Springs of Action and Article on Utilitarianism*, xi.

108 Generally speaking, Bentham (*Preparatory Principles*, 61) defines the cause-effect relation as follows: "That motion, without which some other thing, it is supposed, could not be, is stiled *a cause*: that motion which, without a cause, it is supposed, could not be, is stiled an *effect*." In addition, Bentham (*Preparatory Principles*, 314) remarks that "The relation of cause and effect is within the department of every thing that bears the name of science."

Notwithstanding their expositive difference, due to the point of view chosen, that is, a third-person point of view, corresponding to the legislator or the judge, and a first-person point of view, corresponding to the agent, the two treatments of practical reason and action are based on the same conceptual model, whose distinctive feature is the intimate relation between duty and interest.

The investigation of practical thinking and action carried out in *IPML* might be integrated with certain passages in *Preparatory Principles*. As Long and Schofield, the editors of this text, make clear, *Preparatory Principles* is "a storehouse of ideas," "a mine of raw materials – working documents on which Bentham drew when executing a series of writing projects."[109] Bentham could have regarded "the 'Preparatory Principles' material as a possible starting point for a whole range of works and projects, given the foundational character of much of its content."[110]

No page of *Preparatory Principles* is dated and yet "It seems quite likely [. . .] that the bulk of [the text] was written in and around 1775."[111] The ideas expressed in *Preparatory Principles* are closely related to the content of *IPML* as well as *A Comment on the Commentaries*, *A Fragment on Government*, and *Of the Limits of the Penal Branch of Jurisprudence*, although they "had a profound and enduring value for Bentham's work not only in the 1770s and 1780s."[112] Therefore, the examination of *Preparatory Principles* might help us to reconstruct Bentham's theory of practical reason, because it lays out the tenets of deliberation, which are subsequently expounded in *IPML* in relation to the topic of legislation.[113]

Certain writings of *Preparatory Principles* supply a survey of Bentham's means-end and desire-belief approach in its embryonic stages. Unlike *IPML*, Bentham's remarks on action found in *Preparatory Principles* are directly focused on the pivotal elements of human agency. So, *Preparatory Principles* outlines the theoretical framework for the long treatment of action in *IPML* in which Bentham makes the model sketched out in *Preparatory Principles* suitable to the general reform of legislation.

In the first half of *IPML* Bentham puts forward a sophisticated, detailed and complex theory of action. He identifies and examines the elements which intervene in the formulation of a judgement and are causally connected with the performance of behaviour. Bentham himself provides an overview of the factors which contribute to the construction of a course of action: (1) "the *act* itself, which is

109 *Preparatory Principles*, xi. For an overview of the structure and the contents of *Preparatory Principles* see xi–xxxiv.

110 *Preparatory Principles*, xv.

111 *Preparatory Principles*, xii.

112 Cf. *Preparatory Principles*, xi–xii.

113 *Preparatory Principles*, xvi: "The first six chapters of *An Introduction to the Principles of Morals and Legislation* deal with the principle of utility and its basis in human psychology, reflecting themes addressed in 'Preparatory Principles: Inserenda.' In the seventh chapter of *An Introduction to the Principles of Morals and Legislation*, Bentham deals with aspects of human action, again reflecting themes addressed in 'Preparatory Principles: Inserenda.'" Finally, on p. xvii: "Such connections, of which these are a sample, reflect the fact that [. . .] *An Introduction to the Principles of Morals and Legislation* [. . .] drew on the ideas that had been outlined in the 'Preparatory Principles' material."

done"; (2) "the *circumstances* in which it is done"; (3) "the *intentionality* that may have accompanied it"; (4) "the *consciousness*, unconsciousness, or false consciousness, that may have accompanied it"; (5) "the particular *motive* or motives which gave birth to it"; and (6) "the general *disposition* which it indicates."[114] These elements bring about the consequences or tendency of an act. Inasmuch as the consequences of an act are the concrete outcome of the reflective practical process, they are taken into consideration in the whole planning of conduct.

Bentham outlines a teleological model of action, exemplified by the metaphor of a chain, the links of which are reciprocally related according to a form of practical causality,[115] which has a normative and a motivational value. The above-quoted list is completed in the course of the treatment of the elements intervening in the construction of action in *IPML*.

The understanding and the will

Before examining the ingredients of practical reasoning, it is worth clarifying the faculties operating in it. They are basically the understanding and the will, which correspond to two distinct activities of the mind. The understanding is the faculty of perceiving and thinking: its states or acts are beliefs, consisting in experience-data, sensations, cognitions, suppositions and judgements; they concern the world in which the agent lives and operates. In this sense, the understanding also includes the faculty of sensibility, which sometimes is explicitly distinguished from it by Bentham.

The will or volitional faculty, whose states or acts are desires, motives, appetites, interests and intentions, is the ability to choose a course of action and to act in accordance with it. It is no coincidence that Bentham considers these states of the will as "springs of action."[116] In his works devoted to the exploration of practical reflection, Bentham's main concern is directed toward the clarification of volition, which, even though it "is not to be defined" because of its simplicity, is well known to all of us.[117] Bentham acknowledges the causative function of the will or, more precisely, of its states in the construction and performance of an action. No doubt, he claims the primacy of volition over the understanding in deliberation.

> The object of VOLITION is always some EVENT. We understand tolerably well what an EVENT means. Such a motion, or assemblage of motions, as we take notice of, among things that we take notice of, or the stoppage of such motion or motions, we stile an EVENT. [. . .]

114 *IPML*, 75.

115 Bentham (*De l'ontologie*, 146; Bowring viii, 209) compares the mechanistic explanation of moral causality to the mechanistic explanation of physical causality: "Thus superior is the density of the clouds which overhang the relation between cause and effect in the field of morals as compared with the field of physics."

116 See, for example, *Nomography; or the Art of Inditing Laws*, Bowring iii, 290.

117 *Preparatory Principles*, 443.

> An *event* may be said to be an *object* of our will: our will to be ***directed to*** that event, when *we will*, or, in other words, *when our will is*, that that event should happen.
>
> An EVENT, in the production of which a being capable of volition is instrumental, we stile an ACTION.[118]

In the "Preface" of *IPML* Bentham contrasts the faculty of the will with the faculty of understanding as regards their logical structure. He complains that, in the history of thought from Aristotle, *the logic of the will* has usually been underestimated and neglected to the advantage of *the logic of the understanding*, towards which a great deal of attention has been directed.[119] In the light of this alleged misjudgement, Bentham intends not merely to reappraise the faculty of the will and the knowledge of its machinery, but also to establish the primacy of the will over the understanding, along with their close relation. So, Bentham is committed to deepening the logic of the will, by claiming to be the first to give an account of such a still unexplored field of knowledge.[120]

> Yet so far as a difference can be assigned between branches so intimately connected, whatever difference there is, in point of importance, is in favour of the logic of the will. Since it is only by their capacity of directing the operations of this faculty, that the operations of the understanding are of any consequence.[121]

Bentham attributes to the faculty of the understanding the capacity to steer the will in the decision-making activity. The understanding provides the will with certain beliefs about the context in which a plan of action will be taking place and about the consequences that that action is expected to bring about. The awareness of these beliefs allows the will to make a choice.

The will plays a decisive role in practical reflection by endorsing and implementing a decision concerning what to do. Its primacy "in point of importance"

118 *Preparatory Principles*, 443. An almost identical text is contained on p. 429.

119 For a definition of the logic of the will see Bozzo-Rey 2012, 167: "Contrary to the logic of Aristotle, the logic of the will does not confine itself to the study of sentences understood as affirmative assertions, but seeks to understand logical relations between expressions of will. Expressions of will – that is, laws – will be the new objects of this logic." When clarifying Bentham's logic of the will, Bozzo-Rey makes reference and comments on the following passage from an *IPML*, 299 n. b2: "The subject we are now entering upon belongs to a particular branch of logic, untouched by Aristotle. The main and ultimate business of the school-logic of which that philosopher was the father, is to exhibit the several forms of *argumentation*: the business of the branch now before us is to exhibit the several forms of *imperation*: or (to take the subject in its utmost extent) of sentences expressive of volition: a leaf which seems to be yet wanting in the book of science." Bentham devotes the long note b2, 299–300, to outlining the logic of the will and its distinction from the logic of the understanding.

120 *IPML*, 8. For an overview on the logic of the will and its relation with deontic logic see Bozzo-Rey 2007, 259–88.

121 *IPML*, 8.

consists in its ability to determine the agent to perform a certain action. So, Bentham works out a map of practical reason in which the intellectual section and the volitional section are joined by mutual dependence and complementarity.

Exciting or moderating cause

At the beginning of the deliberative process Bentham places an "exciting cause," which identifies whatever arouses in the agent a feeling of pleasure or pain and impels him/her to act. This cause can also be moderating when it impels the agent to refrain from acting.[122] The perception of a thing as pleasurable or painful depends on the agent, that is, more precisely, on the subjective constitution of his/her sensibility. As circumstances influencing the agent's receptive faculty and thus determining his/her perception of an exciting cause, Bentham mentions physical conditions (health, strength, hardiness and bodily imperfections), mental conditions (the quantity or quality of knowledge, the strength of intellectual powers, the firmness of mind and steadiness), bent of inclination, moral sensibility, moral biases, religious sensibility, religious biases, sympathetic or antipathetic sensibility, sympathetic or antipathetic biases, pecuniary circumstances, education and so forth.[123] For example, an ill man will be "less sensible to the influence of any pleasurable cause" and more sensible to any painful cause than a healthy man.[124] In this way, Bentham aims to provide a "moral physiology,"[125] that is, a study of the physiological bases of morality.

Act

Bentham does not give a definition of *act*, but identifies a series of its specifications, some of them showing further subdivisions. The chief distinctions made by Bentham are the following:

- positive or negative acts, which are characterized, the former, by movement and, the latter, by abstention from movement;[126]
- external or internal acts, pertaining to the physical sphere or the mental sphere;[127]
- transitive or intransitive external acts, if their effects concern a person different from the agent or simply the agent himself/herself;
- transient or continued acts, on the basis of their duration;[128]

122 Cf. *IPML*, 51–2, along with the related notes a and c.
123 Cf. *IPML*, 52.
124 Cf. *IPML*, 53. Bentham deals with the circumstances influencing sensibility in *IPML*, 51–73.
125 *IPML*, 53 n. c.
126 Negative acts are further divided in absolute and relative, according to the extent of the abstention from movement, namely if it regards every movement or only some of them.
127 An instance of mixed external and internal acts is the "acts of *discourse*."
128 Bentham specifies the difference between a continued act and a repetition of acts on the basis of the absence or presence of intervals. Moreover, Bentham also distinguishes between a repetition of acts and a habit or practice according to the length of the intervals and the time of the performance of these acts.

- indivisible or divisible acts, with regard to matter and motion (though indivisible acts, involving the notion of atom, are purely imaginary);
- simple or complex acts, consisting in a single act or in a multitude of simple acts.[129]

It seems clear from all these specifications that with the word *act*, Bentham generally points out movement, also including its negative form, i.e. abstention from movement. Bentham seems to suppose a distinction between act and action here, even though he does not explicitly provide a definition of them. Instead, in *Preparatory Principles* Bentham clarifies that the words action and act "are used in two very different senses, the one an extensive sense, the other a confined one": by act, namely "simple act," he means "nothing more than a mode of motion"; by action, namely "complex action," he denotes "a simple act consider'd as it is, complicated with an indefinite variety of circumstances: i:e: with all those circumstances upon the presence or absence of which depends the influence the act has on the happiness of the agent and the rest of the community."[130] Finally, again in *Preparatory Principles* Bentham distinguishes between an action and a course of action, by defining the latter as "The aggregate assemblage of as many actions as are performed in subserviency to one and the same end."[131]

Circumstances

By circumstances Bentham means certain considerations or situations which accompany the planning and the performance of an act. Moreover, circumstances establish the goodness or badness of an action. They allow us to ascertain the consequences of an act and thus to assess that act as beneficial, indifferent or mischievous. Circumstances are decisive in evaluating what has been done and what will be done. According to Bentham, anything can be a circumstance to the extent that it contributes to the construction of an action.[132]

As in the case of consequences, even the circumstances of an act can be divided into material and immaterial. Generally speaking, the notion of materiality

129 The notion of act is analysed by Bentham in *IPML*, 75–9.

130 Cf. *Preparatory Principles*, para. 511. Philosophers usually tend to distinguish between the notions of action and act. Korsgaard, for example, underlines the inclusive meaning of the word action, which encompasses the notion of act as one of its constitutive elements. In her opinion, an action "involves both an act and an end, an act done for the sake of an end." She exemplifies this definition, by saying that "making a false promise and committing suicide are [. . .] 'acts,'" whereas "making a false promise in order to get some ready cash" and "committing suicide in order to avoid the personal troubles that you see ahead" or "to avoid harming others are 'actions.'" (Cf. Korsgaard 2008, 219). See also Bentham's definition of "a course of action" in *Preparatory Principles*, para. 1252: "The aggregate assemblage of as many actions as are performed in subserviency to one and the same *end*, such an assemblage, consider'd as a whole, may be termed a *course of action*."

131 *Preparatory Principles*, 395.

132 Bentham outlines certain kinds of circumstances (physical and moral circumstances; circumstances of time and place) and their influence on acts in *Preparatory Principles*, paras. 512–13, 923–36, 950.

involves a relation: a material consequence has a relation with pleasure and pain; a material circumstance has a relation with the consequences. Therefore, the materiality of circumstances consists in "a visible relation in point of causality to the consequences."[133]

Bentham explores the causal connection between circumstances and consequences, namely events produced by the agent. He identifies four kinds of relations which a circumstance can have with an event or consequence. A circumstance is related to an event "in the way of causation or production," when the circumstance actively contributes to the production of the event; "in the way of derivation," when the event, produced by the circumstance, produces another event; "in the way of collateral condition," when the circumstance and the event are connected not directly but by means of an object from which they both are produced; "in the way of conjunct influence," when, in whatever way related, they both concur in the production of a common consequence.[134]

In the production of an event there intervene "an indefinite multitude of circumstances,"[135] which are not easy to identify especially because of the remoteness, and thus the obscurity, of some of them. So, "only a very small number [of circumstances] can be discovered by the utmost exertion of the human faculties."[136]

The consideration of circumstances is crucial in the evaluation of an event, especially if it is a crime. In this case, circumstances are qualified as "criminative," since they concur in the commission of a crime. Furthermore, other kinds of additional circumstances interact with the criminative: they are called "exculpative or extenuative," if beneficial, and "aggravative," if mischievous.[137]

A fuller list of the circumstances characterizing an action is provided in *Rationale of Judicial Evidence*, in which Bentham distinguishes between facts having "an inculpative or say criminative tendency" and "an aggravative tendency" and facts having "an exculpative or say justificative tendency," "an exemptive tendency" and "an extenuative tendency." These facts, along with their tendency, "become the subject-matter of regulation to the legislator, and thence of decision and inquiry to the judge." They are, indeed, the evidentiary or principal facts taken into account by the legislator or the judge in the calculation of the quantity of punishment corresponding to a certain crime. The tendency of a fact is established on the basis of two main groups of circumstances: first, the inculpative or criminative and the aggravative circumstances, whose presence is proved through evidence provided by the plaintiff; second, the exculpative or justificative, the exemptive and extenuative circumstances, whose presence is adduced through evidence provided by the defendant.[138]

133 *IPML*, 80.
134 Cf. *IPML*, 80.
135 *IPML*, 81.
136 *IPML*, 82.
137 The examination of the notion of *circumstance* is made by Bentham in *IPML*, 79–82.
138 *Rationale of Judicial Evidence*, Bowring vi, 215.

In *Of the Limits of the Penal Branch of Jurisprudence* Bentham provides a further clarification of the circumstances, that, in general terms, "as mentioned in a law," are defined not as "acts which the legislator wills should be performed or not performed, motions or situations which he wills should take place or not take place in consequence," but rather as "objects the names of which are made use of for the purpose of specifying and characterizing those acts, motions and situations."[139] Therefore, law regards circumstances as "specificant" when they are "specificative or characteristic of the act."[140] More particularly, "The chief use of a circumstance as annexed to the name of an act is to specificate it, that is to distinguish it from acts which in other respects are of the same name."[141] Circumstances not having this effect are distinguished as "unspecificant."[142] Finally, Bentham identifies "exculpative," "justificatory" or "de-obligative" circumstances"[143] and opposes "inculpative" – and sometimes "criminative or criminalizating" – to "exculpative" circumstances[144] and "investitive" to "divestitive" circumstances.[145]

Bentham's previous classification of circumstances fits a legal context. The consideration of circumstances, however, is also fundamental when an agent is deliberating how to behave, as Bentham makes clear in the following lines.

> No effect of this class can, it is believed, be assigned that is not the result of a multitude of influencing circumstances: circumstances, some always in different ways contributing to the production of it, others frequently operating in opposition to it: contributing to it, viz. in the character of promoting and co-operating *causes*; others operating in the opposite character of *obstacles*.[146]

Bentham characterizes circumstances in a slightly different ways when he is dealing with the practical context from the agent's point of view. In his texts on ontology, logic, language and grammar he distinguishes between "influential" and "uninfluential" circumstances; influential circumstances, then, are divided into "promotive" or "obstructive."[147]

Motives[148]

A motive basically consists in a desire for a kind of pleasure or in an aversion to a kind of pain. It prompts the will to act or refrain from acting. Thus, a motive

139 *Of the Limits of the Penal Branch of Jurisprudence*, 66.
140 *Of the Limits of the Penal Branch of Jurisprudence*, 67.
141 *Of the Limits of the Penal Branch of Jurisprudence*, 243.
142 *Of the Limits of the Penal Branch of Jurisprudence*, 243.
143 *Of the Limits of the Penal Branch of Jurisprudence*, 131–2.
144 *Of the Limits of the Penal Branch of Jurisprudence*, 132–3.
145 *Of the Limits of the Penal Branch of Jurisprudence*, 134 n. a.
146 *De l'ontologie*, 140 (Bowring viii, 208).
147 Cf. *De l'ontologie*, 140–2 (Bowring viii, 209); *Essay on Logic*, UC 101.391, editor's note 5 (Bowring viii, 277).
148 I place Bentham's treatment of motive before his treatment of intentionality, because, as he makes it clear, "the causes of intentions are motives" (*IPML*, 134). See also *IPML*, 89.

is the cause of the effects to which the performance of that act or the abstention from it gives birth. In the first pages of chapter x of *IPML* Bentham provides at least three definitions of the notion of motive, which show an increasing level of complexity. The first definition is very general and stresses the dynamic function of a motive in the constitution of a course of action.

> By a motive, in the most extensive sense in which the word is ever used with reference to a thinking being, is meant any thing that can contribute to give birth to, or even to prevent, any kind of action.[149]

A motive is characterized by Bentham as the starting point of a bodily movement or a conscious state of rest. As Bentham observes, the word *inducement* could appear to be "more comprehensive" and in certain contexts "more apposite" than the word *motive*, by including a positive and negative, i.e. active and passive, meaning.[150] However, in his treatment of action Bentham prefers to use the notion of motive, probably because it is more common in the philosophical vocabulary of his time.

Bentham is concerned with *practical motives*, i.e. "motives applying to practice,"[151] which stand out from *speculative motives*, i.e. "motives resting in speculation."[152] The latter remain "in the understanding merely" and exert no "influence in the production of any acts of the will."[153] Speculative motives do not directly affect the agent's will and therefore do not bring forth material consequences. Consequences "can be said to be material" when they "consist of pain or pleasure, or have an influence in the production of pain or pleasure."[154]

The prospect of enjoying pleasure and averting pain, as a consequence of the performance of a type of behaviour, motivates the agent to perform that type of behaviour. Pleasure and pain underpin the planning and execution of a course of action: at the beginning they have an expected form which impels the agent to make a practical decision; at the end they have an actual form, whose production or avoidance depends on the agent's conduct. Only practical motives have a direct influence on agency: they can affect the will because of their close relation with pain and pleasure.

Motives having an intellectual origin may be taken into account in deliberation concerning action if they have a practical bearing, that is, if they exert an influence, though indirect, on the will.[155] In *A Table of the Springs of Action* Bentham contrasts "motives to the *will*" and "motives to the *understanding*." The former correspond to desires "operating in the character of a motive," the

149 *IPML*, 96.
150 Cf. *IPML*, 96 n. a.
151 *IPML*, 97.
152 *IPML*, 96.
153 *IPML*, 96.
154 *IPML*, 74.
155 *IPML*, 99.

latter are considerations "the apparent tendency of which is to give increase to the efficiency of the desire, in the character of a motive to the *will.*" In this respect intellectual motives producing volitional states may be generally regarded as practical: "Motives to the *understanding* operate as such in every case on the *will*: else they would not be *motives.*"[156]

Bentham specifies the practical nature of motives, when articulating a second definition of them in *IPML*.

> The motives with which alone we have any concern, are such as are of a nature to act upon the will. By a motive then, in this sense of the word, is to be understood any thing whatsoever, which, by influencing the will of a sensitive being, is supposed to serve as a means of determining him to act, or voluntarily to forbear to act, upon any occasion.[157]

The practical nature of motives consists in their ability to act upon the will, that is, to influence the agent's will, by determining him/her to act or to refrain him/her from acting.

Bentham makes it clear that in the context of the theory of action the word *motive* might seem "improper" because, according to "the popular usage," it refers to whatever "disposes an object to *move.*" The notion of motive is conceptually connected to the notion of motion: it cannot encompass the idea of abstention from acting, which indeed is opposite to it. This linguistic gap might be filled by adopting the word *determinative*, which however is less usual than motive.[158] Despite this difficulty, Bentham shows again his preference for the term *motive*, arguing that "even forbearance to act, or the negation of [. . .] bodily motion [. . .] supposes an act done when such forbearance is voluntary. It supposes, to wit, an act of the will."[159] The will is thus always actively involved in any practical choice involving movement or abstention from it.

In the third definition of motive Bentham clarifies its intimate connection with the consequences deriving from the performance of an action. These consequences consist in a type of pleasure or pain.

156 *A Table of the Springs of Action*, 92–3.

157 *IPML*, 96–7. Bentham concludes by saying that "Motives of this sort, in contradistinction to the former, may be styled *practical* motives, or motives applying to practice."

158 As Bentham writes in *Preparatory Principles*, 430, para 7.5: "A determinative is a neutral expression, that might be employ'd to signify indifferently a motive or restrictive." However, as he specifies in a note (7.6) related to para. 7.5, "We must submit to usage: the term forbearance is not very common: the terms restrictive and determinative still less so: ‹an› action is commonly used in the sense of a forbearance: a motive in that of a restrictive. To that usage, therefore, it may be often better to submit, rather than, by departing from it, give an air of uncouthness to the discourse. But it may still be convenient to have established these words with an import belonging to them that may be appealed to upon occasion, to clear away any ambiguity that may arise." See also *Preparatory Principles*, 445.

159 Cf. *IPML*, 97 n. b.

> Motive refers necessarily to action. It is a pleasure, pain, or other event, that prompts to action. Motive then, in one sense of the word, must be previous to such event. But, for a man to be governed by any motive, he must in every case look beyond that event which is called his action; he must look to the consequences of it: and it is only in this way that the idea of pleasure, of pain, or of any other event, can give birth to it. He must look, therefore, in every case, to some event posterior to the act in contemplation: an event which as yet exists not, but stands only in prospect.[160]

A motive operates as a stimulus on the agent in order to induce him/her to plan and carry out a kind of behaviour. A motive is connected to an action by means of the will, which, on the one hand, is exhorted to act by that motive and, on the other, turns that motive into a decision concerning action. The agent's decision to be directed or, as Bentham says, governed by a specific motive depends on his/her evaluation of the consequences ensuing from the performance of the action which is caused by that motive. The consideration of the pleasure and pain which a form of conduct can bring forth provides the agent with a motive for adopting that form of conduct. So, a motive consists essentially in the expectation of pleasure and avoidance of pain. That expectation, felt by his/her individual sensibility, exhorts the agent to act; he/she has a reason to act in view of achieving some pleasure or securing himself/herself against pain.[161]

Bentham supplies a series of specifications of the notion of motive, distinguishing between a "literal or unfigurative sense," when a motive corresponds to the real event from which an act derives, and a "figurative sense," when a motive corresponds to a fictitious entity, such as "a passion, an affection of the mind, an ideal being," which operates upon the agent by influencing and prompting him/her to undertake a course of action. Unfigurative motives can in turn be separated into interior, consisting in a perception of pleasure and pain, and exterior, consisting in an event whose occurrence gives rise to that perception.[162]

Bentham makes a distinction between "motives in prospect" and "motives in *esse*" according to the temporality of the object or event, namely if it is future or present, to which they are related. A motive in prospect is linked to "the posterior possible object which is [. . .] looked forward to." A motive in *esse* refers to "the present existing object or event." However, motives in prospect and motives in *esse* are so closely connected that it is difficult, and often unnecessary, to separate them. Finally, motives can be more or less immediate and remote by virtue of the time in which the events related to them happen.[163]

Motives are morally neutral in themselves. They can be qualified as good or bad on the basis of the consequences that the act caused by them brings about.

160 *IPML*, 98.

161 See *A Table of the Springs of Action*, 87: "'Psychological dynamics' (by this name may be called the science, which has for its *subject* these same *springs of action*, considered as such) has for its basis psychological *pathology*."

162 Cf. *IPML*, 97–8.

163 Cf. *IPML*, 98–9.

When that act tends to produce or augment pleasure and to avert or diminish pain, the related motives are good; when that act tends to produce or augment pain and to avert or diminish pleasure, the related motives are bad. The moral evaluation of something, including motives, takes into account the relation that that thing has with pleasure and pain. This is the general criterion which, when applied to motives, enables us to decide whether a motive is good or bad.[164]

Bentham provides a classification of motives: social or sympathetic motives, which are in turn distinguished into the purely social, such as good will, and semi-social, such as the love of reputation, the desire for amity and the motives of religion; dissocial or antipathetic motives, such as the motives of displeasure, i.e. the pleasure or pain of antipathy and resentment; self-regarding motives, such as physical desire, pecuniary interest, love of power and self-preservation.[165]

Intentionality

Bentham qualifies intentionality as a kind of circumstance and intimately connects it with the human will, so that what is intentional is voluntary and what is unintentional is involuntary. While identifying both intentionality and the will as a determination to do something, Bentham casts some doubts on the semantic value of the expressions "voluntary" and "involuntary," which, according to him, show extreme ambiguity.

He singles out at least three common usages of the expression "voluntarily act," pointing out that only one of them is synonymous with "intentional," that is, when it denotes an act in the performance of which the will is somehow involved. In a second sense, this expression signifies an act in the production of which the will has been prompted by motives not having a painful nature; therefore, it is equivalent to "unconstrained" or "uncoerced." In a third sense, voluntary means "spontaneous" and refers to an act caused by a motive occurring to the agent himself/herself and is not suggested by anybody else. Lastly, Bentham notes that "involuntary" is not the corresponding antonym of "voluntary": it is adopted as the opposite of "intentional" and "unconstrained," but not of "spontaneous."[166]

Because of the variety of the usages of the word "voluntary" and in order to escape its ambiguity, Bentham prefers to make use of the notion of "intentional" in his theory of action, by virtue of its unequivocalness. Consequently, the usage of the words "voluntary" and "involuntary" is allowed only when narrowing the meaning of these words.

Bentham analyses the six different kinds of the relation between intention, on the one hand, and the act and its consequences, on the other. First, a consequence can be intentional; second, a consequence can be directly and lineally

164 See, for example, *IPML*, 100, 114 and 116.
165 Cf. *IPML*, 103–22, part. 116; Dinwiddy 2004, 143.
166 Cf. *IPML*, 84 n. a.

or obliquely and collaterally intentional; third, a consequence can be ultimately or mediately directly intentional; fourth, an event can be exclusively or inexclusively directly intentional; fifth, an event can be conjunctively, disjunctively or indiscriminately inexclusively intentional; sixth, two events can be disjunctively intentional with and without preference.[167]

For the sake of clarity, Bentham, by means of an example, explains and also expands the different types of intentionality referring to the consequences or effects of a course of action. During a stag hunt, William II, king of England, was wounded by Tyrrel and then died. Bentham analyses the forms of intentionality that could have accompanied Tyrrel's performance of his action.

1 *Unintentionality.* Tyrrel did not take into account the possibility of the king's death or regarded such an event as out of consideration;
2 *Oblique, i.e. indirect, intentionality.* Tyrrel shot to kill the stag that was running in the same direction and at the same time as the king. Tyrrel was aware of the possibility of killing the king instead of the stag, though this was not his purpose. The consequence of his action was thus supposed, although not wished.
3 *Direct and ultimate intentionality.* Tyrrel killed the king because of the hate he bore him and thus because of the pleasure of putting him to death. The king's death was the purpose of Tyrrel's action.
4 *Direct, not ultimate but mediate intentionality.* Tyrrel killed the king in order to rob him when dead. The king's death was the means to carry out that robbery and is the end of the action performed by Tyrrel.
5 *Exclusive and direct intentionality.* Tyrrel wanted to kill the king and, when doing so, he had no other purpose or desire. Thus his intention was exclusively directed toward the carrying out of that event.

Bentham modifies his example now: the outcome of Tyrrel's action was the wounding of the king's right leg. In this way, he illustrates the kinds of intentionality which guided Tyrrel's action in relation to the production of that consequence.

6 *Conjunctive intentionality.* Tyrrel wanted to shoot the king's hand and, through it, his right leg, but he failed in this purpose. The wounding of the king's right leg and the wounding of the king's hand were two ends conjunctively pursued, even though the latter was not achieved.
7 *Disjunctively concurrent intentionality with preference.* Tyrrel wanted to wound the king either in his hand or especially in his leg, but not in both.
8 *Not exclusive, disjunctive intentionality without preference.* Tyrrel wanted to wound the king indifferently either in his hand or in his leg, but not in both.
9 *Indiscriminately concurrent intentionality.* Tyrrel wanted to wound the king either in his leg or in his hand or in both, without any preference, as it might occur.

167 *IPML*, 85–7.

Consciousness, disposition and consequences

Generally speaking, consciousness is a state of the understanding consisting in the awareness of the circumstances attending an act and influencing its consequences.[168] When planning or performing an act from which some consequences result, an agent can have consciousness, unconsciousness or false consciousness of that act and its consequences. Consciousness consists in the agent's belief in the subsistence of certain circumstances, which actually subsist; unconsciousness depends on the agent's failure to consider or anticipate certain circumstances, which instead subsist or will occur; false consciousness consists in the agent's false belief in the subsistence of certain circumstances, which do not actually subsist.[169]

With reference to his example about the king William II's death at the hands of Tyrrel, Bentham states that "Perhaps [Tyrrel] did not positively wish it; but for all that, in a certain sense he intended it." When shooting the arrow, Tyrrel was aware of certain circumstances dangerous for the king's life: "the direction in which the king was riding up," the direction of his arrow and the probability to shoot the king in a vital point. Tyrrel's performance of the act of shooting his arrow makes his killing of William II intentional, notwithstanding the main end of his action should have been to hunt a stag. Although the consequence of the king's death is "obliquely intentional," it is still "intentional."[170]

After the examination of consciousness Bentham defines a disposition: it is an agent's state of mind when he/she is prompted, by a certain motive, to perform an action having a certain tendency.[171] At the end of the chain structuring an action there are the consequences, which characterize the tendency of an act. A consequence is "the concluding link in all this chain of causes and effects, involving in it the materiality of the whole."[172] Indeed, they correspond to the material effects of an act.

An example of practical reasoning

Let us try to reconstruct and exemplify Bentham's model of practical rationality as set forth in *IPML* from the perspective of the agent who is thinking about what to do and not from the perspective of a judge or a legislator who is evaluating conduct with a view to punishment.[173] The causal chain outlined by

168 *IPML*, 90: "So far with regard to the ways in which the will or intention may be concerned in the production of any incident: we come now to consider the part which the understanding or perceptive faculty may have borne, with relation to such incident."

169 Cf. *IPML*, 75.

170 This example is given by Bentham in *IPML*, 92, from which the quotations in this text are taken.

171 Cf. *IPML*, 125: "Now disposition is a kind of fictitious entity, feigned for the convenience of discourse, in order to express what there is supposed to be *permanent* in a man's frame of mind, where, on such or such an occasion, he has been influenced by such or such a motive, to engage in an act, which, as it appeared to him, was of such or such a tendency."

172 *IPML*, 143.

173 The example examined here is taken from *IPML*, 97–100. Bentham provides and comments on an example of legal reasoning in *Preparatory Principles*, 326–8.

Bentham can, by and large, be divided into three distinct but strictly interrelated phases, i.e. receptive, reflective and active, which basically articulate the scope of practical reasoning.

The first, or receptive, phase (which may also be called sensory or passive) starts with the agent's perception of an event, as in the case of the sight of a fire breaking out in his/her neighbour's house. This event, which is termed the "exciting" or "moderating" cause, provokes in the agent the expectation of a pleasurable or painful sensation, such as the uneasiness "at the thought of being burnt" if the fire spreads to his/her house. In this sense, pain and pleasure are "interesting perceptions,"[174] that is, perceptions that arouse the agent's interest, i.e. his/her motivation, and then impel him/her to act or refrain him/her from acting.[175]

Pain and pleasure reveal a double nature: on the one hand, they are objective springs of action for all humankind; on the other, they are subjective feelings whose experience depends on the single agent's sensibility, namely on his/her disposition to be affected by them. An external incident does not arouse the same quantity of pleasure or pain in every agent who perceives it. The subjective constitution of human sensibility is influenced, and thus individualized, by circumstances such as physical and mental conditions, moral and religious education and attitude, sympathetic biases, and so forth.[176] Hence, in Bentham's approach, the universal pursuit of happiness is joined to the individual's receptiveness to pain and pleasure.

In the second, reflective or deliberative, phase the agent is urged by a series of connected motives, beginning from the recognition of an actual state of affairs and ending in the anticipated perception of pain or pleasure in relation to the occurrence of an expected event. With reference to the example in question, Bentham provides a full list of the motives prompting the agent to act in the same direction, i.e. to run out of his/her own house. He distinguishes such motives by means of the conceptual categories previously introduced and orders them according to relations of antecedence and consequence, in conformity with their proximity to the act. Let us outline Bentham's chain of motives as it follows:

- external motive in *esse*: "The event of the fire's breaking out in your neighbour's house";
- internal motive in *esse*: "the idea or belief of the probability of the fire's extending to your own house";
- internal motive in *esse*: "[the idea or belief of the probability] of your being burnt if you continue" staying in your house;
- internal motive in *esse*: "the pain you feel at the thought of such a catastrophe";
- external motive in prospect: "the event of the fire's actually extending to your own house";

174 *IPML*, 42.
175 *IPML*, 52 n. c.
176 *IPML*, 52.

- external motive in prospect: "[the event] of your being actually burnt by [the fire]";
- internal motive in prospect: "the pain you would feel at seeing your house a burning";
- internal motive in prospect: "the pain you would feel while you yourself were burning."[177]

The above-mentioned motives are causally connected to the same act, to the performance of which, however, they contribute in different ways, according to their distance, i.e. their proximity or remoteness, to that act.

> Of all these motives, which stand nearest to the act, to the production of which they all contribute, is that internal motive in *esse* which consists in the expectation of the internal motive in prospect: the pain or uneasiness you feel at the thoughts of being burnt.[178]

Bentham identifies the last internal motive in *esse* with the pain or pleasure of expectation, derived from imagination:[179] it consists in the actual perception of pain or pleasure in correspondence to the idea of a future event, the occurrence of which is expected to bring forth pain or pleasure. More precisely, the actual perception of the pain or pleasure of this internal motive in *esse* is connected to the apprehension of the anticipated pain or pleasure, in which the last motive in prospect consists: the agent feels pain at the idea of the pain he could feel in case a certain event happens. So, the last internal motive in *esse* intimately refers to the last internal motive in prospect.

> In all this chain of motives, the principal or original link seems to be the last internal motive in prospect: it is to this that all the other motives in prospect owe their materiality: and the immediately acting motive its existence. This motive in prospect, we see, is always some pleasure, or some pain; some pleasure, which the act in question is expected to be a means of continuing or producing: some pain which it is expected to be a means of discontinuing or preventing. A motive is substantially nothing more than pleasure or pain, operating in a certain manner.[180]

The last internal motive in *esse* is the closest to the act and, because of its position, is the triggering cause of that act. However, the last internal motive in *esse* owes its materiality to the last internal motive in prospect. The agent seeing a fire in his/her neighbour's house is compelled to run out of his/her own house

177 All these motives are listed by Bentham in *IPML*, 98.
178 *IPML*, 98–9.
179 Bentham defines the pleasure and pain of expectation, identified as the pleasure of hope and the pain of apprehension, in *A Table of the Springs of Action*, 90.
180 *IPML*, 100.

principally because of his/her fear of feeling pain when dying in flames. The agent's expectation of pain or pleasure relating to a future event puts a constraint on his/her will, leading him/her to perform or to refrain from performing an act aimed at securing him/her from an anticipated suffering or at gaining an anticipated gratification.

Such an expectation of pain or pleasure operates as a motive which determines the direction of the agent's intentionality: he/she wants to act in a certain way with the purpose of preventing the painful consequence of dying in flames from happening and, at the same time, to produce the pleasurable consequence of saving his/her life. In this way the agent moves so as to diminish the pain actually perceived when thinking of a catastrophe threatening him/her. Hence, pain and pleasure, acting in the form of motives, underlie the agent's whole practical reasoning, by giving it a specific orientation. As Bentham makes it clear, "A motive must be the prospect of some pleasure, or other advantage, to be enjoyed in future."[181]

Motives are not only desires, which refer to the will, but also beliefs, which refer to the understanding. Bentham distinguishes two kinds of these latter motives: on the one hand, purely speculative or intellectual motives "of which the influence terminates altogether in the understanding"; and on the other, speculative or intellectual motives having a practical character insofar as they, "through the medium of the understanding, exercise an influence over the will."[182]

> It is in this way, and in this way only, that any objects, in virtue of any tendency they may have to influence the sentiment of belief, may in a practical sense act in the character of motives. Any objects, by tending to induce a belief concerning the existence, actual, or probable, of a practical motive; that is, concerning the probability of a motive in prospect, or the existence of a motive in *esse*; may exercise an influence on the will, and rank with those other motives that have been placed under the name of practical. The pointing out of motives such as these, is what we frequently mean when we talk of giving *reasons*.[183]

The understanding makes an agent aware of the context in which he/she operates. Beliefs, concerning certain circumstances, indirectly affect the agent's will, both by exciting his/her desire for pleasure or his/her aversion to pain and by orienting his/her practical reflection to the pursuit of his/her interest. Intellectual and volitional faculties harmoniously cooperate in the planning of a course of action. The knowledge of a state of affairs can impel the agent to act in order to obtain the pleasure or to avoid the pain deriving from that state of affairs. Beliefs, in the character of external motives in *esse*, take part in the decision-making

181 *IPML*, 145.
182 *IPML*, 99.
183 *IPML*, 99.

process when they arouse the agent's volitional states such as his/her desires and interests. With regard to the previous example, Bentham points out some beliefs, suggested by an interlocutor to the agent. The interlocutor, in other words, gives the agent motives to his/her understanding:

- external motive in *esse*: "the lower part of your neighbour's house is some wood-work, which joins on to yours";
- external motive in *esse*: "the flames have caught this wood-work";
- external motive in *esse*: "if you stay in your house much longer you will be burnt."[184]

> In doing this, then, I suggest motives to your understanding; which motives, by the tendency they have to give birth to or strengthen a pain, which operates upon you in the character of an internal motive in *esse,* join their force, and act as motives upon the will.[185]

By means of these beliefs the interlocutor persuades the agent that he/she is exposed to pain. These beliefs provoke and increase the agent's fear to be burnt and thus to feel pain. They contribute to the creation of the internal motives in *esse*, which directly affect the will by binding and prompting it to act. So, beliefs concerning external events, real or imagined, can have a practical influence only if they arouse a pleasurable or painful sensation in the agent. Properly speaking, beliefs do not seem to have a motivational power in themselves, but only on the basis of the agent's anticipating the experience of certain feelings in correspondence to the events they make known. Actually, what really motivates the agents to endorse a course of action is not the awareness of certain circumstances, but rather the production of pleasure or pain depending on these circumstances.

Bentham is sketching out a clear form of instrumental rationality, which, generally speaking, consists in choosing suitable means to an end. The possibility of being burnt is identifiable as a physical sanction, i.e. a natural calamity or catastrophe, related in the form of a consequence to staying in the house. If the agent does not want to suffer the pain of being burnt, he/she ought to leave his/her house at once. The physical sanction makes that behaviour binding on his/her will and gives it a normative character; the performance of that behaviour is a dictate of prudence ensuing from the physical sanction and endowed with a motivational power.

Finally, in the active phase, the will chooses the course of action supported by the prevailing motive,[186] turns it into an intention and prompts the bodily movement to perform it. The agent's decision to be guided by a specific motive lies in

184 *IPML*, 99.
185 *IPML*, 99–100.
186 As Bentham notes in *A Table of the Springs of Action*, 19: "Commonly an act is the result of the difference in force between an instigating motive or motives and a restraining ditto." *A Table of the Springs of Action*, 20: "Almost on every occasion a man is acted upon by divers motives, concurrent or conflicting."

his/her evaluation of the consequences of the behaviour caused by that motive. The consideration of pleasure and pain, which a type of conduct is supposed to produce, provides the agent with a motive for carrying out or not carrying out that type of conduct. A motive essentially consists in the expectation of obtaining pleasure or avoiding pain. It is, indeed, the anticipated pain deriving from the possibility of being burnt that impels the agent to leave his/her own house at once. A motive compels an agent to act and without it an action is neither feasible nor thinkable.

4.3 Instrumental rationality

Desire-belief and means-end model

Bentham's view of practical reason, as regards its content and structure, is clarified by certain remarks in *Preparatory Principles*, in his writings on ontology, logic, language and grammar, in *A Table of the Springs of Action* and, to a lesser extent, in *Deontology*. Generally speaking, practical reason can be defined as the human self-reflective activity of deliberating and deciding how to behave. Practical reason differs from theoretical reason, because, first, it does not concern only beliefs but also desires and, second, it ends with the action or at least with the intention of acting.[187] Practical reason consists thus in the agent's self-determining ability to think about and decide what to do.

The nature of practical reasoning is an oft-debated issue in the history of philosophy, which has produced a large variety of contributions and conflicting interpretations. Bentham's approach to that issue appears to be consistent with a longstanding desire-based account dating back to Aristotle, including Hume, and was also taken into consideration by Kant with a view to criticizing it. Bentham is in this empirical tradition and yet puts forward an original interpretation of practical reason when accounting for the normative power of morality, law and religion.

Bentham understands practical reason as a calculative activity carried out under the direction of the principle of utility. With reference to action, calculation consists in estimating and taking into account the quantities of pleasure and pain as they seem likely to result from the performance of a type of conduct.[188] In this respect, practical reasoning is comparable to the technical reasoning employed by a mercantile teacher, a pharmacist or a doctor and an architect involving respectively accounts, weights and a foot rule.[189]

187 A definition of practical reasoning is provided by Korsgaard 2008, 207: "Reasoning is self-conscious, self-directing activity through which we deliberately give shape to the inputs of receptivity. This happens both in the case of theoretical reasoning, when we are constructing a scientific account of the world, and in the case of practical reasoning, where its characteristic manifestation is choice." See also Wallace 2014.

188 For the identification between reason and calculation and their dependence on the principle of utility, see for example *A Table of the Springs of Action*, 35, 43 and 58. On Bentham's calculation of pleasure and pain, see Cléro 2015, 229–58.

189 Cf. *A Table of the Springs of Action*, 42 and 44. The relation between calculation and practical reasoning is deepened by Quinn 2014. On the feasibility of the Benthamite calculation of pleasure and pain, see Bozzo-Rey 2007, 349–59, in part. 355–9.

Bentham imports empirical and technical methods of reasoning, belonging not only to applied mathematical sciences, into practical disciplines, especially ethics and politics. According to these methods, motives, actions and duties are understood and balanced in terms of weight or strength. The weight or the strength of practical elements, such as motives, duties and actions, corresponds to their utility, which is consequently measurable. Hence, the activity of practical reason consists in a calculation based on weighing a number of motives supporting alternative modes of conduct.[190]

Bentham sets out a belief-desire, or more precisely a belief-desire-intention, and a means-end model of practical rationality. Roughly speaking, the belief-desire model might be seen as more concerned with the contents of practical reason, whereas the means-end model might be regarded as more involved in accounting for the structure of practical reason. Appearances aside, belief-desire and means-end models are two sides of the same coin: Bentham's treatment of them helps to provide a unified and consistent account of deliberation concerning action and, thus, of the connection between normativity and the motivation that underlies it.

As we have seen, in *IPML* Bentham is aware that the interaction between desire and belief, as states of the will and the understanding, gives shape to the reflection on what to do; however, elsewhere, he emphasizes the instrumental role of motives, namely desires, in the performance of action: "A mode of conduct is producible no otherwise than by motives. A motive is the expectation of Pain or Pleasure."[191]

> The *intellectual instrument* of an action, that *instrument*, or, as would say, *cause* of it, that is in the mind, is stiled a MOTIVE.
>
> A MOTIVE is an idea: it is the idea of some pleasure or some pain: the pleasure conceived as about to exist, or the pain as about not to exist, in consequence of our action.
>
> Cessation of Pain may be spoken of as Pleasure. The Pleasure, then, whereof the idea becomes a MOTIVE, is stiled an END. It is also stiled an *Object*. It may be stiled in either way: thither the mind's prospect is DIRECTED, there it TERMINATES.[192]

> The END of an ACTION may be distant and ill-defined: but no man acts without an END: no man acts without a MOTIVE. Every action has it's END; it's MOTIVE.[193]

190 For an example of calculation as a form of practical reasoning see *Preparatory Principles*, 421–3, in which Bentham observes (421) "In order to see which reason is strongest, it will be necessary to sum up and divide the quantities of pleasure and pain that are the pathological effects of the two different modes of disposition."

191 *Preparatory Principles*, 202.

192 *Preparatory Principles*, 443. An almost identical text is contained on p. 430.

193 *Preparatory Principles*, 445. An almost identical text is contained on p. 430: "The End of an action or forbearance may be distant; and ill-defined: but no man acts or forbears without an end: no man acts without a motive."

Because of its direct influence on the will, which is the faculty for implementing a decision, motives prove to be crucial in the causation of action. In an *Appendix* to *Essay on Logic*, devoted to the study of the phenomena of the human mind, Bentham traces action back to conative states, with particular regard to desire.

> Every operation of the mind, and thence every operation of the body, is the result of an exercise of the will or volitional faculty. – The volitional faculty is a branch of the appetitive faculty: i.e. that faculty in which *desire*, in all its several modifications, has place.[194]

> Desire has for its object either pleasure or pain, or, what is commonly the case, a mixture of both in ever-varying and unascertainable proportions.
>
> The desire which has pleasure for its object is the desire of the presence of such pleasure: desire which has pain for its object is the desire of the absence of such pain.[195]

Bentham establishes a causal connection between desire, the will and action. Desire for pleasure or for the exemption from pain exerts pressure on the will, on which every mental and bodily operation depends, in order to dispose the will to endorse an action aimed at the attainment of that pleasure or the avoidance of that pain. Desire spurs the will to bring such a pleasurable event into reality or to prevent such a painful event from occurring.

Desire turns out to be hope for the happening of a pleasurable event or for the avoidance of a painful event. Desire is aroused by the perspective of a type of pleasure or a type of pain, which can result as a consequence of the agent's action or a natural event. Desire sets the end and impels the will to its accomplishment. When an agent sees an apple, he conceives a desire to possess and eat it. If the agent is not hungry or thirsty, he is moved by the desire to taste the presumedly agreeable flavour of that apple; otherwise, if the agent is hungry or thirsty, he is moved by the desire to free himself/herself from the discomfort of his hunger or thirst. Desire has "an internal object," that is, the enjoyment of a certain pleasure or the reduction of a certain pain, and an "external object," which is the source of that pleasure or pain.[196] Pellegrino argues that in this passage from *Essay on Logic*, Bentham puts forward a non-cognitivist version of motivational hedonism, which differs from his cognitivist versions, explicitly advanced in other of his writings.[197] It is indeed true that Bentham does not take into consideration beliefs here as conceptual elements explicitly intervening in the

194 *Essay on Logic*, UC 101.409 (Bowring viii, 279).
195 *Essay on Logic*, UC 101.410 (Bowring viii, 279).
196 *Essay on Logic*, UC 101.410 (Bowring viii, 279–80).

construction of action: he would seem to suggest that action is merely based on desires. The example of the agent desiring an apple, given in the lines following this passage, however, indirectly throws light on the contribution of the understanding in practical deliberation and decision; in this way, Bentham completes the theoretical treatment of practical reason, making it more consistent with his general desire-belief model.

The vision of an apple, the awareness of its agreeable flavour and the property of an apple to quench hunger or thirst are nothing but beliefs, provided by the understanding, which are certainly taken into account by the agent in that instance of practical reasoning. They arouse the agent's desire to eat that apple, because he/she believes that it has an agreeable flavour or that it satisfies his/her hunger or thirst. In other words, they are motives to the understanding having a practical effect on the will.

It is however undeniable that the pivotal role in the constitution of agency is played by desire: "no act of the will can take place but in consequence of a correspondent desire: in consequence of the action of a *desire* in the character of a *motive*."[198] Action is brought about by desire and only by desire, which can directly affect the will. The causative role acknowledged to desire does not undermine or eliminate the contribution of belief, which can indirectly influence the will by orienting desire. In the above-quoted passage from *Essay on Logic* Bentham seems to be more concerned with clarifying the "results of the exercise of the appetitive faculty,"[199] as he explicitly maintains, than with giving a full account of the elements of agency.

The centrality of desire in determining volition and then action is also similarly stated in the following excerpt from *Essay on Language*.

> A certain event, presented by my imagination as being not yet realized but capable of being realized, becomes the object of my desire – if the event be regarded as capable of being brought into reality by my own agency alone, and my desire of seeing it realized is strong enough, my will, my volitional faculty, and at the same time the appropriate branch of my externally active faculty, are exercised in the production of it.[200]

A desire is a motive operating towards the production of a result, i.e. the presence of pleasure or absence of pain, which is its object.[201] Bentham understands the

197 Pellegrino 2010, 103–6, in part. 105–6. More generally, according to Pellegrino, within Bentham's theory of motivation it is possible to distinguish at least three different versions of motivational hedonism: motivational cognitivist hedonism, motivational sensist hedonism, and non-cognitivist motivational hedonism. For a full discussion of this topic see Pellegrino 2010, 69–138 and, particularly, 83–106, in which he sets out Bentham's versions of motivational hedonism.

198 *Essay on Logic*, UC 101.412 (Bowring viii, 280).

199 *Essay on Logic*, UC 101.409 (Bowring viii, 279).

200 *Essay on Language*, UC 102.457 (Bowring viii, 329).

notion of desire, when involved in the planning of conduct, in terms of motive and also of interest. By interest Bentham means "the universal cause of all action, being the most obvious and surely operative cause of common action of those faculties, volitional and thence of intellectual."[202]

At various points in his writings Bentham makes the semantic affinity of motive, desire and interest explicit. They seem to have two main things in common. First, motive, desire and interest trigger action: they have a causative power on the will, impelling it to act. Second, they consist of and are related to pleasure and pain as regards not only their import and truth but also their motivational and normative force.[203]

Desires, aversions, wants, hopes, fears, motives and interests are *plastosemantic* appellatives, i.e. names of fictitious entities, the roots of which are in *alethosemantic* appellatives, that is, more specifically, in the names of the real entities of pleasure and pain. The "fictitious entity language" needs to be explained through the "real entity language," on which its intelligibility depends. The strategy of paraphrasis, connecting the name of a fictitious entity to the name of a real entity by restating a sentence, uncovers the empirical grounds of psychological fictitious entities.[204]

> On this occasion, as on every other, to understand what *interest* means, we must look to motives: to understand what motive means, we must look to pain and pleasure, to fear and hope; fear, the expectation of pain or of loss of pleasure – hope, the expectation of pleasure or of exemption from pain.[205]

Motives, desires and interests can prompt and give direction to human conduct because they consist of pleasure and pain, which are the original springs of any action, namely the foundations of the ontology of normativity underlying the practical domain.[206]

201 Cf. *Essay on Logic*, UC 101.411 (Bowring viii, 280). Again, Bentham (*Essay on Logic*, UC 101.412; Bowring viii, 280) states that "no desire can have place unless the idea of pleasure or pain, in some shape or degree, has place."

202 *A Table of the Springs of Action*, 38.

203 *A Table of the Springs of Action*, 72: "Correspondent to pleasures and pains are *interests*, *desires* and *motives*."

204 Cf. *A Table of the Springs of Action*, 74–9.

205 *Rationale of Judicial Evidence*, Bowring vii, 393.

206 See *A Table of the Springs of Action*, 98: "Among all the several species of psychological entities, the names of which are to be found either in the *Table of the Springs of Action*, or in the *Explanations* above subjoined to it, the two of which are as it were the *roots*, the main pillars or *foundations* of all the rest, the *matter* of which all the rest are composed – or the *receptacles* of that matter, which soever may be the *physical image*, employed to give *aid*, if not *existence* to conception, will be, it is believed, if they have not been already, seen to be, PLEASURES and PAINS. Of *these*, the existence is matter of universal and constant experience."

Bentham throws light on the constitutive relation that motives have with pleasure and pain.

> But, of the sort of *motive*, which has thus been in operation, no clear idea can be entertained, otherwise than by reference to the sort of *pleasure* or *pain*, which such *motive* has for its *basis*: viz. the pleasure or pain, the idea, and eventual expectation of which, is considered as having been operating in the character of *a motive*.[207]

The motivational or desiderative component of Bentham's theory of action leads to action, i.e. *thelematic motion*, which, unlike *athelematic motion*, is brought about by volition, namely by "the inward act of a sentient and self-moving being." The cause of "a motion of the thelematic class" is "the psychical act – the act of the will of the person by whose will the motion is produced."[208] This state or act of the will is identified with "the desire and expectation of some good, i.e. of some pleasure or of exemption from some pain." Thus, the performance of a specific action is aimed at the attainment of "the good by the contemplation of which this desire has been produced."[209]

The desire to possess or the interest in possessing a certain good makes a certain thing, such as the performance of an action, necessary: the occurrence of that thing is the condition for the fulfilment of that desire or for the satisfaction of that interest. Interest, desire, aversion, want, hope and fear operate on the will as motives for bringing into reality the state of affairs which is conducive to the good from which these conative states are brought about.

> When to a man's enjoying a certain *good*, *i.e.* a certain *pleasure* or *exemption* from a certain *pain*, it has appeared to him to be necessary that a certain *event* or *state of things* should have had place; and, for the purpose of causing it to have place, he has performed a certain act; then so it is, that among the psychological phenomena, which, on the occasion in question, have had place and operation in his mind, are the following, viz. 1. He has felt himself to have *an interest* in the possession of that same good. 2. He has felt *a desire* to possess it. 3. He has felt *an aversion* to the idea of his not possessing it. 4. He has felt *the want* of it. 5. He has entertained *a hope* of possessing it. 6. He has had before his eyes the *fear* of not possessing it. 7. And the *desire* he has felt of possessing it has operated on his will in the character of a

207 *A Table of the Springs of Action*, 98.

208 *De l'ontologie*, 130–2 (Bowring viii, 206).

209 *De l'ontologie*, 112 (Bowring viii, 205): "In the case of human action – a motion, real or fictitious, considered as being produced by an exercise of the faculty of the will on the part of a sensitive being, this action has in every instance for its cause, the desire and expectation of some good, i.e. of some pleasure or of exemption from some pain, and the entity, the good by the contemplation of which this desire has been produced, is in this case, if not the only object, an object, and indeed the ultimate object, the attainment of which is, in the performance of the action aimed at."

> *motive*, by the sole operation, or by the help of which, the act exercised by him, as above, has been produced.[210]

Bentham bases his philosophical system on the "uncontrovertible fact" that "no man ever has done or ever can do any act which at the moment of action is not [. . .] in his own eyes at least, his interest to do."[211] Interest, along with motive and desire, namely two notions with which it is convertible, is the determining cause of action. So, as in the case of desire and motives, Bentham specifies the ontological connection which the notion of interest has with pleasure and pain.

1 A man is said *to have an interest in any subject*, in so far as that *subject* is considered as more or less likely to be to him a source of pleasure or exemption: subject, *viz. thing* or *person* [. . .].
2 A man is said *to have an interest* in the performance of this or that *act*, by himself or any other – or in *the taking place* of this or that *event* or *state of things*, – in so far as, upon and in consequence of its having place, this or that *good* (i.e. *pleasure* or *exemption*) is considered as being more or less likely to be possessed by him.
3 It is said *to be a man's interest that* the act, the event, or the state of things in question should have place, in so far as it is supposed that – upon, and in consequence of, its having place – *good*, to a greater *value*, will be possessed by him than in the contrary case.[212]

Interests are the operating motives for action: "no human act ever has been, or ever can be, *disinterested*." Indeed, as Bentham specifies, "there exists not ever any voluntary action, which is not the result of the operation of some *motive* or *motives*: nor any motive, which has not for its accompaniment a corresponding *interest*, real or imagined."[213] Any action or discourse is "the result of *interest*."[214] Again, in *First Principles Preparatory to Constitutional Code*, Bentham maintains that "On every occasion, the conduct of every human being will be determined by his own interest,"[215] meaning the notion of interest "in its most extensive sense, that in which it is coextensive with the whole aggregate of pains and pleasures."[216]

In Bentham's view, the main components of practical judgment appear to be desires or interests and beliefs, corresponding to motives and circumstances. Desires and interests, in the form of motives, point out the end to attain, i.e. enjoyment of a type of pleasure and exemption from a type of pain. Beliefs and

210 *A Table of the Springs of Action*, 94.
211 *Deontology*, 175.
212 *A Table of the Springs of Action*, 91.
213 *A Table of the Springs of Action*, 99–100.
214 *A Table of the Springs of Action*, 101.
215 *First Principles Preparatory to Constitutional Code*, 68.
216 *First Principles Preparatory to Constitutional Code*, 68 n. a.

circumstances orient the agent in the construction of a course of action, by suggesting to him/her the means for the achievement of his/her own end.

Volitional and cognitive faculties cooperate in the decision-making process, that is, in the deliberation concerning the conduct to choose in order to attain some good. Desire consists in a state of the will tending towards an end, identifiable as a type of pleasure or exemption from a type of pain. Desire activates the cognitive faculties to single out the possibilities for its fulfilment and impels the agent to adopt them. The cognitive faculties explore a set of alternative kinds of behaviour and examine which of them are the best means of achieving, in a particular situation, the desired end. The cognitive faculties alone, however, do not motivate the will to act: if desire is not operative, the consideration of a state of affairs is not sufficient to move the agent.

The cognitive faculties can stimulate the agent's desire, as when the vision of an apple prompts my desire to taste it. However, without desire, the mere vision of that apple does not lead me to eat it. Sense-perception and thought do not impel the agent to act. This prerogative belongs only to the will. The agent finds through volition the purpose of his/her action and through the cognitive faculties the instruments for the attainment of the chosen purpose. Desires and beliefs interact because the former provides the end and the latter the means for its achievement.

According to Bentham, the understanding contributes to the construction of action in two respects. First, the understanding evaluates the object of desire with reference to the pleasure it is expected to bring forth and also to the possible pain associated with it, making known the balance of pleasure and pain. Second, the understanding selects the means to fulfil that desire. In this way, cognitive faculties makes it possible that velleity, i.e. desire for pleasure or aversion to pain not conclusive of action, turns into volition resulting in action.

> To the *will* it is that the idea of a pleasure or an exemption applies itself in the *first* instance; in *that* stage its effect, if not conclusive, is *velleity*: by *velleity*, reference is made to the *understanding*, *viz.* 1. For striking a *balance* between the *value* of this *good*, and that of the *pain* or *loss*, if any, which present themselves as eventually about to stand associated with it: 2. Then, if the balance appears to be in its favour for the choice of *means*: thereupon, if *action* be the result, *velleity* is perfected into *volition*, of which the correspondent *action* is the immediate consequence.[217]

In his account of desire as the starting-point or better the driving force behind reflection and action Bentham appears to be influenced by Hume. In his *Treatise of Human Nature* (ii.iii.3, 413–7), Hume rejects as misleading the common opposition between reason and passion and the traditional preference attributed to reason in guiding human behaviour.[218] Notwithstanding the impressive

217 *A Table of the Springs of Action*, 94.

218 Hume, *A Treatise of Human Nature*, ii.iii.3, 413.

metaphor of reason as "the slave of the passions" that can only "serve and obey them,"[219] Hume establishes a collaborative and harmonious relation between the will and reason, by acknowledging their complementarity in deliberating on what to do. The volitional sphere gives rise to an impulse to act and this impulse is directed by reason.[220] Reason chooses the adequate means for the presupposed end and, thus, orients the agent's behaviour.

Passion is unreasonable when it is based on a false belief or when it does not adopt suitable means. For instance, the desire for a given fruit depends on its good taste, but once I discover that my belief is wrong, my longing ceases. In the same way, I desire the performance of certain actions because I suppose they are suitable means for my designed end; once I realise the falsehood of this supposition because of the inadequacy of these means, they become indifferent to me.[221] Reason investigates the causal relations between states of affairs and, on the basis of this information, influences the will by guiding and changing its direction.

Bentham develops an instrumentalist view of practical rationality: "As *a spring of action*, *a pleasure* cannot operate, but in so far as, in the particular direction in question, action is regarded as a means of *obtaining* it; *a pain*, in so far as action is regarded as a means of *avoiding* it."[222] According to Bentham, the word *end* or *end in view* suggests the idea of some good, consisting in pleasure or in an exemption from pain expected to derive from the performance of an action; the word *means* identifies an object or an action considered as an instrument or an operation tending to the achievement or production of that good having the character of end,[223] that is, of the final cause of the action.[224] Therefore, the will sets out the ends and the understanding identifies the means.

Furthermore, the human mind reflects on and selects the series of secondary or particular ends, along with their related means, structuring the whole course of action aimed at the attainment of the primary end, corresponding to well-being or happiness: "And it is in this sense, that some Ends are said to be ultimate: others to be subordinate. But if we look for the prime and ultimate end of any action (prime in contemplation, ultimate in practise), it is always pleasure."[225]

219 Hume, *A Treatise of Human Nature*, ii.iii.3, 415.
220 Hume, *A Treatise of Human Nature*, ii.iii.3, 414.
221 Hume, *A Treatise of Human Nature*, ii.iii.3, 416–7.
222 *A Table of the Springs of Action*, 89.
223 *De l'Ontologie*, 134 (Bowring viii, 208). See also *Pannomial Fragments*, Bowring iii, 214: "*End* is a word employed to denote a good, the prospect of eventually experiencing which, operates as a motive tending to produce at the hands of any sensitive being, some good which is an object of human desire and hope. *Means* is a word employed to denote any substance, state of things, or matter, considered as contributing to the attainment of the good, which on that same occasion is regarded as an end."
224 About finalism in action see *De l'Ontologie*, 148–50 (Bowring viii, 210): "By final *cause* is meant the *end* which the agent had in view, meaning, as hath been seen, by the *end*, if any thing at all be meant by it, the good to the attainment of which the act was directed: the good, i.e. the pleasure or pleasures, the exemption or security from such or such pain or pains."
225 *Preparatory Principles*, 444. By pleasure, as the prime and ultimate end of action, Bentham means also relief from pain.

In Bentham's teleological view of action, the secondary ends are considered subservient to the universal end, by contributing, in the form of means, to its achievement.[226]

Bentham's practical deliberation seems to have a conditional or hypothetical form. Generally speaking, the hypothetical model is applied to theoretical and practical reasoning, even though they consider different contents. Both patterns of reasoning use a specific concept of necessity, which has a conditional or hypothetical character: in order that Y be the case, it is necessary that X occurs. From the practical point of view, the fulfilment of a desire is subordinate to the performance of an action: if an agent wants something, i.e. to quench his/her thirst, he/she ought to act in a certain way, i.e. to drink water. Desire provides the agent with the normative principle for his/her behaviour: the act of drinking water is the necessary condition for quenching her/his thirst.

In a passage of *Fragments on Universal Grammar*, when outlining a sort of normative vocabulary devoted to the clarification of the meaning of modal verbs, including ought to, should and must, Bentham makes a distinction between the conditional sense and the moral or monitory sense of duty. With reference to the verb should, the conditional sense is exemplified by the sentence "if I should move, I should fall," which is expressed by the agent; the moral or monitory is exemplified by the sentence "You should take heed, lest you should fall," which is expressed by a speaker.[227] Though the passage is not entirely clear, we might suppose that subjective practical reasoning, also when including moral content, has a conditional or hypothetical form. The moral duty, instead, is external to the agent and, in order to be effective, is related to the consequence of its non-compliance.

The hypothetical form of reasoning is deepened by Kant, who, in his *Groundwork for the Metaphysics of Morals*,[228] introduces the notion of "imperative," that is, of a "command of reason" or, in more detail, an "objective principle, insofar as it is necessitating for a will." An imperative is a practical rule, expressed through an *ought*; as Kant says, it "indicate[s] the relation of an objective law of reason to a will, which in its subjective constitution is not necessarily determined by that law."

A hypothetical imperative, in particular, "represent[s] the practical necessity of a possible action as a means to attain something else which one wills (or which it is possible that one might will)." The connection between the fulfilment of the will and the performance of an action is necessary, but the duty to perform the action by itself does not constrain the will to move accordingly. The hypothetical imperative establishes the goodness of an action for a possible or current aim and, by virtue of this, can also be considered an "imperative of skill."

Desires, operating as motives for action, are connected to duties, which stem from them. Desire entails compliance with the condition necessary for its fulfilment. The pursuit of desire, generally consisting in seeking pleasure and avoiding pain, generates a rational requirement by putting a constraint on the agent's will.

226 Cf. *Essay on Logic*, UC 101.147 (Bowring viii, 231).
227 Cf. *Fragments on Universal Grammar*, UC 102.578 (Bowring viii, 353).
228 Kant, *Groundwork of the Metaphysics of Morals*, Ak 4:413–15.

The agent who wants to avert a type of pain ought to act in a certain way. So, Bentham traces the notion of obligation back to the notion of motive, which is ultimately related to pain and pleasure: "Obligation is the action of a motive. A motive is an idea. An idea of Pain and Pleasure. Obligation signifies the act obliged to, the act which is the object of the obligation."[229]

Desire for pleasure and aversion to pain are inherently normative because they compel the agent to perform a kind of behaviour which tends to produce pleasure or prevent pain. The deontic feature of ethics derives from pleasure and pain or, more precisely, from the desire for pleasure and aversion to pain. Normativity turns out to be a requirement of desire-based practical rationality. Put differently, rationality provides agents with the means to their ends and these means obtain their normative, i.e. binding, character from these ends.

Although his account of action seems to leave no room for the agent's freedom when deciding how to behave, Bentham vindicates an autonomist conception of the human will.

> In the production of volition, a desire operating in the character of a motive is either certainly or not certainly effective; if certainly effective, an act of the will is the consequence. The cause of my own act is always my own desire; and in this sense my will is free.[230]

The freedom of the agent's will resides in the fact that his/her choice of a course of action depends on his/her own desire, which is an internal state aroused by his/her perception of an external event in its actual or expected form. The cause of the agent's own action, which is directed to produce or to prevent the production of that event, is his/her own desire; in this sense the agent's will is free because it is not constrained by elements external to it. The external event can indirectly influence the agent's conduct only when he/she begins regarding that event as desirable or undesirable. By itself that event is unable to cause any form of action: it has neither motivational nor normative force without desire, which is an internal state of the will. Hence, "A situation of the parts of a voluntary agent [. . .], such a situation, when brought about by the volition of the agent, may be stiled a Voluntary situation."[231]

229 *Preparatory Principles*, 162.

230 *Essay on Logic*, UC 101.413 n. a (Bowring viii, 280 n. *). This note ends as follows: "But, the cause of that desire, what is it? In some cases, I know what it is; in others, not. When I know not what it is, how is my will free? The action of it is in so far dependent upon an unknown cause, external to myself. When I make my choice amongst a multitude of antagonizing desires, of that choice, what is the cause?"

231 *Preparatory Principles*, para. 937. On the other hand, Bentham (*Preparatory Principles*, para. 924) sees necessity between two events connected according to a relation of antecedence and consequence: "An event that is to come after is supposed to depend upon an event that is to go before when the antecedent is supposed to be among the circumstances necessary to the production of the consequent: in other words, when it is conceived that, if the antecedent does not take place, neither will the consequent take place." In addition, see *Preparatory Principles*, para. 1077: "An event is rather a situation the consequence of an act, than the act itself. For event, we may use consequential situation."

In this way, Bentham saves his theory of agency from the criticism of determinism. Though practical reasoning has a causal form, the original causative element of action is not external to the agent but is one of his/her conative states. The self-determination of the agent's will in choosing a form of conduct and in performing it is guaranteed by the individuality of the desire that gives direction to volition. Ethics, thus, is conceived by Bentham as "the *art of self-government*," that is, "the art of directing a man's own actions" towards the attainment of "the greatest possible quantity of happiness" according to his interest.[232] The agent's self-governance is made possible through the autonomy of his/her will, which is guided by a desire giving rise to an internal obligation.

Scholars discuss the plausibility of the freedom of the will in Bentham's account of action. It seems difficult to reconcile his view of a predictive structure of human behaviour with his idea of the agent's autonomy when deciding how to act. It is probably true that Bentham did not make too much effort to settle the question of the free will, so as to make his causal chain of action compatible with an autonomist conception of the agent. Nonetheless, even though the question of the freedom of the will did not trouble Bentham's mind too much, the passages I have mentioned show that he was more inclined to claim the agent's autonomy in taking a course of action, insofar as the necessary cause of that course of action is a motive consisting in the agent's personal desire.[233]

Bentham seems to solve the free will problem by embracing a compatibilist approach, which is aimed at making the agent's freedom in performing a behaviour consistent with the idea of pain and pleasure, produced by an event external

232 *Of the Limits of the Penal Branch of Jurisprudence*, 4 (also *IPML*, 282): "Ethics at large may be defined, the art of directing men's actions to the production of the greatest possible quantity of happiness, on the part of those whose interest is in view. What then are the actions which it can be in a man's power to direct? They must be either his own actions, or those of other agents. Ethics, in as far as it is the art of directing a man's own actions, may be styled the *art of self-government*, or *private ethics.*"

233 When dealing with Bentham's conception of volition, scholars tend to acknowledge its freedom. See, for example, Roberts Jr 1993, 953–4 (the following quotation is on p. 953): "Just as a modern scientist who makes predictions with regard to the future is not necessarily a determinist, so Bentham's predicting does not necessarily make him a determinist. Indeed, although specific evidence on this point is hard to come by, in all probability he is a believer in free will. Basically he is an individualist who wants each person to decide for himself what he will do; on one level his theory of change is conceived in terms of trying to persuade men to choose one course of action rather than another. If there is any determinism in this, it is internal or self-determinism rather than external." On Bentham's view of free will see Harrison's opinion (*A Fragment on Government and an Introduction to the Principles of Morals and Legislation by Jeremy Bentham*, xlviii–xlix), which is also mentioned by Roberts Jr: "Bentham is again no clearer on the question of the freedom of the will. The will, he says, is moved by motives. [. . .] In his accounts of the 'circumstances affecting sensibility' and in his account of 'disposition,' Bentham appears to give a determinist account of volition; but he says elsewhere that the will, when determined by a pleasurable motive is uncoerced, and in general he writes as though there were no doubt of the freedom of the will of at least censorial jurists and legislators. For the most part, however, Bentham prefers to leave this question on one side and to concentrate his analysis round the meaning of 'tendencies of the acts'."

to the agent, as the causes of action. If, on the one hand, the reason of a behaviour lies in the pain or pleasure expected as a consequence from the performance of that behaviour, then on the other, pain and pleasure are subjective feelings which need to arouse the agent's motivational set in order to be causes of action.

Sanction and obligation

The model of practical deliberation highlighted by Bentham provides him with the theoretical framework to account for any kind of reflective activity undertaken by the agent in deciding what to do. Even though the different cases of deliberation stand out from each other on account of the presence of considerations involving different purviews of the practical domain, they can be traced back to the basic outlined pattern. This pattern enables Bentham to account for any reasoning including physical, moral, legal, religious or sympathetic elements, which require that agents modify their choices and behaviour. Bentham needs to explain the ability of social systems, such as morality, law and religion, to direct their subjects' decision-making process. So, he investigates the foundations of the normative claim entailed by legal, moral and religious orders.

Bentham puts forward a desire-based and instrumentalist account of normativity; it aims at the clarification of the binding character of law, morality and religion, by regarding that binding character as deriving from the particular constitution of human rationality, which is basically pleasure-oriented. Notwithstanding their prescriptive form, moral, legal and religious norms cannot direct the agent's behaviour by themselves.

As we have seen, merely volitional states can move an agent towards an end. These volitional states are aroused by the perception of a kind of pleasure or pain. Moral, legal and religious orders, which claim to be normative, have to be able to affect the agent's sensibility and to influence his/her will. Moral, legal and religious orders can guide human behaviour only if they intervene in the agent's reflective process, by giving him/her motives for action. Bentham identifies the motivational element, which impels someone to comply with an obligation, with a sanction. Sanctions, therefore, are the "sources of obligation and inducement."[234]

> A Sanction is Pain or Pleasure proceeding from an intelligent being in consequence of his approbation or disapprobation of a mode of conduct in the party *pained* or *pleased*.
>
> When it is Pain, it is stiled Punishment: when Pleasure, it is stiled Reward.
>
> It is the expectation of a Sanction that forms what may [be] stiled a determinative: which, if the tendency of it be to determine to action, is a motive: if to forbearance, it may be stiled a restrictive.[235]

234 *Nomography; or the Art of Inditing Laws*, Bowring iii, 290.
235 *Preparatory Principles*, 126–7.

By and large in his writings, Bentham provides conceptually consistent, though slightly different, accounts of the notion of sanction, which proves to be crucial to the understanding of the normative constitution of the practical domain. In *Preparatory Principles: Inserenda*, para. 667 and in chapter iii of *IPML*, Bentham distinguishes four kinds of consequences of an action, i.e. four different sources, from which pleasure or pain derive: they are called the physical, the political, including the legal, the moral or popular and the religious sanction.

In his later paper *Logical Arrangements or Instruments of Invention and Discovery*, contained in *Nomography*, Bentham adds the sympathetic sanction,[236] which is also taken into consideration in his detailed account of the several types of sanction worked out in *Deontology*. Here, as a result of his dichotomic method of exposition, Bentham identifies the physical, the supernatural or religious, the political, distinguished into the legal or judicial and the administrative, the popular or moral, the retributive and the antipathetic or sympathetic sanction.

In *IPML* Bentham characterizes at length the different types of sanction, which basically consist in a punishment or reward from which a certain pain or a certain pleasure ensues.[237] The physical sanction depends on "the ordinary course of nature." An instance of it is a calamity, which strikes an agent either as an accident due to "the natural and spontaneous course of things" or as a negative consequence, that is, a sort of punishment for his/her imprudence. This latter scenario occurs when a fire starts as a result of someone neglecting to blow a candle out. Thus, as regards pain deriving from excessive drinking of intoxicating liquors, "the physical sanction tends in a certain degree to restrain a man from giving into such excess."[238]

The political or legal sanction is dispensed by a judge or a judicial court in compliance with the will of the political authority, namely "the sovereign" or a "supreme ruling power." Pain provoked by this kind of sanction is a punishment inflicted by the sentence of the magistrate. The moral or popular sanction is imposed on an individual by an accidental set of people whom he/she has happened to have a mutual intercourse with during his/her life. This sanction derives not by a "settled or concerted rule," as in the case of law, but rather by a "spontaneous disposition" of some people towards one or more members of the same *moral community*. It can be a form of punishment, consisting, for example, in withholding a friendly assistance to an individual because of his/her misconduct or his/her unpleasant moral character.

The religious sanction is issued by "a superior invisible being" on the basis of certain sins committed by an individual, whose misbehaviour displeases God. Unlike the other kinds of sanction, the religious one can be experienced not only

236 *Nomography; or the Art of Inditing Laws*, Bowring iii, 290–2.

237 The following reconstruction of Bentham's account of the natural, political, moral and religious sanctions is mainly based on *IPML*, 35–6. References to Bentham's other works are explicitly stated.

238 *Nomography; or the Art of Inditing Laws*, Bowring iii, 290.

in the present but also in the future life. This aspect can be cause of distress to the human mind, because of the dread of provoking God's displeasure. It is, in other words, a sort of pain, felt in the present life, for the expectation of a possible transcendent punishment. So, even in its supernatural form, the religious sanction has a natural effect.

> Those which can be experienced in the present life, can of course be no others than such as human nature in the course of the present life is susceptible of: and from each of these sources may flow all the pleasures or pains of which, in the course of the present life, human nature is susceptible.[239]

In Bentham's view the notion of sanction has a very broad meaning, because it encompasses any consequence of a course of action and thus all the kind of pleasure and pain which can be experienced by human beings. Sanction is understood in general terms as the consequence of a type of behaviour, the performance of which produces a certain quantity of pleasure or pain. The evaluation and choice of a course of action, made by the agent, cannot disregard its consequences, having the form of an expected sanction. Every mode of conduct is related to a sanction as its outcome.

With respect to the sensations they provoke, sanctions can be distinguished as punitive, i.e. painful, and remunerative, i.e. pleasurable. The painful sanction or its expectation, however, proves to be "the most effectual and universally applicable"[240] and "acts with more force on a man than that of pleasure."[241] Pain affects the agent's sensibility and influences his/her behaviour in a more successful and efficacious way than pleasure. According to Bentham, one reason for this lies in the fact that "if a man does not receive the pleasure offer'd, he may receive some other; but if he receive pain, while that lasts, he is scarcely susceptible of any pleasure."[242] Consequently, the painful sanction is more capable of producing the results intended by its issuing authority.[243]

The types of pleasure and pain springing from the four sanctions noted above do not differ from each other in kind but only in the circumstances which bring them about.[244] From a qualitative and a quantitative point of view the four sanctions selected by Bentham produce the same feelings. Each sanction may be distinguished chiefly by virtue of its issuing authority, which Bentham identifies with nature, a judge acting in accordance with the political power, a set of people belonging to the same moral community and a deity. Except the

239 *IPML*, 35–6.
240 Cf. *Deontology*, 175.
241 *Preparatory Principles*, 231.
242 *Preparatory Principles*, 231.
243 However, there are certain cases in which reward is preferable to punishment, cf. *Preparatory Principles*, 89–91.
244 Cf. *IPML*, 36.

physical, the several kinds of sanction correspond to a clear division between the three subdomains of practical reality: law, morality and religion. They all claim to direct human behaviour, by providing agents with motives for action related to sanctions.

According to Bentham, each form of sanction, including the religious with reference to the immanent dimension, is basically grounded on a natural element. Moral, political and religious sanctions can be independent, but they cannot operate without the physical sanction, which is therefore embodied in each of them. Hence, practical authorities act "through the powers of nature."[245]

In later works, Bentham deals with the retributive, the sympathetic and, its opposite, the antipathetic sanction: they are regarded as "individually operating" because the pain or pleasure deriving from them depends on an individual. In the case of the retributive sanction, pain or pleasure results or is expected "in consideration of some pain or some pleasure antecedently received or supposed to have been received." Instead, pain, in the case of the antipathetic sanction, and pleasure, in the case of the sympathetic sanction, results or is expected independently of such a consideration.[246]

As Bentham acknowledges, "Few men can contemplate altogether without uneasiness [. . .] pain suffered or supposed to be suffered by a fellow creature." So, the sympathetic sanction, consisting in that uneasiness, "tends on every occasion to restrain the person in question from engaging in any act the tendency of which appears to him to be the giving birth to the sense of pain in the breast of a fellow creature."[247] On the contrary, the antipathetic sanction encourages the individual to engage in any act tending to arouse a sense of pain in his/her fellow.[248]

Harrison notes that "the strongest and most important sanctions are the four [Bentham] cites in the *Introduction* and throughout his life."[249] Bentham expresses the need to distinguish the sympathetic sanction, by virtue of its extra-regarding character, from other kinds of sanction that are "purely self-regarding."[250] Nonetheless, he is aware of the lesser influence of the sympathetic sanction on an individual, whose conduct is generally directed by self-regarding interest.[251]

In *Of Ontology* Bentham acknowledges that the political sanction has a practical primacy over the other types of sanctions. The political sanction is "susceptible of being the strongest and surest in its operation"; consequently, "the obligation derived from it" is "the strongest and most effective, perfect and efficient."[252]

Despite their variety, sanctions are characterized by the same conceptual framework, which basically lies in the intimate connection between interest and

245 Cf. *IPML*, 37.
246 *Deontology*, 176.
247 *Deontology*, 201.
248 An overview of Bentham's treatment of sanction is provided by Schofield 2006, 35–7.
249 Harrison 2001, 95.
250 *Nomography; or the Art of Inditing Laws*, Bowring iii, 291–2.
251 Cf. Dinwiddy 2004, 29–30.
252 *De l'ontologie*, 158 (Bowring viii, 206).

duty, that is, between motivation and normativity. Bentham throws light on this connection in several points of his treatment of sanction, underlining that sanctions provide motives and obligations insofar as they are able both to bind and to prompt an agent to do something.

Bentham plainly states the normative character of a sanction when defining it in *IPML*. He clarifies that "inasmuch as the pleasures and pains belonging to each of them are capable of giving a binding force to any law or role of conduct, they may all of them be termed *sanctions*."[253] By virtue of its relation with pleasure and pain, from which normativity springs, a sanction, consisting in a reward or more frequently in a punishment, enforces any rule of conduct which is associated with it. Bentham specifies such a normative prerogative also by making reference to the Latin etymology of sanction, according to which the word *sanctio* was adopted to mean "the *act of binding*, [. . .] *any thing which serves to bind a man:* to wit, to the observance of such or such a mode of conduct."[254]

This structural relation between a sanction, as a source of pleasure or pain, and the duty to behave in a certain way is also stated by Bentham in *A Fragment on Government*: "That is my *duty* to do, which I am liable to be *punished*, according to law, if I do not do: this is the original, ordinary, and proper sense of the word *duty*."[255] Hence, pain and pleasure are "constitutive" of an obligation by means of a sanction.[256]

The motivational character of a sanction is clarified with reference to its effects or tendency. Bentham explicitly identifies a sanction with an inducement or a motive, when it has the tendency to produce a positive action or motion, and with a restriction, when it has the tendency to produce the negation of an action or motion in opposition to an inducement to positively produce that action or motion.[257] The belief in the occurrence of the sanction, rewarding and praising or punishing and blaming a type of behaviour, induces the agent to perform or to refrain from performing that behaviour.

Bentham gives an example which might be helpful to clarify the motivational mechanism of sanction. He takes into consideration the moral sanction that, by and large, consists in the pleasure deriving from a good name, a good reputation

253 *IPML*, 34.

254 *IPML*, 34 n. a.

255 *A Fragment on Government*, 496. See also 496 n. c.

256 *Essay on Logic*, UC 101.224 (Bowring viii, 247). For the etymology of the word *obligation* cf. J. Bentham, *A Comment on the Commentaries*, 31: "*Obligare*, to oblige, is Latin for to bind. To bind a man to do a thing is to make him to do it: to be the occasion of his doing: to hold him fast in such a manner from doing its contrary, that he does that." In *Preparatory Principles*, 247, Bentham observes that "To one or other of the three Sanctions the words that follow, bound, restrained, &c., must, if they have any meaning, be referable." See also *Deontology*, 207.

257 *Deontology*, 175: "Considered in respect of its effects or tendency a sanction may be termed an inducement, a motive, when the tendency is to give birth to positive action, i.e. to motion in some direction; a restriction when the tendency is to produce the negation of action – not through forbearance – in opposition to whatsoever inducement may be in operation on the other side in the character of motives."

and honour or in the pain deriving from dishonour, disgrace, infamy, ignominy and shame. By virtue of this, the moral sanction generates motives in the agent.[258]

According to "the custom of the country," i.e. its moral code, if a man who suffered an affront does not react, he exposes himself to the pain deriving from "the shame of being thought to bear [that affront] patiently"; if that man reacts, he exposes himself to the pleasure deriving from "the reputation of courage." By means of these sanctions, the agent is motivated to choose the conduct that leads him to enjoy that pleasure and to avoid that pain. Such a motive, regarded by some people as laudable and styled as honour, determines his decision to challenge the individual who made the affront to him to fight a duel.[259]

Generally speaking, sanctions correspond to external events producing a feeling of pleasure or pain in an agent. The awareness of a sanction, as a consequence of the performance of a type of conduct, arouses in the agent an expectation of pleasure and pain which influences his/her practical thinking. By virtue of its causative relation with pleasure and pain, which are the roots of normativity and motivation, a sanction has both a binding and an impelling power. So, Bentham makes clear the connection between obligation and motivation that underlies the notion of sanction.

> A sanction then is a source of obligatory powers or *motives*: that is, of *pains* and *pleasures*; which, according as they are connected with such or such modes of conduct, operate, and are indeed the only things which can operate, as *motives*.[260]

The pleasure and pain produced by a sanction are both binding, inasmuch as they create a duty, and motivating, inasmuch as they entice the agent into conforming his/her behaviour to that duty. With reference to the legal domain, Bentham claims that "A Motive of Law's providing is termed a Sanction" and specifies that "A Sanction is the term given to such a Motive as is produced by operation of Law in the design to give birth to some mode of Conduct commanded by the Law."[261]

The individual desire not to be blamed and to be praised, not to be punished and to be rewarded, and, in short, not to suffer pain and to enjoy pleasure generates the corresponding obligation. The more motivating is that desire, the stronger is the force of the obligation deriving from it. An external rule of conduct, having a legal, moral or religious character, is not normative in itself but according to the ability of its issuing authority to arouse in the individual a desire that directs his/her volition to behave in compliance with that rule. The

258 Cf. *IPML*, 106.
259 *IPML*, 106–7.
260 *IPML*, 34–5 n. a.
261 *Preparatory Principles*, 112.

normativity of an obligation therefore depends on the motivational mechanism brought into play by a sanction.

In Bentham's view, desires have a normative force. The desire to achieve a particular pleasure, having the form of a reward, and the desire to avert a particular pain, having the form of a punishment, creates in the agent an internal duty to comply with the means to fulfil these desires. Hence, the end of an action makes a claim on the will, by requiring the adoption of the means to achieve it.

> When a man is supposed to be prompted by any motive to engage, or not to engage, in such or such an action, it may be of use, for the convenience of discourse, to speak of such motive as giving birth to an imaginary kind of *law* or *dictate*, enjoining him to engage, or not to engage, in it.[262]

Motives provide the agent with obligations: they dictate to him/her the mode of conduct to choose for their fulfilment. As motives basically consist in the desire for pleasure and the aversion to pain, we may conclude that pleasure and pain are the sources of motivation and normativity. The perception of pleasure and pain is at the basis of the linguistic process of construction of fictitious entities, which regulate our practical reason by virtue of their binding and enticing character.

The agent's sensibility to the pain and pleasure flowing from a sanction causes in the agent a motive for avoiding that pain and attaining that pleasure. This motive creates the obligation to adopt suitable means to that end. In Bentham's outline of practical judgement, which is a form of instrumental rationality, desire generates requirements to act or to forbear from acting.

The normative force of a sanction appears to be dependent on its motivational power. Motivation has indeed a causative role in obligation and then action. According to Bentham's principle of self-determination of action, the agent constrains himself/herself to endorse a form of conduct when that form of conduct is instrumental in the achievement of his/her end. Put differently, an agent imposes on himself/herself a duty, compliance with which is aimed at the fulfilment of his/her interest.

Bentham highlights the self-determination or autonomy of practical agents, who have a legislative capacity to the extent that they make their practical world, including obligations and values. Morality, law and religion appear to be the outcome of the fictitious constructive activity performed by self-legislating practical agents, who autonomously decide how to regulate their conduct by creating and imposing duties on themselves.

Bentham establishes a constitutive relation between interest, motive or desire, on the one hand, and duty, on the other. The agent's interest in pursuing a kind of pleasure and averting a kind of pain makes compulsory the choice of the most

262 *IPML*, 116–17 n. t.

suitable means to achieve that pleasure or avoid that pain.[263] The adoption of these means is the necessary condition to the achievement of the desired end. Such a necessity has a practical character, consisting in a requirement provided by the agent's rationality for the fulfilment of his/her desire.

An internal obligation is thus created by the agent's rationality in correspondence to his/her volitional states: "what is not a man's interest is not his duty."[264] Bentham subordinates duties to interests: the normative dimension of the practical domain is made dependent on the individual motivation. An agent acts only when he/she is motivated to act;[265] consequently, external legal, moral and religious authorities have to be able to arouse his/her motivation in order to obtain his/her compliance. An agent is motivated to discharge his/her duty when conformity to it is a means of accomplishing his/her end, viz. of fulfilling his/her desire.

According to Bentham, an agent's conduct can be influenced by intervening in his/her beliefs or in his/her desires, that is, either "by causing him to believe that without any thing done by the party influencing, it is already the man's interest so to do" or "by doing some act in consequence of which it becomes his interest so to do, though it would not have been otherwise: in a word, either by simply indicating inducements, or by creating inducements."[266]

The regulation of individual behaviour can be obtained by interfering in the obligation-creating process, whose basic elements are beliefs and desires. By desiring to avert a particular pain, such as the punishment issued by the legislator, the agent puts himself/herself under the obligation to adopt a type of conduct aimed at the fulfilment of that desire. A duty cannot be merely imposed on an individual by an external authority; indeed, duties are constructed on the basis of the individual motivational structure, which endows them with a binding force. The habit of obedience to particular norms of conduct, for example to legal norms, consists in a series of acts aimed at compliance with those norms. This habit of obedience does not depend on the norm in itself, but resides on

263 In his interpretation of Bentham's thought Bozzo-Rey (2007, 349–66; 2012, 174–82) distinguishes between utilitarian calculus and deontic calculus as components of practical meta-reasoning. According to him, "The specificity of the utilitarian, or felicific calculus, is the desire to measure individual utilities"; more particularly, its aim is "to measure subjective states in order to define which action, between several possible options, an individual agent has to perform if he or she wants to maximise his or her happiness." On the other hand, Bozzo-Rey relates the logic of the will or deontic logic ("as a tool for the legislator in charge of giving structure to reality in order to create a complete code of laws") to the deontic calculus; in this way, he shows that "the logic of the will results in prescriptive statements leading us to act." Thus, Bozzo-Rey concludes that "If utilitarian and deontic calculus can integrate a practical reasoning, one can support the notion that there is in Bentham's thought not two rival reasoning – for that would be nonsense – but a practical meta-reasoning, involving both calculus and authorising action, so an individual knows whether he has to obey a law or not. This meta-reasoning determines what sort of factor should help us to reach practical decisions in a given case; therefore it cannot be merely utilitarian, but should also take into account considerations of deontic logic" (2012, 180–2).

264 *Deontology*, 174.

265 See, for example, the already quoted passages from *Preparatory Principles*, 430 and 445.

266 *Deontology*, 175.

the agent's motivation, which is grounded on his/her desire for pleasure and aversion to pain.

> The obedience paid to any *particular* Law rests ultimately on a circumstance extrinsic to all Laws, a *general habit* of obedience. A habit of executing, upon all occasions and in all points, commands of some one person at least, or body of persons, in the state. [. . .] As every habit consists of acts, and every act must have some motive, and every motive is the expectation of some pain or pleasure, for the origin of this habit we must find the expectation of some pain or pleasure: a capacity of producing most pain or pleasure, such a capacity subsisting in the superior who first began to command.[267]

Bentham exemplifies the relation between a command and pain, which is constitutive of obligation, by making reference to law. So, "the whole business of Law [. . .] consists in nothing more than in setting forth the connection that there is established between punishment and the several modes of conduct that are the objects of Law."[268]

> The instrument the Law has to work with, in creating as well Duties as Restraints, is *Punishment*: or to speak as free as possible from figure, when it imposes duties, it punishes or threatens punishment: when it imposes restraints, it punishes or threatens punishment. 'Tis by punishment that it does both: 'tis by punishment alone that it can do either. Punishment is pain. Of pain, the idea is a simple one.[269]

Pain, as the consequence of the performance of a certain behaviour, creates the duty to refrain from that behaviour, which can be also explicitly forbidden by the law. So, if a child does not want to suffer pain as a consequence of an action, he/she will feel constrained not to carry out that action leading to pain. Therefore, pain is generative of obedience; indeed, pain gives rise to an internal duty not to perform the conduct productive of it. Moreover, compliance with a duty is supported by motivation, since no individual wants to experience the pain ensuing from disregarding that duty.

> What produces obedience to a Law is the expectation of punishment for disobedience. When action or forbearance is produced by a Law, it is no otherwise than by the expectation of pain which the Law excites. It is not difficult, therefore, to understand how the same expectation should produce the same action or forbearance even without a Law. Command a child to forbear reaching out at the window, if he has found punishment has been

267 *Preparatory Principles*, 343.
268 *Preparatory Principles*, 249.
269 *Preparatory Principles*, 102.

> usually the consequence of disobedience, he will forbear. But, without saying any thing to him in the way of command, punish him whenever he goes to reach out at the window, he will in like manner also forbear. He will forbear in this case reaching out at the window, just as he will forbear meddling with the flame of the candle, when his hands have been two or three times slightly pained by it.[270]

Similarly, moral or religious obligation depends on the individual acknowledgement of the pain and pleasure deriving from compliance or non-compliance with the conduct prescribed by the related moral or religious rule. Pain or pleasure makes a moral or religious command binding *in foro conscientiae*.

> By Conscience is meant the faculty of judgment, upon the occasion of it's pronouncing that an action is of that sort, which is apt to be follow'd by pain or pleasure from either of the two Sanctions, the Moral or the Religious: or else it is a judgment that the individual action in question will be follow'd by such Pain or Pleasure: in other words, it is the expectation of Pain or Pleasure as about to ensue from one or other of those sources.
>
> The phase '*forum conscientiae*' is plainly metaphorical. '*Forum*' is a Court of Justice. When we speak, therefore, of the *Forum Conscientiae*, we take the faculty of conscience and suppose it to be a person. We suppose it to be a Judge sitting in his court, and decreeing that the person in whose mind all this is supposed to pass shall experience a certain allotment of Pain or Pleasure accruing from one or other of these sources.
>
> When we speak of an obligation *in foro conscientiae*, we mean the idea of Pain or Pleasure as about to accrue from one or other of them in consequence of the action in question, according to the decree of this imaginary judge.[271]

As a result, common expressions such as "love of duty," "sense of duty," "Sacrifice [. . .] interest to duty" and "Duty can not be made to coincide with interest" are meaningless in Bentham's opinion.[272] "Love of duty," for example, is "an impossible motive" because it is tantamount to "love of the pains employed in coercion"; indeed, duty, which is synonymous with obligation, involves coercion.[273] An agent cannot obtain pleasure from that which he/she is forced to do. Similarly, "sense of duty" properly means "*fear* of the several pains," such as "fear of *legal punishment*," "fear of *loss of amity*," "fear of *loss of reputation*" and "fear of the wrath of God," which, "in the character of *evil consequences* to the individual in question, may (as it appears to him) befall him, in case of a neglect on his part, in relation to that same duty."[274]

270 *Preparatory Principles*, 184.
271 *Preparatory Principles*, 162.
272 Cf. *A Table of the Springs of Action*, 20, 49 and 114. See also *Deontology*, 121.
273 Cf. *A Table of the Springs of Action*, 20.
274 Cf. *A Table of the Springs of Action*, 114.

Duties derive from individual interest, that is, from the individual perception of pleasure and pain, the prospect of which orients the agent's decision. Sanctions act as inducements or restraints, by indicating pleasure or pain as the consequence of a course of action: they exhort the agent's will to conform his/her behaviour to the mode of conduct which is conducive to anticipated pleasure or aversive to anticipated pain.

An obligation is thus a fictitious entity resulting from a constructive process carried out by instrumental rationality which connects, in the form of a condition, the performance of a certain behaviour to volitional and perceptual elements, i.e. aversion to pain and desire for pleasure. Hence, as regards the notion of obligation, "Whoever wishes to see it dispelled must call in the principle of utility, and from the system prescribed by that [principle] borrow the word 'motive'."[275]

The obligation to act in a certain way depends on its related sanction, whose avoidance or achievement provides the agent with a motive for compliance with that obligation. On the basis of the origin of that motive, namely if it belongs to the political, moral or religious sanction, the obligation consequent to it can be political, moral or religious.[276] By means of the sanction, consisting in the prospect of pain or also pleasure, the individual is duty-bound to obey the corresponding moral, legal or religious norm.

> An obligation – understand here that sort of obligation which through the medium of the will operates on the active faculty – takes its nature from some act – from the act to which it applies itself: it is an obligation to perform or to abstain from performing a certain act.
>
> A legal obligation to perform the act in question is said to attach upon a man, to be incumbent upon him, in so far as in the event of his performing the act at the time and place in question he will not suffer any pain, but in the event of his not so performing it he will suffer a certain pain – viz. the pain that corresponds to it, and by the virtue of which, applying itself eventually as above, the obligation is created.[277]

Obedience to a legal, moral and religious rule cannot be obtained through the subject's passive submission because it requires the active involvement of his/her will.[278] The creation of an obligation depends on the ability of a sanction to give

275 *Deontology*, 207.

276 Cf. *Deontology*, 207. Here Bentham employs the particular expression "creating an obligation," which hints to the rational process of the construction of fictitious ethical entities such as obligation. Similar expressions also occur in *Preparatory Principles*, 259–60; *Of the Limits of The Penal Branch of Jurisprudence*, 317; *De l'ontologie*, 160 (Bowring viii, 206).

277 *De l'ontologie*, 160 (Bowring viii, 206).

278 See, for example, *Of Promulgation of the Laws and Promulgation of the Reasons Thereof*, Bowring i, 161: "But the greatest advantage is that which results from conciliating the approbation of all minds, by satisfying the public judgment, and obtaining obedience to the laws; not from a passive principle of blind fear alone, but with the concurrence of the will also." See also, *A Table of the Springs of Action*, 64: "Fancy not, not pretend to fancy, that by saying 'ought' or 'ought not' you can create a duty."

rise to the agent's motivation. The threat of a painful sanction or the enticement of a pleasurable sanction backs a mode of conduct which is instrumental in the avoidance of that painful sanction or in the attainment of that pleasurable sanction.

Conformity to a certain mode of conduct is the necessary means for the fulfilment of the desire, aroused by sanction, to avoid a certain pain and to achieve a certain pleasure. The mode of conduct aversive of pain or conducive to pleasure becomes binding by virtue of its relation with pain and pleasure. The perception of pain and pleasure endows that mode of conduct with a normative and a motivational force. Pleasure and pain are indeed the foundations of the practical domain and of its distinctive normative claim.

The law as a real entity

For the sake of accuracy and completeness, it is worth noting that in two passages from his text *Of the Limits of The Penal Branch of Jurisprudence* Bentham regards the law as a real entity to which he relates the notion of obligation or duty as its corresponding fictitious entities.

> An act is a real entity: a law is another. A duty or obligation is a fictitious entity, conceived as resulting from the union of the two former. A law commanding or forbidding an act thereby creates a duty or obligation.[279]

> What is it that every article of law has in common with the rest? It issues command, and by so doing it creates *duties*: or, what is another word for the same thing, *obligations*. The idea of duty is concerned in every thing that belongs to law. It is from hence that the differences and resemblances of the various branches of law are to be traced as from their common source.
>
> The notion of command leads to that of duty: that of duty to that of exemption, that of power and that of right: that of exemption to that of privilege: power and duty together, that of trust.[280]

Bentham places the law at the origin of the legal fictitious chain, made up by the consequent notions of command, duty, exemption, power, right, privilege and trust. By issuing a command, the law creates an obligation which gives rise to the other above-mentioned legal fictitious entities. Such a view, sketched out by Bentham, raises two important interpretative difficulties, which challenge the overall consistency and uniformity of his philosophical system, though they do not question the basic distinction between real and fictitious entities.

The first difficulty concerns the puzzling nature of the law as a real entity.[281] Actually, the law, along with the act prescribed by it, has neither a perceptible nor

279 *Of the Limits of The Penal Branch of Jurisprudence*, 316.

280 *Of the Limits of The Penal Branch of Jurisprudence*, 317.

281 Some scholars also, such as Bozzo-Rey (2009b, 34 n. 28) and Edvinsson (2009, 5–14), cast doubt on Bentham's consideration of the law as a real entity.

an inferential character, which, according to Bentham's ontology, distinguishes a real entity. The law has no empirical nature: unlike pain and pleasure, it cannot be an object of experience. In the same way, the law has no inferential nature, which belongs to certain metaphysical creatures.[282] The law appears to be more similar to a fictitious than a real entity. Its import and truth seem to depend on pain and pleasure, which makes it effective.

The second difficulty, deriving from the first, concerns the foundation of obligation, as a fictitious entity, on the law, as a real entity. In the previously quoted passages, an obligation is considered to be the product of the law. No doubt, one of the main purposes of the law is to impose a duty by means of a command. However, an obligation is not binding by itself but by virtue of the relation it maintains with certain real entities from which it receives its normative value. When related to the notion of law, the obligation still needs to be clarified. Indeed, the law cannot fulfil the foundational function generally ascribed to real entities. The law in itself is not normative. Moreover, even if the law were able to explain the notion of obligation, it would concern only legal obligations and not moral and religious obligations.

Some interesting suggestions to solve these interpretative difficulties seem to come from an excerpt from *Pannomial Fragments*, in which Bentham characterizes the relation between an obligation and the law in a slightly more detailed way.

> Obligation – a fictitious entity, is the product of a law – a real entity.
>
> A law, when entire, is a command; but a command supposes eventual punishment; for without eventual punishment, or the apprehension of it, obedience would be an effect without a cause.
>
> [. . .]
>
> Obligation has place, when the desire on the part of the superior, the obliger, being signified to the obligee, he understands at the same time, that in the event of his failing to comply with such desire, evil will befal him, and that to an amount greater than that of any evil which he could sustain in compliance with that desire.[283]

Again, Bentham points out the real nature of the law and the derivation of an obligation from the law. However, the law is not merely a command prescribing an act, but a command prescribing an act and making explicit the sort of punishment applied when disregarding that act. Hence, the law in its full form contains a reference to a punishment, that is, to a type of pain.

In order to provide an effective exposition of the notion of obligation, we have to relate it to pain and pleasure. When examining a legal obligation, the notion of the law contributes to its exposition, by establishing the connection between

282 See, indeed, *IPML*, 301: "What is a law? What the parts of a law? The subject of these questions, it is to be observed, is the *logical*, the *ideal*, the *intellectual* whole, not the *physical* one: the *law* and not the *statute*."

283 *Pannomial Fragments*, Bowring iii, 217.

the performance of a type of behaviour which is forbidden and the application of a sanction corresponding to a certain pain or sometimes to a certain pleasure.

Stating that the law creates an obligation is absolutely consistent with the idea that pleasure and pain are the foundations of the notion of obligation. By imposing a punishment, the law creates and makes explicit the relation between an obligation to act in a certain way and a sort of pain expected to be felt in case of non-compliance. Nevertheless, the statement concerning the reality of the law remains puzzling, as the law does not fit Bentham's definition of real entities and cannot serve their foundational function.

Probably the ability of law to create fictitious connections between duties and punishment induced Bentham to distinguish the law, as a real entity, from the notions of duty and obligation, as fictitious entities. This operation, however, would entail a general revision of the concept of a real entity, which, as it is outlined by Bentham, seems to be unable to successfully incorporate the notion of law.

Conflicting motives in practical reasoning

In *IPML*, at the conclusion of his treatment of motives, Bentham gives an illuminating and intriguing case of practical reasoning,[284] enabling him to illustrate the causative relation between an external event, consisting in a sanction, motives, duties and action. By doing so, he exemplifies the process underlying the constitution of agency and throws light on the pivotal connection between obligation and motivation.

Generally speaking, practical reasoning often involves a "variety of contending motives, by which a man may be acted upon at the same time."[285] Conflicts among motives are common in practical deliberation. Motives urge the agent to behave in different ways and consequently need to be evaluated and balanced in order to decide the conduct to carry out.

> When a man has it in contemplation to engage in any action, he is frequently acted upon at the same time by the force of divers motives: one motive, or set of motives, acting in one direction; another motive, or set of motives, acting as it were in an opposite direction. The motives on one side disposing him to engage in the action: those on the other, disposing him not to engage in it.[286]

With reference to an action of the positive kind, resulting in bodily movement, Bentham distinguishes between "impelling motives," "the influence of which tends to dispose" the agent to engage in that course of action, and "restraining

284 *IPML*, 122–3. The quotations contained in this paragraph, referring to Crillon's practical reasoning, are taken from here if not otherwise specified.
285 *IPML*, 122.
286 *IPML*, 122.

motives," "the influence of which tends to dispose" the agent not to engage in it. With reference to an action of the negative kind, resulting in abstention from movement, those appellations are interchanged: impelling motives tend to influence the agent not to engage in that action, whereas restraining motives dispose him/her to engage in it.

Bentham's example of practical judgment is based on a reworked anecdote, set in the context of the ideological dispute between Catholics and Protestants in the sixteenth century, when, according to the Catholic custom of that time, the elimination of Protestant believers was regarded as meritorious. Crillon, a Catholic, is ordered by his king, Charles IX of France, to suddenly attack and kill Coligny, a Protestant. Bentham focuses on Crillon's reasoning, whose conclusion partly disregards the king's order.

Instead of suddenly assassinating Coligny, Crillon prefers to challenge him in a formal duel, in conformity with his moral code of honour. This is the outcome of Crillon's deliberation, characterized by a number of "repugnant dictates," namely competing obligations to perform alternative courses of action. Bentham expands Crillon's reasoning, by identifying at least three "forces" exerting a pressure on his will. They generate five dictates, flowing one from the political (1), another from the religious (2) and the other three from the moral sanction (3).

1 By the political sanction, that is, by the sovereign's dictates, Crillon is "enjoined to put Coligny to death" by assassination.
2 "[B]y the religious sanction, that is, by the dictates of religious zeal," Crillon is "enjoined to put" Coligny "to death in any way."
3a "[B]y the moral sanction, or, in other words, by the dictates of honour, that is, of the love of reputation," Crillon is permitted and then, in accordance with his sovereign's mandate, enjoined "to fight the adversary upon equal terms."
3b By another moral sanction, or, more precisely, "by the dictates of enlarged benevolence," consisting in "respecting the interests of a certain set of persons,"[287] Crillon is enjoined not to attempt Coligny's "life in any way, but to remain at peace with him."
3c By still another moral sanction or, more precisely, "by the dictates of private benevolence" Crillon is enjoined "not to meddle with [Coligny] at any rate."

Deliberation pertains to the ends and their related means. In a process of evaluation and weighing up, the understanding considers different and often conflicting ends. So, when deciding how to act among possible alternatives connected to different ends, the agent makes "the balance on the side of happiness,"[288] i.e. "the balance on the side of pleasure or pain."[289]

287 *IPML*, 117.
288 *Essay on Logic*, UC 101.148 (Bowring viii, 232).
289 *A Table of the Springs of Action*, 67.

In his deliberation Crillon is faced with conflicting duties, deriving from different kinds of sanction. The dictates of honour, first, and those of benevolence, then, tip Crillon's balance in favour of fighting his adversary if he accepts his challenge; otherwise Crillon would remain at peace. The obligations created by the moral sanction outweigh the obligations created by the political and religious sanctions. The binding power of each obligation depends on the motivational ability of the corresponding sanction backing it.

Bentham analyses the different motives impelling Crillon to comply with each of the related above-listed duties and consequently restraining him from conforming to the opposite duties. Such motives are aroused by different types of sanction or, properly speaking, by Crillon's sensibility to the pain and pleasure flowing from these sanctions as consequences of his performance of a certain action.

In order to be normative, that is, to put a constraint on the agent's will by claiming conformity, an obligation needs to be joined to a sanction, which produces the feelings of pain and pleasure. The expectation of the pain and pleasure ensuing from a sanction gives rise to motives which enforce obligations.

1 The political sanction generates in Crillon self-regarding motives for abiding by the sovereign's order, if Crillon is aware that the sovereign has the power "to punish him for non-compliance, or reward him for compliance."

2 The religious sanction motivates Crillon's obedience to the corresponding dictates, if Crillon believes that it is "God's pleasure he should comply with them," that is, if he believes that the person who pleases God, by conforming his/her behavior to his will, is expected to be rewarded by him or that the person who displeases God, by disregarding his will, is expected to be punished by him.

3a The moral sanction generally consists in his/her peers praising or blaming the individual who is responsible for a type of conduct. Moral sanction arouses in Crillon the love of reputation as a motive for obeying its related dictate, if Crillon believes that his/her peers in the community to which he belongs "would expect and require" that obedience.

3b–c Other moral sanctions provoke motives of benevolence in Crillon, if he believes that his community would benefit from his compliance with the duties corresponding to these motives. These motives might be labelled as extra-regarding inasmuch as the expected pleasure deriving from the action they support concerns not only the individual who carries out that action but a certain set of people belonging to his/her community.

Crillon's practical balance is focused not on the action in itself but rather on the consequences following its performance. Such pleasurable or painful consequences motivate and bind Crillon to perform the conduct which enables him to obtain or avoid them. Motives and duties arise from the desire for pleasure and aversion to pain.

Crillon's decision is directed by the consideration that the consequences springing from the moral sanction, corresponding to the pleasure of honour in case of compliance with the related duty or to the pain of bad reputation in case of disregard for that duty, are weightier or stronger than the consequences springing from the political and religious sanctions, corresponding to the pleasure of a legal or divine reward or to the pain of a legal or divine punishment.

The criterion of Crillon's practical judgement lies in the utility of an action, that is, in the consideration, in quantitative terms, of pleasure or pain that the performance of an action is anticipated to bring about. The assessment of motives and, then, of dictates is based on the quantity of pleasure or pain their related sanctions produce or are expected to produce.

> Seldom (it will readily be seen) does it happen, that a man's conduct stands exposed to the action of no more than one motive. Frequently, indeed – not to say commonly – does it happen, that, on one and the same occasion, it is acted upon by a number of motives, acting in opposite directions: in each of those two opposite directions respectively, sometimes by one, sometimes by more than one motive: and, on every such occasion, be it what it may, the action is, of course, the result of that one motive, or that group of simultaneously operating motives, of which on that same occasion, the force and influence happen to be the strongest.[290]

The strength of the moral obligation to fight a duel according to a formal protocol depends on Crillon's sensibility either to the pleasure of the esteem of his fellows or to the pain of dishonour and a bad reputation. In other words, the sanction or, more precisely, the subjective perception of pleasure or pain, expected from the application of the sanction, establishes and enforces the related mode of conduct to the extent that it is contributive to that pleasure or helps to avoid that pain. The prospect of pleasure and pain stemming from a sanction arouses Crillon's desire to conform his behaviour to the mode of conduct backed by that sanction. Pleasure and pain are the sources of motivation and normativity: the desire to enjoy a kind of pleasure and avert a kind of pain makes binding the action which is instrumental in its fulfilment.

The actual or anticipated sensation of pleasure or pain, ensuing from different sanctions, generates opposite duties supported by different motives. Crillon chooses not to assassinate his religious opponent, disregarding the king's command, but to fight him in a duel, in agreement with the duty imposed by the moral sanction. In Crillon's view, the motive of the love of reputation prevails over the political and religious motives, because it is weightier or stronger and thus more influential than them. The quantitative evaluation of each of these motives is determined by the subjective perception of the weight or strength of their related pleasures and pains. Notwithstanding the varieties of duties and of the corresponding sanctions to which Crillon's conduct is exposed, the freedom

290 *A Table of the Springs of Action*, 112.

of his will remains unchallenged: the direction of Crillon's action is caused by his volitional states, i.e. desires or motives, which actually dictate to him how to behave.

Duty and interest junction principle

The binding power of a normative order such as law, morality or religion lies in its ability to provide the agent with motives for compliance. A legislator who intends to guide his/her subjects' conduct has to take into account their reflective self-governing nature and the corresponding individual process of the construction of an obligation.

This aspect is remarked upon by Bentham in his definition of a law in *Of the Limits of the Penal Branch of Jurisprudence*. A law is in fact regarded as the expression of the sovereign's volition aimed at guiding the conduct of a person who is subject to his power. This volition should be accompanied or enforced by "the expectation of certain events" in the form of sanctions, "the prospect of which it is intended should act as a motive upon those whose conduct is in question."[291]

Moreover, among the different respects in which a law may be considered, Bentham points out its force, consisting of "the *motives* it relies on for enabling it to produce the effect it aims at."[292] At the basis of this conception of law there is the practical principle according to which "The forces, and the only forces, by which the human will is influenced are *motives.*"[293]

Bentham underlines the need for a law to motivate its subjects in order to gain compliance: he is aware that without a motive there is neither action nor law. So, Bentham distinguishes the law into two parts: the *directive* part, corresponding to the legislator's will, serves "to make known to you what the inclination of the legislator is"; the *sanctional* or *incitative* part serves "to make known to you what motive the legislator has furnished you with for complying with that inclination." The former part is addressed to the subject's understanding whereas the latter part is addressed to his/her will.[294] These faculties cooperate in the construction of action.

As Bentham makes clear in a passage from *Deontology*, "it never is, to any practical purpose, a man's duty to do that which it is his interest not to do."[295]

291 Cf. *Of the Limits of the Penal Branch of Jurisprudence*, 24–5.

292 *Of the Limits of the Penal Branch of Jurisprudence*, 41.

293 *Of the Limits of the Penal Branch of Jurisprudence*, 91.

294 *Of the Limits of the Penal Branch of Jurisprudence*, 143: "In this case, the law may plainly enough be distinguished into two parts: the one serving to make known to you what the inclination of the legislator is: the other serving to make known to you what motive the legislator has furnished you with for complying with that inclination: the one addressed more particularly to your understanding; the other, to your will. The former of these parts may be termed the *directive*: the other, the *sanctional* or *incitative*." For an analysis of Bentham's conception of a law as composed by a directive and a sanctional or incitative part, see Tusseau 2014a, 80–9, 95–102; see also Zhai 2014. A critical examination of Bentham's notion of command is provided by Hart 1982, 241–68.

295 *Deontology*, 121.

A legislator should try to align pursuance of a duty with individual interest. In other words, Bentham suggests that the legislator join duty to interest: this is what he calls the "*Duty and Interest* junction principle."[296] Bentham gives a political application to the practical principle of the subordination of obligation to motivation: "That which the ruler has endeavoured to make it the subject-citizen's *interest* to do, he calls his *duty*. In so far as this endeavour has been successful, *duty* and *interest* have been made to coincide."[297]

The task of the legislator is to artificially harmonize the different interests of the members of his/her community through rewards and especially punishments.[298] The purpose of the work of the legislator has to consist in coordinating and regulating individual desires in order to make them consistent with the pursuit of the final and universal common end, corresponding to the happiness of the whole community, that is, to the greatest happiness of the greatest number. Bentham does not undermine individual interests in favour of general interests but subsumes the former to the latter, bringing both of them into agreement through the intervention of the legislator. The legislator's ability to coordinate his/her people's behaviour basically lies in the possibility of constructing ethical values and standards and thus in the manipulation of particular ends in the light of pleasure and pain.

In this sense, we can understand Bentham's conception of obligation as service, which is put forward in *General View of a Complete Code of Laws*. Bentham complains that in texts about legislation and jurisprudence, "the idea of obligation is too often independent of the idea of service." Bentham instead intends to reappraise the notion of service, which "can serve as a limit and a guide in the establishment of obligations." The purpose of an obligation should be to render a service: "there ought never to exist any obligation which is not founded upon a service received or to be received"; consequently, a bad law is a law "which imposes an obligation without rendering any service." The law makes the individual subject to the obligation to perform a certain act and this performance is backed by a sanction which is evil, that is, pain. As Bentham observes, "the principle of utility requires that the evil of the obligation, whatever it be, should be compensated by the good of the service."[299]

296 See for example *Tracts on Poor Laws and Pauper Management*, Bowring viii, 380: "*Duty and Interest* junction principle – No means to be omitted that can contribute to strengthen the junction between *interest* and *duty*, in the instance of the person intrusted with the management: – *i.e.* to make it each man's *interest* to observe on every occasion that conduct which it is his *duty* to observe. Application of this principle to practice – All means of action upon a man's interest, reduceable to the two heads of *punishment* and *reward*." For a comprehensive study of the duty and interest junction principle, as regards its foundations and application, see Harrison 1983, 106–34.

297 *A Table of the Springs of Action*, 72.

298 Cf. Halévy 1995, vol. i, 27. Halévy examines Bentham's *principle of the artificial identification of interests*. The overcoming of the opposition between the interests of the rulers and the interests of their subjects by means of the promotion of the general interest pursued by the rulers is examined by Schofield 1996. On the same topic see Postema 2006 and also 1998. For an examination of Bentham's theory of institutional design as an instrument for directing people's decision at the pursuit of general well-being see Elster 2013, 140–90.

299 Cf. *General View of a Complete Code of Laws*, Bowring iii, 180–1.

Only by motivating its subjects to conform their behaviour to its rules, can a code fulfil its function of providing guidance. Bentham rejects the idea of obligation as adequacy to a standard of behaviour external to the agent; instead, he puts forward an internalization of the notion of obligation, by tracing it back to the individual desire to obtain pleasure and avoid pain. The dependence of obligation on motivation is, then, the foundational practical concept which a legislator should bear in mind in his/her work of codification.

From Bentham to the normative question

In the introductory remarks to this book I tried to outline a path starting from the contemporary philosophical scene and turning to seventeenth- and eighteenth-century British moral thinkers. The objective was to understand the current so-called normative question as an investigation pertaining to the foundations of practical reality and, then, to trace it back to the historical context from which it arose. By exploring its origins and especially by focusing on Bentham's original and unfortunately ignored contribution to it, I claimed that it was possible to provide new insights to solve the normative problem and, consequently, to illuminate the foundations of ethics from a different point of view.

As a conclusion to my work devoted to the examination of Bentham's ontology of normativity, I attempt to go from Bentham's treatment of the notion of obligation to contemporary reflections on the nature and sources of normativity. This attempt offers me the opportunity to recapitulate Bentham's main ideas concerning obligation involved in ethical standards and, then, to enhance his legacy with reference to the normative question.

The research conducted in this book was mainly aimed at reconstructing Bentham's idea of obligation characterizing the ethical realm. Bentham maintained a lifelong commitment to assessing the nature of various practical domains such as morality, law and also religion. As their distinctive property, the elements making up practical domains are characterized by a basically linguistic ontology, which is endowed with normativity, that is, with the property to make claims on the agents' behaviour to require obedience. In other words, concepts such as duty, goodness, rightness and virtue have a directive or guidance function, because they prescribe or recommend the performance of the act to which they refer. The normative claim essentially characterizes ethical standards and, thus, any investigation into their authoritative feature is an investigation into the foundations of ethics and the obligation entailed by them.

More than his principle of utility, the distinction between real and fictitious entities provides Bentham with the ontological and epistemological framework to outline the structure of normative domains such as morality and law and then bring about their reform. My examination of Bentham's ontology of normativity was committed first to clarifying his fictionalism by defining the notions of a real entity and a fictitious entity along with their relationship. Then, I concentrated my attention on the specific nature of ethics, which is identified and characterized by a normative claim. Bentham's conception of normativity entirely depends on his doctrine of real and fictitious entities, which concerns all the areas of human knowledge. Therefore, I tried to show the intimate connection between Bentham's moral and legal theory with his view of ontology and epistemology.

We can single out certain crucial points in the path that lead us from Bentham's philosophy to the current normative question: the theory of real and fictitious entities, the introduction of a linguistic notion of existence, the combination of an empirical and a constructivist perspective in representing and thinking of the natural and the practical world, and the internalist approach to ethics. Let us re-examine these points in short, thereby exploring how they are related to the controversy on the status of normativity. Bentham's strategy to clarify the normative claim of morality, law and religion is directed to disclosing the ontological and epistemological bases on which this distinctive property of the ethical domains resides. Consequently, we cannot understand Bentham's idea of normativity if we do not appreciate his ontology and epistemology.

Bentham provides a systematic and consistent account of the fictitious character of mathematical objects, physical properties, moral values, legal rules and religious norms. In the history of thought the originality and importance of Bentham's idea of a fictitious entity can scarcely be overstated, notwithstanding certain precursors of his view. Bentham is convinced of the falseness of certain linguistic constructs with an ontological claim. He understands a fictitious entity as something false, which is however regarded as if it were true. Bentham's fictionalist approach questions the ontological and epistemological nature of the elements making up the mathematical, the physical, the moral, the legal and the religious domains of knowledge. In particular, it challenges the effective correspondence of beliefs and statements to an alleged external reality, on which the idea of truth resides, thereby assuming that the human mind has through language autonomous constructive ability in conceiving of the world.

Terms such as motion, quality, relation, cause, virtue, goodness, obligation, right and power represent mere artefacts characterized by a mental or, more precisely, a linguistic form of existence, as they are names produced by the activity of the human mind carried out on perceptual elements. On the other hand, real entities, by and large, have an empirical character and their existence lies in human perception. Bentham stresses the linguistic nature of real and fictitious entities which are, precisely speaking, names of real entities and names of fictitious entities included in a sentence on which their meaning depends. Real and fictitious entities, along with their relations, are resolved in language which accounts for them as nouns.

In Bentham's philosophy then, language has an ontological and epistemological function, since it contributes to the knowledge and interpretation of reality. Our imagining of the external world is shaped by language which plays a performative role, by providing a form of existence, though fictitious, to the natural and practical framework of reality. This linguistic ontology, depending on the creative power of the human mind, is complementary to and interrelated with the empirical ontology captured by sense-perceptions. Bentham emphasizes the existence-conferring ability of language, which enables human beings to consistently structure their knowledge and coordinate their behaviour in society.

The relation that a fictitious entity maintains with its empirical source, identified as a real entity, is constitutive of its import and truth. Divorced from reality, a fictitious entity is nothing but falsehood and nonsense. Paraphrasis, as a linguistic method to disentangle the obscurities and ambiguities of fictitious entities, reveals the empirical foundations on which the construction of practical reality resides.

Fictitious objects are contrivances with a theoretical and a practical function. From a theoretical standpoint, they are instrumental in our image of the world, giving an order to perceptions and making sense of experience; consequently, the physical world or, more precisely, our representation of it is artificial, since it is the outcome of an organizational process of the human mind. From a practical standpoint, fictitious objects make reasoning and decision possible, by orienting and directing people's individual and collective behaviour. According to Bentham, the activity of the human mind consists in creating fictitious entities; without these entities knowledge and action, and more generally social life, would be impossible. In other words, fictitious objects allow people to think, communicate and act.

The theory of real and fictitious entities lies at the very basis of Bentham's account of the natural world and of the science of morality and law. Bentham's fictionalism not only provides the framework for his political and legal reform, but also puts forward a constructivist ontology based on language, which underlies the various subsets of reality. Bentham's approach to fictitious entities, thus, affords an original and critical point of view to rethink the constitution and the structure of the mathematical, the physical, the moral, the legal and the religious realms. One of Bentham's major contributions to philosophy is the multidisciplinary application of the notion of a fictitious entity and the interdisciplinary identification of the foundations of our knowledge. Bentham intertwines different disciplinary perspectives in working out the structure of reality, which appears to be a human creation produced by cooperation between the sensory faculties and the intellectual faculties.

Bentham conceives of values, duties, virtues and standards of behaviour as fictitious entities, namely as linguistic elements, whose import and truth depend on the empirical perceptions of pain and pleasure, which are real entities. Ethical standards turn out to be human artefacts, related to perceptions; more precisely, their guidance claim on us lies in the constitutive relation ethical standards have with pain or pleasure. Indeed, pain and pleasure are the foundations of the ethical domain and of its peculiar normative claim.

Normativity, as the distinctive property of the ethical area, consists in providing an agent with reasons for action. From Bentham's perspective, these reasons for action are normative inasmuch as they are based on pain and pleasure. Values, virtues, norms, commands and standards of behaviour purport to direct an agent if they are connected with pain or pleasure; their normative, that is, their action-guiding prerogative derives from these perceptions. In Bentham's view normativity has naturalistic foundations which, though external to the agent, rely on his/her psychological structure: the desire to enjoy or maximize pleasure and the desire to avoid or minimize pain direct and guide the agent to choose the course of action which leads him/her to the achievement of that pleasure or to the avoidance of that pain.

By putting forward his model of normativity, Bentham contributes to the shaping of the early modern idea of obligation as an internal requirement of a self-governing moral agent's thinking. The creation of an obligation, along with the notions involving it, such as rights, values and virtues, depends on the ability of its issuing authority to arouse in the agent his/her desire to avoid punishment, deriving from disregarding that obligation, or his/her desire to gain praise, deriving from complying with that obligation. Punishment and praise are sanctions, consisting in pain or pleasure, which drive the agent to choose a course of action. An obligation is then the result of the agent's practical reasoning concerning the evaluation and the balance of the consequences that the performance of a certain behaviour or several types of behaviour will bring forth.

The connection that an obligation has with motivation is crucial. In order to feel the pressure to conform his/her action to a standard of behaviour, a pressure in which the normative claim resides, an agent needs to perceive the pain and the pleasure related to that standard and, then, to be motivated to act from that perception. Ethical values provide the agent with guidance, by recommending him/her to behave in a certain way; their guidance function springs from the pain or pleasure that the conformity with these values is expected to bring forth.

The relation between normativity and motivation, namely between duty and desire, is thus fundamental to understanding Bentham's idea of ethics and of its decision- or action-guiding claim. Something can bind an agent to adopt a certain behaviour inasmuch as this thing motivates the agent to behave accordingly. Motivation consists in the desire to achieve the pleasure or escape the pain stemming from the adoption of that behaviour. Therefore, one can say that desire makes an action binding. The agent's volition and, thus, his/her behaviour is moved by his/her desire to avoid pain and to gain pleasure. As they are the motivating factors of deliberation and action, pain and pleasure can be considered the sources of the normativity of practical reality; indeed, obligation springs from desire for pleasure and aversion to pain.

Bentham openly embraces an internalist position, by regarding ethical entities and the normative phenomena characterizing them as resulting from the agent's motivation. Moral and legal obligation or, more generally, normativity is a linguistic creation based on the real entities of pain and pleasure, which excite the individual motivational set. The motivating aspect of pain and pleasure turns out to be the key to understanding Bentham's ontology of normativity.

An action is right and thus worthy to be performed inasmuch as it leads to pleasure or, at least, it entails the reduction of pain. The rightness of that action resides in its utility and this utility is measured by the agent himself/herself according to his/her receptiveness to a certain pleasure or a certain pain. Despite appearances, Bentham does not put forward a merely reductionist theory of normativity, according to which obligation depends on an external fact, i.e. a sanction. No doubt, it is true that a sanction, as a source of pain or pleasure, is an objective event related, for example, to the compliance or non-compliance with a command prescribed by an authority. However, it is also true that the pain and the pleasure deriving from a sanction are subjective perceptions; in other words, pain and pleasure need to be felt by the agent so that they can make their normative claim. Bentham upholds an internalist position, since he traces back normativity to the agent's conative states, such as desires, interests, dispositions and wants.

According to Bentham's view, moral values and legal norms are not normative in themselves, but inasmuch as they are taken as normative by the agent. Bentham's internalism lies in this subjective constitution of the practical world. His version of internalism nourishes his constructivist approach, which consists in the fundamental idea that the practical world is a creation of the human mind on the basis of the perceptions of pain and pleasure. Bentham's fictionalism turns out to be a form of constructivism: reality, or at least its representation, is the result of the activity of the cognitive human faculties which, by means of fictitious entities and their connections with real entities, give sense and truth to the world in which human beings live and interact.

Bentham's internalism is originally joined to the idea that the ethical domain, including its normative claim, is a fictitious construction of the human mind. Bentham does not limit himself to tracing obligation back to desire, as early modern British internalists do, but he rethinks this connection between normativity and motivation within a general fictitious context. Bentham combines empicirism, fictionalism, constructivism and internalism in conceiving of ethics. His idea of obligation, as a fictitious creation of the human mind depending on naturalistic foundations, is a unique position in the debates on normativity. By virtue of this, Bentham's approach enables us to re-assess the premises of the normative question and to explore it from a new perspective.

Bentham's idea of the ontology of ethics as a linguistic creation of the human mind underpins his theory of normativity. The ethical domain, however, is not an arbitrary construction; this is the reason why Bentham levels his criticism against the deceptive use of fictitious entities which is aimed at the protection of the interests of the ruling few. On the contrary, ethics has a firm foundation in empirical reality or, more precisely, in the psychological constitution of human nature, which is naturally oriented to pursue happiness, namely to seek pleasure and avoid pain. The empirical roots of the practical realm provide the guidelines for the legislator's and judge's decisions, so that they can achieve the greatest happiness of the greatest number.

By taking advantage of Bentham's perspective on fictionalism and constructivism, one can try to throw light on the normative question and to advance new insights for its settlement. The moral, legal and religious orders, including their prerogative to claim conformity, rely on the agent's desire for pleasure and, similarly, aversion to pain. Bentham's duty and interest principle summarizes the constitutive relation between normativity and motivation, which allows us to clarify the foundations of practical reality. The individual perception of pain and pleasure endows something with the property to guide human behaviour.

The power to make a claim to guide human behaviour, in which normativity resides, is related to the agent's feeling of pain and pleasure. Pain and pleasure provide the agent who perceives them with various reasons for his/her action and these reasons for action, having both a binding and a motivating force, are liable to be balanced according to the quantity of actual or expected pain and pleasure from which they arise. Agents regulate their conduct in compliance with the standards of behaviour that they believe conducive to happiness, by meaning with happiness both the enjoyment of pleasure and the reduction of pain. When reasoning about what to do, the agent deliberates on the utility of different and often conflicting courses of action, by taking into account the effects that these courses of action will bring forth.

Due to the extremely limited circulation of his manuscripts, along with their textual difficulties, Bentham's fictionalism was not so influential as it could have been and would have deserved. Today, thanks to the enormous editorial and interpretative work carried on by Bentham leading scholars and specialized research teams, such as the Bentham Project in London and the Centre Bentham in Paris, we are able to have an increasing knowledge of Bentham's ideas, which can provide new insights into crucial topics in philosophy and law.

Bentham's fictionalism offers a cutting-edge approach to examine the structure and the roots of the several ethical domains and, then, to settle the normative question. To the best of my knowledge, the attempt to explain the normative claim of morality and law, along with its constitutive connection with motivation, in the larger framework of the distinction between real and fictitious entities has never been pursued. Therefore, one of Bentham's major philosophical legacies is his project to understand the obligation which is at the heart of ethics as a fictitious construction of the human mind; in other words, by conceiving of the core notion of obligation in terms of fictitious entity, Bentham laid the foundations for illuminating the idea of normativity from a fictionalist point of view. This project is still worthy to be pursued in all its depth, complexity and fruitfulness.

Bibliography

Primary sources

The following volumes are included in ***The Collected Works of Jeremy Bentham***, general editors Burns J. (1961–79), Dinwiddy J. (1977–83), Rosen F. (1983–95), Rosen F. and Schofield P. (1995–2003), Schofield P. (2003–), London: The Athlone Press, 1968–81; Oxford, UK: Clarendon Press, 1983– in progress.

Chrestomathia, edited by Smith M. and Burston W., Oxford, UK: Clarendon Press, 1993.

A Comment on the Commentaries and A Fragment on Government, edited by Burns J. and Hart H., London: The Athlone Press, 1977.

The Correspondence of Jeremy Bentham. Volume 1: 1752–76, edited by Sprigge T., London: The Athlone Press, 1968.

The Correspondence of Jeremy Bentham. Volume 2: 1777–80, edited by Sprigge T., London: The Athlone Press, 1968.

The Correspondence of Jeremy Bentham. Volume 8: January 1809 to December 1816, edited by Conway S., Oxford, UK: Clarendon Press, 1988.

The Correspondence of Jeremy Bentham. Volume 10: July 1820 to December 1821, edited by Conway S., Oxford, UK: Clarendon Press, 1994.

Deontology together with A Table of the Springs of Action and Article on Utilitarianism, edited by Goldworth A., Oxford, UK: Clarendon Press, 1983.

First Principles Preparatory to Constitutional Code, edited by Schofield P., Oxford, UK: Clarendon Press, 1989.

An Introduction to the Principles of Morals and Legislation, edited by Burns J. and Hart H., London: The Athlone Press, 1970.

Of Laws in General, edited by Hart H., London: The Athlone Press, 1970.

"Legislator of the World": Writings on Codification, Law and Education, edited by Schofield P. and Harris J., Oxford, UK: Clarendon Press, 1998.

Of the Limits of the Penal Branch of Jurisprudence, edited by Schofield P., Oxford, UK: Clarendon Press, 2010.

Preparatory Principles, edited by Long D. and Schofield P., Oxford, UK: Clarendon Press, 2016.

Rights, Representation, and Reform: Nonsense Upon Stilts and Other Writings on the French Revolution, edited by Schofield P., Pease-Watkin C. and Blamires C., Oxford, UK: Clarendon Press, 2002.

Other editions of Bentham's works

Bentham's Manuscripts, University College London Library (unedited).

Bentham's Theory of Legislation being Principes de législation and Traités de législation civile et pénale, translated and edited from the French of É. Dumont by C. Atkinson, vol. 1, *Principles of Legislation, Principles of the Civil Code*, London: Oxford University Press, 1914.

De l'ontologie et autres textes sur les fictions, texte anglais établi par Schofield P., traduction et commentaires par Cléro J. et Laval C., Paris: Éditions du Seuil, 1997.

A Fragment on Government and an Introduction to the Principles of Morals and Legislation by Jeremy Bentham, edited with an Introduction by Harrison W., Oxford, UK: Basil Blackwell, 1948.

Jeremy Bentham's Economic Writings, edited by Stark W., 3 vols., London: Allen & Unwin, 1952–54.

Logic and Universal Grammar, transcribed by Schofield P., Bentham Manuscripts, University College London Library.

Traités de législation civile et pénale, préface de Bozzo-Rey M., Brunon-Ernst A, De Champs E., Paris: Dalloz, 2010.

The Works of Jeremy Bentham, Published under the Superintendence of his Executor, John Bowring, 11 vols., Edinburgh: William Tait, 1838–43.

Other sources

Berkeley G., *A Treatise Concerning the Principles of Human Knowledge*, in *The Works of George Berkeley, Bishop of Cloyne*, edited by Luce A. and Jessop T., 9 vols., London: Nelson, 1948–1957, vol. 2.

Blackstone W., *Commentaries on the Laws of England*, 4 vols., Oxford, UK: Clarendon Press, 1765–69.

Clarke S., *A Discourse Concerning the Being and Attributes of God, the Obligations of Natural Religion, and the Truth and Certainty of the Christian Revelation*, Edinburgh: A. Allardice, 1823.

Encyclopédie ou Dictionnaire raisonné des sciences, des arts et des métiers, par une société de gens de lettres, mis en ordre & publié par M. Diderot [. . .] & quant à la partie mathematique, par M. d'Alembert [. . .], 28 vols., Geneva, Paris, Neufchatel: Briasson and others, 1754–72.

Hartley D., *Observations on Man, His Frame, His Duty, and His Expectations*, 2 vols., London: Richardson, 1749.

Hume D., *Enquiry concerning the Principles of Morals*, in Hume D., *Enquiries concerning Human Understanding and concerning the Principles of Morals*, edited by Selby-Bigge L., revised by Nidditch P., Oxford, UK: Clarendon Press, 1975[3].

Hume D., *A Treatise of Human Nature*, edited by Selby-Bigge L., revised by Nidditch P., Oxford, UK: Oxford University Press, 1978[2].

Hutcheson F., *An Inquiry into the Original of Our Ideas of Beauty and Virtue in Two Treatises*, edited by Leidhold W., Indianapolis (IN): Liberty Fund, 2004 (1725).

Kant I., *Gesammelte Schriften*, Berlin: de Gruyter, 1902-.

Kant I., *Groundwork of the Metaphysics of Morals*, translated and edited by Gregor M. and Timmermann J., with an introduction by Korsgaard C., Cambridge, UK: Cambridge University Press, 2012.

Locke J., *An Essay Concerning Human Understanding*, edited by Nidditch P., Oxford, UK: Clarendon Press, 1975.

Porphyry, *Introduction*, translated, with a commentary, by Barnes J., Oxford, UK: Clarendon Press, 2003.

Sanderson R., *Logicae Artis Compendium*, edited by Ashworth J., Bologna, Italy: CLUEB, 1985.

Lord Shaftesbury, *Inquiry Concerning Virtue or Merit*, in Shaftesbury, *Characteristics of Men, Manners, Opinions, Times*, edited by Klein L., Cambridge, UK: Cambridge University Press, 1999, 163–230.

Studies

Ayer A. (1954), *The Principle of Utility*, in Id., *Philosophical Essays*, London: Macmillan, 250–70.

Bagnoli C. (2015), *Constructivism in Metaethics*, in Zalta E., ed., *The Stanford Encyclopedia of Philosophy*. http://plato.stanford.edu/archives/spr2015/entries/constructivism-metaethics/.

Baranger D. (2014), *The Legislator's Tormented Soul (Utility in Bentham's Of the Limits of the Penal Branch of Jurisprudence)*, in Tusseau 2014, 375–95.

Baumgardt D. (1952), *Bentham and the Ethics of Today*, Princeton, NJ: Princeton University Press.

Bouriau C. (2013), *Le "comme si": Kant, Vaihinger et le fictionalisme*, Paris: Les Éditions du Cerf.

Bouveresse J. (1993), *La théorie des fictions chez Bentham*, in Mulligan K. & Roth R., eds., *Regards sur Bentham et l'utilitarisme*, Genève: Librairie Droz, 87–98.

Bozzo-Rey M. (2007), *Le statut du principe d'utilité dans la philosophie politique et juridique de Jeremy Bentham*, Thèse de doctorat, Université Paris 10 – Nanterre.

—— (2008), "De la estructura de la sociedad política a la construcción Del discurso jurídico. Nueva aproximación a la teoría benthamiana de las ficciones," *Anales de la Cátedra Francisco Suárez*, 42, 95–118.

—— (2009), "Entre analyse linguistique et théorie générale du droit: La *Nomographie* de Jeremy Bentham," *International Journal for the Semiotics of Law*, 22, 425–36.

—— (2009a), *Loi et volonté chez Bentham et Rousseau*, in De Champs & Cléro 2009, 35–51.

—— (2009b), "Loi, fiction et logique dans la pensée juridique de Jeremy Bentham," *Annales de Droit*, 3, 27–50.

—— (2012), *Social Control and the Legal Panoptic Paradigm*, in Brunon-Ernst 2012, 161–84.

—— (2014), *Reducing the Limits of the Realm of Possibilities: Law, Action and Will in Jeremy Bentham's Thought*, in Tusseau 2014, 338–57.

—— (2017), "Indirect legislation: it is just a question of time", *History of European Ideas*, 43, 106–21.

Bozzo-Rey M. & Tusseau G. (2011), eds., *Bentham juriste: l'utilitarisme juridique en question*, Paris: Economica.

Brunon-Ernst A. (2012), ed., *Beyond Foucault: New Perspectives on Bentham's Panopticon*, Farnham, UK: Ashgate.

Burns J. (1989), "Bentham and Blackstone: A lifetime's dialectic," *Utilitas*, 1, 22–40.

—— (1993), "Nature and natural authority in Bentham," *Utilitas*, 5, 209–19.

—— (2005), "Happiness and utility: Jeremy Bentham's equation," *Utilitas*, 17, 46–61.
Campos Boralevi L. (1984) *Bentham and the Oppressed*, Berlin: de Gruyter.
Cléro J. (1993), "La théorie des fictions chez Jeremy Bentham," *Nouvelles de la République des Lettres*, 2, 47–71.
—— (1998), "La réflexion benthamienne sur les mathématiques," *Revue de synthèse*, 119, 447–84.
—— (2000), "La valeur d'une théorie des fictions," *Laval théologique et philosophique*, 56, 439–61.
—— (2004), *Les raisons de la fiction: les philosophes et les mathématiques*, Paris: Colin.
—— (2006), *Bentham: Philosophe de l'utilité*, Paris: Ellipses.
—— (2007), "Quelques difficultés symptomatiques de la théorie benthamienne des fictions," *Cahiers critiques de philosophie*, 4, 73–84.
—— (2012), *Penal Theory without the Panopticon*, in Brunon-Ernst 2012, 79–114.
—— (2014), *Essai sur les fictions*, Paris: Hermann.
—— (2014a), "On the ambiguous status of pleasure in Bentham's theory of fictions," *Utilitas*, 26, 346–66.
—— (2015), " Le calcul benthamien des plaisirs et des peines," *Archives de Philosophie*, 78, 229–58.
Copp D. (2004), *Moral Naturalism and Three Grades of Normativity*, in Schaber P. (2004), ed., *Normativity and Naturalism*, Heusenstamm, Germany: Ontos Verlag, 7–45.
Darwall S. (1989), "Motive and Obligation in the British Moralists," *Social Philosophy and Policy*, 7, 133–50.
—— (1995), *The British Moralists and the Internal "Ought": 1640–1740*, Cambridge, UK: Cambridge University Press.
—— (2004) *Autonomy in Modern Natural Law*, in Brender N & Krasnoff L. (2004), eds., *New Essays on the History of Autonomy: A Collection Honoring J. B. Schneewind*, Cambridge, UK: Cambridge University Press, 110–29.
De Champs E. (1999), "The place of Jeremy Bentham's theory of fictions in eighteenth-century linguistic thought," *Journal of Bentham Studies*, 2, 1–28.
—— (2015), *Enlightenment and Utility: Bentham in French, Bentham in France*, Cambridge, UK: Cambridge University Press.
De Champs E. & Cléro J. (2009), eds., *Bentham et la France : fortune et infortune de l'utilitarisme*, Oxford, UK: Voltaire Foundation.
Del Mar M. & Twining W. (2015), eds., *Legal Fictions in Theory and Practice*, London: Springer.
Dinwiddy J. (2004), *Bentham on Private Ethics and the Principle of Utility*, in Twining 2004, 134–54 (first published in *Revue Internationale de Philosophie*, 36, 1982, 278–300).
Edvinsson R. (2009), *The Quest for the Description of the Law*, Berlin-Heidelberg: Springer.
El Shakankiri M. (1970), *La Philosophie juridique de Jeremy Bentham*, Paris: LGDJ.
Elster J. (2013), *Securities Against Misrule: Juries, Assemblies, Elections*, Cambridge, UK: Cambridge University Press.
Fuller L. (1967), *Legal Fictions*, Stanford, CA: Stanford University Press.
Fuller G., Stecker R. & Wright J. (2000), eds., *John Locke. An Essay Concerning Human Understanding in Focus*, London: Routledge.
Goldworth A. (1972), "Bentham's concept of pleasure: Its relation to fictitious terms," *Ethics*, 82, 334–43.
—— (2002), "The meaning of Bentham's greatest happiness principle," in Postema 2002, vol. i, 129–35 (first published in *History of Philosophy*, 7, 1969, 315–21).

Guidi M. (1987/8), "Linguaggio, Logica, Etica: Bentham e l'interpretazione causale dell'azione umana," *Quaderni di storia dell'economia politica*, 5/6, 253–83.

Haakonssen K. (1996), *Natural Law and Moral Philosophy: From Grotius to the Scottish Enlightenment*, Cambridge, UK: Cambridge University Press.

Hacker P. (1993), *Bentham's Theory of Action and Intention*, in Parekh 1993, vol. ii, 160–78 (first published in *Archiv für Rechts und Sozialphilosophie*, 62, 1976, 89–109).

Halévy E. (1995), *La Formation du radicalisme philosophique*, 3 vols., Paris: Presses universitaires de France, 1995 (first edition published 1901–1904).

Harrison R. (1983), *Bentham*, London: Routledge & Kegan Paul.

—— (2001), The Sanctions of Utilitarianism, in Harrison R. (ed.), "Henry Sidgwick", *Proceeding of the British Academy*, 109, New York: Oxford University Press, 93–116.

Hart H. (1982), *Essays on Bentham: Jurisprudence and Political Philosophy*, Oxford: Clarendon Press.

—— (1996), "Il concetto di obbligo," *Rivista di filosofia*, 57, 125–40.

Hofmann W. (2002), *Politik des aufgeklärten Glücks: Jeremy Benthams philosophisch-politisches Denken*, Berlin: Akademie Verlag.

Hume L. (1981), *Bentham and Bureaucracy*, Cambridge, UK: Cambridge University Press.

Jackson B. (1998), "Bentham, truth and the semiotics of law," *Current Legal Problems*, 51, 493–531.

Joyce R. (2001), *The Myth of Morality*, Cambridge, UK: Cambridge University Press.

—— (2005), *Moral Fictionalism*, in Kalderon 2005, 286–313.

Kalderon M. (2005), ed., *Fictionalism in Metaphysics*, Oxford, UK: Clarendon Press.

—— (2005a), *Moral Fictionalism*, Oxford, UK: Clarendon Press.

—— (2008), "Moral fictionalism, the Frege-Geach problem, and reasonable inference," *Analysis*, 68, 133–43.

Kelly P. (1990), *Utilitarianism and Distributive Justice: Jeremy Bentham and the Civil Law*, Oxford, UK: Clarendon Press.

Kelsen H. (1945), *General Theory of Law and State*, translated by Wedberg A., Cambridge, MA: Harvard University Press.

Kervégan J. (2010), *La théorie kantienne de la normativité*, in Kervégan J. (2010), ed., *Raison pratique et normativité chez Kant*, Lyon: ENS Éditions, 89–109.

—— (2015), *La raison des normes. Essai sur Kant*, Paris: Vrin.

Korošec G. (1994), "The role of fictions in law: Hume, Adam Smith and Bentham," *Filozofski Vestnik / Acta Philosophica*, 15, 151–68.

Korsgaard C. (1996), *Creating the Kingdom of Ends*, Cambridge, UK: Cambridge University Press, 1996.

—— (1996a), *The Sources of Normativity*, Cambridge, UK: Cambridge University Press.

—— (2008), *The Constitution of Agency: Essays on Practical Reason and Moral Psychology*, Oxford, UK: Oxford University Press.

Laval C. (1994), *Jeremy Bentham. Le pouvoir des fictions*, Paris: Presses Universitaires de France.

Leroy M. (2007), "La "dynamique psychologique" selon Bentham: une théorie de la motivation," *Cahiers critiques de philosophie*, 4, 85–94.

Lieberman D. (1989), *The Province of Legislation Determined: Legal Theory in Eighteenth-century Britain*, Cambridge, UK: Cambridge University Press.

Lillehammer H. (2011), *Constructivism and the Error Theory*, in Miller 2011, 55–76.

Long D. (1977), *Bentham on Liberty: Jeremy Bentham's Idea of Liberty in Relation to his Utilitarianism*, Toronto: University of Toronto Press.

Lyons D. (1972), "Logic and coercion in Bentham's theory of law," *Cornell Law Review*, 57, 335–62.

—— (1991), *In the Interest of the Governed: A Study in Bentham's Philosophy of Utility and Law*, Oxford, UK: Clarendon Press (first edition 1973).

Mack M. (1962), *Jeremy Bentham: An Odyssey of Ideas 1748–1792*, London: Heinemann.

Mackie J. (1977), *Ethics: Inventing Right and Wrong*, New York: Penguin Books.

Mathieu M. (2014), *Les représentations dans la pensée des juristes*, Paris: IRJS Éditions.

McReynolds P. (1993), *Jeremy Bentham and the Nature of Psychological Concepts*, in Parekh 1993, vol. ii, 144–59 (first published in *Journal of General Psychology*, 82, 1970, 113–27).

—— (1993a), *The Motivational Psychology of Jeremy Bentham*, in Parekh (1993), vol. ii, 179–213 (first published in *Journal of the History of the Behavioral Sciences*, 4, 1968, 349–64).

Miller C. (2011), ed., *The Continuum Companion to Ethics*, London: Continuum.

Mulgan T. (2007), *Understanding Utilitarianism*, Stocksfield, UK: Acumen.

Murphy J. (2014), *The Philosophy of Customary Law*, New York: Oxford University Press.

Niesen P. (2014), *Benthams Rechtspositivismus*, in Schmidt R. 2014, ed., *Rechtspositivismus: Ursprung und Kritik. Zur Geltungsbegründung von Recht und Verfassung*, Baden-Baden, Germany: Nomos, 37–62.

Nolan D., Restall G. & West C. (2005), "Moral fictionalism versus the rest," *Australasian Journal of Philosophy*, 83, 307–30.

Ogden C. (1932), *Bentham's Theory of Fictions*, London: Kegan Paul, (reprinted 2000 and 2001 Abingdon, UK: Routledge).

Olivier P. (1975), *Legal Fictions in Practice and Legal Science*, Rotterdam: Rotterdam University Press.

Olson J. (2011), *Getting Real about Moral Fictionalism*, in Shafer-Landau R. (2011), ed., *Oxford Studies in Metaethics*, vol. vi, Oxford, UK: Oxford University Press.

Parekh B. (1974), *Bentham's Justification of the Principle of Utility*, in Parekh B. (1974), ed., *Jeremy Bentham: Ten Critical Essays*, London: Frank Cass, 96–119.

—— (1993), ed., *Jeremy Bentham: Critical Assessments*, 4 vols., London: Routledge, 1993.

—— (1993a), *Bentham's Theory of Virtue*, in Darling-Smith B. (1993), ed., *Can Virtue be Thought?*, Notre Dame: University of Notre Dame Press, 53–68.

Pellegrino G. (2010), *La fabbrica della felicità: Liberalismo, etica e psicologia in Jeremy Bentham*, Napoli, Italy: Liguori.

Pink T. (2007), "Normativity and reason," *Journal of Moral Philosophy*, 4, 406–31.

Poggi F. (2006), "Cosa esiste? Un'introduzione all'ontologia di Jeremy Bentham," *Materiali per una storia della cultura giuridica*, 36, 39–53.

Posner R. (1976), "Blackstone and Bentham," *Journal of Law and Economics*, 19, 569–606.

Postema G. (1986), *Bentham and the Common Law Tradition*, Oxford, UK: Clarendon, 1986.

—— (1998), "Bentham's equality-sensitive utilitarianism," *Utilitas*, 10, 144–58.

—— (2002), ed., *Bentham: Moral, Political and Legal Philosophy*, 2 vols., Aldershot, UK: Dartmouth Publishing.

—— (2002a) "Facts, fictions, and law: Bentham on the foundations of evidence," in Postema 2002, vol. ii, 401–28 (first published in *Archiv für Rechts- und Sozialphilosophie*, 16; 1983, 37–64).

—— (2006), "Interests, Universal and particular: Bentham's utilitarian theory of value," *Utilitas*, 18, 109–33.

Quine W. (1981), *Five Milestones of Empiricism*, in Quine W. (1981), *Theories and Things*, Cambridge, MA: Belknap Press, 67–72.

Quinn Malcolm (2011), "The invention of facts: Bentham's ethics and the education of public taste," *Revue d'études benthamiennes*, 9, https://etudes-benthamiennes.revues.org/346.

Quinn Michael (2012) "Which comes first, Bentham's chicken of utility, or his egg of truth?," *Journal of Bentham Studies*, 14, 1–46.

—— (2014), "Bentham on mensuration: Calculation and moral reasoning," *Utilitas*, 26, 61–104.

—— (2015), *Fuller on Legal Fiction: A Benthamic Perspective*, in Del Mar & Twining 2015, 55–82 (first published in *International Journal of Law in Context*, 9, 2013, 466–84).

Raphael D. (1969), ed., *British moralists: 1650–1800*, 2 vols., Oxford, UK: Clarendon Press.

Rawls J. (1980), "Kantian constructivism in moral theory," *Journal of Philosophy*, 77, 515–72.

—— (1999), *A Theory of Justice: Revised Edition*, Cambridge, MA: Belknap Press.

Raz J. (1990), *Practical Reason and Norms*, Oxford, UK: Oxford University Press (first edition 1975).

—— (1999), *Engaging Reason: On the Theory of Value and Action*, Oxford, UK: Oxford University Press.

Redondo M. (1999), *Reasons for Action and the Law*, Dordrecht, the Netherlands: Kluwer Academic Publishers.

Roberts Jr W. (1993), *Bentham's Conception of Political Change: A Liberal Approach*, in Parekh 1993, vol. iii, 952–65 (first published in *Political Studies*, 9, 1961, 254–66).

Rosen F. (1998), "Individual sacrifice and the greatest happiness: Bentham on utility and rights," *Utilitas*, 10, 129–43.

—— (2003), *Classical Utilitarianism from Hume to Mill*, London: Routledge.

—— (2007), ed., *Jeremy Bentham*, Aldershot, UK: Ashgate.

Rosen G. (2005), *Problems in the History of Fictionalism*, in Kalderon 2005, 14–64.

Samek Ludovici G. (2004), *L'utilità del bene. Jeremy Bentham, l'utilitarismo e il consequenzialismo*, Milan, Italy: Vita e Pensiero.

Scanlon T. (1998), *What we owe to each other*, Cambridge, MA: Belknap Press.

Schneewind J. (1995), "Voluntarism and the origins of utilitarianism," *Utilitas*, 7, 87–96.

—— (1998), *The Invention of Autonomy: A History of Modern Moral Philosophy*, Cambridge, UK: Cambridge University Press.

—— (2003), *Seventeenth- and Eighteenth-Century Ethics*, in Becker L. and Becker C. (2003), eds., *A History of Western Ethics*, New York: Routledge, 79–93.

Schofield P. (1987), "A comparison of the moral theories of William Paley and Jeremy Bentham," *The Bentham Newsletter*, 11, 4–22.

—— (1996), "Bentham on the identification of interests," in *Utilitas*, 8, 223–34.

—— (1999), "Political and religious radicalism in the thought of Jeremy Bentham," *History of Political Thought*, 20, 272–91.

—— (2003), "Jeremy Bentham, the principle of utility, and legal positivism," *Current Legal Problems*, 56, 1–39.

—— (2006), *Utility and Democracy: The Political Thought of Jeremy Bentham*, Oxford, UK: Oxford University Press, 2006.

—— (2009), *Bentham: A Guide for the Perplexed*, London: Continuum.

—— (2014), *Jeremy Bentham and James Mill*, in Mander W. (2014), ed., *The Oxford Handbook of British Philosophy in the Nineteenth Century*, Oxford, UK: Oxford University Press, 347–64.

—— (2014a), *A Defence of Jeremy Bentham's Critique of Natural Rights*, in Zhai & Quinn 2014, 208–30.

—— (2015), "Jeremy Bentham on utility and truth," *History of European Ideas*, 41, 1125–42.

Selby-Bigge L. (1987), ed., *British Moralists: being Selections from Writers principally of the Eighteenth Century*, 2 vols., Oxford, UK: Clarendon Press.

Sgarbi M. (2013), *The Aristotelian Tradition and the Rise of British Empiricism. Logic and Epistemology in the British Isles* (1570–1689), Dordrecht, the Netherlands: Springer.

Shafer-Landau R. (2011), *Constructivism*, in Miller 2011, cvii–cviii.

Shapiro L. (2014), *Pleasure, Pain and Sense Perception*, in Garrett A. (2014), ed., *The Routledge Companion to Eighteenth Century Philosophy*, London: Routledge, 400–17.

Smart J. & Williams B. (1973), *Utilitarianism for and against*, Cambridge, UK: Cambridge University Press.

Sprigge T. (2002), *The Relation between Jeremy Bentham's Psychological, and his Ethical, Hedonism*, in Postema 2002, vol. i, 177–200 (first published in *Utilitas*, 11, 1999, 296–319).

Stearns J. (1975), "Bentham on public and private ethics," *Canadian Journal of Philosophy*, 5, 583–94.

Steintrager J. (1977), *Bentham*, London: Allen and Unwin.

Stemmer P. (2008), *Normativität. Eine ontologische Untersuchung*, Berlin: de Gruyter.

Stolzenberg N. (1999), "Bentham's theory of fictions: 'A curious double language'," *Cardoza Studies in Law & Literature*, 11, 223–61.

Stone M. (1985), "Dickens, Bentham, and the fictions of the law: A Victorian controversy and its consequences," *Victorian Studies*, 29, 125–54.

Street S. (2008), *Constructivism about Reasons*, in Shafer-Landau R. (2008), ed., *Oxford Studies in Metaethics*, vol. iii, Oxford, UK: Oxford University Press.

Tarantino P. (2017), "La fondazione benthamiana dello statuto etico e giuridico degli animali," *Bioetica. Rivista Interdisciplinare*, 1, 79–96.

Tusseau G. (2001), *Jeremy Bentham et le droit constitutionnel : une approche de l'utilitarisme juridique*, Paris : L'Harmattan.

—— (2002), "Jeremy Bentham et les droits de l'homme: un réexamen," *Revue trimestrielle des droits de l'homme*, 13, 407–31.

—— (2007), "Jeremy Bentham on power-conferring laws," *Revue d'études benthamiennes*, 3, 48–77.

—— (2009), *La réception de l'œuvre de Jeremy Bentham par les juristes français: l'exemple de Michel Villey*, in De Champs & Cléro 2009, 243–58.

—— (2011) *Jeremy Bentham et les fictions du droit*, in Darcy G. & Doat M. (2011), eds., *L'imaginaire en droit*, Bruxelles: Bruylant, 383–433.

—— (2011a), *Jeremy Bentham: la guerre des mots*, Paris: Dalloz.

—— (2014), ed., *The Legal Philosophy and Influence of Jeremy Bentham: Essays on "Of the Limits of the Penal Branch of Jurisprudence"*, London: Routledge.

—— (2014a), *An Old English Tale? Bentham's Theory of the Force of a Law*, in Tusseau 2014, 80–133.

Twining W. (2004), ed., *Bentham: Selected Writings of John Dinwiddy*, Stanford, CA: Stanford University Press.

Tyler C. (2003), "Jeremy Bentham, social criticism and levels of meaning," *Journal of Bentham Studies*, 6, 1–18.

—— (2004), "'A foundation of chaff'? A critique of Bentham's metaphysics, 1813–16," *British Journal for the History of Philosophy*, 12, 685–703.

Vaihinger H. (2001), *The Philosophy of "As if". A System of the Theoretical, Practical and Religious Fictions of Mankind*, translated by Ogden C., Abingdon, UK: Routledge (first published 1924, London: Routledge and Kegan Paul).

Voltolini A. (2006), *How Ficta Follow Fiction: A Syncretistic Account of Fictional Entities*, Dordrecht, the Netherlands: Springer.

Waldron J. (1987), *Natural Rights in the Seventeenth and Eighteenth Centuries*, in Waldron J. (1987), ed., *Nonsense Upon Stilts: Bentham, Burke and Marx on the Rights of Man*, London: Methuen, 7–21.

Wallace J. (2014), "Practical reason," in *The Stanford Encyclopedia of Philosophy*, in Zalta E. (2014), ed., http://plato.stanford.edu/archives/sum2014/entries/practical-reason/.

Yelle R. (2005), "Bentham's fictions: Canon and idolatry in the genealogy of law," *Yale Journal of Law and the Humanities*, 17, 151–79.

Zhai X. (2014), *Bentham's Command versus Hart's Authoritative Reason: An Examination of the Principal Interpretations of Bentham's Imperative Theory of Law in Hart's "Commands and Authoritative Legal Reasons"*, in Tusseau 2014, 170–95.

Zhai X. & Quinn M. (2014), eds., *Bentham's Theory of Law and Public Opinion*, Cambridge, UK: Cambridge University Press.

Index

For Product Safety Concerns and Information please contact our EU representative GPSR@taylorandfrancis.com
Taylor & Francis Verlag GmbH, Kaufingerstraße 24, 80331 München, Germany

www.ingramcontent.com/pod-product-compliance
Ingram Content Group UK Ltd.
Pitfield, Milton Keynes, MK11 3LW, UK
UKHW011001180926
475701UK00004B/491
9780367589349